1806158450
WITHDRAWN FROM STOCK
AF805183
ABERYSTWYTH

Learning for a Future: Refugee Education in Developing Countries

Edited by Jeff Crisp, Christopher Talbot and Daiana B. Cipollone

LC
3715
L4

UNHCR
The UN Refugee Agency

Don
Dec '07

Learning for a Future:
Refugee Education in Developing Countries

Evaluation and Policy Analysis Unit
Health and Community Development Section
United Nations High Commissioner for Refugees

Cartography — UNHCR Geographic Information and Mapping Unit [PGDS/GIMU], Global Insight Digital Mapping @ Europa Technologies Ltd. The maps in this document do not imply the expression of any opinion on the part of UNHCR concerning the legal status of any country, territory, city or area, of its authorities, or the delimitation of frontiers or boundaries.

Photographs — UNHCR Photolibrary

Design — Mine de Rien - conception visuelle

Printing — Presses Centrales Lausanne, Switzerland

© United Nations High Commissioner for Refugees 2001

Cover photo — Afghan refugee girls. Munda Refugee Village, Peshawar District, Pakistan. UNHCR/03.1990/A. Hollmann

Back cover photos — Sudanese refugees at a Vocational Training Centre, Bonga Camp, Gambella Region, Ethiopia. UNHCR/02.2001/B. Neeleman

Returnee children at a pre-school in Asi-Kulam Camp near Vavuniya, Sri Lanka. UNHCR/03.1995/H. J. Davies

---

First printed December 2001

For details, contact — UNHCR, Case Postale 2500 / CH-1211 Geneva 2 / Switzerland
E-mail: hqep00@unhcr.ch / E-mail: hqts00@unhcr.ch
http://www.unhcr.ch

How to order — United Nations Publications
Sales + Marketing Section
Room C-113
Palais des Nations / 1211 Geneva 10 / Switzerland
E-mail: unpubli@unog.ch
http://www.un.org/pubs/sales.htm

Sales No. GV.E.01.0.17
ISBN 92-1-101044-6

Foreword

Contrary to popular opinion, visiting a refugee camp or settlement is frequently an inspiring experience. For while refugees undoubtedly suffer a great deal of hardship and trauma, they also show tremendous determination to make the best of a bad situation and to prepare for the day when they can resume a normal way of life.

This determination is to be seen most clearly in the very high value which refugees place on all forms of education. Indeed, experience shows that once refugees have met their basic need for food, water and shelter, their primary concern is to ensure that their children can go to school.

Tragically, the international community has tended to place less value on education than refugees themselves. With humanitarian needs growing in many parts of the world, the funding available for refugee assistance programmes has become progressively tighter. In many situations, this has meant that the resources available for education have declined.

It is impossible to calculate the immense costs that are incurred by depriving refugees of education. A refugee who goes without education cannot look forward to a more productive and prosperous future. A refugee who is unable to attend school or a vocational training course is more likely to become frustrated and involved in illegitimate or military activities. A refugee who remains illiterate and inarticulate will be at a serious disadvantage in defending his or her human rights.

The education of refugees is an important but neglected humanitarian issue. I therefore welcome the publication of this stimulating new book, and hope that it will be instrumental in bringing new ideas, information and resources to the challenge of providing education to the world's refugees.

Ruud Lubbers
United Nations High Commissioner for Refugees

Acknowledgements

This volume is the product of a research programme undertaken by UNHCR's Evaluation and Policy Analysis Unit, in conjunction with the organization's Health and Community Development Section. The programme was generously funded by the U.S. State Department's Bureau of Population, Refugees and Migration, where Nan Kennelly, Allan Jury and Mark Walkup provided valuable support.

The papers presented in the volume were commissioned by UNHCR and presented at a March 2001 workshop on 'Refugee Education in Developing Countries: Policy and Practice', kindly hosted by the George Washington University in Washington D.C., in association with UNHCR's Washington office. The papers have been revised for publication, taking into account the workshop discussions, as well as comments submitted by UNHCR's Senior Education Officer, Christopher Talbot.

The production of this book would not have been possible without the hard work of Elizabeth De Leon-Jones, who assisted with the organization of the workshop; Sue Mulcock, who administered the research programme; and Daiana B. Cipollone, who served as the volume's Production Editor.

Full details of UNHCR's research, evaluation and policy analysis activities can be found on the UNHCR website, www.unhcr.ch.

Jeff Crisp
Head, Evaluation and Policy Analysis Unit
UNHCR, Geneva

Preface

Healthy, cognitive and emotional development of children and adolescents is promoted by a secure environment and opportunities for learning. Yet there are many hundreds of thousands of children living in refugee camps and settlements, or internally displaced, whose security has been shattered, often violently, and who have been separated from friends and family members. Education provides a vehicle for rebuilding refugee children's lives, through social interaction and gaining knowledge and skills for their future lives. For some, the alternative is depression and idleness, and for others, a range of anti-social activities and the thought of revenge through a renewal of armed conflict.

UNHCR decided therefore to review the state of the art, identifying key issues and best practices, to assist in updating its guidelines for assistance to refugee education in developing countries. Margaret Sinclair prepared an overview of education response in the early stages of emergency situations in developing countries. Jim Williams reviewed research findings on factors promoting educational quality in Third World schools, to identify principles that might raise the effectiveness of refugee schools. Tim Brown visited refugee schools in Nepal, to examine issues of quality. Marc Sommers assessed the impact of UNHCR's innovative peace education programmes for refugee schools and communities in Kenya and Uganda. Erik Lyby evaluated skills training programmes for refugees in Tanzania.

In the first paper, Margaret Sinclair reviews the rationale for education in situations of emergency and crisis, in terms of the protection and psychosocial needs of displaced children and adolescents, the need to maintain and develop study skills as a contribution to individual and national development, and the dissemination of key messages regarding health, environment, conflict resolution and citizenship. All these are aspects of the rights of the child. The paper identifies key principles such as rapid educational response, using a community-based approach, with capacity-building through training of refugee teachers, youth leaders and school management committees. The debate on 'education kits' is reviewed. The objective of promoting durable solutions implies a curriculum similar to that in the area of origin, including survival and peace-building skills. The paper examines ways of promoting the participation of girls, adolescents, persons with disability and ex-combatants in refugee education programmes. Special attention is given to the situation of ongoing education programmes that receive a continuous or intermittent influx of new refugees from an unstable neighbouring country or region. The study looks at these elements of education response in several recent emergency situations. Recommendations include the strengthening of institutional commitment and preparedness, in terms of policy, staffing arrangements and training, and funding.

The focus of Margaret Sinclair's paper is on emergency response. Often, however, refugee situations continue for years or even decades, while refugees are unable to return to their homeland in dignity and security. In this situation, efforts must be made progressively to raise the quality of schooling, building on the foundations laid by appropriate rapid education response. In his paper on school quality and attainment in developing countries, Jim Williams looks at research on education in developing countries, to see what lessons can be learned for refugee education in 'care and maintenance' situations. He notes that there are many interpretations of educational quality, from schools' reputation to levels of inputs, from process to content and outcomes. He examines the core dimensions of quality, linking research findings to recommendations for policy. A first theme is the influence of individual characteristics on educational attainment, including student age, gender, health status, parental support and so on. At system level, school quality reflects supporting and enabling dimensions such as community support, teacher competencies and training, material inputs and administrative structures. Teaching and learning processes are, of course, the essence of school effectiveness and quality, and should include well-designed assessment procedures. A separate dimension of quality is inclusiveness, with gender-sensitive approaches and participation of vulnerable groups. The paper concludes with suggested strategies for improving school quality and attainment in refugee situations.

Tim Brown reviews the theme of quality from a field-based perspective. He begins by drawing attention to the lack of consistent donor funding to maintain even the low-cost models of refugee education supported by UNHCR. This is an ongoing hazard for refugee school programmes worldwide, due to unified multi-sectoral budgets at global and country level, which mean that a refugee education project's budget can be cut whenever there is a funding crisis anywhere in the world. The shortfall in funding experienced by UNHCR in recent years has prevented the introduction of consistent programming standards, as recommended in UNHCR's internal evaluation of the education sector in 1997. Tim Brown visited one of the better-resourced programmes, serving Bhutanese refugee children and young people in Nepal, but focused on the elements of quality that were transferable at limited cost. He structures his analysis in terms of actors, tools, environment and outcomes. He found that the strengths of the Bhutanese programme include positive attitudes towards education on the part of children and youth, families and teachers, strong systems for teacher training and support, and good organization, including provision for certification of students' achievements. Weaknesses of the programme reflect factors not under the control of the implementing agency, notably the refugee situation itself, the decline in funding and the lack of further education opportunities for school graduates. Tim Brown recommends that actors in other refugee situations learn from the Bhutanese case study by building on such strengths as refugees' strong motivation to succeed in education, refugee teacher training and support, and cost-effective approaches.

The humanitarian community can contribute to a more peaceful future simply by supporting refugee education and ensuring that it does not contain negative messages of hate and revenge for ethnic or other groups perceived as enemies. More positively, the education programme can incorporate life skills needed for conflict prevention. Marc Sommers looks at the conceptual framework underlying 'education for peace', a term not popular with some analysts but greatly appreciated by refugee participants seeking a peaceful solution to the conflicts that have led to their refugee status. He distinguishes the field of conflict resolution, which often involves adults seeking ways to end specific conflicts, from education for peace, which seeks to promote skills, understandings and attitudes promoting non-violent resolution of conflicts in general. He endorses the approach taken by UNHCR, that peace education in schools needs to be supported by education for the wider community. This is happening in the peace education programmes recently developed by UNHCR in the refugee camps in Kenya, and subsequently being adapted for other countries, including Uganda. His field visits indicated that participants identified with the UNHCR peace education initiative, and that its impact was strongly positive. His suggestions for improvement focus on ensuring wider access to the programme, notably finding ways to increase female participation. The paper also urges measures to incorporate school drop-outs, including the use of mother tongue where needed and practicable. He recommends the inclusion of this model of peace education as a standard component of refugee education programming, and the development of specific UNHCR peace education guidelines for this purpose.

Out-of-school refugee adolescents and youth often face very limiting life situations, if there is little possibility for them to enter the labour force due to lack of skills, political or economic constraints. This can lead to anti-social behaviour, such as excessive drinking, taking drugs and sexual violence. Alienation can also lead to recruitment into forced labour, military forces or prostitution. Such concerns underlie the initiation of skills training programmes, but these programmes often have limited impact, due to poor quality of training and lack of opportunities to use it. Erik Lyby evaluated the ongoing vocational training programmes for Burundian refugees in Tanzania, both formal and non-formal, to assess their functioning and propose a more comprehensive approach. He examined further the vocational training structures and economic opportunities in Burundi, with a view to linking training in exile to the needs of reconstruction after repatriation. He distinguishes three training structures, namely pre-entry institutional training, group-based training (for cooperative production), and enterprise-based training. Erik Lyby recommends the development of a camp-based training strategy incorporating these approaches. Enterprise-based apprenticeships should represent a strong element of this strategy, given its higher level of effectiveness in many situations. Group-based training in employable skills such as horticulture, useful after repatriation, represents another approach. Finally, he recommends the organization of group activities to occupy out-of-school youth who otherwise have little else to do, including the organization of sports teams and exploring the idea of computer centers or internet cafes which could provide the opportunity for informal learning.

The research papers presented here represent a step forward in the task of developing deeper professional insights into the field of refugee education and education in emergency situations in general. It is hoped that they will be of assistance to field practitioners and programme managers, but also to donors in understanding the need for consistent and adequate funding for refugee education.

Christopher Talbot
Senior Education Officer
UNHCR, Geneva

Notes on contributors

Margaret Sinclair is currently an independent consultant on education in humanitarian emergencies. She works in the field of educational planning, policy and programming. Since 1987 she has worked on issues of refugee education, training and income generation, including assignments in UNHCR's Peshawar office (1988-1993) and as UNHCR's Senior Education Officer (1993-1998). In 1997, she organised a design workshop on education for peace, conflict resolution and human rights in the refugee context, and helped set up UNHCR's programme of life skills and peace education. She can be reached by e-mail at: margaret_sinclair@yahoo.com

James H. Williams teaches at The George Washington University, where he directs the International Education Program at the Graduate School of Education and Human Development and the International Education concentration of the International Development Studies Program at the Elliott School of International Affairs. Professor Williams received his doctorate from Harvard University in administration, planning and social policy. His dissertation research examined the cross-national impact of educational expansion on health 1965-1990. He has worked for USAID; Obirin University, Tokyo; Ohio University. He has undertaken studies for numerous international organizations including UNHCR, UNICEF, the World Bank, USAID, UNESCO, CARE, and the International Institute of Research.

Dr Williams has written on diverse subjects in educational development including: approaches to improving educational quality; management issues in the decentralization of education; collaborative programs in education and health as a cross-sectoral development strategy; education in contexts of refugees, crisis, and reconstruction; best practices in girls' education; and the use and misuse of indicators and information systems. He is currently editing a book on education for social reconstruction. He can be reached by e-mail at: jhw@gwu.edu

Timothy Brown is currently Education Officer for the Refugee Education Trust at UNHCR in Geneva. He helped establish the independent Trust in December 2000 on the occasion of the 50th Anniversary of UNHCR by carrying out a feasibility study and authoring the blueprint documents. He received his B.Sc. (Hons) in Physics (1971) and Ph.D. in Mathematics (1978) in London, United Kingdom.

Dr Brown has spent over 20 years in Africa in the field of education – as a lecturer, teacher trainer and education officer. He has been associate professor at Juba University in Southern Sudan, senior lecturer at Kenyatta University in Nairobi, and education adviser for UNHCR in Uganda. He is committed to the work of the Trust which advocates for, and researches into, refugee education. The Trust also fundraises for, and provides, post-primary education for refugees in less developed countries. He can be reached by e-mail at: brownt@unhcr.ch

Marc Sommers is an international consultant and Research Fellow at Boston University's African Studies Center. He has explored the impact of war on children and youth in Africa as well as Colombia, El Salvador and Kosovo. He has also worked on emergency and peace education, the human rights of forced migrants, urban refugees and migrants, community reconciliation and post-war transitions. Publications include a book:"Fear in Bongoland: Burundi Refugees in Urban Tanzania," (Berghahn, 2001); a monograph: "The Dynamics of Coordination" (Humanitarianism and War Project, Tufts University, 2000); and a report: "Emergency Education for Children" (Center for International Studies, MIT, 1999). He can be reached by e-mail at: msommers@bu.edu

Erik Lyby received his B.Sc. in Architecture and Civil Engineering from Aarhus Polytechnic (1965) in Denmark. He then went to Zambia as a bilateral volunteer in 1969. Inspired by his first African sojourn, he took up the study of social anthropology in 1972 and spent the next ten years studying and teaching at the university, including two years of field research in Botswana in preparation for his thesis on labour migration in Southern Africa. He received his Mag. Art. (magister artium) in social anthropology from the University of Aarhus (1982).

Between 1984 and 1992, he worked for the International Labour Organization in Geneva on programmes for the creation of employment for the unskilled in developing countries through the use of labour-intensive technologies – first in rural areas and later also in the exploding cities of Asia and Africa. Between 1993 and 1999, he was chief consultant in a Danish consulting firm. This included another two-year posting to Zambia, after which he established his own firm, Jacaranda Consult. Most of his work in more than 25 countries has been related to human resource development and job creation for the poor with special emphasis on vocational education and training systems as the entrance to a changing labour market. He can be reached by e-mail at: erik.lyby@inet.uni2.dk

Contents

Chapter 1
Education in Emergencies

margaret sinclair

Summary

This paper reviews the rationale for education in situations of emergency and crisis, and the basic principles for emergency education. It examines how these principles were reflected in some recent emergencies. The intense 1990s debate on education kits is revisited. A final section examines the implications of the study for preparedness and cooperation.

Reasons for education in emergency include the psychosocial needs of children and adolescents affected by trauma and displacement, the need to protect them from harm, and the need to maintain and develop study skills and disseminate key messages such as how to avoid HIV/AIDS, landmine awareness, environmental education and education for peace and citizenship. All these are aspects of the rights of the child.

A key principle for education in situations of emergency and crisis is rapid response, using a community-based approach, with capacity-building through training of teachers, youth leaders and school management committees. Education should support durable solutions and should normally be based on the curriculum and languages of study of the area of origin. Survival and peace-building messages and skills should be incorporated in formal and non-formal education. Programmes must progressively promote the participation of under-represented groups, including girls, adolescents and persons with disability. Ongoing refugee programmes should develop procedures for rapid response to the needs of newly arriving refugee children and adolescents.

Recommendations include the strengthening of institutional commitment and preparedness, in terms of policy, staffing arrangements and training, and funding. There should be no question that UNHCR has a vital role to play in the education sector, along with its UN and NGO partners, since the international community provides it with the physical and human resources for a strong field presence in refugee, returnee and some other situations. Inter-agency cooperation, strengthened by the year 2000 World Education Forum and Inter-Agency Consultation in Situations of Emergency and Crisis, can help emergency education fulfil its humanitarian and peace-building roles.

Introduction

The end of the Cold War did not mean the end of conflict and population displacement. Many of the countries which gained (or regained) their independence in the latter decades of the twentieth century are multi-ethnic in nature and have not yet developed stable systems of governance. The 1990s saw numerous conflicts with an ethnic dimension, which led to suffering and displacement for millions of children and young people, often under horrific circumstances. Their lives were disrupted and their education abruptly terminated.

This has coincided with the enhanced awareness of children's needs and rights, following nearly universal ratification of the 1989 Convention on the Rights of the Child. Graça Machel's *Report on the Impact of Armed Conflict on Children* highlighted the needs for education in emergency situations (Machel, 1996). These needs were reiterated at the World Education Forum held in Dakar in April 2000.[1]

Education is increasingly viewed as the "fourth pillar", or a "central pillar", of humanitarian response, alongside the pillars of nourishment, shelter and health services (Norwegian Refugee Council et. al., 1999: 26; Midttun, 2000a: 3–4; ICWAC, 2000: 9). Children are vulnerable and dependent, and they are developing, not only physically but mentally and emotionally. "The sudden and violent onset of emergencies, the disruption of families and community structures ... deeply affect the physical and psychological wellbeing of refugee children" (UNHCR, 1994: 5–6). Education provides opportunities for students, their families and communities to begin the trauma healing process, and to learn the skills and values needed for a more peaceful future and better governance at local and national levels.

The present paper, commissioned by UNHCR, is intended to support the updating of the UNHCR guidelines on assistance to the education sector, to better meet the needs of communities displaced by conflict.[2] The main focus of the paper is on preparedness for new population movements such as refugee influxes, and on rapid response to meet the psychosocial and educational needs of the emergency-affected children and adolescents. This entails a perspective on the longer-term situation, however, since a false step at the beginning can lead to problems later.[3]

The paper reviews approaches to education in a wide range of emergency situations not limited to refugees. Innovative programmes are being developed for internally displaced populations and for those living in disturbed or temporarily failed states such as Somalia. Some of these new approaches are relevant to refugees. Moreover, UNHCR and other organizations with a refugee service mandate often assist populations that are internally displaced, or in areas receiving returning refugees, or in areas where government has broken down.

---

1 See the Forum's declaration, Dakar Framework for Action – Education for All: Meeting our Collective Commitments (World Education Forum, 2000a), and the Thematic Studies published for the Dakar meeting. The Framework includes a pledge to meet the needs of education systems affected by conflict, natural calamities and instability, and to conduct educational programmes in ways that promote mutual understanding, peace and tolerance. A follow-up Inter-Agency Consultation on Education in Situations of Emergency and Crisis was held in Geneva in November 2000.

2 UNHCR has commissioned parallel research papers on the themes of the quality of refugee education (Brown, 2001, Williams, 2001) and education for peace (Sommers, 2001).

3 UNHCR's recent Briefing Paper on The Education Sector in UNHCR's Programmes, in its section entitled "Emergency educational response", notes the need for inter-agency cooperation, institutional preparedness, standby staffing arrangements, emergency supplies of learning and teaching materials, a phased strategy, and work with refugee and local communities and educators to define needs and design appropriate responses (UNHCR, 2000a).

Refugee and returnee children at school in Madhu, Sri Lanka UNHCR/07.1999/M. Kobayashi

The paper focuses on education specifically organized for emergency-affected children and young people,[4] and does not cover the topic of scholarships or other arrangements for displaced children to attend local schools or colleges.[5] Furthermore, it adopts a descriptive approach, being more a survey of the state of the art than testing hypotheses, not least because there is very little feedback in terms of published monitoring data or evaluation studies with which to verify results.[6] The underlying hypotheses are as follows:

First: it is possible and psychologically beneficial to refugee and other crisis-affected children and adolescents to participate rapidly in community-based healing activities including elements of education and recreation, with subsequent systematization of these activities. Second: these psychological benefits together with learned knowledge, skills and values can contribute to peace-building and to social and economic development. Third: in many situations, education can serve as a tool of protection and of prevention of harm.

4 Space does not permit the coverage of adult education or vocational training and apprenticeships. For a broader overview of refugee education issues, see UNHCR (1995a), Avery et al. (1996), Retamal and Aedo-Richmond (1998b), and Sinclair (1998a, 1999).

5 As emphasised in the Machel report, individual refugees and internally displaced children and young people can face problems of enrolment in local schools because of lack of proper documentation, not being residents of the area or inability to pay school fees. Bridging programmes may be needed, and ways to lessen harassment at local schools (Machel, 1996: 57). Local schools may need assistance to cope with additional students (UNHCR, 1995a: 14–15).

6 The paper draws on four intensive evaluations, relating to use of education kits in Somalia (Eversmann, 2000) and in Angola (Johannessen, 2000), to psychosocial benefits of emergency education in Sierra Leone (Gupta, 2000), and to pre-schools in Bosnia (Burde, 1999); and on a review of lessons learned in early response in East Timor (Nicolai, 2000) (none of these focused on refugee education). It draws on multi-country overviews by Marc Sommers (1999) on refugee education, and by John Richardson (1998) on psychosocial programmes in the former Yugoslavia.

The paper does not attempt comprehensive coverage of past or ongoing programmes or of implementing agencies. The research was based in UNHCR and draws heavily on information from UNHCR staff and records. Especial thanks are due to staff of other organizations who gave their time for telephone interviews or answered written queries, notably staff of UNICEF, UNESCO, the Norwegian Refugee Council, the International Rescue Committee (IRC) and Jesuit Refugee Service (JRS). Time did not permit contacting a wider range of agencies, but this is a priority for future research.

The paper attempts to answer five questions. First, why is education necessary in emergency situations and when? Second, what are the basic principles for education assistance in emergency situations? Third, how were these principles reflected in recent emergencies? Fourth, what use should be made of education kits? And fifth, what are the implications of the analysis for emergency preparedness in UNHCR, the sponsor of the study, and for other concerned organizations?

As will be seen, UNHCR did not play a prominent role in the education sector in the two most publicised recent emergencies (Kosovo and Timor), although it will be argued in this paper that it has an indispensable role even in circumstances where another agency takes the lead in the education sector. In order to reflect the role of UNHCR, which has the primary responsibility for refugee education in many of the most desolate locations on earth, the answer to question three includes not only a brief description of education response in the Kosovo and Timor crises but also of refugee education in Tanzania, Pakistan and the Democratic Republic of Congo (DRC) (which received large influxes of refugees in 1999) and of the response to the Eritrean refugees entering Sudan in May and June 2000.

Different uses of the term "education in emergencies"

The term "emergency education" is used at inter-agency level to refer to education in situations where children lack access to their national education systems, due to man-made crises or natural disasters. Its precise interpretation varies, from a concern with emergency education during the first few months after a crisis, to the years taken to restore normal education systems after a "complex humanitarian emergency". In UNHCR "emergency response" is technically a matter of months, essentially referring to the time required to get the organization's normal systems in place and operational. However, the tasks set forth in the education section of the UNHCR *Handbook for Emergencies* (UNHCR, 1999a: 106–109) take longer than this. UNHCR also recognizes that mass repatriation, albeit welcome, can create what is termed an "emergency-like situation" requiring "emergency-like" support. Almost all UNHCR education assistance is "emergency education" in the broad sense of the term, as used by many other organisations.

For UNESCO, an educational emergency is a crisis situation created by conflicts or disasters which have destabilized, disorganized or destroyed the education system, and which require an integrated process of crisis and post-crisis response (UNESCO, 1999). For UNICEF "emergencies include natural disasters such as floods and earthquakes, and human-made crises such as civil strife and war", as well as silent emergencies such as HIV/AIDS, extreme poverty and children living in the streets (Pigozzi, 1999: 1).

As will become evident during the presentation, the term "education in emergencies" increasingly serves as shorthand for schooling and other organised studies, together with "normalising" structured activities, arranged for and with children, young people and adults whose lives have been disrupted by conflict and major natural disasters.

Dimensions of the problem

Comprehensive statistics are not available on the numbers affected by conflict and disaster, and there are serious problems of definition. The 1990s saw new and sometimes very complex displacements, including those arising from the break-up of the Soviet Union and of the former Yugoslavia (UNHCR, 1995b, 1997a). As of December 1999, there were some 15 million refugees in the world,[7] including about 7 million in populations categorized as "assisted by UNHCR". Other populations "of concern" to UNHCR included over 2 million refugees who had repatriated during the previous two years; 4 million internally displaced persons (IDPs) in areas where UNHCR had been asked to provide support, and over 1 million recently returned IDPs (UNHCR, 2000b).

A decade ago, the countries that had generated the most refugees were Afghanistan (over 6 million refugees), Ethiopia, Iraq, Mozambique, Liberia, Sudan and Somalia (all with over 400,000) (UNHCR, 2000b: 38–39). By 2000, many of these populations had trekked home and begun the difficult task of rebuilding their communities, and the largest refugee groups (over 400,000) were from Afghanistan, Iraq, Burundi, Sierra Leone, Sudan, Somalia and Bosnia-Herzogovina. Other places generating over 400,000 refugees during the 1990s were Rwanda and Kosovo.[8] These 12 countries also suffered major internal population displacement and disruption of national services such as education. This is true also of many of the 39 other countries which generated 10,000 or more refugees in any one year during the 1990s.

The world total of internally displaced persons has been variously computed as between 20 million and 50 million.[9] In a recent study, Save the Children UK estimated that 13 million children have been violently displaced within the borders of their own country.[10] It seems that in the 1990s as many as 1 per cent of the world's population have been displaced from their home areas by conflict or other disasters, or have returned and are attempting to rebuild their communities under usually adverse circumstances. Populations affected by a breakdown of governance due to conflict, and consequently deprived of national services such as education in their home areas, can be added to this roll-call of emergency-affected populations.

In 1999 alone, a total of 1,688,000 persons left home situations so grim that they were recognized as prima facie refugees.[11] This included 411,000 in Africa, 409,000 in Asia and 868,000 in southern and eastern Europe. The countries receiving the most new arrivals (in descending order of magnitude) were Albania, Macedonia, Indonesia (West Timor), Tanzania, Pakistan, Bosnia and the Democratic Republic of the Congo (DRC) (UNHCR, 2000b: 24).

---

7 This figure includes 11.7 million in the UNHCR refugee statistics (UNHCR, 2000b) plus 3.7 million Palestinian refugees under the aegis of UNRWA. The latter benefit from extensive education provision, as compared with more recently displaced refugee populations (see www.un.org/unrwa).

8 Some 500,000 refugees living in the Sudan were reclassified as Eritrean in 1991, when Ethiopia recognized Eritrea's right to secede. Please note that in this paper all statistics have been rounded.

9 See the website of the Global IDP Project of the Norwegian Refugee Council, at www.db.idpproject.org.

10 From Children and armed conflict: report of the Secretary General (United Nations, 2000a: 10), which also cites the Office for the Coordination of Humanitarian Affairs (OCHA) estimate that children comprise 75 per cent of the 2.5 million people in Angola displaced since hostilities resumed in December 1998.

11 UNHCR (2000b); there were an additional 176,000 refugees accorded individual recognition. ("Prima facie" refers to refugees recognized on a group basis.)

Refugee children line up in front of temporary school tents provided by UNHCR. Until school buildings can be constructed, UNHCR and its partners are providing basic education for refugee children at New Shamshatoo camp. UNHCR/04.2001/L. Boscardi

In many displaced populations, about one in three persons are in the age group for schooling and other child and adolescent activities.[12] Thus in the refugee populations recorded in the 1999 UNHCR Statistical Overview as "UNHCR-assisted" (UNHCR, 2000b: 3), totalling 6.9 million, there would be a total of about 2.3 million in the child and adolescent age group. This may be compared with the total of nearly 800,000 children and young people recorded as beneficiaries of UNHCR-funded education programmes,[13] to which must be added an unknown number who benefit from other assistance programmes or participate in schooling in the host country without special assistance. These very approximate statistics suggest that one-third of refugee children (excluding infants) and adolescents in populations categorized as "UNHCR-assisted" are in UNHCR-supported schooling,[14] and that perhaps 40 per cent are in school altogether. Girls represent about 40 per cent of UNHCR-funded students (UNHCR, 2000a). These figures reflect the observation of the author and many colleagues that most children in UNHCR-assisted populations do

12 In many developing countries children aged under 16 to 18 years are estimated to comprise about one-half of the population. Looking at an age group of concern for emergency schooling, from 3 to 6 years as the lower limit to 15 to 18 years (with a few who are a bit older) at the upper end, one is looking at about two-thirds of one-half which is one-third of the whole. Given that education starts late in many developing and crisis-affected countries, that schooling is often interrupted by crisis and also that exact ages are not known where birth certificates are missing, there should be no precise upper limit for young persons benefiting from emergency schooling (UNHCR, 1999a: 108).

13 A survey of UNHCR support for refugee schooling in 1999 in 27 major country programmes gave a total of about 754,000 beneficiaries. The total varies according to the pattern of refugee movements, with a figure of 773,000 estimated for all programmes in 1995/6 (UNHCR, 1997b: 11), and a lower figure of 650,000 for 1997/8. The total recorded for 1990 was 330,000. Interpretation of refugee education and population statistics is complex (Sinclair, 1999: 10–18, 50–52; UNHCR, 2000b: 1–4; WEF, 2000b: 16–19).

14 The majority of these students are at primary school level. Most attend refugee primary or secondary schools, but substantial numbers attend local schools (1997c: 13–24). The widespread belief that UNHCR does not support secondary education, or refugee secondary schools, is untrue, although of a total of 77,000 recorded in major programmes in 1999, over half were Afghan students attending government schools in Iran (UNHCR, 2000a: 6).

indeed enrol in school but that many drop out quickly due to poverty and other factors. Refugees are often from poor rural areas with low previous enrolment rates. Often, the adults in the family have not completed primary school and do not press their children to do so.

Education in emergencies: why and when?

Is education needed in emergency situations? Is there a need to do more than feed, shelter and provide medical services to displaced emergency-affected populations? Is there a need to do more than stop them dying? Can displaced children and adolescents be kept in some kind of storage, without harmful long-term effects, until they can return home?

These may seem rhetorically harsh questions, but there are donors and even staff of humanitarian institutions who do not see education as part of a humanitarian intervention, or who do not think that it is urgent, or who do not think that it should be professionally organized and monitored even if their own organization is funding it.

Trauma and child development

> Armed conflict affects all aspects of child development – physical, mental and emotional – and to be effective, assistance must take each into account … *ensuring, from the outset of all assistance programmes,* that the psychosocial concerns intrinsic to child growth and development are addressed. (Machel, 1996: 49, emphasis added)

The strongest reasons for supporting organized activities such as education early in an emergency situation are to lessen the psychosocial impact of trauma and displacement and to protect at-risk groups (see below). UNHCR's *Refugee Children: Guidelines on Protection and Care* emphasises that "refugee children's wellbeing is as important as their physical health". The guidelines note that children have a unique psychological characteristic: their personalities are being formed and their coping skills developed almost daily. The disruption and insecurity inherent in refugee situations can harm children's physical, intellectual, psychological, cultural and social development. And this disruption can lay the foundations for another generation to engage in revenge, conflict and displacement (UNHCR, 1994: 38–39).

The 1990s saw a "take-off" in concern over psychosocial impacts of trauma.[15] Work with child soldiers in Mozambique and with war-affected youth in Guatemala showed the importance of activities such as education and training in promoting psychological healing (Boothby, 1992, 1996; Herbst, 1995). The work of Swedish Save the Children and UNICEF with boys who survived a dangerous trek from southern Sudan to Ethiopia in 1988, and who had to return in traumatic circumstances in 1991, and then move on to Kenya, helped bring the psychosocial needs of refugee children to the fore. Impacts of such experience include withdrawal from social contact and from activities such as playing, laughing and expressing emotions, together with sadness and guilt, aggression, sleeping difficulties, nightmares and bedwetting,

15 As of 1981, manuals on refugee health did not mention this aspect (Summerfield, 1999). The Harvard Program in Refugee Trauma developed from the Indochinese Psychiatry Clinic, founded in 1981, which was one of the first to work with victims of mass violence and torture (Harvard School of Public Health, 1998).

psychosomatic disorders, flashbacks, and inability to concentrate in school (Zutt, 1994: 37–40; Tefferi, 1999: 17). Schooling was an integral part of the varied activities organized for this group in Ethiopia and in Kakuma refugee camp in Kenya (Swedish Save the Children, 1999a).

The break-up of the former Yugoslavia led to numerous psychosocial interventions.[16] Child psychologists at the University of Belgrade found that many refugee children in collective centres were unable to play, and that their parents were unable to provide normal parenting. The psychologists developed programmes of art, clay modelling, storytelling and expressive games and exercises to build children's self-esteem and social interaction, and a sense of mastery over difficult circumstances (Tolfree, 1996).

The UNICEF survey of Rwandan children showing that more than two-thirds of the sample had witnessed someone being killed or injured during the 1994 genocide publicized the fact that war-affected children's psychological development was in danger (UNICEF, 1996). The UNICEF and UNESCO response in Rwanda included support for the rapid restoration of schooling, as a means of mass outreach to children, as well as training of teachers to understand the effects of trauma (Aguilar and Richmond, 1998). The Rwanda experience, and the horrific experiences of children in conflicts such as those in Mozambique, Liberia and Sierra Leone led to the UN study on the impact of armed conflict on children, led by Graça Machel. Her report emphasized that:

> All phases of emergency and reconstruction assistance should take psychosocial considerations into account ... Programmes should aim to support healing processes and to establish a sense of normalcy. This should include establishing daily routines of family and community life, opportunities for expression and structured activities such as school, play and sports. (Machel, 1996: 53)

One input to the study was a Save the Children Working Group's enunciation of the principles of a community-based approach. "In addition to family routines, organized activities, especially educational ones, are important for children; even without a school building, lessons and play groups can be held and sports and games organized" (ISCA, 1996: 8). Ellen Lange (1998: 12), reviewing the needs of refugee children newly arrived in Guinea from Sierra Leone, recommended that:

> In future refugee emergency situations, some structured recreational as well as educational activities should take place in a school-like setting. School-like settings allow children to (re-)establish a student identity, which should be considered an important step towards a normal child life.

Other psychosocial benefits of early educational response may be noted. Education restores an element of hope: it is forward-looking and constructive, as contrasted to talk of revenge, joining militias or participating in other harmful activities. Moreover, for older children and adolescents, the sudden ending of their studies represents an additional trauma in itself, perpetuating hopelessness, and should be remedied. As noted in the UNHCR Education Guidelines, "the trauma of exile should not be aggravated by the trauma of loss of educational opportunity" (UNHCR, 1995a: 12).[17] Further, the content of structured

16 Agger (1995: 26) categorised these interventions according to a pyramid, moving from help with worrying practical problems, and "task-oriented group interventions" for the many, to psychologically oriented group interventions, counselling interventions and intensive psychotherapy, for smaller numbers. The category of task-oriented group interventions for the many included educational activities, recreational activities and training of staff working with refugees.

17 See also UNHCR, 1994: 111. A review of education following national upheaval by Phillips and colleagues emphasizes "psychological restructuring" on a par with the restoration of physical infrastructure and capacity-building for teachers (Arnhold et al., 1998).

activities and education programmes can be designed to help develop coping skills (see below), much needed in an emergency situation.

Re-establishment of the routine of schooling is felt by many agency staff to have a beneficial effect on the mental state of adults as well as of children. It also has practical benefits, in that mothers are able to concentrate on their tasks, such as queuing for food and water, and so on, without having to worry that their young children will get lost in the camp or come to harm. The parents or other relatives caring for children may initially be depressed and unable to cope with children's emotional needs themselves. For this reason, structured activities for children have an additional importance. Education can partially substitute for poor child–adult interactions in the family, a role which is less important for most children in normal times. This is the reverse of the "macho" philosophy that education is a luxury in emergencies, and not a humanitarian requirement.

When? The importance of rapid action to meet the needs of crisis-affected children was emphasized in the 1997 "Evaluation of UNHCR's efforts on behalf of refugee children and adolescents", prepared by UNHCR's Inspection and Evaluation Unit in partnership with the International Save the Children Alliance. This crucial document highlighted social and psychological needs not only of younger children but especially of adolescents, "often the age group most psychologically affected by war". The report recommended community-based "daily structured activities [for] the large majority of children and adolescents" as "an integral part of emergency response ... as soon as a food distribution system is in place". These structured activities, including education, were seen as the "first line of response for promoting the recovery and wellbeing of children and adolescents who have suffered losses, displacement and often horrific experiences" (UNHCR, 1997c: 18–21). Much of the present paper consists of an analysis of how these recommendations might be implemented quickly and on a sustained basis.

Physical and social protection

> Uprooted adolescents are at risk of sexually transmitted diseases, unwanted pregnancies, mental health problems, violence and substance abuse ... social stigmatization [and] ... recruitment into armed forces or groups. (United Nations, 2000a: 11)

Bringing together children and adolescents for structured activities has a protection role, in early emergency and thereafter. Apart from revealing that some children have severe physical or mental health problems that need specialist attention, a serious attempt to bring all young persons into these activities may reveal children subject to abuse, such as harmful labour, exploitation of foster children for domestic labour (so that children of the household can attend school), and so on. Education can provide a constructive alternative for young people who might otherwise find their fulfilment in joining armed forces or militias, especially if confined to a refugee or IDP camp and without access to employment opportunities.[18] Education is likewise a forward-looking activity that can lessen the incidence of alcohol and drug abuse, teenage pregnancies, prostitution and so on.

18 It is true that, in some instances, well-established schools can be recruiting grounds for military forces or armed groups. In this case precautions must be taken as appropriate, and students must be educated about their rights under the 1989 Convention on the Rights of the Child not to be recruited for military activities before they are adults.

Moreover, the act of attending school brings awareness of the wider world and of personal rights, such as the equal right of girls to attend schools and the new roles and lifestyles for women modelled by female teachers. Most schools have elements of human rights in their "hidden curriculum", and it is increasingly the case that education for peace, tolerance, child or human rights and citizenship are included as explicit awareness-raising features of the school programme.

Sustaining study skills and re-introducing schooling

Displaced communities are normally anxious to reintroduce schooling quickly, as soon as food and shelter are provided. They ask their educated members to start classes for the younger children on a voluntary basis. In many cases people fled without their belongings, so that it is difficult for classes to begin without external assistance. A flexible approach is needed so that students who were in upper primary and secondary school or higher education can also maintain and develop their study skills. There are various ways of doing this, such as involving youth in helping with younger children for part of the time and providing interim courses in languages or other subjects to maintain their study skills until they can resume their courses of study.

Rapid intervention of this kind is important, so that the benefit of past schooling is not lost and time is not wasted. Time is short for many of these young people, especially girls, who often have to leave school at puberty or early marriage, and boys from poor families, who have to work full-time as soon as they are old enough to do so. Trauma can have a negative impact on study skills, as can a long gap in studies. Hence, the restoration of some kind of studies is urgent.

Restoration of schooling brings the widely recognized benefits of schooling as such, including its contribution to productivity and economic development. It can contribute to social stability through engaging young people in sustained constructive activity. There are also long-term implications for social cohesion: it is undesirable for one group of the population to be severely under-educated relative to other groups, especially when there is an ethnic dimension. Schooling for girls leads to lower child and maternal mortality rates and increased female participation in economic and political decision-making.[19]

Conveying survival and peace-building messages and skills

In early emergency, camps are dangerous places. Cholera and other diseases can easily take hold. Malaria is often a hazard. In many places, sexual activities including rape can lead to HIV/AIDS. There is usually an incipient environmental crisis, with the neighbouring land being stripped of trees for firewood, construction of temporary shelter and so on. Rapid organization of school-like activities for children and adolescents, working with community volunteers, can provide an excellent channel for conveying survival messages on these matters.

For internally displaced persons, and for refugees who may soon return home, there is often the need for education about landmines and the dangers of unexploded ordnance. Besides mine awareness programmes for adults, the messages need to be skilfully conveyed to children, in ways that will have a lasting effect on their behaviour.

---

19 See, for example, the Concept Paper for the UN Ten-Year Programme on Girls' Education (United Nations, 2000b), as well as the annual UNICEF report, The State of the World's Children.

Conflict-affected people also need help in discussing the situation they are in, and in identifying constructive ways to build a better future. This discussion needs to be attuned to the experiences they have gone through and to be sensitively developed with local educators. For lack of a better name, the 'participative' approaches to such discussions developed in recent years are often known as "peace education", although they can serve to improve much needed coping skills in general. Peace education does not "produce" peace but is an enabling factor. Peace education in the Kenya refugee camps has transformed the way in which many refugees see their situation and their plans for the future (Baxter, 2000: 9–11). There is a need to build on this approach to incorporate elements of citizenship and governance in situations of national reconstruction (see below).

Human rights

The 1989 Convention on the Rights of the Child is the most widely ratified human rights document ever, with only two countries not having signed.[20] It is binding on states that are party to it and has been adopted as a normative framework by UN agencies. Under the convention, priority must be given to the best interests of the child (Article 3). Every child has the right to a standard of living adequate for physical, mental, spiritual, moral and social development (Article 27). All appropriate measures must be taken to promote the physical and psychological recovery and social reintegration of child victims of abuse or armed conflict (Article 39). Children have the right to play, recreation and cultural activities (Article 30). All of these rights have been addressed above: the rapid introduction of structured activities including education can help in meeting these objectives.

The Convention reaffirms that children have the right to education as such (Article 28), supporting the fullest development of their personalities, talents and mental and physical abilities, and promoting peace and tolerance (Article 29). States party to the convention are required to promote and encourage international cooperation in matters related to education, to eliminate ignorance and illiteracy, and to help developing countries achieve better levels of education provision (Article 28) for all children within their jurisdiction regardless of status (Article 2).

Education is a progressive right, and most countries are trying to improve the coverage and quality of education provision for their own citizens. Governments of developing countries, having signed the convention, should not refuse international assistance in providing education to refugees, asylum-seekers or the internally displaced, if they lack the funds to provide it themselves. Denial of access to primary education occurs rarely, but in some locations governments restrict refugee access to secondary education as a matter of policy, which is also contrary to the convention.[21]

---

20 Somalia and the United States. See also Article 22 of the 1951 Convention Relating to the Status of Refugees. Other human rights instruments likewise incorporate the right to education: for the work of the UN Special Rapporteur on the Right to Education, see www.unhchr.ch

21 For example, there are restrictions on refugee access to secondary education in the DRC; and in Tanzania, formal refugee secondary education is not permitted in the new caseload Burundian and Congolese refugee camps (the refugees themselves organize self-help secondary classes but with inadequate resources).

UNHCR SUPPORTED EDUCATION PROGRAMMES 2000

UNHCR
The UN Refugee Agency

UNHCR Geographic Information and Mapping Unit - November 2001
The boundaries shown on this map are those used by the UN Cartographic Section, New York
The boundaries and names shown and the designations used on this map do not imply official endorsement or acceptance by the United Nations.

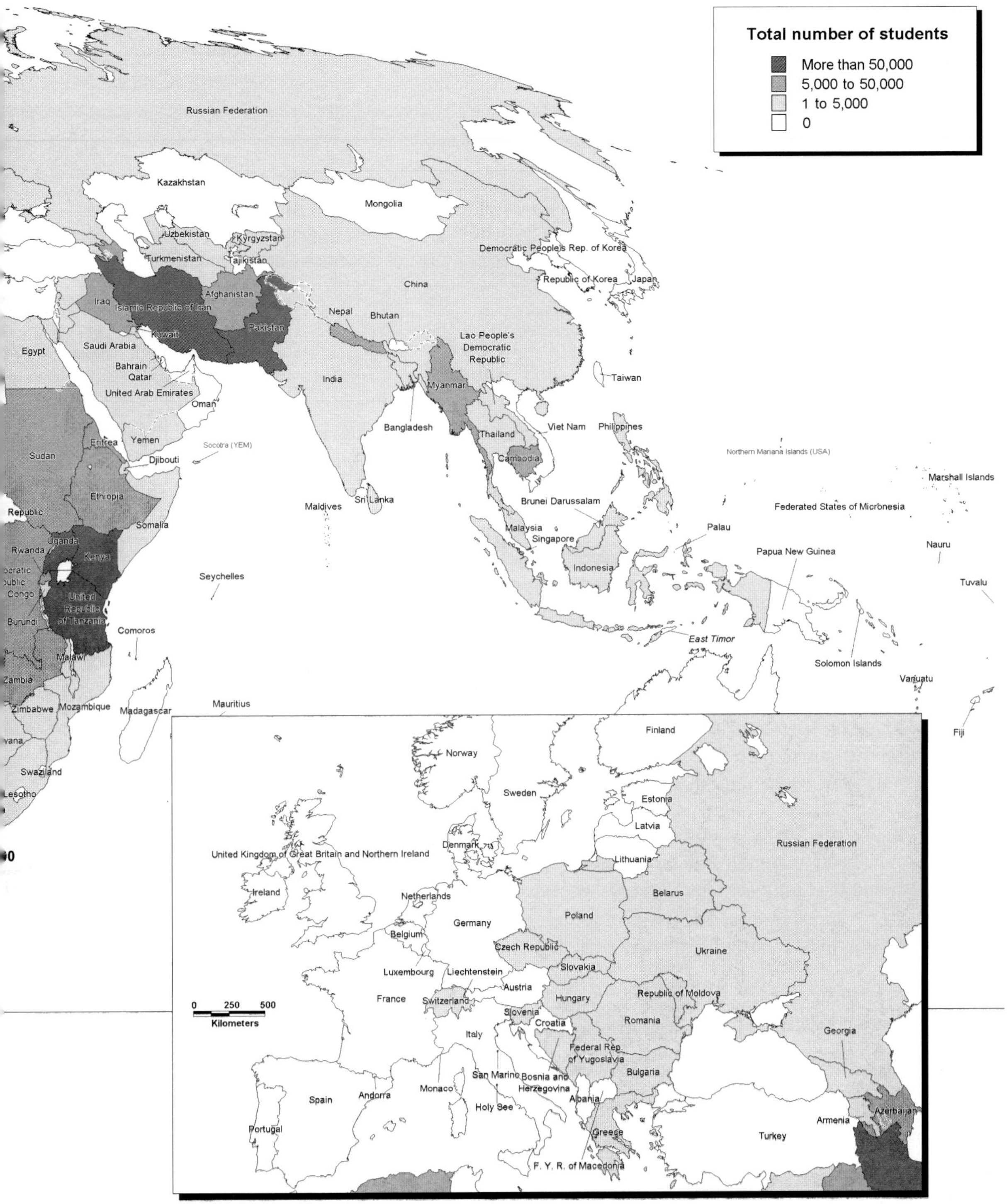

PGDS/GIMU - October 2001

Spurious arguments against rapid educational response in refugee emergencies

Several arguments are advanced for delaying education to newly arrived refugees. The most influential arguments are as follows:

- Education may prevent rapid voluntary repatriation;
- Staff are too busy, there are insufficient vehicles or staff housing;
- Education is not urgent, not life-saving.

In fact, refugees are normally homesick and their return from mass exile in neighbouring countries is delayed primarily by political and economic factors, and security issues. Decisions about repatriation are made by political leaders or tribal or family elders, many of whom have little concern over how young children spend their days.[22] The type of education that can take place in the first weeks of a refugee situation is very non-formal, with often unqualified teachers gathering children to play games, learn the alphabet, practice reading, writing and arithmetic, and so forth. It is unlikely to delay repatriation. Any items distributed are portable and can be taken back to the home country. (When refugees have been in exile for many years and a system of primary and secondary education has been established, then the situation is different. In this case, careful planning is needed to ensure that education is quickly developed in returnee areas, or to allow older students to complete their courses before repatriating, so that students are not cut off in the middle of a course of studies.)

Some people imagine that rapid education response means "building schools", but emergency education frequently takes place under trees or plastic sheeting. School construction may happen later, in months or years (and by then, formal education would have started anyway). The argument that emergency education means "building schools" and will give a "feeling of permanence", is thus unrealistic.[23]

Agency staff are indeed very busy in an emergency. This is one major reason for accepting the services of emergency education specialists from standby rosters such as that maintained by the Norwegian Refugee Council. These specialists (often funded by the Norwegian government) may come with logistical support and with money to spend on educational procurement and teacher training.

Regarding the lack of urgency, as noted earlier, schools represent a mechanism to get "survival messages" to the community and to identify and protect at-risk children. Children are in the process of psychological development, and the best way to provide psychosocial support on a large scale is to introduce structured group activities, including education. This is especially important for adolescents, who may otherwise be prone to engage in militia training and other antisocial activities, or to suffer depression.

Moreover, where the crisis arises due to ethnic conflict, it is crucial for humanitarian agencies to participate in the emergency education process rather than leaving it only to the community. Otherwise, schools can become channels for transmitting hatred to the next generation, leading to new crises in the future.

---

22 Statement based on the author's many conversations with refugees, UNHCR and NGO staff. Statistical analysis of the mass repatriation to Afghanistan from Pakistan in 1992 showed that non-repatriants were often from areas with minefields or damaged water supply, or from villages occupied during the war by other tribal groups. Education played little part in decisions to repatriate.

23 Similarly, it is unrealistic to delay emergency education on the grounds that this could mean host government pressure for "jobs". Teachers are not paid incentives early in an emergency – this normally takes place later, after a process of professional testing, selection and training.

The stories of Rwandan refugee children in Goma sitting on hard volcanic rocks in front of refugee teachers, neither children nor teachers having any materials, not even slates or a blackboard, are memorable (Rille, 1995: 9; LaPrairie, 1995: 4). They encapsulate the rationale for education as a humanitarian and peace-building response. It is not difficult to imagine that some teachers, lacking any educational materials, would have led songs and told stories reflecting the views of their ethnic group (these camps were under the influence of the leaders of the genocide). In fact, most refugee camps and settlements reflect one side of a conflict. It is thus important to link refugee teachers to the humanitarian community through employment by humanitarian organizations and to provide training to discourage them from using school to reinforce messages of hate.[24]

Policy commitments to education in emergencies

> Support for the re-establishment and continuity of education must be a priority strategy for donors and NGOs in conflict and post-conflict situations. (Machel, 1996: 59)

The United Nations has endorsed the findings of the Machel Report and has appointed a Special Representative of the Secretary-General for Children and Armed Conflict. The *Report of the Secretary-General to the General Assembly and Security Council on Children and Armed Conflict*, published in July 2000, in a section headed "Education and adolescents: two neglected concerns", recommends that governments, UN agencies and NGOs,

> Should collaborate to ensure that children are provided with educational materials and opportunities, at both the primary and secondary levels, as a priority throughout and after periods of armed conflict; with especial attention to displaced children, adolescents, girls, disabled children, former child soldiers and victims of sexual violence.

States, donors and international NGOs are encouraged to provide the "technical and financial resources required for sustained education for all children, both during and after conflict" (United Nations, 2000a: 17–19).

Relevant organs of the United Nations have integrated these concerns into their programming. UNICEF states that "in emergency situations, educational activities must be established and restored as soon as possible". The activities, though beginning very simply, should be developed professionally so as to help transform education methods and content and help solve the problems that gave rise to conflict (Pigozzi, 1999: 4–6). The World Food Programme often contributes food for students and teachers to maintain education systems in situations of emergency (WEF, 2000b: 25).

UNHCR is committed to education and supports refugee primary and secondary schools, as well as other refugee education programmes. In 1994, the Executive Committee noted that "education programmes for refugee children contribute enormously to their wellbeing and towards finding a durable solution for them", and requested the High Commissioner "to continue her efforts to give higher priority to the education of all refugee children, ensuring equal access to girls". The committee further urged UNHCR

24 In some situations, refugee teachers are employed by the host government, which may likewise tend to restrain the impulse to use schools to inculcate hatred and the desire for revenge, especially if in receipt of funding from donors who emphasise this.

"to identify educational requirements in the early stages of an emergency so that prompt attention may be given to such needs" (UNHCR, 1995b: 6). Rapid educational response in emergencies is stressed in UNHCR's guidelines on refugee children (1994) and education (1995b: 25–39) and in its *Handbook for Emergencies* (1999a: 106–109).

Among the specialized UN agencies, UNESCO has a mandate based on the assumption that wars begin in the minds of men and that the foundations of peace must be laid there also. The UNESCO Programme for Education in Emergencies and Reconstruction (UNESCO-PEER) has undertaken major emergency education programmes in East, Central and Southern Africa.[25] UNESCO has likewise provided technical support for emergency and post-emergency education in other regions, and is seeking to extend this work, including exploration of the possible use of modern technologies for this purpose (Kacem Bensalah, personal communication). UNESCO provides the education component of the United Nations Mission in Kosovo (UNMIK).

National governments are obliged by the Convention on the Rights of the Child to permit the education of child refugees within their borders. In many countries the government is actively engaged in or supportive of refugee education programmes, while, in contrast, some governments place restrictions on the education of child refugees and asylum-seekers. Within the donor community, some governments and multilateral bodies support education in emergencies, while some hesitate (Sommers, 1999: 19–22); this topic was not researched for the present study but merits detailed review.[26]

Some donors may not realize that education is the main organized activity in refugee and other displaced communities receiving external assistance. It is the main outreach activity for children and adolescents, and often involves almost every family in the community. Often children and adolescents who had missed out on schooling before displacement enrol or re-enrol and then stay in school for several years, while it is hoped that a new generation of six-year-olds will enter school each year. The resourcing needs thus grow with time, unlike costs for health (which should diminish as preventive health measures take effect), shelter and water supply. Some donor governments now realize that the 1990s concern for children, and for girls' education, translates into the need for consistent resourcing, and are examining ways of sparing education from the endless financial crises that make the management of emergency education programmes so difficult. The fact that education is in effect a "development" expenditure, an investment with both private and public benefits over the students' lifetimes, may also be mentioned here.

Regarding the policy commitments of non-governmental organizations, several major NGOs are committed to emergency education as a core activity and strongly advocate rapid and effective educational response, including psychosocial and peace-building elements. And many NGOs implement emergency education programmes in one or more locations.

---

25 UNESCO-PEER's activities in Somalia, Yemen, Djibouti, Burundi, Kenya, Tanzania, Ethiopia and Sudan are described in UNESCO-PEER (2000).

26 A website-based review of donor policies on another education topic, namely secondary education in developing countries, showed that there was limited public information on the details of education assistance policies, at least on the web (Dampare and McClure, 2000). The list of "eligible expenditure" on the European Community Humanitarian Office website (www.europa.eu.int/comm/echo) includes staff, food, medical, relief items, shelter, water and sanitation, training and other relevant headings, but appears to have inadvertently (?) omitted education, a very serious omission. The ECHO office did, however, support a Psychosocial Unit in the European Community Task Force working in Bosnia and Croatia (after a mission by a female expert to investigate rape), and this too is not listed explicitly as an eligible item (Agger and Mimica, 1996).

The Norwegian Refugee Council (NRC) has made a major impact in the 1990s, largely due to Eldrid Midttun, its Education Coordinator, whose wide travels have made her one of the leading specialists on education in emergencies. Since 1994, NRC has seconded 34 education experts to UN agencies, mostly to UNHCR, UNICEF and UNESCO, for six to 18 months to meet emergency needs and begin local capacity-building.[27] In 1998 NRC, Norwegian Save the Children and UNHCR jointly hosted an international conference on the follow-up to the Machel Report, which recommended that in emergency situations education should start immediately, and that education is a professional task, to be handled by educationalists (NRC et al., 1999: 20–22).

The IRC, UNHCR's largest implementing partner, set up a Children and Armed Conflict Unit following the Machel Report, and in 1999 hired an education specialist for this unit. It is committed to rapid education response, and has emergency education projects in 16 countries.[28]

The Jesuit Refugee Service (JRS) has a strong commitment to refugee education world-wide, with programmes in 13 countries in Africa. It has developed an education resource centre in Nairobi which houses materials on education for refugees and from emergency-prone countries.[29] Many other NGOs should also be mentioned here, but space does not permit.

Returnees at the Club Mamans Sportives, a Rwandan Women's Initiative for adult literacy training, Rwanda. UNHCR/12.1998/R. Chalasani

27 Since 1994 NRC has had emergency education programmes in Tanzania, Rwanda, Sierra Leone, Angola, Uganda, Burundi, Zaire/DRC, and Afghanistan, as well as secondments to UN agencies in some of these and other countries (Eldrid Midttun, personal communication).

28 IRC has refugee education programmes for children and young people in Albania, Azerbaijan, Bosnia, Burundi, Ingushetia/Chechnya, Cote d'Ivoire, Croatia, East Timor, Guinea, Guinea-Bissau, Indonesia (West Timor), Kosovo, Liberia, Pakistan, Rwanda and Thailand, with psychosocial programmes in some of these countries and in DRC, Sierra Leone and Uganda.

29 Angola, Burundi, DRC, Ethiopia, Kenya, Namibia, Rwanda, South Africa, Sudan, Tanzania, Uganda, Zambia and Zimbabwe. In different locations these programmes cover pre-primary, primary and secondary education, teacher training, literacy, languages, computer studies and tuition for tertiary distance students. The largest programme is in Uganda, where JRS supports over 9,000 students in pre-school and over 27,000 in UNHCR-funded primary schools (Sister Lolin Menendez, personal communication).

Education in emergencies: what are the basic principles?

Community-based approach and capacity-building

Soon after a displaced community has solved the problems of food, water and shelter, there is usually a desire to restore educational activities. Often refugees or IDPs themselves initiate simple educational activities on a voluntary basis and without any materials. For example, in Peshawar, Pakistan, in 1993 and 1994, newly arrived Afghan refugees from Kabul developed "self-help" community-based schools within weeks, seeking donations of materials such as tents and writing materials from UNHCR and other sources.[30] Burundi refugees reaching Tanzania in 1996 were not permitted to start schools at first but established community-run "children's activity centres" which provided informal schooling, with limited international support. This community-based approach has been replicated in the subsequent response to major new influxes (UNHCR, 1999b; Bird, 1999). Following the large refugee influx into Zambia in 1999 and 2000, community education committees were established to organize recreational activities and prepare sites for emergency schooling.

The involvement of the community in the establishment and management of its schools represents a step forward, from the helplessness of being displaced to gaining control over one element of social function, even if classes have to be held in the open air and are cancelled when there is rain. Because education is a fundamental right, and to ensure that it develops in an orderly fashion and meets humanitarian criteria, these initial schools are later incorporated into an organized system, normally led or supported by an NGO or government agency. This is necessary also because of the value of the resources needed for education, from writing materials and shelter to teacher "incentives" (see below), and because of the need to ensure ethnic and gender balance among teachers.[31]

Training refugee teachers and youth leaders. Community members have a vital role to play in the wider range of "structured activities" needed to involve both children and adolescents (see below). The IRC project proposal for emergency response in West Timor, for example, had specified one community educator and four community youth leaders per 100 refugee children and adolescents, to lead two daily sessions of structured activities including drawings, group discussions, theatre and music, sports, recreation and basic educational activities.[32] It is interesting to consider whether these parameters could be of more general application in early emergency.

In some cases, there are many trained and/or experienced teachers among the refugees, as with the intact Rwandan communities which took refuge in Tanzania in April 1994. Almost always there are educated refugees who take up teaching for the first time. In-service teacher training therefore plays a vital role. At the point where education programmes are being systematized, there is (or should be) a selection test to identify teachers for the post-emergency phase. Often there is a brief "new teacher training" and then systematic in-service training and mentoring; there is also, training of mentors and head-teachers (Lange, 1998). After the testing and preliminary training sessions, it is normal to pay "incentives" (in cash or kind)

30 Personal observation.

31 Management by an outside organisation protects community educators from pressures to favour particular community members and groups with jobs or other benefits, under conditions of insecurity and resource scarcity.

32 The proposal mentioned an initial "theme-based" curriculum integrating psychosocial needs, and relevant topics such as health, civics, human rights or conflict resolution, relevant to the Timor situation.

to the selected full-time teachers, to ensure continuity of service.[33] Otherwise, teachers' families will ask them to do petty trade or manual labour to earn cash for basic necessities instead of teaching, and the training they have received will be lost to the system.

Training community members in school management. It is important to prepare communities to play an ongoing role in the management of schools. The school education committee or parent–teacher association can be a grassroots training ground for improved local and national governance (Vargas-Baron and McClure, 1998; WEF, 2000c: 18–23). In many cases this idea is welcomed by programme managers and teachers, but there may be little concept of the role of such a committee (beyond asking for labour on school buildings and for fees).[34] UNICEF Somalia has produced an illustrated book for sharing with parents and community leaders, indicating how they can contribute to the quality of school life. The GTZ refugee education programme in Pakistan has recently prepared a manual for community support to schooling, based on the work of its community mobilization unit.

Community members understand the reasons for non-enrolment or drop-out of children, notably children from the poorest families and girls, and can help overcome these problems. They can also assist the school in recruiting students who have disabilities and in coping with ex-combatants. The Community Education Committee can help to bring about changes regarding participation in schooling of teenage mothers and regarding HIV/AIDS awareness and attitudes to students with AIDS. Involvement of the community in school management can facilitate communication of survival and peace-building messages to adults. Since many displaced persons will return to countries and districts where education cannot be adequately supported by government, this is an area for more research and dissemination of good practice.

Community-based rapid response in Zambia

Following the refugee influx in 1999 and early 2000, education committees were organized in all camps to initiate recreational activities and prepare sites for emergency schooling. Learning processes took the form of simple lessons combined with recreation activities. Well-qualified refugee teachers from DRC organized a structured programme for Congolese refugee students, using photocopies of the DRC curriculum obtained from UNHCR Tanzania, where CARE International staff visited to study "education for repatriation arrangements". UNICEF later procured DRC textbooks ... Because of the unavailability of resources for secondary education, some of the refugee teachers have organized private tuition for refugee secondary school students ... Levels of literacy among the newly arrived Angolan refugees in Mayukwayukwa camp are very low, and children aged 7 to 17 registered for schooling have begun emergency education with singing, literacy classes, recreational activities, Portuguese, and a few greetings in English ... In Nangweshi camp, new Angolan refugees have begun classes incorporating elements of the UNESCO-PEER approach (Chanda, 2000: 1–4).

33 "Normal" especially for refugee populations which have limited earnings possibilities. "Incentives" should at least compensate for "earnings foregone" from unskilled work, should be modest enough to be fundable and should preferably not be such as to deter repatriation when this becomes a realistic option (though lack of security in the home area is more often the deterrent nowadays).

34 The author spoke recently to a number of urban Afghan refugee educators who asked what parent–teacher associations or school management committees would actually do (education in Afghanistan had been directed by the state).

Strengthening local education administration. In post-conflict situations, national- and district-level education authorities may be functioning with new staff and without basic office equipment or transport. Yet they may be asked to present strategies to donors and to coordinate the actions of UN agencies, NGOs and community groups. Training as well as modest material assistance should be envisaged in the early stages of reconstruction.

Many of the children are traumatized by the ordeal of their flight. This $3\frac{1}{2}$ year old girl and her family just arrived in Kukes, northern Albania, after an arduous five-day trek inside Kosovo. UNHCR/04.1999/U. Meissner

Some issues for consideration. There is no consistency between emergency education programmes in the importance given to the above capacity-building measures. Much depends on the experience of project staff. Some programmes give teacher training for only 10 days in the long vacation, while for others training is a major feature of the whole programme, with courses and in-school mentoring for teachers, mobile trainers and school clustering arrangements. IRC in Guinea and JRS in Uganda have had good results with a separate teacher training unit, using mobile trainers who are distinct from field supervisory staff (Lange, 1998: 39–40; Tim Brown, personal communication). Some programmes in Pakistan have separate staffing for training of teachers and training of community education committees. Elsewhere, many programmes integrate teacher supervision and training, and community mobilization. The precise arrangements will depend on scale and logistics, but training should be a major feature of emergency education programmes, incorporating the elements mentioned above.

Another dilemma is the sharing of responsibility between the community and the implementing agency, and between international and national or refugee staff. Progressive devolution is desirable, as a capacity-building measure and for reasons of sustainability.

Meeting psychosocial needs of the child–adolescent age group

Psychologists and psychoanalysts working in the field of emergency response are deeply preoccupied with a debate regarding the universality or otherwise of the concepts of psychiatry and psychology in non-Western cultures. For some experts, elements of the Western approach must be used, while for others the focus should be the restoration of supportive social structures broken by conflict and displacement (Summerfield, 1999; Bracken et al., 1997; Parker, 1996; IFRCS, 1999).[35] The large-scale use of individualized therapies is not practicable in such situations, and a community-based approach is needed. UNICEF's support for community-based psychosocial projects was one of its main interventions during the conflicts in Bosnia-Herzegovina and Croatia, following the break-up of Yugoslavia. Local psychologists were hired to train school teachers and primary health care workers in the basics of psychological trauma. A 1998 review concluded that teachers were given valuable information about behavioural changes in their students at an important time and felt better able to cope (Richardson, 1998: 38–40).

As noted earlier, the 1997 evaluation of UNHCR's programmes for refugee children and adolescents recommended the early introduction of structured activities, tailored to the needs, concerns and resources of the population, and including such elements as "structured play and safe spaces to play; separate sports activities for boys and girls; literacy and numeracy instruction; key health, sanitation and nutrition messages; mine awareness and other safety information; drawing and painting; traditional songs, dance, theatre and story telling; lessons in traditional knowledge and skills; community service activities; and training in such conflict resolution skills as communication, negotiation and decision-making" (UNHCR, 1997c: 18).

Psychosocial issues were to the fore in the Rwandan crisis. In the Lumasi refugee camp, in Ngara, Tanzania, the NGO responsible for community services, Norwegian People's Aid, organized simple recreational activities for children within two months of the arrival of the Rwandan refugees in April 1994. This laid the

35 This has perhaps distracted them from a professional concern with emergency education programmes. Two symposia were held in Washington under the auspices of the Congressional Hunger Committee in March 1999. Some participants in the "Education in Crisis and Transition" meeting stayed on for the symposium on "Psychosocial Effects of Complex Emergencies". But the report of the latter does not discuss education as such, even though at least two key participants were strong supporters of rapid educational response on psychosocial grounds.

foundations for the subsequent inter-agency consensus on phased response to education in emergencies. Phase One focuses on generalized psychosocial response through simple community-based recreational and educational activities, while preparations are made for organized schooling. Phase Two corresponds to simple schooling accessible to all, and Phase Three is achieved with reintroduction of a unified system of curriculum, teacher training and examinations (UNHCR, 1995a: 25–37: Aguilar and Retamal, 1998). The Rwandan refugee schools in Tanzania each had a "psychosocial teacher", but problems were encountered, not least because the schools were very large and operating on a shift system. The role of the psychosocial teachers was not clear to many refugee staff, but was beneficial (Stolte, 1996: 33). In Rwanda, UNICEF initiated training of teachers in basic trauma theory and appropriate school activities in August 1994, leading to a nation-wide Trauma Recovery Programme, including the training of over 8,000 primary and secondary school teachers (Aguilar and Richmond, 1998: 132–133).

Jacinta Goveas, UNHCR's Community Services Officer in Macedonia from April to June 1999, commented that children serve as a "release mechanism" for adults' feelings of anger and hatred, and that the adults' conscious or unconscious indoctrination of children might lead to renewal of conflict in 20 years' time. She noted that even in refugee pre-school groups, children were singing songs about blood and revenge. The teachers needed consciousness-raising about this (they responded favourably to her suggestions that such songs might be harmful), and trauma counselling for themselves. She recommended that emergency kits should include materials to help teachers deal with their own post-traumatic problems (Jacinta Goveas, personal communication).

Some issues for consideration. There are vast areas of virgin territory to be explored concerning the effectiveness of structured activities including education in healing the effects of trauma, displacement, breakage of social networks and so on, among child and adolescent populations in emergency situations.[36,37] Education and social work are often more art than science, however, so that it is better to introduce constructive social activities of the type discussed above rather than wait for "scientific proof" of effectiveness (which will be difficult to achieve, given widely varying situations and cultures, and ethical considerations in establishing valid control groups). Another area to consider is how to bring structured activities to out-of-school children and adolescents as well as to school pupils over the longer term, rather than seeing them as a gap-filler for young children until schools are established.

Carl Triplehorn, IRC's Education Officer in Kosovo, noted that reconstruction programmes for 2000/2001 include psychosocial training for teachers. He drew attention to the question of whether "psychosocial" experts should train teachers, or whether it would be better for experienced teacher trainers with psychosocial exposure to train teachers in how to bring the psychosocial dimension into their daily teaching. He tended to favour the latter (Carl Triplehorn, personal communication).

---

36 The territory referred to here concerns child and adolescent populations in general rather than specific groups of individuals such as child soldiers, for whom there is more documentation: see, for example, McCallin and Jareg, 1996, and the ARC Training Module on Child Soldiers (UNHCR and SCA, 2000).

37 The International Children's Institute has prepared a generic manual on psychosocial programming for children in refugee camps which can be a useful resource in programme development (ICI, 2000). The initial version is designed for, and under trial in, the Balkans, and adaptations are envisioned for other regions.

Psychosocial components of emergency education programmes in Sierra Leone

Pilot education programmes have been developed to meet the psychosocial needs of children in Freetown, Sierra Leone. Following the attack on Freetown in early 1999, with its killings, rapes, amputations and abductions, a joint initiative for rapid education response was developed over the period April to July 1999 and initiated in August 1999 by UNESCO's Gonzalo Retamal, working with the NGO Plan International, the Education Ministry, UNICEF and the Federation of African Women Educators (FAWE). A teacher's guide was prepared which covered two "domains". Domain One comprised core literacy and numeracy. Domain Two comprised six elements: trauma healing, physical education and corporal expression, art, music, drama and peace education. Domain Two began with a trauma healing module of four weeks, comprising "structured trauma activity", plus modelling with clay, songs and music, drama and role playing, local games, cultural dance (one of these activities each morning), and jump-rope, throwing and catching balls, athletics, volleyball and football (one of these each afternoon).

Evaluation of the psychological state of the children before and after the trauma healing module and the literacy/numeracy lessons indicated a dramatic reduction in troubling symptoms, which had persisted for months until the course began. The children had been exposed to very traumatic events (80 per cent lost a nuclear family member, more than two-thirds had witnessed people being killed or attacked, and almost all had expected to die). In a pre-test before the "rapid education" course began, 95 per cent of the interviewed children had reported thinking about the most traumatic event when they did not want to. This number was reduced by 37 per cent in post-test interviews, held two to six weeks after the trauma healing module was completed. In the pre-test, 71 per cent had reported experiencing recurrent mental pictures of the worst event. This was reduced by 63 per cent in the post-test. In terms of arousal symptoms, 80 per cent of children reported difficulty concentrating at the first interview, when the courses had just begun. This was reduced to 10 per cent at the post-test. There was also a 49 per cent reduction in sleep difficulties, a 47 per cent decline in irritability, a 29 per cent decline in startle reactions and 38 per cent reduction in bad dreams. More than half the children stated that they felt a sense of relief while drawing pictures, talking or writing about their bad memories from the war. The limited timeframe and lack of a control group mean that this valuable study needs follow-up by the "psychosocial" community.

The Norwegian Refugee Council and UNICEF initiative for re-insertion of older Sierra Leonean children into schooling was developed in early 2000 by local educators (with facilitation from NRC), drawing on the "rapid education" programme just described and other materials. It comprises six strands: literacy; numeracy; trauma healing; physical and health / AIDS education; religious and moral education; and peace and human rights education. This Rapid Response Education Programme aims to help children aged over 10 years of age re-enter schooling that was disrupted by nine years of conflict. This programme should permit (re-)insertion of children into the regular school system at the beginning of the next school year, or into an accelerated learning programme for adolescents. Due to a general lack of school places, younger children seek to join also. (Gupta (2000), Retamal (1999), Mette Nordstrand and Eldrid Midttun (personal communications)).

Rapid response

A major focus in emergency education policy during the 1990s has been to develop modalities of rapid educational response, to meet the psychosocial and educational needs of crisis-affected children. A working group called "RAPID ED" held a series of meetings in the early 1990s on emergency response.[38] Examples of speedy response include education for Kosovar refugees in Albania and Macedonia in 1999, newly arriving Burundi and Congolese refugees in Tanzania since 1996 and recent influxes of Angolan refugees in Zambia. In these cases, and no doubt in many more, there was response to the needs of some new arrivals within the first two months.

As will be seen below, there has been much debate as to whether pre-assembled education kits can contribute to rapid response (as compared to local procurement and distribution of educational materials). Of the above-mentioned cases, UNICEF kits were supplied in Tanzania, Albania and Macedonia, although response may have pre-dated their arrival. UNICEF has recently adopted a core corporate commitment to supply some education and recreation kits by air within a few days and a larger number, as required, by sea or land within a month.[39] Deployments from the standby roster maintained by NRC have contributed to rapid education response in sudden crises such as Kosovo in 1999 and Eritrean refugee movements in 2000.

Some issues for consideration. It is often difficult to be precise about the speed of response retrospectively, as emergencies may arise gradually and population displacement may continue over months or years, while education response tends to build up gradually, in terms of geographic coverage and activities undertaken. Hence data was not to hand for the present study systematically to review achievements in speed of response. However, it would be most desirable for future emergency education programmes to document in "real time" the dates of crisis onset and subsequent population movements and crises, of needs assessments and actions taken in the various relevant locations. This would help "ground" the concept of "rapid" response, and perhaps show which factors make for speed and effectiveness.

Relating response to the school year

A welcome trend has been to take note of the timing of an emergency in relation to the school year, and to develop emergency response programmes that not only meet the psychosocial needs of children and adolescents quickly (see below) but also lead to completion of unfinished studies in time for a new school year. As noted below, the Albanian government formulated a plan for "catch-up" classes so that Kosovo refugees could be ready for the new school year in September 1999, whether in Albania or Kosovo. In 2000, the Eritrean government likewise arranged vacation classes for schoolchildren to make up the last three weeks of the school year, disrupted by conflict. This permitted students to sit school examinations needed for promotion to the next year of schooling.[40] Alternatively there can be a road-map for resumption of formal studies, with an "emergency phase" until the beginning of the next school year, as in refugee programmes in Tanzania (see below).

---

38 This was a sub-group of the International Multi-channel Action Group for Education (IMAGE), based at the International Council for Distance Education, Oslo.

39 Personal communications from Pilar Aguilar and Peter Buckland (2000).

40 In Rwanda, the school year beginning in September 1993 was extended to December 1994, because of the genocide. The next school year was compressed to run January–July 1995 inclusive, after which the normal timings resumed (Mark Richmond, personal communication).

Some issues for consideration. Initial emergency assessments could perhaps focus more strongly on a detailed understanding of the pre-emergency education system. Educators in the affected population can advise on how to restore a sense of normalcy in terms of school years, examinations and so on, given the practical constraints of the particular situation.

Education for durable solutions

UNICEF has emphasized that long-term education development objectives should guide even the earliest phase of emergency education response (Pigozzi, 1999). Refugee agencies seek durable solutions to refugee problems, namely voluntary repatriation, local settlement in the country of first asylum or resettlement in a third country. Opportunities for local settlement and resettlement are limited, and most refugees in any case long to return to their homeland, if they can do so in safety and dignity. Hence the durable solution for most refugee populations has to be return to their own country; but while this may in some circumstances be possible in a matter of weeks, in other circumstances it can take years or even decades.

At the UN–NGO Consultation on Refugee Education convened by UNHCR after the Jomtien Conference on Education for All in 1990, a major focus was on strengthening the concept of "education for repatriation". Participants described how the education programme for Mozambican refugees in Malawi and Zimbabwe was being developed on this basis. The refugee schools followed the Mozambican curriculum, using Portuguese as the medium of instruction. Textbook supply, in-service teacher training and school examinations were organized in coordination with the Mozambican Ministry of Education. In consequence the students were in a position to re-enter the school system in Mozambique after repatriation (Smawfield, 1998).[41] The smaller numbers of Mozambican refugees in Zambia and Tanzania, who were following the national curricula there, did not study Portuguese, and therefore may have had to repeat lower primary school classes in Mozambique after repatriation. The other cases presented at the consultation were the education of Afghan refugees in Pakistan (also following the principle of education for repatriation) and emergency education in the Horn of Africa.

The concept of "education for repatriation", using the home country curriculum, gained recognition during the 1990s (Preston, 1991; UNHCR, 1995a: 14, 28; Retamal and Aedo-Richmond, 1998a). Besides preparing students to re-enter schooling in their areas of origin, it also permits the employment of educated refugees as teachers. Familiar classroom materials and teachers provide a sense of security and identity for the displaced students.

The most important aspect of the curriculum from the viewpoint of repatriation is the language(s) used for study. Thus the Afghan refugees who fled to Pakistan in the 1980s studied in their own language (mostly Pushtu), while following a curriculum based on their religious beliefs, rather than the Marxist curriculum adopted in Afghanistan at that time. They also study Pakistan's national language, Urdu. This is an example

41 Gonzalo Retamal and Ruth Aedo-Richmond (1998) describe the attempts of the consultation to establish inter-agency cooperation on refugee education, but the mechanism devised (a UN–NGO Working Group on Refugee Education to meet between consultations) did not prove viable, due to factors such as staff rotation and the inability of NGOs to meet travel costs. Cooperation may be easier in the age of e-mail.

of a curriculum that "faces both ways", providing needed linguistic skills for children, some of whose families are likely to repatriate and some not.[42] In the case of refugees from southern Sudan, the previous curriculum had been anglophone, similar to that in Kenya and Uganda, their principal asylum countries. Based on the wishes of the refugees, the refugee schools follow the curriculum of the host country: studies are thus linked to the education tradition of the area of origin rather than to the current national curriculum of the country of origin.

There has in the past been some feeling of national pride, requiring that refugees should follow the host country curriculum.[43] This is still the case in the DRC, where students from southern Sudan and from Angola have to follow the francophone national curriculum, even though their own education traditions are based on English and Portuguese respectively. It is true for Sudan, where the government schools for refugees use Arabic medium and the national curriculum.[44] There are human rights issues to be considered here (see below). In the case of very long-stay refugees there is some rationale for following the host country curriculum plus the language of the area of origin, but a bridging phase is needed to help children make the transition.

Regional approach and certification. The regional approach to Mozambican education has just been noted. In 1994 there was inter-agency cooperation and a regional approach to emergency education from the beginning of the Rwandan emergency. UNICEF and UNESCO-PEER shared an office in Kigali and supported the distribution of education kits and associated teacher training for Rwandan students in Rwanda itself, in Tanzania and in eastern Zaire (Aguilar and Richmond, 1998). Currently, a regional approach to certification of examinations has been developed by UNHCR and UNICEF in Tanzania, working with education authorities in Burundi and DRC (see Tanzania case study below). UNESCO-PEER is leading a process to examine modalities of certification of refugee studies in East Africa (UNESCO-PEER, 2000: 3).

The IRC refugee education programme in Guinea gave early priority to producing a curriculum that incorporated the requirements of both countries of origin, Liberia and Sierra Leone, leading to recognition of school attainments by the education authorities of these countries. The refugee school examinations are administered by the West African Examinations Council. IRC's strong refugee teacher training programme in Guinea did not meet the precise specifications for teacher qualifications in Liberia, however, and could not be recognized in the early stages of repatriation. After prolonged negotiations, the Liberian Education Ministry agreed that IRC's teacher training programme in Guinea was acceptable as a qualification for a "C-level" teacher training qualification in Liberia. The refugee teacher training programme in Cote d'Ivoire was deemed insufficient for accreditation. This is an example of how a decision taken early on – to design the in-service training of refugee teachers so that it cumulatively covers the teacher training curriculum of the country of origin – could contribute to a durable solution (Nordstrand, 2000: 13).

---

42 For a review of current curriculum issues see Education for Afghans: a strategy paper (Rugh, 1998) and follow-up papers in preparation by Ellen van Kalmthout of UNICEF Afghanistan and Andrea Rugh of Save the Children. These papers describe inter-agency collaboration to identify grade-wise "basic competency" objectives and produce shared supplementary materials.

43 Use of the host country curriculum may create more teaching jobs for nationals, but may disempower refugees who could otherwise teach. Use of some host country nationals as teachers, for subjects such as their own language, represents a compromise, but there can be disquiet if they are paid more than refugee teachers.

44 Some refugee families sent their children to informal schools following the Eritrean curriculum (Appadu and Retamal, 1998: 48–50).

Opportunity for positive change. Crisis can provide the opportunity to upgrade education programmes, providing long-term benefits. Don Foster-Gross (2000: 2–4) cites USAID's support to the Honduran Education Ministry for curriculum revision as well as infrastructure reconstruction after Hurricane Mitch and USAID's wider efforts to promote participatory planning and local contributions to educational governance. UNICEF emphasizes emergencies as an "opportunity for educational transformation" (Pigozzi, 1999). UNMIK's "Developing the Education System in Kosovo" (DESK) initiative in Kosovo comprises a system design team of 25 Kosovar educators (inclusive of women and minorities) and 22 international educators working to analyse education problems and develop strategies for transformation to meet the needs of the twenty-first century (Daxner, 2000: 10–11).

Some issues for consideration. UNHCR should look more closely at situations where refugees are forced to follow the host country curriculum, in languages different from their previous languages of instruction. There are several important human rights issues that would support freedom to use the previous medium of instruction (Bruce Abramson, personal communication). Another important concern is to ensure that school studies and teacher training in emergencies are recognized after the emergency is over, for example after repatriation. Regarding emergency as an opportunity for positive change, can norms be developed from analysis of recent emergencies that will encourage major donors to fund renovation of education systems (and not merely reconstruction of buildings)?

Survival and peace-building messages

> The difference between education in emergencies and in a normal situation, is that the target group's needs are taken more into account more than the [normal] curriculum would. Basic learning and basic knowledge for coping mentally and physically is given priority along with knowledge and practice that will help promote a peaceful and values-/rights-based rebuilding of the war-torn communities. (Midttun, 2000b: 2)

Health education. Throughout the 1990s there has been a growing awareness of the need to convey information to crisis-affected communities.[45] Some senior managers see this as a justification for maintaining refugee education budgets in times of acute funding constraints.[46] UNESCO-PEER has prepared booklets in Somali on "Cholera Awareness", "A World without Polio", "HIV/AIDS and Other Sexually Transmitted Diseases", and charts on sexually transmitted diseases, acute respiratory infections and diarrhoea, as well as health education textbooks and teacher guides (UNESCO-PEER, 2000).

---

45 "Supplementary survival packages: Around the basic core of non-formal responses [recreation, literacy/numeracy], important subjects or "emergency themes" are crucial in order to heighten awareness of the affected populations and especially for the children and youth who have been the victims of armed conflicts. The research and assessment of these "generative themes" are an important part of the dialogue between the educators and the populations affected by the humanitarian crisis. These contents constitute the foundation for developing a basic safety net of knowledge and understanding for the populations that are confronted with extreme situations, and the daily threat of land mines, cholera, waterborne diseases, and/or the degradation of the environment ... The theme of becoming aware about the horror of war, the desire for peace and reconciliation, can be 'generated' from the active realization of the perils left by these confrontations, such as land mines, cholera, famine, HIV/AIDS etc." (Aguilar and Retamal, 1998: 33).

46 Kolude Doherty, Director of the Africa Bureau, UNHCR: personal communication.

UNHCR is developing programmes to sensitize refugee communities to the dangers of HIV/AIDS and sexual and gender-based violence, and has prepared a "how to" guide on reproductive health education for adolescents based on the IRC programme in Guinea (Flax and James-Traore, 1998). UNICEF has supported governments and NGOs in developing health education materials in many countries, adapted for emergency situations as necessary, and with especial attention to HIV/AIDS education. The package of HIV/AIDS education materials developed by the World Health Organization (WHO) and UNESCO is a useful resource that should be widely distributed for local adaptation (WHO and UNESCO, 1994).

Returnees from Mozambique in a mine awareness class by a Zimbabwean Demining Company. Espungabera Transit Centre. UNHCR/05.1994/L. Taylor

Environmental awareness. UNHCR and UNESCO-PEER have worked together to prepare environmental education materials for years one to eight of schooling in refugee camps in east Africa; these materials are designed to enrich the teaching of school subjects with key environmental messages affecting children's lives (Talbot and Muigai, 1998).[47] Follow-up activities are needed to make such materials available in more countries and to ensure that the materials are actually used, despite the difficulties of integration into an overloaded school programme.

Mine awareness. Mine awareness has received much attention recently (Baxter et al., 1997; Baxter and Hoffmann, 1998; Swedish Save the Children, 1998, 1999b; UNICEF, 1999a; UNHCR and SCA, 2000). UNICEF is the designated lead agency within the UN system (see www.unicef.org). The University of Pittsburgh's Global Information Network In Education (GINIE) website has a strong focus on this topic (www.ginie.org).

Education for peace and citizenship. Conflict has become less a matter of geopolitics and more a matter of disputes between neighbouring countries or neighbouring citizens. This has led to increased emphasis on education to build skills and attitudes supportive of tolerance and peace. UNESCO has developed the theme of a Culture of Peace, and is responsible for the Decade of Education for the Culture of Peace and Non-Violence for the Children of the World, 2001–2010. UNESCO-PEER has worked with Somali educators to develop peace education materials for Somalia (UNESCO-PEER, 2000: 6–7). UNICEF has developed a peace education teachers' training manual (Fountain, 1997) and has worked with governments and NGOs to promote peace education (Fountain, 1999). NRC has produced a Human Rights Education Resource Book, which includes peace education and human rights messages.[48] Since 1999, the International Committee of the Red Cross and Red Crescent (ICRC) has established a network of 15 sites for its "Exploring humanitarian law" project, which has produced a manual for testing with adolescents in secondary and non-formal education programmes (Tawil, 2000: 590–91).[49]

Thanks to earmarked funding, UNHCR's peace education consultant has been able to work with a multinational group of refugee educators to develop a set of generic peace education teachers' guides, with a complete set of lesson plans for years one to eight of schooling, and a facilitators' manual for concurrent training sessions in the community (Baxter, 2000). Such foundational materials should in future be supplemented by modules focusing on specific health behaviours and coping skills, environmental behaviour, humanitarian law, and citizenship issues, including an understanding of global human rights dialogue as a guide to building democratic governance locally and nationally. There should be linkage to psychosocial programming, and a guide to phasing, from modules catering to early emergency through to post-crisis situations.[50]

47 For Ethiopia materials see UNESCO-PEER and UNHCR (1999).

48 Originally developed for use in Albania, NRC has introduced the programme jointly with the respective education ministries in Armenia, Georgia, Azerbaijan and Angola, and provided it to the OSCE Human Rights Education programme in Kosovo (Midttun, 1999).

49 Humanitarian law is especially relevant for populations in conflict-prone areas, and can be linked to peace education, citizenship education and human rights education, as appropriate to local conditions.

50 At a key RAPID-ED meeting in 1995, the working group on education for conflict resolution and peacebuilding, facilitated by Eldrid Midttun, suggested that, "Initial peacebuilding curricula for refugees should include stress reduction, communication skills, information management, information on the refugee camp and refugees' rights. Curricula for refugees while in exile should include dealing with conflict and conflict resolution, mediation skills and an attempt to create normalcy through activities such as sports and music. Curricula designed to prepare refugees for repatriation should include reconciliation skills, education for democracy-building and human rights education" (Tilson, 1995).

Peace education in practice

UNHCR peace education materials are used in all refugee schools in Kenya, where some 42,000 children have a peace education lesson period each week and where more than 3,000 young people and adults have followed the community training (12 half-day sessions plus periodic follow-up sessions). Peace education has a separate lesson period, and separate well-trained teachers, since it requires a different, skill-based approach, compared with the rote learning or "chalk and talk" approach used in most refugee schools (Baxter, 2000). Peace education "lessons" in fact give many students and teachers a first insight into participative methods in education, which are strongly emphasized in the peace education teacher training. "The peace education teachers are now considered to be the best-trained teachers in the camp and they have taken on roles which were not envisaged, such as peer training, counselling and mentoring" (Baxter, personal communication).

Young people can be confined to the camps for many years, with little intellectual stimulation, and the opportunity should be taken to prepare the next generation for seeking ways of rebuilding their societies rather than perpetuating conflict.

The skills included in peace education programmes are also known as "life skills". They include active listening, understanding emotions, cooperation, problem-solving, prejudice reduction, negotiation and mediation, and are developed through class activities followed by discussion. As noted during an inter-agency meeting convened by the World Health Organization, these skills are needed for positive goals such as gender equality, democracy and peace, as well as for prevention of HIV/AIDS, teenage pregnancy, substance abuse, racism, environmental damage, depression, suicide and conflict (WHO, 1999).

Some issues for consideration. Making room for these messages and for skills training in emergency education situations is not easy. In a developing world situation especially, teachers are often under-educated and under-trained, reference books for teachers and students are few, hours of study are often limited by a shift system or lack of school lunches, studies are examination-oriented, and much time is needed for students to copy notes down from the blackboard, the normal means of knowledge transfer. Much emphasis is laid on rote-learning, and many teachers lack professional questioning skills and awareness of the value of discussion in the classroom. Given resource and teacher limitations and the overloaded curriculum, the Western approach of "integrating" messages and skills into the teaching of normal subjects can be difficult. On the other hand, it is difficult to find a classroom period for a new topic. From the point of view of programme management, it is easier to do the latter, since it is a one-off decision and relatively easy to monitor. It can be acceptable to the teachers and community if the topic is deemed important, such as health or peace education.

Another question is whether to use special teachers. IRC's health education programme in Guinea and UNHCR's peace education programme have used this approach, so that there are staff with skills and motivation (their job) to give most or all of their time to health or peace respectively. Another requirement for effectiveness is to reach out-of-school peers and adults, so that the messages are reinforced: this can be problematic where a topic is introduced in a national education system.[51] After-school clubs, vacation workshops, and youth clubs or study circles are other ways of reaching children and young people.

---

51 As in the tolerance education programme developed for young adolescents in government schools in Kyrgyzstan with support from UNHCR (Jenkins, 1997). There is now some wider outreach through the Kyrgyz NGO Foundation Tolerance International (Barbara Smith, personal communication).

Broadening the concept of education

As is evident from the above examples, key agencies now identify "education in emergencies" with the range of activities needed to normalize the state of traumatized and/or displaced children and adolescents. In some cases (in refugee camps in Tanzania, for example), the same organization looks after "Community Services" and education, and arranges recreational, cultural and other healing activities for young refugees, without having to draw a boundary between what is "education" and what is something else. In some cases, however, an organization which does not specialize in education and children's programming is given a budget for "education". The agency may not be aware that "education" in emergency has the wider dimensions noted above, even for its own school students. And there may be no organization to support non-formal education and recreation, cultural and other healing activities for out-of-school children and adolescents. It may be argued that non-formal education should be a "default" responsibility of the NGO responsible for schooling, if no other agency is systematically covering the needs of out-of-school children and adolescents.

Questions for consideration. Some of the leaders in the field of "emergency education" have moved to this broader approach, and hopefully others will follow. This may require a clearer focus in the policy guidelines of donor and implementing agencies. It will be desirable to include "real-time evaluation" in these innovative programmes, so that lessons learned can be quickly shared elsewhere.

Attention to specific groups: gender, early childhood, adolescents, minorities, children with disability, separated children, ex-combatants

Education programmes can easily overlook the special needs of specific groups. Under-representation of girls is widely reported and discussed (Stromquist, 1997; WEF, 2000d). Belated attention has been paid to the needs of adolescents. In some emergencies, special measures are needed to promote the access of minority group children to education. Special measures may be needed to bring children with disability, separated children and ex-combatant children into the education process. Efforts of this kind are important as examples of human rights in practice for crisis-affected populations that may have suffered from human rights abuses.

Refugee children from Mali at a school in M'Berra Camp, Mauritania. UNHCR/10.1996/J. Brigou

Gender. A growing international consensus on the importance of girls' education led the UN Secretary-General to devote most of his opening speech at the Year 2000 World Education Forum to this topic, at which he launched a special UN Girls' Education Initiative. Gender equity, or promoting the participation of girls, features as an objective in almost every emergency education programme.

Many of the issues affecting girls' education in poor countries affect refugee girls also. The most prominent reason for the under-representation of refugee girls in school affects boys also, namely family poverty. However, the poverty factor has a gender bias.[52] In some cultures, the most traditional families hold back from girls' education or withdraw their daughters from school before puberty.[53] There are many ways in which girls' participation in schooling can be promoted in refugee and other emergency situations (Sinclair, 1998b). For example, older girls are reluctant to attend school if they do not have clothing that preserves their decency, and they need soap and sanitary materials. Where adolescent boys have to work, special late afternoon classes can be held for them, as in the GTZ refugee programme in Pakistan (GTZ, 1999a: 3).

A broader concept and wider outreach

"Structured normalizing activities for children and adolescents that address their protection and developmental needs" is the key objective of the "Consortium" programme in East Timor, the consortium comprising Save the Children/US, Christian Children's Fund and IRC. Many children and adolescents in East Timor are out of school (sometimes out of reach of school, since many schools were destroyed and many teachers have left). The project "trains community adults and youth leaders [to lead] appropriate games and activities for children and youth in post-conflict settings", issuing each with a "psychosocial kit" comprising "basic education supplies, recreation and sports equipment". There is support for parent–teacher associations or education committees (to help restore schooling), support and capacity-building for youth clubs and organizations, training of youth to work with younger children or vulnerable peers, and so on. The project goal is "to enable East Timorese children and adolescents to resume healthy development through community-based protection, psychosocial and reconciliation programmes"(CPPPS, 2000: 1). These "normalizing" programmes can not only help children recover from trauma and move forward, but provide a training ground for youth and adults to learn the skills of constructive participation in the work of civil society, in the competencies needed for democratic local and national governance.

52 Investment in boys' education is seen as bringing greater long-term benefits to the family. Poverty also means that girls have more household chores than boys, since many of the chores confronting poor families are very time-consuming and are seen as female tasks. WHO's provision of a monthly tin of edible oil to Afghan refugee girls attending school regularly in Pakistan, has had a dramatic positive effect on girls' attendance (Geert van der Casteele, personal communication).

53 In many societies there is concern that girls will be sexually active or harassed if they attend school after puberty. There are often strict rules against the participation of pregnant girls or teenage mothers in school, but in some locations an effort has been made to overcome this tradition. Special measures may be needed to prevent harassment by teachers and students in school, and by students or others on the way home from school.

Early childhood. There are several views on pre-school education in emergency settings. For some, it seems a luxury. The best way to overcome this problem is to help the community organize simple kindergarten or pre-school activities, as happens in many refugee situations. This can sometimes be done even in the midst of conflict, as shown by the work of Save the Children in Bosnia (Nuttall, 1999, Burde, 1999).[54] It is preferable to train community volunteers for this work, so that it can continue when funding is no longer available. Training, supervision and the supply of simple materials need to be funded, however, to ensure effective programme development. These issues need to be discussed with the community in the context of promoting girls' education. Girls commonly have to look after younger siblings, which is especially important in the confusion of early emergency. Hence, the introduction of simple kindergarten and pre-school activities can contribute to girls' enrolment and retention in school.

Adolescents. Adolescents are at a particularly vulnerable stage of their personal development in psychological terms, as well as at risk of being raped, forced into early marriage, recruited into militias and so on. There has been a tendency in emergencies to ignore them: it is much easier to organize classes for very young children.[55] Influenced by the children's lobby seeking to promote the wellbeing of persons up to 18 years of age (the age group covered by the Convention on the Rights of the Child) and by the Machel Report, with its explicit concern about the neglect of adolescents, agencies are now attempting to broaden the initial response to crises, to provide educational and related activities for adolescents (Lowicki, 2000: 12–18; UNHCR, 1997b, 1997c; UNHCR, 2000c). As noted above, the "Consortium" programme in East Timor provides for outreach to adolescents. The same is true, for example, for the IRC project "Emergency education and psychosocial support for Chechen children and adolescents in Ingushetia"[56] and the Save the Children/US programme in eastern Ethiopia.[57]

In many developing countries, education begins late or has been interrupted, with the consequence that many of the children in primary school are adolescents. For older adolescents needing to begin schooling, special classes separate from very young children are sometimes arranged. For example, an accelerated learning programme for adolescents, which covers the first six years of schooling in three years, initially developed in Liberia, has recently been adapted by the Ministry of Youth, Education and Sports in Sierra Leone (Mette Nordstrand, personal communication).

It is not always easy to attract the intended age group to an activity. NRC reports that some students following its emergency school programme in Angola are at the lower end of the intended age bracket of 6 to 14 years, although one objective had been to promote the insertion of older children into regular schooling (Johannessen, 2000: 12–13). Likewise, in Sierra Leone, the programme intended to support re-insertion into schooling of children aged 10 to 13 (or older) is "finding it difficult to avoid children under 10 when regular schooling is insufficient"(Mette Nordstrand, personal communication). For more educated

54 For examples of early childhood work with refugees in Guatemala and Zambia respectively, see Dagnino (1996) and Fozzard and Tembo (1996).

55 For recreational, cultural and voluntary service activities for adolescents, promoted by UNHCR Community Services staff in Rwandan refugee camps in Tanzania, see Blomquist (1995: 23–26).

56 The objectives specified in the project document are "to rapidly provide normalising structured education activities for children and adolescents that address their cognitive and developmental needs", to establish "Parent-Education Committees", and "to respond to the protection and psychosocial needs of vulnerable adolescents through the establishment of theme-based clubs and the promotion of positive leadership roles".

57 The multisectoral UNHCR-funded programme includes under "education" activities the promotion of youth education centres, sports and cultural activities for youth as well as training for primary school teachers and other activities.

young people the creative writing workshops developed by Carl Solomon and Naomi Flutter working with refugees in Nepal have led to ongoing writing and community education activities by participants, with the age group 15 to 30 showing the greatest commitment to follow-up (Solomon, personal communication).[58]

Minorities. In some emergencies, minorities have to be protected by separation, as in the case of mixed-marriage Hutu–Tutsi Rwandan refugee families in Tanzania. In Kosovo UN agencies and OSCE are currently promoting schooling for minority families which are threatened by the Kosovo Albanian population. In one area the peacekeeping troops had to start patrolling a local school road to allow Roma children, who were harassed by other children, to resume school attendance. In another area, a survey on access of Roma and Ashkalija children to school was postponed due to their families' fear that they would be harassed.[59] UNHCR undertook a needs assessment for Roma education and developed a plan of action for raising the education level of this community (Lange, 1999a).

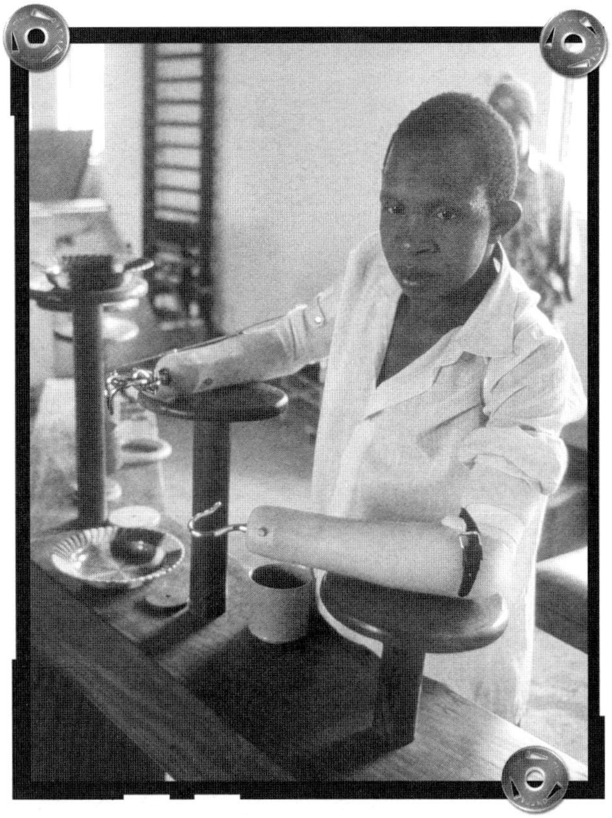

A mutilation victim receiving help at the National Pediatric Center in Conakry. UNHCR provides therapy and medical aid, including artificial limbs, to dozens of the victims who fled to Guinea from Liberia and Sierra Leone. UNHCR/06.1999/P. Stromberg

Children with disability. In principle the emergency education approach of working with the community should facilitate the participation of children and adolescents with disability. During her mission to refugee schools in Guinea in 1998, Ellen Lange had noted that parents of disabled children often did not choose to send them to school, and stressed the importance of discussing these issues with the community.[60] In Bhutanese refugee schools in Nepal, there is systematic provision for the education of children with disability (Brown, 2001).

58 See their Creative Writing Manual (forthcoming), and Nepal creative writing project evaluation report (forthcoming).

59 See Kosovo Humanitarian Update, February 2000.

60 A volunteer informed her that there were students with reduced eyesight among the refugees, who could see by day and not by night and would have difficulty seeing the blackboard inside the often dark school rooms. Eyesight and hearing issues need attention (Lange, 1998: 32–33).

The UNHCR adviser for education in Kosovo (seconded by NRC) focused on disability and minority issues. She recommended that the UN Standard Rules on the Equalization of Opportunities for Persons with Disabilities were taken into account in the reconstruction of schools destroyed by conflict or damaged by use as residential centres (Lange, 1999b).

Separated children. There have been unfortunate experiences in which orphanages established in emergency situations have led to family separations, as parents place their children there for food security, access to education or for other reasons. Where possible, the policy of placing separated children with families in the community and providing guidance and support is much preferred (UNHCR, 1999a: 102–104). However, this does entail monitoring that the fostered children have access to education equally with other children.

Ex-combatants:

> Education [for child soldiers], and especially the completion of primary education, must be a high priority ... to normalize life and to develop an identity separate from that of the soldier. The development of peer relationships and improved self-esteem may also be facilitated through recreational and cultural activities ... Former combatants may have fallen far behind in their schooling, and may be placed in classes with far younger children. Specific measures may then be required, such as establishing special classes for former child soldiers who can then progressively be reintegrated into regular schools ... Many teachers and parents may object to having ex-combatants enrol in school, fearing that they will have a disruptive effect. Programmes must address these wider community concerns ... For older children especially, effective education will require strong components of training in life skills and vocational opportunity. (Machel, 1996: 20)

In Liberia, 77 per cent of demobilized soldiers stated that their foremost desire was to return to school. UNICEF helped supply primary schools with materials, train teachers and support peace education (in Monrovia up to 60 per cent of school children were reported to be former child soldiers, who often resorted to violence). UNICEF's Support for War Affected Youth (SWAY) project provided a regular day programme of counselling and vocational and literacy training, in three accessible counties. Graduates of the Zion Community College three-month course in trauma healing were used as counsellors. An accelerated curriculum was developed for child soldiers and others whose education had been disrupted by the conflict.[61]

Key requirements for ex-combatants are the re-establishment of trust, self-esteem, identity and attachment, self-control (rather than aggression), and recognition of their own resources and strengths. Save the Children/UK, working with Liberian child soldiers, stressed the need to create a normalized setting and wait until the children are ready to talk. The talk would not be of "trauma healing" but issues of suffering, loss, loneliness, terror and anxiety. Community members were trained to hold "supportive

61 The accelerated learning project condenses the six years of primary schooling into three. The curriculum focuses on skills development, and teaching methods are pupil-centred. The success of the programme lies in the students' motivation, their readiness to learn because they are older, and support from their families and communities. In Sierra Leone, the UNICEF Children Associated with War (CAW) demobilization process included access to a six-month programme of education, group counselling, play, recreation, vocational skills and apprenticeship training. (From UNICEF's assistance to ex-child soldiers, at www.ginie.org)

conversations" (avoiding the stigmatization of "trauma counselling"). It was found useful to have a goal in mind, such as controlling aggression or increasing concentration in class. Such practical discussions and goals enable children to gain gradual control of the problem.[62]

Some of the lessons learned in demobilization and similar education programmes could be useful in helping schoolteachers deal with conflict-affected students and ex-soldiers. In Guinea, IRC teachers reported motivating young fighters who came out of the forest to stay in school, rather than returning to fight. They also reported violent incidents involving former child soldiers unable to cope with their situation. Being able to talk to teachers unconnected with their former military life may be a crucial factor in the students' mental development, but their confidences can endanger teachers. Moreover, teachers need support when faced with claims from one student that another is responsible for the death of his or her family members (Lange, 1998: 32).

Children and adolescents involved in substance abuse or prostitution. These are important problems in current emergency situations, but have not been well documented in relation to emergency education.

Some issues for consideration. There are often simplistic approaches to estimating how many children are missing out on education, based on statistics comparing enrolment and population estimates. These give misleading results when there is a backlog of unmet demand for education and when population statistics are weak. Based on his experience with refugee programmes in Uganda, Tim Brown recommends that linkages should be built to the community to find out who is *not* in school (personal communication). Emergency programmes should have a systematic plan to extend progressively the coverage of schooling, based on local circumstances. Insights into local culture and the situation of poor families are vital here: this is an area where sensitive researchers with an anthropological methodology could make a contribution.[63] The broad understanding that participation is limited by poverty could be fine-tuned, for example, leading to locally workable ideas for action.

Reaching out to less accessible and insecure places

In many war-torn and insecure places such as Angola, southern Sudan, DRC, Sierra Leone and Chechnya, there are major problems of access and security. Some places become accessible for a time and then perhaps less accessible again. An example from the year 2000 was the arrival of about 100,000 refugees from DRC in remote and insecure parts of the Republic of Congo and the Central African Republic. Even the most basic assistance is difficult under such conditions, and it is not clear whether NGOs will be willing or able to implement education programmes in such locations. Another example is the situation of refugees from East Timor, confined to camps in West Timor, and without international support at the time of writing, due to security concerns. In such situations efforts may be made to assist self-help or local government schooling through distribution of education and recreation kits, although the monitoring of their distribution and use may be difficult, and pilferage probable. There are many questions for consideration here and no easy answers.

62 From the Action for the Rights of the Child (ARC) training module on child soldiers (UNHCR and SCA (2000).

63 Such research is to be funded in 2001 by the Mellon Foundation.

Preparing ongoing refugee or IDP programmes to receive new arrivals

Often, refugees or internally displaced persons arrive in locations where emergency programmes are already in place. For example, refugees continue to arrive in Tanzania, Pakistan, Zambia and Guinea (respectively 142,000, 93,000, 38,000 and 23,000 new arrivals in 1999), countries with well-established refugee education programmes. In contrast, the continuing arrival of refugees in DRC (65,000 in 1999) presents more problems of response, since even ongoing refugee education programmes (and national schools) face problems due to lack of access to insecure areas as well as funding constraints.

From the personal viewpoint, an emergency occurs when the life of an individual or family is threatened or disrupted. It is therefore important to prepare existing refugee or IDP programmes to meet promptly the psychosocial and educational needs of new arrivals. Ellen Lange's mission to study the well-established IRC refugee education programme in Guinea included a review of the education situation of the newly arrived refugees from Sierra Leone. Teachers felt that they lacked the competence and resources to meet the psychosocial needs of the recently traumatized students. They were uncertain how to cope with incidents of violence in the classroom linked to the newly arrived students, and noted that the admission of these students could revive feelings of trauma among fellow students. Based on this experience, Lange recommended training existing teachers in appropriate response, in identifying and reporting students with special problems, and in ways to ask for and use assistance from the refugee community when necessary. She stressed that this should be a standard component of emergency response, helping the students and preventing the teachers from feeling incapable of addressing a major problem. She suggested that girls who had been raped would benefit from even a short time in a peer group led by an experienced person (Lange, 1998: 31).

Discussions with NGO staff implementing refugee education programmes in Pakistan[64] indicated the need to balance rapid access to education for newly arrived children and the problems of introducing children to a class in the middle of the school year, which could disturb the progress of the other students and increase class size. If a large number of new arrivals enter a camp or settlement together, then for some grades new schools or classes can be started, even during the school year, and the opportunity taken to meet the special needs of these students. But what should be done when the number of new arrivals seeking admission to a given year of schooling is insufficient to justify starting a new class? Headteachers need guidance on this.

Some issues for consideration. Education NGOs need to develop policy guidelines on response to new arrivals, in consultation with their programme managers. For example, all in-service teacher training could include training on the psychosocial needs of newly arrived refugee or internally displaced children. Headteachers could be trained on the approaches needed and to ensure that education opportunities are made known to newly arrived families. If admission mid-year to ongoing classes is not considered advisable, then separate multi-grade new arrivals classes with trauma healing and basic study skills components may be appropriate. Programmes could carry a stock of books and materials sufficient to permit distribution to newly arrived students during the school year. Monitoring and reporting activities could also indicate the numbers of newly arrived or newly displaced children. Likewise, community and youth volunteers could develop complementary programmes for newly arrived out-of-school children and youth. Donors should be sensitive to requests for additional funding to meet the immediate needs of newly arrived children and adolescents. These points are further discussed in the case studies of Tanzania and Pakistan below.

64 Salimah Ikram and S. Junaid Shah, personal communications.

Principles for the longer term: improving quality, coverage and management

The principles presented above, mostly in the context of early emergency for displaced populations, need to be enriched to cover the longer term and a wider range of emergency education and post-crisis situations. Over the longer term, there should be progressive improvement in the quality and coverage of emergency education, and upgrading of the capacity of local professionals[65] to manage the programme. The 1997 internal evaluation of UNHCR's education programmes set out prototype guidelines and resourcing standards for refugee primary and secondary schooling and in-service teacher training (UNHCR, 1997b). The primary education standards are reproduced in the discussion document by Pilar Aguilar and Gonzalo Retamal (1998), which sets out further important principles and standards for each phase of response, including the need for an "educational development centre" with a heavy-duty Gestetner to make copies of educational materials. Schools should gradually collect textbooks, supplementary reading materials, education aids, basic science equipment, sports equipment and so on. Programmes should develop and equip teachers' centres, and resource centres open to students and teachers.[66] In-service training and certification of teachers should be systematically developed.

This paper focuses on principles that are relevant from the early stages of an emergency. More work is needed to develop a more comprehensive set of principles covering the various types and phases of education in situations of crisis and post-crisis reconstruction.

Inter-agency cooperation

An inter-agency consultative process, supported by field research, is needed to establish principles, standards and best-practice models covering the field of emergency education, from early crisis to post-crisis reconstruction and transition. The Inter-agency Consultation on Education in Situations of Emergency and Crisis, held in November 2000, led to the establishment of an Inter-Agency Network for Education in Emergencies, which will undertake this work.[67]

Often there is a communication gap between different agencies working at field level. In the best instances, there are regular coordination meetings of field project staff, chaired or attended by the local education authorities, and concerned UN agencies. These may need to be weekly in new emergencies. The mature refugee education programme in Uganda has quarterly education coordination meetings, including the concerned government departments, NGOs implementing programmes, UNHCR (convenor) and UNICEF. Particular themes are discussed as well as current issues. In some cases, there is a lack of dialogue between organizations working for refugees and those working to support national and local development programmes of the host country. This can be a deliberate policy of the host country, if there is a fear that refugees may not repatriate, as in the case of Pakistan. The strengthening of field-level partnerships will be considered in the follow-up to the Inter-Agency Consultation.

---

65 In this paper the term "local professionals" includes refugee professionals.

66 For an account of resource centres in Uganda see Sesnan (1998: 69–71).

67 For details see www.ineeweb.net or contact the Network Coordinator (e-mail: n.drost@unesco.org).

Were these principles reflected in recent refugee emergencies?

In 1999, eight countries each received new refugees numbering more than 20,000: Albania (435,000), the Former Yugoslav Republic of Macedonia, Indonesia (West Timor), Pakistan, Bosnia-Herzegovina, Tanzania, DRC, Zambia and Guinea.[68] The places from which most of the refugees came (Sierra Leone, Angola, southern Sudan, Republic of Congo, Burundi, DRC, Kosovo, East Timor and Afghanistan) suffered internal turmoil also, with internal displacement and disruption of normal government services; many of these flows continue in 2000. In May 2000 there was a new flow of refugees from Eritrea into Sudan, this time displaced by international conflict. Some aspects of education response to various of these emergencies have been touched upon above. The following brief case studies may give a further picture of the reception accorded to some of the new refugees (including also education in the early post-conflict situations in Kosovo and East Timor). A brief note is added on the Eritrean refugees who entered Sudan in May and June 2000.

Psychosocial response for children and youth in a "popular" emergency

"CRS organized drawing activities in Tirana, Kavaj and Durres District as part of their PTSD screening, extending their services to Elbasan and Fier. SCF Alliance started its Non-Formal Education (NFE) in Kukes and plans to do the same in Kavaja, Fier and possibly Korce. Albanian Centre for Human Rights is also preparing for summer school activities in Tirana, Durres, Kruja and other districts. Relief International just started its children's activities (recreation/sport) in Korce. More and more agencies for this category (NFE or children) are being identified in recently built camps, including CARE and MED-AIR … Sports associations have received various offers: … Albanian Olympic Committee with IOC funds plans cross-country races and with funds from Italian Olympic Committee has organized one. European Football Association and International Volleyball Association made similar offers, facilitated by UNHCR" (Shimizu, 1999).

It has proved difficult to find comprehensive data on emergency education response even for these refugee programmes. Data on non-refugee emergencies is often much less accessible than for refugee situations, and time did not permit case studies of such programmes, although these are badly needed.

The Kosovo crisis

The Kosovo crisis began in 1998, and UNICEF and UNHCR cooperated to supply education kits to vulnerable or internally displaced Albanian communities. During the NATO campaign from late March to early June 1999, more than 750,000 ethnic Albanians fled Kosovo, mostly to Albania (435,000, joining 22,000 who had arrived in 1998), Macedonia (355,000) and Bosnia-Herzegovina (72,000). Many refugees stayed with families or in collective centres, while others stayed in camps. Following a UN Security Council resolution on 10 June, K-FOR troops arrived in Kosovo on 12 June, and within three weeks 500,000 Kosovar refugees had returned. By November 1999 more than 800,000 had returned (HIWG, 1999: 1; UNHCR, 2000b). The Security Council resolution established the UN Interim Administration Mission in

68 Data from UNHCR (2000b). Kenya could be mentioned here also, but the statistics are ambiguous.

Kosovo (UNMIK), coordinating a humanitarian assistance pillar (led by UNHCR and with UNICEF as the lead agency for education), a civil administration pillar (with UNESCO responsible to UNMIK for the education sector), a democratization and institution-building pillar (led by the Organization for Security and Cooperation in Europe (OSCE)) and an economic development pillar (managed by the European Union). [69]

Damage assessment in Kosovo was divided between UNHCR (homes) and UNICEF (schools). A July 1999 UNICEF/NGO assessment showed that 37 per cent of schools were destroyed or in very bad condition. As of January 2000 a total of 362 buildings had been fully repaired, funded mainly by the European Community Humanitarian Office (111 school buildings), UNHCR (96) and UNICEF (43); with more than 400 buildings still in the process of being repaired or awaiting repair, UNESCO was undertaking a school mapping exercise and developing standards for future school construction (Daxner, 2000: 7–8).

Community-based approach and capacity-building. UNHCR funded many "Community Services" activities for Kosovo refugees, including recreational and other activities benefiting children. A lead actor was Catholic Relief Services, which in the field of education had been promoting "parent–school partnerships" in Albania since 1996. The Soros Albania Education Development Project (AEDP) had likewise been promoting teacher–parent organizations in Albania for five years, as well as other aspects of school excellence.[70] These and other agencies promoted a community-based approach to refugee education. In Macedonia, the Norwegian staff seconded to UNICEF worked with communities to achieve rapid education response (see below).

Meeting psychosocial needs. As noted by one of UNHCR's Community Services Officers, psychosocial activities (recreation, sport, culture and non-formal education) were organized by many agencies and were of especial interest to donors. Some agencies made arrangements through UNHCR while others were funded bilaterally, making coordination difficult. UNICEF promoted the concept of "child-friendly spaces" (described below), where conditions permitted. After the return to Kosovo, similar programmes were introduced there, and UNMIK produced psychosocial guidelines for staff of relevant organizations, and promoted the training of teachers in psychosocial methods (Daxner, 2000: 10).

Rapid response. Mark Richmond, comparing his experience in the Kosovo emergency with that of Rwanda, noted that many of the lessons learned during the 1990s were applied in the Kosovar refugee camps, such as phasing of response, with an emphasis on early introduction of structured activities (personal communication). The NATO intervention began part-way through the school year, and the Albanian Ministry of Education and Science proposed a three-phased approach: preparatory (April–May 1999), summer "catch-up" schools (June–August), and return to school, in either Albania or Kosovo (September). Textbooks originally intended for Albanian children were instead given to Kosovar children attending the summer schools.[71] Coordination of education response in Albania was led by the Ministry, assisted by AEDP.

69 See www.un.org/peace/kosovo. UNMIK set up a Regional structure with five Regional Administrators and 30 Municipal Administrators, plus central departments such as the Department of Education and Science. On 15 December it set up the Joint Interim Administrative Structure to share responsibility with representatives of all of Kosovo society. Each of the Administrative Departments is led by two heads, a Kosovar official and an UNMIK official.

70 See Albania update: May 1999 at www.ginie.org and AEDP (1999).

71 See Albania update: May 1999 at www.ginie.org; MOES (1999); Ruka (2000). The summer schools had no specific teachers' guide for working with refugee children, as they were furnished with regular Albanian textbooks and were supposed to run "catch-up" classes (Ellen Lange, personal communication).

Returnees arrive at their heavily damaged homes or schools in Mitrovica, Kosovo. UNHCR/06.1999/R. LeMoyne

In Macedonia, UNICEF served as the lead agency for education and achieved rapid education response. Secondment of five education specialists to UNICEF by the Norwegian Refugee Council enabled education response to begin in a matter of weeks. The NRC staff moved quickly, identifying and mobilizing teachers, space, tents and chairs.

> Education as a concern and necessity was introduced a couple of weeks after the exodus/influx and was being organized one month after the bombing started. Evaluations among our educators who went there, and comments from the refugees, leave no doubt that these activities considerably brightened and relieved the minds of the teachers and the children and had a positive effect on the families as well – even with the restrictions placed by the host government. (Eldrid Midttun, personal communication)

UNICEF also supplied materials to assist the already strained education system in Bosnia-Herzegovina in coping with the influx of Kosovar refugees.

Backpacks of student materials were supplied during both the refugee and the returnee phases, by UNICEF (using their normal international procurement system) and to a lesser extent, UNHCR. UNHCR contributed to school textbooks and school rehabilitation.[72] IRC Kosovo's Carl Triplehorn commented to the author that backpacks have high psychosocial benefit, establishing a personal space for private writing and so on, but take time to assemble.[73]

Soon after the return to Kosovo many teachers held classes outdoors or in tents, if schools were badly damaged. Non-formal schooling and related activities started early, not least because a condition for being paid a stipend (by UNMIK) was that a teacher had resumed teaching. Many Albanian teachers "took back" the place they had lost in 1989, and others resumed the activity they had performed in the parallel school system.

Relating response to the school year. The "catch-up" second phase of the refugee education response in Albania was designed specifically to enable refugee children to cover studies interrupted by the outbreak of hostilities in the middle of their school year.[74] Similar "catch-up" studies were organized informally by teachers in Kosovo, as just noted.

Education for durable solutions. During the 1990s there had been a parallel system of education in Kosovo, run by Kosovo Albanians (Davies, 1999: 5–10). Hence there was no curriculum problem when refugees arrived in Albania, and most refugees used the same system in Macedonia. The curriculum adopted in Kosovo for the new school year commencing October 1999 was based for practical reasons on the existing school textbooks. UNICEF and UNESCO staff met teachers' organizations, government educators and others to agree on curriculum principles, notably to avoid materials harmful to ethnic relations, while the process for curriculum renewal was put in place.[75] Jennifer Ashton, UNHCR's Senior Community Services Officer, in an internal e-mail from Kosovo dated August 1999 stated:

> UNMIK has agreed that for the next year ... textbooks in Serbian will be obtained from the Ministry of Education in Belgrade, Albanian textbooks will be those from the parallel system ... the latter were developed in Tirana but printed in Kosovo in the past ... UNMIK is drawing together a consortium of donors who can fund textbook production this year ... and will screen all textbooks for offensive material.

Survival and peace-building messages. Given the tasks for coping with a much larger number of refugees than had been foreseen and the speedy repatriation to Kosovo, UN agencies did not have time to promote emergency-wide strategies for conveying survival and peace-building messages. These would have been present in many locations but subsumed under "psychosocial" and health interventions. There is a need to work towards education for tolerance, peace and human rights in Kosovo, but this must be developed participatively and sensitively (Davies, 1999: 21–22). After many years of Serb–Albanian conflict, about 58 per cent of Kosovar Albanian men and 56 per cent of women felt extreme hatred (86 per cent

72 For example, UNHCR received a donation of $1,000,000 from the "Pavarotti and Friends" June 1999 concert, disbursed for 50,000 backpacks of student supplies, establishment of two youth centres and reconstruction of 33 schools.

73 In future, they should have luminescent strips for road safety reasons, especially in latitudes where the journey back from school may end in the dark.

74 In some localities in Albania, children were bussed daily from refugee camps to national schools (Jon Rothenburg, personal communication).

75 This approach had been used earlier in South Africa, where apartheid books were used during the slow and political process of post-apartheid transition (personal communication from Peter Buckland, who led UNICEF's initial work in Kosovo).

and 89 per cent respectively felt either "extreme" hatred or "a lot of" hatred), while 50 per cent of men and 43 per cent of women had feelings of revenge all the time or a lot of the time (CDC, 1999: 7–8).

The multi-agency Psychosocial Assessment Mission to Kosovo in September 1999 noted that "hatred is an accepted norm, a value passed from adults to youth". They cited a poem recited proudly by a six-year-old girl which demonized Serbs; she had learned it in school. The Mission commented that talk of reconciliation would be premature and that "It is more appropriate now to focus on steps toward reconciliation, such as building tolerance and respect for human rights [and] critical reflection on what Kosovar society is becoming" (IRC, 1999: 7).

Attention to specific groups: gender. Gender appears not to have been a major concern in the education sector during the brief duration of the refugee emergency. Education among the Kosovar Albanians had been co-educational. In Kosovo there may be gender issues such as the earlier withdrawal from school of girls as compared with boys among poor families, for economic reasons (Davies, 1999: 23). In rural areas where girls have to travel a long distance to school, the participation of girls at secondary levels is said to be poor.[76]

Pre-school age group and adolescents. There were many NGO projects catering to early childhood, and to adolescents and youth. UNICEF promoted the creation of Kosovar Youth Councils in six refugee camps near Kukes in northern Albania in May 1999, which organized sports, music, cleaning the camps, helping to integrate new refugees, fund-raising for the poorest families, setting up camp schools, disseminating information on landmines, organizing psychosocial and recreational activities for younger children, and influencing decision taken by camp managers (e.g. asking for increased patrolling to improve security). These activities were discussed each week at meetings of the six councils (Bainvel, 1999). There was no specific report available on secondary education for Kosovar refugees in Albania, but in principle government activities also covered education at this level.[77]

Minorities. A major UNMIK concern in Kosovo has been the security and access to education of the ethnic minority groups, such as Croatian Serb refugees, Serbs, Roma, Ashkaelia, and a Turk minority. UNHCR's seconded Education Officer made suggestions for the development of education for Roma and related minority groups, recommending in-service training of Roma teachers and other measures to build an interest in formal education (Lange, 1999a).[78]

Trauma and disability among Kosovar refugee children

"The largest group of refugee children with special needs during the crisis were the traumatized children ... problems with concentration among students, and students reporting problems with sleeping at night ... According to the teachers at Kavajes the heavily traumatized children were given education in small groups in private homes ... [they] reported no children with physical or mental disabilities among refugee students, ... probably related to disabled students not being included into Albanian schools." (Lange, 1999c: 2)

76 Cited from an internal UNHCR memorandum from Ellen Lange, 4 Aug. 2000.

77 "According to oral reports from UNHCR staff and NGOs, the drop-out rate of adolescent Kosovars from school in Kosovo was substantial. This is probably related to the fact that the parallel Kosovar education system reportedly concentrated mainly on primary level" (Lange, 1999b:1).

78 Gradual progress in minority education has been reported in the monthly Kosovo Humanitarian Update (www.reliefweb.int).

Children with disability. Lange (1999b) noted that access to schools for physically disabled students in Kosovo needed to be significantly improved, and recommended that participation of students with disability be included in education statistics.

Progressive improvements in quality, coverage and management. The international community is working to restore and improve education in Kosovo, including school reconstruction, teacher training, curriculum review and the "DESK" programme mentioned above (Daxner, 2000).

Lessons learned. This was an unusual emergency, and exceptionally well-resourced, with "warehouses full of toys and clothes" (Jacinta Goveas, personal communication) and many agencies seeking to help. At one level, this reflected genuine concern stimulated by massive television coverage, while at another level it reflected political commitment to the NATO action and the desire of European governments to avoid a massive flow of refugees into western Europe. It is difficult to quantify how quickly refugee children had access to structured activities and education, due to their diverse situations and the many organizations involved. However, many refugee children benefited from emergency response, and more would have done so if repatriation had been delayed. Education response after return home was quite rapid. It may be noted here that the education programmes of UNMIK illustrate a new role for the UN, helping to create a new education system in an area affected by conflict, working with local counterparts to permit handover and sustainability. A similar situation obtains in East Timor.

Two international staff (one UN, one NGO) with long emergency experience commented to the author in confidence that there were insufficient international education staff on the ground in Kosovo after the repatriation, and that they were overwhelmed with issues such as "physical resources and teachers: rehabilitate schools, get furniture in, hire teachers back" and unable to attend quickly to issues such as the needs of the population, trauma and teacher training. Relevant here was the need to meet time pressures because of the approach of the new school year, which should perhaps have triggered stronger "standby" staffing inputs.

It may be noted further that education coordination was something of a problem in Albania, where the government gave technical leadership but lacked UNHCR's experience of coordinating large numbers of NGOs.[79] However, the education officer seconded to UNHCR by NRC reached Tirana only on 16 June, after repatriation had begun.[80] This is understandable given the difficulties experienced in the whole operation (Suhrke et al., 2000), but would have been avoided if there had been an automatic "trigger" mechanism for a deployment request when the number of refugees exceeded a certain threshold (see below).

The Timor crisis

The referendum on independence for East Timor in August 1999 was followed by violence, internal displacement, and the voluntary and forced movement of about 280,000 residents of East Timor to camps in West Timor. Access to these camps was difficult, and at the time of writing became impossible, for security reasons. About 15,000 children attended local schools in West Timor, which in some areas

79 As mentioned in an internal UNHCR Community Services situation report dated 13 May 1999.

80 Internal UNHCR correspondence indicates that NRC had offered in early April 1999 to second an Education Officer at no cost to UNHCR, that the busy Community Services Officer in Tirana assumed that this was proceeding (personal communication), was "desperately wanting" an Education Officer (e-mail of 25 April 1999) and drafted terms of reference for such a deployment on 29 April 1999.

The homes and schools of many East Timorese were devastated during the militia rampage following the August 30 ballot on self-determination. UNHCR is supplying timber, nails and plastic sheeting to help returnees build shelters. Dili, East Timor. UNHCR/10-11. 1999/M. Kobayashi

increased schools' student numbers by a factor of five times the normal enrolment. UNICEF and other agencies provided tents and other support, but an estimated 12,000 children of primary school age remained out of school.[81]

In East Timor itself there was an educational emergency, with many internally displaced and repatriating refugees returning to their home areas in East Timor to find that infrastructure such as schools had been destroyed. Many teachers had returned home to Indonesia or were in West Timor. UNICEF has been the lead agency for education and community services within the UN Transitional Administration for East Timor (UNTAET), providing education kits to the UNTAET schools, and convening regular inter-agency Education Coordination Meetings and Psychosocial Coordination Meetings.[82]

Community-based approach and capacity-building. As noted earlier, a "Consortium" of agencies, funded by the US Bureau of Population, Refugees, and Migration and other NGOs have worked to support community-based recreational and cultural activities, in cooperation with the CNRT (National Council of Timorese Resistance). IRC has documented the experience of its start-up project, based mainly in the enclave of Oecusse. At the assessment stage, local organizations, especially youth groups, came forward

81 Based on an e-mail reporting on the Community Services Working Group meeting in Kupang on 24 February 2000, which noted that some organizations were leaving and asked "will UNHCR urgently fund simple education activities for [out-of-school] refugee children?".

82 As in Kosovo, UNHCR was made the lead agency for shelter.

with ideas for action, leading IRC to direct its support through existing community organizations. Subsequently, the project provided training for youth leaders in sports management, grant applications and study circle materials development (Nicolai, 2000: 18–19).

Meeting psychosocial needs. UNICEF convened the regular inter-agency Psychosocial Coordination Meetings, and quickly provided three-day trainings for teachers and community workers on trauma identification in children. UNHCR's East Timor programme had the benefit of a series of community services specialists, seconded by Swedish and Norwegian Save the Children. They had advised that UNHCR should contract international NGOs to undertake capacity-building, focused on trauma healing and psychosocial needs, for local NGOs. This was cancelled due to the UNHCR budget crisis (Eva Nordernsjold, personal communication).

The NGO "Consortium" focused strongly on meeting the psychosocial needs of children and adolescents, especially through support to local NGOs. For example, the IRC project quickly helped the local young women's group to provide daily structured activities for 400 pre-primary children, including recreation, music, art and health care, at a children's centre established in Oecusse. It provided supplies that enabled about 2,500 children and youth to play soccer, basketball, volleyball and jump-rope through a male youth group and development of organized sports practice and tournaments for younger children and girls.

UNICEF is working with NGOs to promote the concept of child-friendly spaces, at least one per district, physically bringing together health care, and activities for primary school children after school and for adolescents, including non-formal education, and recreational and peace-building activities.[83]

Rapid response. Susan Nicolai (2000: 12) noted that "communities took surprising initiative in opening schools, with most starting instruction within 1–2 months of returning. Although some teachers were not qualified and none were initially paid, classes for primary school ages were taught in homes or under trees for several hours a day ... language study of Tetum, Portuguese or English taught from memory ... Part of the reason for this rapid community-led response was the fact that the East Timorese were a repatriating rather than a refugee population" and that most had not been absent from their homes for long.

Lack of school materials was a constraint. After on-the-ground consultation, IRC ordered materials from Darwin, which took time because of the necessary paperwork, purchasing, shipping and delivery. Nicolai concluded that the materials ordered were not much different from what would have been ordered prior to local consultation, and suggested that,

> Factoring in the time-consuming procurement process, it would have been better to place an order for materials immediately upon arrival. Using perhaps one third of the materials budget for generic items such as notebooks and balls straight away would have speeded the arrival of a first order of materials and still left a significant portion to be identified by the community. (Nicolai, 2000: 27)

Delays in access and delivery were caused in some locations by the rainy season.

83 Personal communications from Pilar Aguilar, Wendy Smith, Susan Nicolai.

Education for durable solutions. Choice of the future language of instruction and curriculum is a politically sensitive issue in East Timor. Thus the year 2000/2001 is to be a transitional year in terms of curriculum, using the previous textbooks while curriculum strategies are developed and decisions taken.

Survival and peace-building messages. Activities promoting awareness of HIV/AIDS and promoting reconciliation and peace were included in the planned emergency response (United Nations, 1999: 96–110). IRC's Nicolai notes that instead of the original plan to provide workshops for young people, it seemed better to work with the local tradition of youth study circles.

> In partnership with six local groups, curriculum materials were developed in topics including reconciliation, indigenous culture, traditional story writing, literacy campaigns, gender and conflict resolution. Designed as simple interactive and discussion-based activities, the 18 lessons were prepared at a level easily understood and led by a facilitator without much background in the subject … they will be used by youth groups in organizing and facilitating study circles in their home communities. (Nicolai, 2000: 24)

Lessons learned: IRC start-up project in East Timor

- Emergency education operates best under a set of guiding principles allowing room for the design of context-appropriate interventions;
- Procurement of capital goods and a small amount of programme materials prior to staff arrival will greatly speed assessment and implementation; an initial order of basic education and recreation materials should be placed [before detailed need assessments are made on the ground];
- Involvement of local groups in conducting assessments and the participation in project planning [benefit the project and the groups];
- Repatriated communities will often take the lead in structuring activities for their children and youth but may lack the material resources to do so;
- Capacity among local populations for care of children and youth may be high, but assistance is needed to organize and communicate that knowledge;
- Systems of monitoring and evaluation, including decisions on project indicators, should be established with input from local beneficiaries or partner groups.

Selected from the Project Coordinator's list of lessons learned (Nicolai, 2000: 34–35)

Broadening the concept of education. The East Timor "Child Protection and Psychosocial Programs Consortium" project was cited earlier as an example of the broader concept of education, covering a wide range of structured activities for children and young people and helping to meet their psychosocial and learning needs (CPPPC, 2000).

Attention to specific groups. As already mentioned, support was given to activities for adolescents and youth of both sexes, empowering local youth groups through training and provision of needed resources, including a scheme for young women, under the guidance of teachers, to work with pre-school children.

In East Timor, there has been a tradition of sending children away for schooling, to boarding schools and so-called orphanages. This tradition has been reinforced by the recent crisis. The education and other social systems have been disrupted on the one hand, and there is donor sympathy for "orphanages" on the other, so that there are now schools linked to "orphanages" serving non-orphaned children. However, there does not seem to be any danger of these children losing contact with their families.[84]

Lessons learned. The emerging principles noted in this paper were reflected in the actions of the humanitarian community in the Timor emergency. Information is not available, however, on the proportion of the population reached by initiatives of the type described above, or the timeframe for their wider outreach. Information is likewise lacking on the situation in refugee camps in West Timor.

Tanzania

Tanzania ranked fourth in terms of the prima facie refugee arrivals for 1999. (It had been fourth in 1998 also, with a smaller influx). There were 64,000 new refugees from Burundi and 76,000 from DRC. There are no statistics on how many of these refugees entered school. However, in December 1999 the total number of children, adolescents and youth (aged 3 to 25) enrolled in pre-school, school and other education programmes was 131,000 or one-third of the refugee population. This included 49,000 boys and 43,000 girls in refugee primary schools. There were also 25,000 children (about 12,000 boys and 13,000 girls) in pre-schools and 8,000 in self-help secondary schools (not recognized by the government).

Community-based approach and capacity-building. In Tanzania, each camp has an NGO implementing both "community services and education", supporting many non-formal education, recreation, cultural and peace-building activities as well as formal schooling.[85] NGOs encourage refugee communities to undertake these activities on their own initiative. When large numbers of refugees arrived in 1997 and the government delayed permission for formal schooling, education activities were conducted by the communities for a full year with voluntary teachers, in "children's activity centres" that subsequently became schools. Post-primary and pre-school classes continue to be run by the community on a voluntary basis, with guidance from the NGOs. Capacity-building includes a comprehensive training programme for unqualified teachers.

84 Eva Nordenskjold, end-of-mission debriefing, August 2000.

85 The programmes are implemented by NGOs, namely Tanganyika Christian Refugee Service, UMATI (Chama Cha Uzazi na Malezi Bora Tanzania), Diocese of Western Tanzania, Africare Tanzania, Dutch Relief Agency and Christian Outreach, Norwegian People's Aid and Southern Africa Extension Unit.

Peace education for refugees from Burundi and Rwanda, Ngara Camp, Tanzania. UNHCR/08.2000/L. Boscardi

Meeting psychosocial needs. According to the Senior Community Services Officer:

> The training of teachers includes lessons on how to cope with the psychosocial needs of newly arrived refugees. We hope to organize more structured activities in this area through UNICEF. In all the camps new students are admitted throughout the year and the teachers are trained to cope with this. (Ethel Nhleko, personal communication)

Rapid response: preparing ongoing programmes to receive new arrivals. The refugees arriving in 1999 were accommodated in existing camps (and the children in existing schools) until these were full to overflowing and then in Karago camp, established in December 1999, for Burundi refugees and Lugufu camp for Congolese refugees. Following the procedure established earlier, the refugee community in each new camp was mobilized to help establish schools. In Karago camp, with about 40,000 new refugees, some 10,000 students were immediately registered for schooling by the NGO UMATI, which already implemented the community services and education programmes in another camp. Before the end of the first month 71 refugees had been identified to serve as teachers and had received a 10-day introductory training, coordinated by UNICEF and given by trainers from neighbouring camps. UNICEF supplied emergency classroom kits and contacted schools in other camps to loan textbooks. The emergency phase led on to a "curriculum phase" at the beginning of the new school year in September 2000, with about 8,000 students and 96 teachers. As in many refugee schools, there is a two-shift system.

Education for durable solutions and regional approach. The refugee students follow their home curriculum and, as noted earlier, continuing efforts and cross-border missions by UNHCR and UNICEF staff have enabled them to sit their national examinations. In May 2000 the grade 6 Burundi examination papers were taken by 1,874 students, two days after their counterparts had taken them in Burundi. A team of five persons from Burundi (education officials, UNICEF and UNHCR) supervised the process. The results have been issued on an unofficial basis: UNHCR and UNICEF are advocating for formal certification. The Education Inspector from Lumumbashi in DRC took grade 6 and grade 12 examination papers to Tanzania, where 1,577 refugees sat the former and 444 the latter (Nhleko, 2000: 2–6). There are continuing efforts to obtain more textbooks and teachers' guides from the education authorities in Burundi and DRC.[86]

Survival and peace-building messages. Non-formal and informal education events conveying preventive messages related to health, sexual and gender-based violence, environmental awareness and so on, take place regularly, assisted by the combined NGO mandates for community services and education. Health personnel visit schools to educate the students on HIV/AIDS. A strengthened HIV/AIDS information campaign is planned for 2001, and funding is currently being sought to involve refugee youth in developing posters and leaflets relevant to their age group (Nhleko, personal communication).

Refugee schools in Tanzania use environmental education materials developed under a UNHCR–UNESCO-PEER project. Ethel Nhleko (personal communication) comments:

> There should be somebody to coordinate the project. A consultant should be hired to work on a proposal which should handle the implementation and monitoring aspect. We do not have the capacity to handle this … there is only one officer to cover both community services and education at each field office, and both are large fields on their own.

Following a UNHCR- and UNICEF-sponsored workshop in 1996, led by Susan Fountain, there have been a number of community-based workshops and special events promoting the concepts of peace and conflict resolution.[87] A technical team of refugees, facilitated by UNICEF and UNHCR, has developed a teachers' manual and a student "catalogue" including songs, poems, short plays and artwork, which will be used in refugee schools in 2001 (Nhleko, personal communication).

Broadening the concept of education. Due to the restrictions on post-primary education in the camps, an open-learning "distance" education programme was introduced for the study of English language. Graduates from this course can enter distance education programmes for Tanzanian nationals, and have also entered vocational training and obtained jobs with NGOs. Some have been awarded UNHCR "DAFI" scholarships for higher education. Youth centres have been constructed in the camps, and youth groups are involved in skills training, sports, culture, debates and social service (UNHCR, 1999b: 7).

Special groups. Efforts are made to engage adolescents in formal schooling and other activities, as mentioned above. Girls' education is promoted through meetings of leaders, parents' committees and so on. In each school two female teachers serve as focal points for the promotion of girls' education. Lack of

86 See also Bird (1999), UNHCR (1999b, 2000), and Eric Eversmann's unpublished 1999 report for UNICEF on quality aspects of the programme.

87 The workshop was for Rwandan and Burundi refugees. The initiative was continued by Burundi refugees, supported by UNICEF and UNHCR, after the repatriation of Rwandan refugees in late 1996.

decent clothing is one of the main causes of drop-out; funds are needed to buy cloth for school uniform projects and sanitary supplies for older girls (Nhleko, personal communication). Parents are encouraged to send children with disabilities to school and each primary school has a class for those who cannot join in normal classes.

Progressive improvement in quality, coverage and management. Under-resourcing of the Tanzania programme means that textbooks are in short supply and that there is often a delay in payment of incentives to newly hired refugee teachers. The equipment at the "educational development centre" in Ngara, left from the earlier Rwandan refugee programme, permits heavy-duty copying of textbooks but is too slow to meet the needs. The school examinations show that most students reaching grade 6 have low achievement levels, though two pupils achieved marks of over 90 per cent. Lack of recognition of secondary education by the host government is a disincentive to achievement in primary school. There are self-help secondary schools, but they lack resources and the teachers are unpaid: this situation should be remedied.

Lessons learned. Overall, the Tanzania programme is well attuned to the needs of newly arrived refugee students, including training of teachers to meet their needs and the existence of a range of non-formal education and recreational activities for out-of-school youth. The programme has suffered greatly from lack of resources, and from an inability to access additional funds during the year to meet the needs of extra students. Communities are quick to make mud-brick walls for classrooms, but the UNHCR budget is insufficient to pay for corrugated sheet roofs, leading to oversized classes. There have sometimes been delays in paying incentives to new teachers and shortages of educational materials. The post-primary classes need official permission to operate and then resourcing to permit payment of incentives and provision of education materials. This will help improve performance and retention in primary schools (as students work to qualify themselves for secondary school) as well as in the secondary schools themselves.

Pakistan

Pakistan received the fifth-largest number of new refugees in 1999 (92,700). There were already large and long-established UNHCR-funded refugee education programmes in Pakistan at primary level, mostly catering to Pushtu-speaking refugees The refugee schools had initially been managed by the respective provincial governments, but management was transferred in 1996 to GTZ, Save the Children/US and Ockenden International, with the intention of developing a more community-based approach. UNHCR had (controversially) discontinued its support to middle and secondary refugee education in 1995, due to perceived donor pressure to phase down assistance to long-term refugee populations and to immediate budget constraints. Some of these schools have been kept operating by a special refugee fund, administered by the government.

Several other organizations support refugee schools. The Female Education Programme of IRC, established during the 1990s, provides secondary education to Afghan girls as well as primary education to boys and girls, in 30 schools in and around Peshawar, with classes in Dari and Pushtu languages of instruction. Many of the new refugees have settled near Peshawar and those who were from Dari-speaking regions have benefited from the Dari-medium schools run by IRC. The large number of urban refugees, mostly from Kabul, means that many children attend poorly resourced Afghan private schools while children from the poorest families often have no schooling.

Community-based approach and capacity-building. In the early 1980s newly arrived refugee communities began their own small schools, according to tribal, religious and political affiliation, and those wishing for UNHCR support were then grouped into more viable and cost-effective entities (Khalid Mahmud Shah, personal communication). After these schools were transferred from management by the provincial governments to NGOs, steps were taken to prepare communities for participation in school management. The NGOs employ community animation staff to help establish and train school management committees (GTZ, 1999b).

As mentioned earlier, new schools for urban refugees were established in and around Peshawar on a self-help basis during the 1990s; many were subsequently supported and absorbed by larger programmes. The Social Welfare Cell of the North West Frontier Province Commissionerate for Afghan Refugees still motivates newly arrived refugee communities, or those with a new interest in girls' education, to form "self-help" schools for the early classes of primary school, again with the need to link with larger programmes to have access to materials, teacher training and so on.

An estimated 170,000 Afghans have fled to Pakistan since September 2000, escaping both war and drought. The majority are housed at two large sites near the city of Peshawar, Shamshatoo and Jalozai. Refugees prepare pit latrines at the New Shamshatoo camp. UNHCR/04.2001/C. Shirley

Psychosocial needs. A recent World Bank study of teacher training needs gave as its first recommendation the development of a teacher training module on meeting the affective needs of Afghan refugee students (Spicer, 2000: 34). This is all the more important for newly arrived refugee children.

Rapid response: preparing ongoing programmes to receive new arrivals. When a new camp is established, one or more of the education-sector agencies is assigned responsibility for schooling and it can start at any convenient time. For example, a planning meeting for Akora Khattak New Camp in 1998 assigned GTZ to establish a Pushtu-medium school and IRC to establish a Dari-medium school. As noted earlier, the arrival of new families in existing camps presents different problems. There is concern about balancing the desire of these families for schooling and the possible deleterious effect of children entering existing classes during the school year. This problem needs to be solved, with measures ensuring some kind of education access for newly arrived children, and training of headteachers and teachers accordingly.

The Afghan Social Animators working with the Social Welfare Cell could usefully be sensitised to the psychosocial and educational needs of newly arrived students.

Education for durable solutions. The curriculum in all Afghan refugee schools is a variant of the pre-war curriculum of Afghanistan. In the 1980s there were several curriculum development initiatives, leading to different sets of textbooks and supplementary materials. An inter-agency workshop in 1990 led to the adoption of the "University of Nebraska" textbooks for use in UNHCR-funded schools, but since then the emphasis has shifted towards workbooks prepared by GTZ's Afghan educators.[88] Refugees in UNHCR-funded schools also study Urdu (the national language of Pakistan) as a subject. As noted earlier, the curriculum thus supports repatriation but provides language skills for students who stay in Pakistan.

Regional approach. There was an inter-agency meeting in 1998, for exchange of experience between education programmes for Afghans in Pakistan and Afghanistan (see Rugh, 1998). This has led to an inter-agency effort to develop supplementary learning materials, aligned to "basic competency" objectives, led by UNICEF Afghanistan in cooperation with Save the Children/US. These materials, initially covering mathematics and mother tongue for grades 1 to 6, have been developed in writing workshops attended by educators from NGOs aligned to the Taliban authorities in Afghanistan as well as from Western NGOs. Through avoiding depiction of living beings, the materials meet the strict religious views of some participants. This work provides technical skills and materials that can be a useful input to the future development of education in Afghanistan. A programme for pilot testing of the new materials is planned for 2001 (Ellen van Kalmthout, personal communication).

Survival and peace-building messages. The Pakistan refugee programme developed a network of community health supervisors, attached to clinics, and volunteer community health outreach workers. Health messages form a large part of the science curriculum in the "Nebraska" primary school textbooks. Social Animators from the Social Welfare Cell sponsor child and adolescent groups in some of the refugee schools, which convey health messages including information about HIV/AIDS. Considerable attention is given to environmental awareness, through tree-planting days and so on. An independent Afghan NGO

88 The author co-facilitated this workshop. The "Nebraska" materials were prepared by a group of Afghan educators from all the seven Afghan political parties recognized by the Pakistan government. They are acceptable to the Taliban authorities and therefore widely used. They have strong points, eg. health education, but have gaps in content. The accompanying teacher guides were not updated and are not in use.

based in Peshawar is developing peace education programmes on a pilot basis in 30 private and NGO schools in and around Peshawar, under a capacity-building grant for Afghan NGOs. Consideration might be given to the development of a programme reaching a larger number of students, perhaps drawing on the UNHCR peace education materials as well as on the UNHCR tolerance education materials from Kyrgyzstan and the initiative just mentioned. The complex political issues would require a very sensitive approach, however, perhaps integrating environmental and health messages also.

Attention to specific groups. Coverage for girls has increased dramatically since the mid-1990s, thanks to a range of measures and perhaps general social change, possibly the desire of educated young refugee men for literate wives. It was much helped by the decision of the World Food Programme to provide about 4 kg of edible oil per month to girls who attend school regularly. This helped to overcome the perception that it is pointless for Afghan girls to attend school, and too costly for poor families, in terms of requirements for decent clothing and so on. There is heavy drop-out of boys from poor families, since there is no restriction on participation in the labour market by Afghans; and the youngest boys earn money for their families by scavenging. As noted earlier, GTZ runs late-afternoon basic education classes for working boys. The Social Welfare Cell has promoted the participation of children with disability in non-formal or regular education activities.

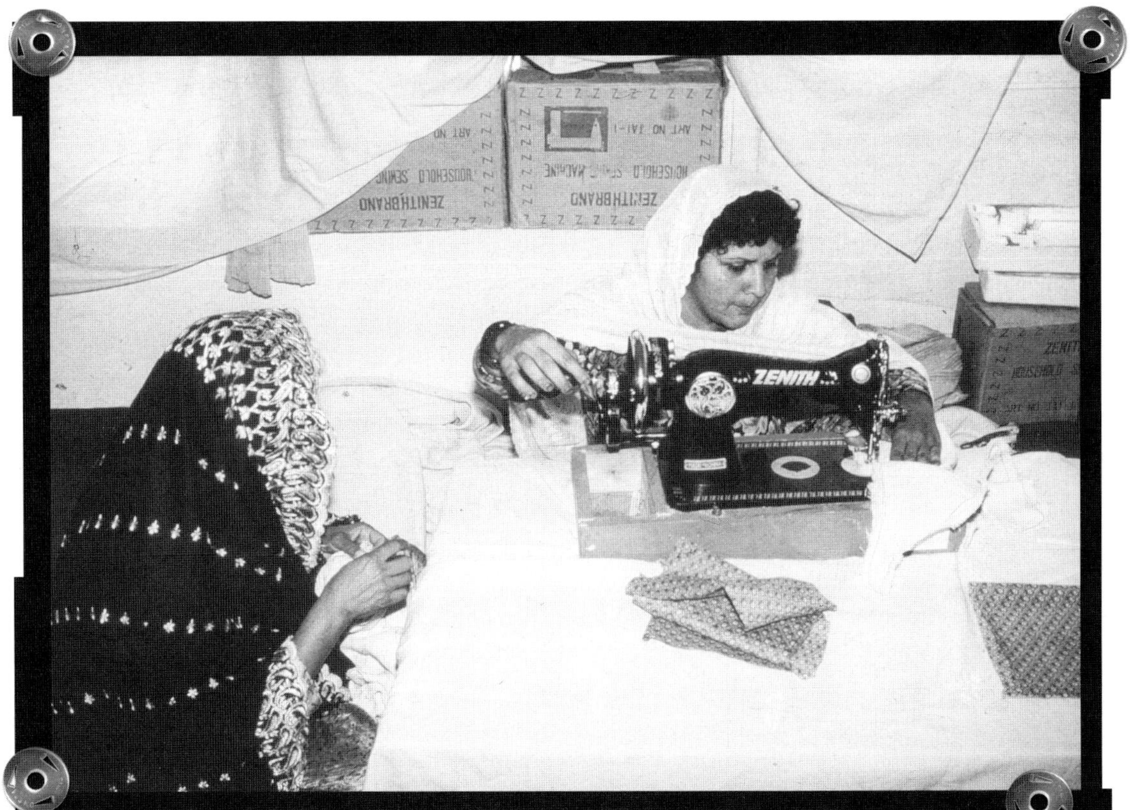

An income-generating project for women at the Kunduz Refugee Dpt., Kunduz Province, Afghanistan. UNHCR/05.1995/A. Hollmann

Progressive improvement in quality, coverage and management. The refugee education programme has benefited from various teacher training initiatives, including a massive GTZ teacher training and materials development programme. All children receive a complete set of locally printed textbooks or workbooks. Other steps taken to improve quality include the achievement testing used in Baluchistan Province, which helped justify a decision to eliminate unsuitable teachers, and the development of supplementary course materials aligned to basic competencies, as described above. Programmes are almost exclusively staffed by Afghan professionals, who benefit from internal and external training programmes.

Lessons learned. Overall, the refugee education programme in Pakistan refugee camps is well developed, and there is an inter-agency initiative to improve programmes both in refugee camps and inside Afghanistan. However, there is no systematic approach to the educational needs of newly arrived refugees, except where they arrive as a large group and are assigned to a particular camp. In many locations, there are several schools supported by different agencies, and no single agency or school feels responsible for scattered groups of new arrivals. Hence there is a situation where parents have to bargain with individual heads of school when requesting admission of their children during the ongoing school year. Under such circumstances there may be little attention to psychosocial needs or bridging arrangements. Since there has been a continuing stream of new arrivals over the years, dispersed over a wide geographic area, it would be useful to develop a policy on new arrivals and train school heads accordingly. Recent NGO efforts to upgrade the many (mostly under-resourced) private Afghan refugee schools in Peshawar and Islamabad could also include sensitization on these issues.

Democratic Republic of Congo

DRC received the sixth-largest number of new arrivals in 1999 (65,000). (It was third in 1998, with 52,500.) During 1999 some 49,000 refugees arrived in DRC from the Republic of Congo but most of them repatriated by year's end. 1999 also saw the return to Aru district in northern DRC of many south Sudanese, who had left in 1998 due to conflict. "As these are long-staying refugees located in rich agricultural areas, UNHCR will implement a local settlement programme which will also benefit local communities, including education." (UNHCR, 2000f). In an innovative programme, over 200 post-secondary students in this district are studying English by "open learning" or "tele-education", using video-cassettes and local tutors to obtain a diploma from the University of Quebec (Gueye, 2000:11).

Operational conditions in DRC are very difficult, with some areas inaccessible due to conflict. Government services such as education are no longer state-funded, parents having to pay teachers themselves. In these circumstances UNHCR pays fees for some refugee children to attend state schools and constructs schools in camps. The number of students supported at primary level in 1999 was 23,000, while for 2000 it was 25,000. Secondary education enrolments are limited to 1,800, since high fees have to be paid ($184 per year), and there are restrictions on refugee admission to government secondary schools. Within its limited budget UNHCR also provides education materials, school furniture, school repairs etc. No additional funds are provided during the year on account of new arrivals.[89]

89 The implementing agencies in the various locations include World Vision, IFRC, three religious bodies, Association pour le Développement Social et la Sauvegarde de l'Environnement and the NGO HDW.

As noted earlier, the national curriculum is followed even in refugee schools. So far it has not been possible formally to introduce Portuguese language as a subject for Angolan refugees (as happens in Zambia) or English in schools for south Sudanese. Much remains to be done to improve refugee education in DRC, depending on improvement in security and access, and on the availability of sufficient funding; support for education for internally displaced young people is needed also.

The Eritrea crisis

In Eritrea, the outbreak of renewed hostilities with Ethiopia in May 2000 happened about three weeks before the end of the school year. Internal displacement increased and some 90,000 refugees crossed the border into Sudan, where three refugee camps were established. Many refugees repatriated within a few months. Refugee communities discussed education, but there was not much action since this was school vacation time. Among the Muslim boys and younger girls, there was daily traditional religious instruction at the mosques, providing a structured group activity.

The Eritrean government decided to reconvene schools during the summer vacation to enable students to prepare for and sit their end-of-year examinations, so that they could be assigned to the appropriate class for the next school year. UNHCR was supporting repatriation and felt that refugees could return in safety to Eritrea to take advantage of these arrangements. It was planned that refugees who do not return to Eritrea will be relocated to an older camp in the same locality (where there is refugee schooling that follows the Sudanese curriculum). At the time of writing this relocation has been delayed by insecurity.

Somali refugees and returnees at the Emkulu Camp, Eritrea. UNHCR/09.2000/W. Rappeport

There was considerable discussion within UNHCR field offices regarding the possible need for education officers in Eritrea and the three refugee camps, especially as NRC had offered to make these specialists available at no cost to UNHCR. Given the pattern of repatriation, a decision was finally made to deploy a single Norwegian education specialist on secondment to UNHCR in early August 2000, to assist in meeting the needs of children remaining in the camps (Susanne Kindler-Adam, personal communication). However, debriefing of this secondee on 12 December 2000 revealed that he and his Community Services colleague had been instructed not to promote any child or adolescent activities in the camps because there had been strong repatriation in July, although it became clear after a while that the repatriation had slowed down. Refugee parents were requesting education or other activities to occupy their children. In this situation, the education and community services specialists undertook repatriation-oriented community-based activities, of which the education component included documenting the resourcing needs of schools in returnee areas. However, the limited funding required by these schools was not made available.

How can assistance organizations prepare for emergency educational response? The debate on kits

The establishment of emergency activities for children and adolescents often requires a major feat of organization. Sometimes refugees or internally displaced persons (IDPs) arrive in remote locations with poor access by road or air, and in the middle of a rainy season. Sometimes a country has been badly affected by war, and there is a shortage of basic materials. In such situations, what procedures should be adopted for the procurement and distribution of educational and recreational materials? Should this be achieved through the use of kits? This has been the subject of heated debate during the 1990s, and thus merits a separate section here. It should be emphasized that, as far as refugees are concerned, the use of kits has not been and should not be a major feature of refugee education, since local procurement of materials through NGOs is normally a better option. There may, however, be some difficult refugee situations where kits could be of use, and they are found helpful for some non-refugee situations of chronic emergency, where normal procurement and distribution systems have failed.

This section begins with a brief history of some 1990s kits, and then reviews some strengths and weaknesses of the kit approach, in relation to refugee and non-refugee situations.

The UNESCO "Teacher Emergency Package". The civil conflict and breakdown of government in Somalia in 1991 led UNESCO to send a refugee education specialist, Gonzalo Retamal, to Mogadishu to organize emergency education programmes. A "Teacher Emergency Package" (TEP) was developed, which could be transported to any community group willing to establish a simple school. Disruption of education during the previous decade meant that there were few qualified teachers and that most students would be complete beginners. Retamal collected examples of education materials such as cloth alphabet charts from other refugee programmes to guide local production of similar materials. A teacher's guide for initial literacy and numeracy was prepared by Somali educators. The TEPs, each comprising a box of education supplies for one classroom and a shoulder-bag of teacher materials, were assembled by suppliers in Nairobi. Kits were distributed to community schools after the teachers had received a four-day training (Retamal and Devadoss, 1998: 81–3).

This Somalia operation, which began in 1993, became the first activity of UNESCO's Programme for Education for Emergencies and Reconstruction (PEER). In June 1994, UNESCO-PEER worked with Rwandan educators to prepare a Rwandan version of the teacher guide, and the TEP was used with Rwandan refugees and in Rwanda. By March 1995, some 7,400 TEPs had been distributed in Rwanda and 1,300 in refugee camps in Tanzania, and in Goma and Bukavu in eastern Zaire (now DRC) (DANIDA, 1996: IV, 56–57).

The TEP has been adapted for use in conflict-affected areas of Angola (Midttun, 1998). A TEP has also been prepared with a teachers' guide in Uduk language, for use in Ethiopia. A Kirundi version is in use in rural Burundi (Midttun, 2000a: 5). In a recent pilot project initiated by Gonzalo Retamal and Plan International, a TEP kit was flown from Nairobi to Freetown, Sierra Leone, to facilitate local design and production of a rapid response kit for use in Plan's work for internally displaced children (see www.ginie.org).

The use of kits by UNICEF. UNICEF has been providing educational and recreational materials to developing countries and in emergencies for many years, as part of its mandate to help children. It has a large warehouse in Copenhagen, which issues a price-list for all items stored there. Field offices normally procure supplies from Copenhagen, unless the UNICEF Supply Division has authorized local purchase, on the basis of proven cost-effectiveness.[90] In accordance with its current move towards a predictable minimum response to emergencies, UNICEF has recently defined standard kits, which can be shipped from its Copenhagen warehouse in the first days or weeks of an emergency. These include a classroom kit, a recreation kit and an early childhood kit. For the long-term support needed in Somalia, UNICEF has recently worked with Somali educators to design a "teachers and school kit" and a "pupils' supplies" classroom kit, procured in Nairobi (Geeta Verma, personal communication). In some situations, UNICEF supplies individual "student kits".

Mention may be made also of UNICEF's work with the government of Zambia to develop "Zedukits", linked to training of unqualified volunteers under the "sPARK" project, to help develop community schools, and to cope with the loss of teachers due to the AIDS emergency. Zedukits, given to schools not run by the government, contain the official textbooks (Barry Sesnan, personal communication).

The healing role of various forms of play has led to the concept of issuing a recreational kit to support organized recreational activities in the earliest weeks of an emergency, as a first step leading to the restoration of schooling. A kit was developed in Rwanda with UNICEF support, incorporating local games and costumes as well as volleyballs, skipping ropes and so on, together with an instructor's guide. This model, not extensively used in Rwanda, was advocated in Aguilar and Retamal's 1998 discussion paper, which suggested the contents of a recreation kit and recommended that it be issued (preferably) after a short training of those who are to organize its use. It has now been adopted by UNICEF as a standard component of rapid emergency response.

From kits to child-friendly spaces

UNICEF, working in collaboration with NGOs such as Save the Children/US, has recently adopted the concept of Child-Friendly Spaces or Safe Spaces for Children, with its broader approach to emergency response, including the creation of a sense of security for mothers and children. The child-friendly space recommended by UNICEF Albania includes a minimum of four tented spaces of 70–75 sq m for pre-primary and lower primary classes, three similar spaces for upper primary classes, a play area of 50 sq m, a well baby area of 50 sq m, a water point, and a small women and children's "adult" area, all set in 1,700 sq m for a population

90 See www.supply.unicef.dk/specialprojects.htm

of 2,500 refugees (UNICEF, 1999b: 9). This approach was adopted in several locations, where space permitted. The schools were supplied with UNICEF classroom and recreation kits, similar to those used elsewhere.

Other kits. As mentioned above, the Norwegian Refugee Council uses an adapted version of the TEP in Angola, for "TEP schools", which are established in villages where no normal school is operating. The TEP programme is implemented jointly with UNICEF and the Ministry of Education. In 1999–2000, NRC has collaborated with the Ministry of Education in Sierra Leone and UNICEF to develop a Rapid Response Education Programme kit for use with children aged 10 to 13 whose schooling has been interrupted. The aim is to prepare them for re-entry to primary school. This kit integrates both classroom supplies and recreational materials (as do UNICEF's new kits for Somalia, mentioned earlier).[91]

Should supplies be pre-assembled into kits?

The normal procedure in times of peace and with efficient distribution mechanisms is to send cartons of exercise books, cartons of chalk, cartons of balls and so on to schools and youth centres, according to their particular needs. What are the advantages then of preparing kits suited to a single classroom, youth group or student?

"Kitting" can be helpful when there is no established or efficient system for supplies procurement and distribution. This can be the situation in some early emergency situations and in some situations of chronic emergency. In his study of kit use in Somalia over recent years, Eric Eversmann (2000: 17) notes that kits have the advantage of keeping related items together. Some field staff stated that they preferred pre-packaged materials, as "staff did not have to deal with the physical and time demands of assembling materials from individual boxes across a warehouse or storage centre for distribution".

Eversmann adds, however, that "Given sufficient personnel, UN and NGO staff both felt that it would be more efficient to send bulk materials". This comment reflects the chronic under-supply of basic education materials. NGOs reported that when there were insufficient education kits to meet the needs of all schools, some kits had to be disassembled in the warehouse, so that the contents could be distributed fairly between the schools that they were supporting. The same kind of disassembly of classroom kits occurs if a school receives fewer kits than there are classes. He comments that "This means that the expenses incurred in packaging the materials into kits in the first place have been lost and the programme is rendered increasingly inefficient".

In resource-poor contexts, the pre-assembly of kits has the advantage of discouraging diversion to the local market of valuable and compact items, such as boxes of pencils or scissors, and tins of blackboard paint. Nevertheless, some of the kits in Angola arrived in the school already opened and lacking various items. Teachers did not always communicate to supervisors that items were missing or that the actual number of students meant that more items were required (Johannessen, 2000: 20). In a further measure to limit pilferage, UNICEF Somalia presents education kits to the receiving school during a ceremony to which community members are invited, so that parents are aware of the items transferred to the schools, such as slates for their children (Geeta Verma, personal communication).

91 The Sierra Leone NRC kit includes: 40 pencils, 40 exercise books, 40 erasers, 40 slates, 3 boxes of chalk, a cloth number chart, a cloth multiplication chart, a cloth alphabet chart, a clock face, 5 sets of small wooden "scrabble cubes", a measuring tape, 3 pencil sharpeners, a football, a softball, 4 short skipping ropes, 2 long skipping ropes, a whistle, a football pump and 5 packets of crayons (and for the teacher an attendance register, a notebook, a can of blackboard paint with paint brush, 5 ballpoint pens, a packet of coloured chalk, a bag and a padlock). For other kit specifications, catering to 80 students in two shifts, see Aguilar and Retamal (1998) and UNHCR (1999a: 116–117).

Pre-assembly of kits also has the advantage that materials in the kit boxes are protected from rain and other damage when in transit, even when handled by workers unfamiliar with such materials. Supervised preparation of kits including books can help avoid the situation where books are left for months or years in warehouses, and the situation where the wrong items are delivered to schools (e.g. the primary school that received enough textbooks, but they were all for year 1).[92]

Pre-assembly of standard kits makes for complexity in respect of "refills", however, if the kit approach is used on a prolonged basis. The diverse items in the kits described earlier need to be replenished or replaced at different rates. UNICEF Somalia's new school and teacher kits are designed to meet the start-up needs of new classes or schools. There is a hope that replenishment of consumable items will be undertaken at community level, but schools in situations of "abject poverty" will require external support. NRC kits shipped to Angola from Nairobi require replenishment through additional in-country purchase of chalk, exercise books and pencils during the school year.

Inflexibility of pre-assembled contents in relation to different users

A major problem is that pre-designed kits never quite fit any user situation.[93]

Class size. Kits mostly assume that there are 40 students per class (25 for NRC's programme in Angola), while the real figure may be much higher than this. Yet the kit should not be designed in a way that signals approval of over-sized classes. This is a major problem of using the classroom kit approach, and could be used to argue in favour of individual "student kits".

Slates. There is wide variation in the use of slates and chalk in primary schools. Some school systems use them extensively, while others regard them as suited only to pre-school, or to grades 1 or 2 of primary. Since francophone systems may use slates throughout primary school, UNICEF plans to make slates an optional component of its emergency education kit. UNICEF Somalia has included slates in kits for students in years 1 and 2, on sustainability and pedagogical grounds (Geeta Verma, personal communication). The NRC evaluation consultant in Angola noted that some teachers had absorbed the training on the use of slates more effectively than others, and emphasized that slates were superior to notebooks for the first four to five months of the TEP year (Johannessen, 2000: 28). "Slate pencils" as available from UNICEF Copenhagen have certain advantages, but cannot normally be replenished locally, which constitutes a disadvantage.

Exercise books. The amount of exercise book space required by students increases steadily throughout primary and secondary school. The TEP, and UNICEF's standard "education kit" as described earlier, provide the same amount of writing space for every child, which tends to be unsatisfactory above grades 2 or 3. In many countries, education above this level relies extensively on pupils copying notes from the blackboard, and students at higher levels need at least one exercise book per subject per year, possibly one per term, depending on the number of pages.

---

92 Great Lakes example, cited by Barry Sesnan (personal communication).

93 Comment by Peter Buckland (personal communication).

"Quick Impact Projects" (QIPs) funded under UNHCR's Cross-Border Operation include the rehabilitation of schools as well as "Food for Work" schemes and training for teachers. Bardera Camp, Gedo Region, Somalia. UNHCR/01.1994/B. Press

Two approaches have been advocated to overcome this problem. One is to purchase additional supplies locally, to supplement standardized kits. (However, this presents problems if procurements need to go through a lengthy approval process.) Another is to develop separate kits for each grade and situation, as for grades 1 to 4 in Somalia (see above).

Recreation materials. The problems of local appropriateness are even more acute with recreational materials. Forms of recreation vary widely, as do the discrepancies between activities considered appropriate for girls and for boys. UNICEF "recreation kit" specifications indicate that musical instruments should be procured locally and distributed with the kit. In Sherkole camp, Ethiopia, Swedish Save the Children has organized refugee youth production of leather footballs, which are cheaper than those in the market and well used. This may be worth exploring more widely, given that balls deteriorate when used on rough ground, and need replacement (Lobo, 2000).

Sanitary materials. Kits have not so far addressed the issue of sanitary materials, which are important if older girls are to attend regularly. Schools often lack soap, even though they teach about washing hands after using the toilet.

Clothing. Lack of decent clothing is a barrier to participation in schooling and other activities for older children in displaced communities. UNHCR's "peace packs", donated by the Girl Guide movement, include tee-shirts, but these have not normally been included in emergency response.

Shelter, blackboards and school furniture. These are not normally supplied in education kits but are procured separately, providing work for local craftsmen or businesses. Sometimes refugee craftsmen prepare school furniture, with refugee youth as apprentices receiving training. Blackboards are included in the kits being supplied by UNICEF for Somali schools, although not in the main "package" box. The TEP and the UNICEF emergency kits include tins of blackboard paint, for painting surfaces or packing material to serve as blackboards.

Other materials. In his description of "dream kits" for southern Sudan, Barry Sesnan (n.d.) lists what are really specifications for reasonable equipment of emergency schooling, including a school establishment pack, a classroom supplies pack, a teacher's pack and personal pack, a pupil's pack, a science and mathematics (very basic) pack, a sports pack, an income generation (very basic) pack, an English-language pack, a mini-library pack and "awareness messages" packs. Unfortunately there are few crisis-affected or refugee schools with all the basic items listed by Sesnan. Education assistance programmes should try, however, to identify locally relevant resourcing needs in this fashion, and meet them through local or regional procurement, "kitting" them for distribution if this is helpful.

Sourcing and costs

UNESCO-PEER typically contracts suppliers in Nairobi to assemble kits. Local materials are used, meaning that standards are comparable in quality with items for sale locally (diminishing the risk of diversion to the local market). There will be no disappointment at a later date when imported items are not available. On the other hand, there can be problems of quality, such as slates that are or become difficult to clean.

The TEPs for the Somali and Rwandan emergencies were transported by road from Nairobi. Transport costs add substantially to the cost of the kits themselves. Nevertheless, NRC found in 1996 that the costs of procuring TEPs in Angola would be higher than procurement from Nairobi and shipping by container to Luanda.

The current cost of a TEP for Angola, if procured from Rymans in Nairobi, is about $280, or $3.50 per student (this assumes 80 students using the kit during two shifts). The cost of shipping a container of 230 kits to Angola is about $4,000, or $17 per kit. Air freight of the 40 kg TEP kit from Nairobi to Luanda would cost about $80 per kit (which would raise the cost to $4.50 per student). UNESCO-PEER policy is now to conduct a local market survey and to produce some kit components locally, where possible (Mudiappasami Devadoss, personal communication).

As noted above, UNICEF's procurement procedures are centralized at its Copenhagen warehouse, although efforts are being made to decentralize. Time is needed to gain approval for local procurement, meaning that emergency response tends to use materials from Copenhagen. If air freight from Copenhagen is used, this adds costs of the order of $1 per kilogramme. Freight costs can be much higher in conflict-affected areas, however, due to insecurity. The current cost of the UNICEF education and recreation kits are $287.80 and $269.36 respectively. If the education kit is used by 80 students in two shifts this means a per student cost of $3.60. The recreational kit could be shared by more children and adolescents and therefore has a lower cost per user (Pilar Aguilar, personal communication).

Purchase in the country or region of use is commendable in terms of supporting local markets. In terms of purchase costs, however, there is not necessarily any saving. Comparison of costs of typical items included in PEER and UNICEF kits shows that some are more expensive in Nairobi than through UNICEF Supply Division procurement procedures, and vice versa.

Printed materials and education aids: should they be included in the kits?

A distinguishing feature of the TEP is the inclusion of a teacher's guide and other printed materials such as cloth wall-charts and small wooden cubes that can be used for word formation games such as "scrabble". Where possible it also includes or is accompanied by "supplementary survival messages" (Aguilar and Retamal, 1998: 33–44). The teachers' guide was initially developed in 1993 in Somalia, where the level of education in rural areas was very low and where classes were being taught by inexperienced teachers (Retamal and Devadoss, 1998: 74–83).

The Somali teachers' guide was used as the model for the Kinyarwanda teachers' guide prepared by Rwandan and Somali educators employed by UNESCO-PEER in summer 1994. The guide became somewhat controversial at this point. One reason was that the Rwandan refugees in Ngara, Tanzania, included almost intact populations who had crossed the border to avoid the approaching army of the Rwandan Patriotic Front. Hence the population included trained teachers and even school inspectors. As they crossed the border, a humanitarian worker overheard a school inspector asking "What can we do? It is time for the school examinations."[94] Another difference from Somalia was the presence of a considerable number of students who had been attending upper primary classes.

There was thus resistance to the TEP guide from some teachers, who were reported as saying, "Why are you giving us [TEP]? It is not Rwandan." (Sommers, 1999: 9). The level of suggested activities was deemed inappropriate by teachers of older children and by some teachers in Rwanda when TEPs were issued there. Of course, the function of the kit as a source of writing materials was valid, even if some teachers were uninterested in the emergency guide. The TEP initiative in Ngara and Karagwe camps, in Tanzania, permitted the re-establishment of schooling in October 1994, with as many as 58,000 students in 40 refugee schools by March 1995, just before the first anniversary of the genocide (Aguilar and Richmond, 1998: 137).

The inter-agency evaluation of the Rwandan emergency noted "serious shortcomings" in the TEP response in Rwanda. The emphasis in the TEP approach and teacher's guide on introductory literacy and numeracy meant that the package was distributed mainly to lower primary classes, whereas writing materials were needed by all classes.

> The TEP was distributed only to the lowest grades, covering about three-quarters of the children ... In June 1995, the TEP packets were still being distributed to some communes despite the fact that more substantial education programmes had since been established. Second, this late diffusion underscores questions about the TEP's appropriateness to begin with. The programme attempts to shape a prefabricated intervention to needs of the country. For instance, the limited teacher training that accompanies the TEP enables teachers to use the packet; however, that training should be adapted to the needs of the country's existing programme. Children in Rwanda would have been better served if the international community had focused on rehabilitating the indigenous education system rather than investing scarce resources in the TEP programme, particularly so many months after the emergency. (DANIDA, 1996: IV, 92)

94 Narrated to the author by a UNHCR field staff member in 1994.

A feature of the TEP approach has been the provision of at least two days initial training for teachers on the use of the teachers' guide and the TEP materials (Aguilar and Retamal, 1998: 26). The Angola version of TEP incorporates enriched teachers' guide and a longer period of initial training (five weeks), due to the low level of education of the rural population from whom teachers are recruited (Midttun, 1998: 6). The training and guide do not always lead to the use of child-centred teaching methods, as intended, but there is more success when groups of teachers prepare their lessons together (Johannessen, 2000: 27). The Angola TEP project has been extended to include grades 1 to 4 in some locations, and additional training has therefore been given (two-week training courses for each of grades 2 to 4), and textbooks and supporting materials supplied for grades 1 to 4 (Midttun, 1998: 5). In other cases, TEP students are encouraged to enter regular government schools – and there is then the problem of these students transferring at appropriate levels (Johannessen, 2000: 17–18). In Sierra Leone NRC has recently begun courses for children over 10 years of age, using the TEP Angola manual, translated and adapted by US and British educators to introduce literacy in English. Enrichment modules from its Rapid Response Education Programme are also being used with these students (Mette Nordstrand, personal communication).

With the increasing emphasis on rapid response, and to meet the needs of diverse operational situations, agencies have tended to separate the supply of kits from the processes of developing the educational and recreational programmes themselves. The development of materials for NRC's Rapid Response Education Programme for older children in Sierra Leone took approximately three months, including needs assessment, cooperative design of curriculum outlines, and teacher recruitment and training (Mette Nordstrand, personal communication). It is difficult to move faster than this. UNICEF, for example, has decided to separate the supply of emergency materials from the process of teacher training:

> The reason that we [UNICEF] have moved away from the name "school-in-a-box" is that, despite its appeal to donors, it tends to create the impression that the box contains a school, when it can only contain supplies. No amount of kits will replace all the other work that it takes to get education going – community mobilization, identifying an appropriate curriculum, obtaining or developing learning and teaching materials, identifying, orienting and training teachers, monitoring standards and so forth.[95]

UNICEF Somalia is combining the distribution of the education kits with a brief training of principals and teachers on their use. A "user's manual" of a few pages explains the contents of the kits.[96] Despite initial training where TEP has been used, evaluation of the programmes in Somalia and Angola have shown that unfamiliar items such as the "scrabble cubes" and cloth charts have been under-used, by teachers used to blackboard-based teaching (Eversmann, 2000: 27–30; Johannessen, 2000: 28).

Intended duration of use of "kitted" items

The UNESCO-PEER kit was designed to serve the needs of lower primary children and to last for a few months. The duration of use was controversial in the Rwandan refugee camps in Tanzania, where teachers complained that they had "finished the TEP", meaning that they had finished using the teachers' guide that came with the kit. It was intended that textbooks would be in place within a few months, but these were delayed, and interim materials were developed by refugee educators.

95 Peter Buckland, personal communication. UNICEF plans to develop a start-up workshop manual for initiating this collaborative process early in an emergency.

96 Details supplied by Geeta Verma, UNICEF, Somalia.

In contrast, kits (and replenishment packages) are seen as a long-term approach in situations where there is no established and reliable distribution system in place, as in the case of UNICEF Somalia and NRC's work in Angola and Sierra Leone.

Preparedness

There has been much discussion of the issue of "preparedness". This is an area where UNICEF Copenhagen is able to benefit from its dual role in supplying development programmes and emergency programmes. Suppliers are often willing to promise emergency supplies provided that there is an ongoing annual procurement. Thus, UNICEF Copenhagen has the capacity to respond to emergency demands for the types of item needed for its education and recreation kits. Likewise, UNESCO-PEER in Nairobi is able to procure education kits quickly, by dealing with known suppliers, who have valued its substantial past orders.

Advantages of standby stocks. In some cases it is not possible to procure the needed items quickly from the local market. In some cases there may not be a known implementing partner that could quickly make the local purchases. In these circumstances pre-assembled materials may reach crisis-affected communities more quickly than would be possible with local procurement. In practice it may not be possible quickly to increase the budget line for education in an agency's programme. An existing education budget may have been used up, and/or the emergency may be too small to justify budget revision to accommodate new arrivals. If standby stocks can be used, budget issues can be handled later.

Managers in an emergency situation may be more willing to say "yes" to a Headquarters' request to receive pre-assembled activity kits for children than to initiate immediate local procurement. Moreover, preparedness may create awareness. The existence of kits to meet the needs of children and adolescents for structured activities may create a positive climate of opinion among agency staff, reminding them that children and adolescents have special needs to restore their wellbeing after trauma and displacement. And kits are widely considered to be attractive to donors.

Disadvantages of standby stocks. A classroom education kit is like a large heavy suitcase or trunk. This can mean high storage costs and high transport costs. Also, deterioration may be a problem. Some materials deteriorate with storage (especially in hot climates). Paper may become mouldy, ball-point pens may dry up. Moreover, it is hard to predict the nature and location of future emergencies, which means that the volume and type of supplies needed are uncertain, and it is difficult to know what emphasis to give to possible regional storage sites. If a small volume of supplies is needed, they can probably be purchased in the local capital. If a large volume of supplies is needed, then this would exceed the likely capacity of standby stocks.

Another factor that is uncertain is access to emergency sites. If road conditions are poor and air access is overloaded with other relief goods, it may take time before bulky trunks of educational materials can be given space on crowded flights or road transport schedules. By the time access becomes practicable, it might have been possible to procure the items in the affected country or region.

When to use kits. It may be concluded that there is a rationale for the large-scale use of imported, pre-assembled kits, when procurement and distribution are the responsibility of a government system that is not reliable, or where there are security problems. At the other extreme, there will rarely be a justification for imported kits when one or more efficient NGOs are already on the ground and able to make local purchases.[97] Whether such local purchases would be "kitted" in the location of purchase or field office or are distributed item by item to schools would depend on local circumstances, as would the contents of such kits.

Experience suggests that having samples of education and recreation kits to show to local educators (and craftsmen) can facilitate decision-making early in emergency situations on items needed and on whether they can be assembled locally. It could be useful therefore for agencies such as UNHCR to have a limited stock of kits that could be sent to new emergencies for demonstration and trial use, while local supply mechanisms ("kitted" or otherwise) are decided upon. UNHCR might consider developing a standby agreement with UNICEF Supply Division (see below).

What are the implications for humanitarian response? Preparedness and cooperation

International consensus is needed on the principles of educational response in crisis situations. The "Sphere" consultative process which produced a Humanitarian Charter and Minimum Standards in Disaster Response set an unfortunate example here by limiting itself to the fields of food and water, health and shelter. Resource and time constraints led the Steering Committee for Humanitarian Response to focus only on the above-mentioned topics (Joel McClellan, personal communication). However, the Sphere standards, on their own, could give the impression that humanitarian assistance to a population escaping from conflict or oppression means keeping everyone physically alive (but with young people not constructively occupied and breeding thoughts of revenge). This is despite the first principle in the associated Humanitarian Charter, "the right to life with dignity" (Sphere Project, 2000: 1–10)!

There are many agencies engaged in emergency education, and some have limited awareness of current best practice.[98] They request funds from donor personnel who are non-specialists and who cannot advise them on improving their proposals. Ways are needed therefore of establishing international principles and standards. The matter was raised at the recent Inter-Agency Consultation on Education in Emergency and Crisis, and follow-up activities may permit some progress in this direction.

The core principles identified in this limited study may be viewed as possible elements of the emerging international consensus.

- ***The right of access*** of all children and adolescents to education, including post-primary education, needs to be reiterated, since some governments refuse to acknowledge this.
- ***The community-based approach to education*** represents an investment in future capacity and in sustainability, a training ground for working together in civil society. Training of teachers, headteachers and school education committees is crucial. Involvement and training of youth leaders is needed for reaching out-of-school children and adolescents.

97 Two senior Africa-based emergency educators have recently communicated to the author their frustrations about the cost and inappropriateness of importing UNICEF kits in situations where competent NGOs implementing refugee programmes could have purchased materials in the country of asylum.

98 And, due to staff turnover, their project managers are often new to the field.

Young adolescents and their teacher at Madhu, Sri Lanka. UNHCR/07.1999/M. Kobayashi

- ***Meeting the psychosocial needs*** of children and adolescents through a range of structured activities such as education, recreation, expressive activities and community service, is a humanitarian duty and should be a "default" responsibility of the organization(s) responsible for schooling, unless other agencies are providing the needed services on a widespread basis.
- ***Rapid response*** is vital to meet psychosocial and protection needs. Where local materials procurement or distribution is likely to be difficult, pre-assembled imported kits may be helpful
- ***Relating response to the school year*** is important in meeting the concerns of the affected communities and in showing the importance of emergency education to policy-makers and donors.
- ***The principle of education for durable solutions,*** primarily refugee education in the languages of study used in the area of origin, should be internationally accepted. A regional approach, embracing countries of origin and asylum of refugees, can help solve problems of textbooks and certification and promote a durable solution. Emergency programmes should provide the foundation for positive change.
- ***Including survival and peace-building messages and skills*** in emergency education programmes can help save lives (health education and mine awareness) and prepare the coming generation of young adults to work for reconciliation, responsible government and sustainable development.

- ***The concept of emergency education should be broadened*** to embrace all the above-mentioned concerns, including both school-based programmes and programmes for out-of-school children and adolescents.
- ***Ensuring the participation of special groups*** including girls, adolescents, persons with disabilities and others is a primary concern, to be tackled jointly by education programme staff, other humanitarian programmes, community groups (leaders, youth, women, religious and other groups) and community education committees.
- ***Ongoing refugee education programmes*** should make special arrangements for rapid and broad-based response to the needs of newly arriving refugee children and adolescents.
- ***Efforts should be made to provide schooling*** for children and adolescents, even in less accessible and insecure places.
- ***In prolonged emergencies,*** there should be steady improvement in education quality, coverage and management.
- ***Vigorous field-level partnerships and coordination mechanisms*** are needed to achieve the above objectives.[99]

The most controversial of these principles among policy-makers concerned with refugees is likely to be rapid response to the needs of newly displaced populations, for fear that this will deter return. The solution here is to emphasize the broader approach to meeting psychosocial needs that is envisaged. Policy-makers should understand that a "real" emergency education system takes at least a year to establish, more often several years.

The most controversial of these principles among educators is likely to be the integration of responsibility for organized child and adolescent activities in general into the sphere of "emergency education". It is argued here that "structured normalizing activities for children and adolescents that address their protection and developmental needs" (see the case study on Timor above), including education, should be what emergency educators are talking about and doing. Donors fund "emergency education" programmes which have to be within walking reach of every child. Given current funding constraints, these programmes must assume "default" responsibility for the broader agenda of child and adolescent or youth activities.

In general, it is probably wise to keep the title "education" for this broader approach, as has been done by the Norwegian Refugee Council, for example, especially since teachers and classroom materials account for the bulk of the costs. However, in situations where emergency schooling is being tackled (often partially) by host governments, or where newly arrived refugees may be still thinking about an immediate return home, it may be more diplomatic to use a term such as "child and youth activities".

UNHCR's role

The roles of the UN agencies concerned with emergency education should build on their strengths. UNESCO has special expertise in supporting national education programmes in situations of chronic crisis and of reconstruction, for example. There is a Memorandum of Understanding between UNHCR and

99 For another, similar, list of principles see Retamal et al. (1998: 213–214).

UNICEF on situations and sectors of mutual concern, based on their strengths and mandates. It assigns the primary role to UNHCR in refugee situations, and to UNICEF for in-country situations, but allows for flexibility. This flexibility has meant that UNICEF has largely handled humanitarian education in the recent high-profile crises in Kosovo and Timor (likewise in Tanzania, where UNICEF took an active role in the education of the large numbers of Rwandan and subsequently Burundi refugees, in cooperation with UNHCR). UNHCR, however, continues to be actively responsible for the education of almost a million refugee children.

UNHCR's responsibilities for education cannot be abdicated, as they relate to its field presence. The international community expects UNHCR to be present in almost every location where refugees need protection and assistance, and equips the agency with field offices, field staff, vehicles and communications equipment accordingly. In most of these locations, therefore, it is cost-effective for UNHCR to be the lead agency for emergency educational response.

The invisible activity

Although education is one of the main activities in refugee camps over the longer term, it is sometimes almost invisible in the discourse on policy. An examination of UNHCR evaluation reports in recent years (see www.unhcr.ch) shows little mention of education except for specific evaluations on children and education. The DANIDA-led multinational evaluation of the international response to the Rwanda emergency made only passing reference to education in the refugee camps, some 37 words in a detailed four-volume report (DANIDA, 1996), and these words were in the chapter on reconstruction inside Rwanda, not in the discussion of refugee operations.

The international community provides these resources to UNHCR in areas of repatriation and in specific internal displacement scenarios also. In such situations, UNHCR is not normally the lead agency for education, but UNHCR's field resources and protection mandate mean that it should attend to the specifics of ensuring that children "of concern" have access to school, without discrimination.[100] Returnee teachers should likewise have access to employment, without discrimination. UNHCR frequently gives funds for physical reconstruction, and these funds should support enlightened educational response, including education materials and teacher training as well as school buildings. (They should not be used for a few expensive school buildings benefiting the elite.) UNHCR should represent the interests of returnee districts in discussions of the allocation of donor funds generally (UNICEF in this case has country-wide responsibilities and has to build a long-term relationship with the central government, which may favour other districts).

All these responsibilities mean that UNHCR staff in general need an awareness of emergency education issues; and that specialist education officers are needed for major refugee programmes and for the initial period after repatriation (see below).

100 UNHCR refers to non-refugees benefiting from its protection or assistance as "persons of concern".

Strengthening institutional policies

Institutional policy is not always clear, since decisions derive from different sections within a headquarters bureaucracy. Moreover, organizations such as UNHCR and UNICEF decentralize interpretation of policy as much as possible, to take account of the very different regional and national situations affecting refugees and children respectively. Matters are complicated further by the frequent job-rotation and sometimes high staff turnover in field-oriented humanitarian organizations. This can lead to inconsistent application of policy within countries over time and between countries. As noted above, UNHCR's Inspection and Evaluation Service found gross disparities in UNHCR's resourcing and speed of response to the education and psychosocial needs of children and adolescents (UNHCR, 1997b, 1997c). There cannot be rapid education response, or adequate subsequent emergency education unless there is a clear institutional commitment from the top, not just to the word "education", but to specific principles and standards and to giving feedback to donors if these standards cannot be met.

Institutional support for rapid response. UNICEF's "core corporate commitments" include shipment of the first emergency education and recreation kits within 72 hours. Norwegian Refugee Council standby educators are likewise available for deployment within 72 hours, which has greatly improved the capacity of the UN system for emergency response: funds have been obtained from the Norwegian government to provide quickly educators with relevant experience to UNHCR, UNICEF and UNESCO.

In the case of UNHCR, there is, or should be, a debate regarding the possibility of inclusion of an education specialist in the earliest stages of emergency response, to undertake needs assessment, prepare plans and help communities with early structured activities for children and adolescents. Currently, a Community Services specialist is included in the first emergency response team, often through a deployment from the standby team led by Swedish Save the Children.[101] In most situations, however, the Community Services Officer is busy with identifying and briefing NGOs to work with separated children, women victims of violence and rape, elderly refugees and so on. In these circumstances the officer is expected to indicate the need for an education specialist to support the development of activities for children and adolescents. This can be difficult, however, if there is a hesitation at management level to begin "education" because of the belief that it might deter an expected immediate repatriation.[102] Hopefully, this paper helps to clarify that emergency educators are expected to have important "soft" emergency response skills for working with the community, and are not about to build costly school classrooms enticing people to stay.

If UNHCR is to live up to its policy commitments to rapid education response, it needs to avoid the situation where e-mails about the possible "rapid deployment" of an education officer go back and forth for weeks or months, between overloaded staff (who are not educators) – as happened with Albania 1999 and the Eritrean crisis, 2000. UNHCR senior management should review the issue and consider adopting a trigger mechanism whereby the movement of more than 15,000 (or some other number of) refugees would automatically require deployment of a standby emergency education expert.[103] The trigger mechanism should also ensure the immediate dispatch (or immediate local procurement) of basic educational and

101 A total of 39 such deployments have been made since January 1996 (up to August 2000), of whom one-third were from Norwegian Save the Children.

102 Regarding the objection that education may delay voluntary repatriation in an early refugee emergency, see comments earlier in this paper.

103 This topic could be discussed by the UNHCR Executive Committee's Standing Committee in its regular reviews of child policy issues.

recreational materials, based on population estimates; which would be deployed under the guidance of the emergency education specialist.

Accessing supplies in early emergency. As noted above, UNICEF has developed standardized emergency kits and has suppliers contracted to supply more kits at short notice. UNHCR, having the advantage of working often through competent NGOs, relies on local purchasing by these NGOs for the bulk of its education supplies.

The best form of rapid response is indeed for a competent organization to start working with the refugee or internally displaced community as soon as possible, and to purchase simple supplies locally. However, there is not always a competent implementing partner on the spot, and large-scale local purchases can be difficult. UNHCR might therefore consider procuring and stocking a small stock of emergency education and recreation kits, which could be dispatched to small emergencies and, as part of the start-up process, to larger ones (but unless there is NGO back-up, the kits sent to crisis-affected locations may get lost). The kits would cover only about three months of initial operation and would not be a substitute for normal local procurement. The kits could be used quickly without waiting to establish an education budget line. If the emergency is large, feedback would indicate whether to order more and whether modifications are necessary. Local production may often be possible, once samples of the kits are available.

One option for refugee emergencies would be to design a combined education and recreation kit, to save space and to avoid the impression that permanent schools are being established for newly arrived refugees who may still be considering return home. The kits could be called some variant of "Child and Adolescent Activity Kits", and the initial centres of activity could be called something like "Child and Adolescent Activity Centres".[104] On balance, however, it would probably be simpler for UNHCR to develop institutional arrangements to procure the standard UNICEF education and recreation emergency kits, through an arrangement with UNICEF Supply Division.

Rapid access to funds. Regarding donor policy, Nicolai (2000) commends "up-front" seed money given by the Banyan Tree Foundation for IRC to start its programme in East Timor, as contrasted with situations where need assessments for early emergency interventions lead to the submission of proposals to donors and finally to the receipt of funds when the time for "phase one" interventions is past (Wendy Smith, personal communication). The high-speed response of the Norwegian Ministry of Foreign Affairs to funding requests from NRC is also noteworthy. The lack of effective mechanisms in UNHCR for meeting mid-year additional funding requirements for education of newly arrived refugee children and adolescents has been noted above.

Institutional commitment to maintaining and improving standards. Consistency of institutional support is another huge challenge. UNHCR and many NGOs operate under perpetual resource constraints and insecurity of funding. UNHCR, for example, raises almost all its resources through fund-raising from governments during the current calendar year. Field budget proposals are effectively limited in advance to an estimate of the funds that donor governments may be willing to provide during the coming year, rather than indicating what is needed to achieve agreed minimum standards. Information on the actual needs of education and youth programmes rarely reaches headquarters, or donors.

---

104 The "resource box for recreational and other activities" proposed in the 1999 edition of UNHCR's Handbook for Emergencies, is of this type (UNHCR, 1999a: 116–17).

Additionally, agencies such as UNHCR normally experience funding crises during the year, when programmes are asked to reduce their budgets due to an expected shortfall of resources.[105] NGOs likewise often operate on faith alone, unsure whether the next tranche of funding will arrive until the last moment or even later! Under no circumstances should teacher posts be cut with the constant ups and downs of budget projections and crises, otherwise education will not be worth the name and teachers and children will not learn the lessons of orderly institutional management and trust that they often badly need.[106] The impact of financial crises should be limited to temporary reductions in infrastructure budgets, which should be part of every education project after the initial phase, if only for this reason.

The incipient donor interest in multi-year funding is very necessary in the field of education (and should be on a rolling basis, so that there is always a two- or three-year future funding profile). As noted earlier, donors have also begun earmarking funding for refugee education programmes in several African countries to give a secure resource base. It is hoped that these donors will invest in a study of the true resourcing needs of these programmes, in ongoing monitoring and reporting and in periodic independent evaluation of programme achievements (as well as solving problems of budget structure that can constrain expenditure of the donated funds).

Attitudes to staffing the education function. Humanitarian organizations have few staff with expertise in education in situations of emergency and crisis. The most lacking is UNHCR, which has only one senior post for education, despite a case-load of over two million children and adolescents in refugee populations assisted by UNHCR.[107] Many of the educators working within UNICEF and UNESCO lack emergency experience. And the NGOs which undertake front-line work in this field have difficulty in retaining international staff to work in difficult field locations.

In UNHCR, the lack of international education posts at field level means that UNHCR cannot properly fulfil its coordination and monitoring role in this sector, and cannot actively promote quality improvement and certification of schooling or dissemination of life-saving messages (including HIV/AIDS education, and environmental and peace education). Moreover, without specialist staff, there is no professional advice to non-specialist field programme officers on how to minimise the impact of the frequent budget cuts on education programmes. Steps are needed to overcome this ambivalence about education, such as the creation of posts of Regional Education Officer, and the deployment of seconded education experts at country level.[108]

Linkages between education and related specialists. It is vital to make good linkages between education, youth services, community services and child policy specialists. All have a concern with the

---

105 The author conducted training for UNHCR field staff on programming to meet the resourcing standards set out in the 1997 education sector evaluation. Within weeks, the usual spring announcement of a financial crisis meant that education budgets had to be reduced. This meant a reduction in books and education aids, since there is usually an attempt to preserve teachers" incentives. "Progress" has meant that in November 2000 there was already an assumption of 20 per cent under-funding of approved budgets for 2001.

106 The year 2000 saw a new "low" in this respect, with some teacher posts being cut.

107 This position needs to be restored to "specialist" status, lost during an interval of 20 months when there was no senior post at all, due to restructuring during a funding crisis. In addition to the one senior specialist, the German funding for higher education scholarships includes a non-specialist post funded to administer the scholarships. And there is a United Nations Volunteer Education Adviser post in UNHCR Kampala. Some years back some field offices had Junior Professional Officers for the education sector, seconded by their governments, although this mechanism often led to the deployment of social scientists rather than educators. Donors should be requested to reactivate this arrangement, but with recruitment of education specialists.

108 NRC has deployed some education specialists to non-acute emergency programmes. See also the previous footnote.

programmes discussed here. The post-Machel establishment of units relating to children affected by armed conflict in NGOs such as Save the Children/US and IRC is a big step forward in this direction. In UNHCR, the Regional Child Policy Officers and Regional Community Services Officers have an important role to play in promoting earlier, better and more comprehensive approaches to emergency education.

Staff training. Training needs include those of staff directly managing education in emergency situations and staff at management and programme level who influence education policy and budget allocations. The ARC (Action for the Rights of Children) training materials, developed jointly by UNHCR and the Save the Children Alliance, include a module on education (UNHCR and SCA, 2000). Other training initiatives are under consideration, such as a distance education module linked to the GINIE website (Maureen McClure, personal communication).

Inter-Agency cooperation

Sharing teaching-learning materials, guidelines and manuals. Many organizations have produced education materials for use in emergencies, in the early phase and during subsequent periods. These materials tend not to be published and hence vanish when there are no longer funds to keep them in use, or when their authors or promoters move on. This can lead to waste and duplication and to slow or less than optimal results. There has been discussion about a repository of emergency education materials at least since the "RAPID-ED" meeting in Washington in 1995 that led to the establishment of the GINIE database. The JRS Regional Resource Centre in Nairobi represents a regional resource of this type.[109] Copies of certain documents have been hand-carried to certain emergencies, or downloaded from GINIE, but there has been no comprehensive approach to this matter.[110] The recent Inter-Agency Consultation included a working group discussion on this topic and a Task Team is being established to identify materials for sharing. Another Task Team will work with GINIE on web-based approaches to sharing.

There is a strong case for bringing together a set of resource materials to assist in the development of emergency education programmes. Some education materials are generic and easily adaptable to new situations, while some mention a particular country or group, but could serve as models and handy reference materials. A first step would be to review existing education materials (other than national textbooks) and prepare an annotated bibliography. The languages in which the materials are available should be documented, and in some cases translations may be felt to be useful. This activity was envisaged as part of the follow-up to the November 2000 consultation.

In a stronger version of the sharing process, some core materials could be adapted for inter-agency use, published with multiple logos, and made commercially available (at least in UNESCO and UNICEF bookshops), so that they are available to a wider range of users, are not dependent on individuals for their continued existence and become part of the public record. A useful starting point could be peace education in humanitarian situations, where UNHCR, UNICEF, UNESCO and other agencies have developed materials in recent years, rather similar in approach but with slightly different orientations. The author's

109 For contents of the Resource Centre see JRS (2000).

110 As in Sierra Leone in 1999, when psychosocial and peace education materials were downloaded in Freetown (see www.ginie.org/Sierra Leone). In many places, Internet access and printing of long documents might be difficult, although print-outs can be made by international staff before departure.

experience of visiting an Afghan NGO in Peshawar, which was translating American school textbooks to serve as a model when developing a peace education programme for Afghan refugees, reinforced this idea, since the UNHCR materials had already been structured to meet the concerns of displaced Third World populations (including Muslim as well as Christian religious leaders in the Kenya refugee camps).

Sharing information about needs and programmes. It has proved difficult to conduct the present research on education in emergencies because much of the relevant information is either lost in the mists of time, and/or scattered in files across the globe. It was extremely difficult, for example, to find out what programmes were in place at the beginning of a year and what changes were made during the year to meet the educational needs of new arrivals.[111] Difficulties in profiling emergency education world-wide were experienced by the working group convened by UNESCO in 1999 to develop the Thematic Study on education in situations of emergency and crisis.[112]

As discussed at the recent Inter-Agency Consultation, there should be a database on emergency education programmes, using a standard format. The database should be relatively simple, so that field staff have time to assemble and present the required information. Because emergency situations are so diverse, and education programmes so different, the database would be rather misleading unless there were qualitative documentation widely available to back it up. The easiest way to make such qualitative information available would be for organizations implementing emergency education programmes to put their quarterly and annual reports, and occasional evaluations and special studies, routinely on to their own or the GINIE website (excluding sensitive information).

GINIE itself needs multi-agency endorsement and input; an arrangement of this type is likely to be instituted in 2001, through the follow-up to the recent Inter-Agency Consultation. GINIE performs a useful but limited function in the field of emergency education at present, pending a stronger and more secure funding base. If the site is to provide the information services required in the field of education in crisis and transition, there is work initially for two educators with emergency experience (and different language skills) to meet the backlog of documentation work and to build networks, and on a continuing basis thereafter for at least one.

Field and headquarters inter-agency cooperation. Until recently, communication and cooperation between agencies has been weak. One consequence has been that a core group of technical specialists from each major player does the rounds of prominent new emergencies, looking at issues of education, child protection and gender. They often do not share their experiences outside their own agencies. Sometimes, but not always, the agencies are competing for funds. With the greater cooperation now envisaged, it may be possible to establish a "hotline" for communications, such that the multiplication of uncoordinated visits and initiatives could be avoided. This hotline might also be used to promote attention to the needs of "unpopular" and less "mediatized" emergencies, where education may otherwise be tacked on to the assignments of an organization whose primary concern is shelter, camp management, or water and sanitation.

111 It became clear during the present research that this exercise could not be conducted at UNHCR Headquarters, due to the decentralization of preparation of sub-agreements (and revisions thereof) with implementing partners and of records generally.

112 As observed by the present author, the difficulties ranged from knowing which organizations to contact, and non-response, to lack of standardized interpretations of basic parameters such as "duration of project" (overall duration versus current funding cycle(s)).

Plans for inter-agency cooperation in sharing materials and sharing information about ongoing programmes have been noted above. It will be a challenge for this inter-agency work to avoid being labelled a "headquarters" exercise, and to find ways of reaching deep into the field staff networks of the various partner organizations. It is hoped that there will be emergency education networks at regional level also. And the importance of inter-agency cooperation at country level has been stressed earlier in this paper.

Education as a humanitarian pillar, a human right and a cornerstone of peace-building

Education in emergencies is a pillar of humanitarian assistance, enabling services to be provided to children and young people from early in an emergency onwards. Speedy access to education and other activities which help to restore the child's development after trauma is a human right which must be respected by agencies, guided by a normative framework based on international human rights law. And education in crisis and transition can be enriched (if certain minimal resources are available) to serve as a cornerstone for building a new social order, promoting mutual respect and tolerance, peaceful discussion and problem-solving at local level, and an understanding of the role of law and of representative and honest systems of governance in problem-solving at national level.

A cornerstone is a lesser part of the whole than a pillar. Many factors contribute to the future of a country, and education, preferably peace-oriented education, is only one. But in the long run it is the next generation who will determine a country's pain or gain. And the foundations of future response to present troubles are being laid in the daily lives of emergency-affected children and young people cared for or neglected by the international community. May donors concerned with humanitarian values, human rights, long-term development and non-fissiparous governance work together to fund education in emergency, crisis and reconstruction, following principles developed through professional discussions to which this paper is a humble contribution.

References

AEDP (1999). *An integrated approach to educational assistance for Kosovo refugees in Albania.* Albania Education Development Project, Tirana; see www.aedp.soros.org

Agger, I. (1995). *Theory and practice of psycho-social projects under war conditions in Bosnia-Herzegovina and Croatia.* European Community Task Force Psychosocial Unit, European Community Humanitarian Office, Zagreb.

Agger, I and Mimica, J. (1996). *ECHO psychosocial assistance to victims of war in Bosnia-Herzegovina and Croatia: An evaluation.* European Community Task Force Psychosocial Unit, European Community Humanitarian Office, Zagreb.

Aguilar, P. and Retamal, G. (1998). *Rapid educational response in complex emergencies: a discussion document.* UNESCO International Institute of Education, Hamburg; see www.ginie.org

Aguilar, P. and Richmond, M. (1998). "Emergency educational response in the Rwandan crisis", in G. Retamal and R. Aedo-Richmond (eds.). *Education as a humanitarian response.* Cassell, London/UNESCO International Bureau of Education, Geneva: 119–41.

Appadu, K. and Retamal, G. (1998). "Education for Eritrean and Ethiopian refugees in Sudan", in G. Retamal and R. Aedo-Richmond (eds.). *Education as a humanitarian response.* Cassell, London/UNESCO International Bureau of Education, Geneva: 45–58.

Arnhold, N., Bekker, J., Kersh, N., Mcleish, E. and Phillips, D. (1998). *Education for reconstruction: the regeneration of educational capacity following national upheaval.* Symposium Books, Wallingford.

Avery, A., Bobiller, C. and Sinclair, M. (1996). *Source book for refugee skills training.* UNHCR, Geneva.

Bainvel, B. (1999). "Kosovo crisis inspires youth participation project", in *UNICEF Education Update, July 1999;* see www.unicef.org

Baxter, P. (2000). *UNHCR peace education programme.* UNHCR Regional Services Centre, Nairobi.

Baxter, P., Fisher, J., and Retamal, G. (1997). *Mine awareness education.* UNESCO-International Bureau of Education, Geneva.

Baxter, P. and Hoffmann, K. (1998). "Awareness campaigns versus education programmes: experiences developing mine awareness education for children", in G. Retamal and R. Aedo-Richmond (eds.). *Education as a humanitarian response.* Cassell, London/UNESCO International Bureau of Education, Geneva: 248–61.

Bird, L. (1999). *The Tanzanian experience.* UNICEF, Dar es Salaam; see www.ginie.org

Blomquist, U. (1995). *Community participation in a refugee emergency: focusing on community mobilisation, women and youth: a report from the Rwandan camps in the Kagera Region of Tanzania.* Swedish Save the Children, Stockholm.

Boothby, N. (1992). "Displaced children: psychological theory and practice from the field", *Journal of Refugee Studies,* 5, 106–22.

Boothby, N. (1996). "Children of war: survival as a collective act", in M. McCallin (ed.). *The psychosocial well-being of refugee children.* International Catholic Child Bureau, Geneva: 136–49.

Bracken, P., Giller, J. E. and Summerfield, D. (1997). "Rethinking mental health work with survivors of wartime violence and refugees", *Journal of Refugee Studies,* 10, 431–42.

Brown, T. (2001). "Improving quality and attainment in refugee schools: The case of the Bhutanese refugees in Nepal", in Jeff Crisp, Christopher Talbot and Daiana B. Cipollone (eds.). *Learning for a Future: Refugee Education in Developing Countries,* UNHCR, Geneva.

Burde, D. (1999). *Communities, conflicts and pre-schools: an evaluation of Save the Children's Early Childhood Education Programme in Croatia and Bosnia-Herzegovina.* Save the Children Federation, Westport, CT.

CDC (1999). *A mental health assessment in Kosovo.* Centers for Disease Control and Prevention, Atlanta, GA.

Chanda, M. (2000). *Report on emergency education for refugees in Zambia.* UNHCR, Lusaka.

CPPPC (2000). *Care and protection of children, youth and families in East Timor: project proposal.* Child Protection and Psychosocial Programs Consortium: Christian Children's Fund, Richmond, VA, International Rescue Committee, New York, Save the Children Federation, Westport, CT.

Dagnino, N. (1996). "Responding to the psychosocial needs of refugee children: a multi-faceted approach", in M. McCallin (ed.). *The psychosocial well-being of refugee children.* International Catholic Child Bureau, Geneva: 150–67.

Dampare, C. and McClure, M. (2000). *Secondary education reform: policy briefing paper for the Secondary and Youth Education Reform Consultation, February 2000.* UNESCO, Paris; see www.ginie.org

DANIDA (1996). *The international response to conflict and genocide: lessons from the Rwanda experience.* see www.um.dk/danida

Davies, L. (1999). *Education in Kosova: report to the British Council.* University of Birmingham, UK.

Daxner, M. (2000). *Education in Kosovo: from crisis to recovery and transformation.* UN Mission in Kosovo, Department of Education and Science, Pristina.

Eversmann, E. (2000). *Education kits in Somalia.* Forthcoming.

Flax, V. and James-Traore, T. A. (1998). *How to guide: reproductive health education for adolescents.* IRC, New York/UNHCR, Geneva.

Foster-Gross, D. (2000). *Bilaterals and crisis education: USAID activities.* USAID paper for the World Education Forum, Dakar.

Fountain, S. (1997). *Education for conflict resolution: a training for trainers manual.* UNICEF, New York.

Fountain, S. (1999). *Peace education in UNICEF.* UNICEF, New York; see www.unicef.org

Fozzard, S. and Tembo, L. (1996). "Promoting a caring environment for the children: a community-based model for intervention", in M. McCallin (ed.). *The psychosocial well-being of refugee children.* International Catholic Child Bureau, Geneva: 110–125.

GTZ (1999a). *Basic education for Afghan refugees: project brief.* Deutsche Gesellschaft fur Technische Zusammenarbeit/German Agency for Technical Cooperation, Peshawar, Pakistan.

GTZ (1999b). *Community participation annual report: Community-Oriented Primary Education Programme.* German Agency for Technical Cooperation, Peshawar, Pakistan.

Gueye, A. (2000). *Report of mission to Aru, Democratic Republic of Congo, 23 July – 5 August 2000.* UNHCR, Kinshasa.

Gupta, L. (2000). *Psychosocial assessment of displaced children exposed to war-related violence in Sierra Leone.* Plan International, Freetown; see www.ginie.org

Harvard School of Public Health (1998). *Harvard Program in refugee trauma: program overview.* Harvard School of Public Health, Cambridge, MA.

Herbst, L. (1995). *Children in war: community strategies for healing.* Save the Children Federation, Westport, CT/University of Zimbabwe, Harare/Duke University, Durham, NC.

HIWG (1999). *Update on the situation in Kosovo, 29 November 1999.* Humanitarian Issues Working Group, Geneva.

ICI (2000). *Crossing bridges: a guidebook to psychosocial programming for children in refugee camps.* International Children's Institute, Montreal.

ICWAC (2000). *Caught in the crossfire no more: a framework for commitment to war-affected children – Summary by the Chairs of the Experts' Meeting 13–15 Sept. 2000.* The International Conference on War-Affected Children, Winnipeg.

IFRCS (1999). *Psychosocial assistance for children affected by armed conflict.* International Federation of Red Cross and Red Crescent Societies, Geneva.

IRC (1999). *Kosovo psychosocial needs assessment mission report.* International Rescue Committee, New York.

ISCA (1996). *Promoting psychosocial well-being among children affected by armed conflict and displacement: principles and approaches.* International Save the Children Alliance, Geneva (now London).

Jenkins, S. (1997). "Education for prevention: a case study from Kyrgyzstan", in *Education for Peace, Conflict Resolution and Human Rights: papers from a design workshop.* UNHCR, Geneva: 35–44.

JRS (2000). *Resource Base for Refugee Education News, Fifth Edition.* Jesuit Refugee Service, Nairobi.

Johannessen, E. (2000). *Evaluation of TEP in Angola.* Norwegian Refugee Council, Oslo.

Lange, E. (1998). *The IRC education programme for refugees in Guinea, 1991–1998: a best practice study.* UNHCR, Geneva.

Lange, E. (1999a). *Improving the access to education for the Roma minority in Kosovo.* UNHCR, Pristina/Geneva.

Lange, E. (1999b). *Deployment Report No. 1, July 1999.* UNHCR, Pristina/Geneva.

Lange, E. (1999c). *Deployment Report No. 1, Sept. 1999.* UNHCR, Pristina/Geneva.

LaPrairie, M. (1995). *Assessment and coordination of UNHCR refugee education programmes in Eastern Zaire/Rwanda.* UNHCR, Geneva.

Lobo, M. (2000). *Report of community services mission to the camps in Western Ethiopia.* UNHCR Regional Services Centre, Nairobi.

Lowicki (2000). *Untapped potential: adolescents affected by armed conflict,* Women's Commission for Refugee Women and Children, New York.

Machel, G. (1996). *The impact of armed conflict on children.* United Nations, New York; see www.unicef.org

McCallin, M. and Jareg, E. (1996). "The rehabilitation and social reintegration of child soldiers", in M. McCallin (ed.). *The psychosocial well-being of refugee children.* International Catholic Child Bureau, Geneva: 192–217.

Midttun, E. (1998). *Brief history and main features of the TEP for Angola 1995–98, as developed and extended by the Norwegian Refugee Council, by arrangement with UNESCO-PEER.* Norwegian Refugee Council, Oslo.

Midttun, E. (1999). *Concept paper on human rights education.* Norwegian Refugee Council, Oslo.

Midttun, E. (2000a). *Education in emergencies and transition phases: still a right and more of a need.* Norwegian Refugee Council, Oslo.

Midttun, E. (2000b). *Clarification regarding components and aspects of core activities in various phases of emergency.* Norwegian Refugee Council, Oslo.

MOES (1999). *Study of the educational needs of Kosovo children settled in Albania.* Ministry of Education and Science, Tirana.

Nhleko, E. (2000). *Education programme in the refugee camps in Kigoma and Kagera regions of Tanzania: report on primary and post-primary examinations in the year 2000.* UNHCR, Dar es Salaam.

Nicolai, S. (2000). *Emergency education in East Timor: lessons learned.* International Rescue Committee, New York.

Norwegian Refugee Council, Redd Barna and UNHCR (1999). *Protection of children and adolescents in complex emergencies: conference report.* Norwegian Refugee Council, Oslo.

Nordstrand, M. (2000). *End of mission report.* UNHCR, Monrovia.

Nuttall, J. (1999). *Bosnia pre-school programme: some lessons learned about design and management.* Save the Children Federation, Westport, CT; see www.ginie.org

Parker, M. (1996). *The mental health of war-damaged populations,* Institute for Development Studies, Bulletin 27, University of Sussex.

Pigozzi, M. (1999). *Education in emergencies and for reconstruction: a developmental approach.* UNICEF, New York.

Preston, R. (1991). "The provision of education to refugees in places of temporary asylum: some implications for development", *Comparative Education,* 27, 61–81.

Retamal, G. and Aedo-Richmond, R. (1998a). "Education as a humanitarian intervention: some reflections on policy and practice", in G. Retamal and R. Aedo-Richmond (eds.). *Education as a humanitarian response.* Cassell, London/UNESCO International Bureau of Education, Geneva: 1–26.

Retamal, G. and Aedo-Richmond, R. (eds.) (1998b). *Education as a humanitarian response.* Cassell, London/UNESCO International Bureau of Education, Geneva.

Retamal, G. and Devadoss, M. (1998). "Education in a nation with chronic crisis: the case of Somalia", in G. Retamal and R. Aedo-Richmond (eds.). *Education as a humanitarian response.* Cassell, London/UNESCO International Bureau of Education, Geneva: 74–93.

Retamal, G., Devadoss, M. and Richmond, M. (1998). "UNESCO-PEER: lessons learned in East Africa", in G. Retamal and R. Aedo-Richmond (eds.). *Education as a humanitarian response.* Cassell, London/UNESCO International Bureau of Education, Geneva: 210–22.

Richardson, J. (1998). *A critical review of UNICEF's support to psychosocial and peace education projects in the countries of the former Yugoslavia.* UNICEF, Geneva.

Rille, F. (1995). *Regional emergency education mission to Tanzania, Rwanda and Zaire.* UNHCR, Geneva.

Rugh, A. (1998). *Education for Afghans: a strategy paper.* Save the Children, Islamabad/UNICEF Afghanistan Office, Islamabad.

Ruka, E. (2000). "L'éducation basique en situation d'emergence et de crise". Paper presented by Albanian Education Minister at the Global Education Forum, Dakar.

Sesnan, B. (1998). "Push and pull: education for south Sudanese in exile 1986–1996", in G. Retamal and R. Aedo-Richmond (eds.). *Education as a humanitarian response.* Cassell, London/UNESCO International Bureau of Education, Geneva: 59–73.

Sesnan, B. (n.d.). *Designing an emergency primary school kit: with particular reference to Southern Sudan.* Operation Lifeline Sudan/UNICEF, Nairobi.

Shimizu, Y. (1999). *Community Services situation report.* UNHCR, Tirana.

Sinclair, M. (1998a). "Refugee education in the mid-1990s", in G. Retamal and R. Aedo-Richmond (eds.). *Education as a humanitarian response.* Cassell, London/UNESCO International Bureau of Education, Geneva: 262–70.

Sinclair, M. (1998b). *Promoting refugee participation in schooling: a sourcebook.* UNHCR, Geneva.

Sinclair, M. (1999). *Refugee education in the 1990s and issues for the next decade.* UNHCR, Geneva.

Sinclair, M. (2001). "Education in emergencies", in Jeff Crisp, Christopher Talbot and Daiana B. Cipollone (eds.). *Learning for a Future: Refugee Education in Developing Countries,* UNHCR, Geneva.

Smawfield, D. (1998). "Refugee education in an international perspective: the education of Mozambican refugees in Malawi, 1987–1993", in G. Retamal and R. Aedo-Richmond (eds.). *Education as a humanitarian response.* Cassell, London/UNESCO International Bureau of Education, Geneva: 27–44.

Sommers, M. (1999). *Emergency education for children.* Mellon Foundation/MIT, Cambridge, MA.

Sommers, M. (2001). "Peace education and refugee youth", in Jeff Crisp, Christopher Talbot and Daiana B. Cipollone (eds.). *Learning for a Future: Refugee Education in Developing Countries,* UNHCR, Geneva.

Sphere Project (2000). *Humanitarian Charter and minimum standards in disaster response.* The Sphere Project of the Steering Committee for Humanitarian Response, Geneva.

Spicer, B. J. (2000). *Report of a mission to review teacher training programmes for Afghans.* World Bank, Islamabad.

Stolte, M. (1996). *Guidelines on a psychosocial assistance programme for refugee children.* Dutch Relief and Rehabilitation Agency, The Hague.

Stromquist, N. P. (1997). *Increasing girls' and women's participation in basic education.* UNESCO International Institute of Education Planning, Paris.

Suhrke, A., Barutciski, M., Sandison, P. and Garlock, R. (2000). *The Kosovo refugee crisis: an independent evaluation of UNHCR's emergency preparedness and response.* UNHCR, Geneva; see www.unhcr.ch

Summerfield, D. (1999). "The nature of conflict and the implications for appropriate psychosocial responses", in M. Loughry and A. Ager (eds.). *The refugee experience; psychosocial training modules.* Refugee Studies Programme, University of Oxford: I, 28–55.

Swedish Save the Children (1998). *Mine awareness for children: a discussion of good practice.* Radda Barnen/Swedish Save the Children, Stockholm.

Swedish Save the Children (1999a). *The unaccompanied minors of southern Sudan.* Radda Barnen/Swedish Save the Children, Stockholm.

Swedish Save the Children (1999b). *Mines beware! Starting to teach children safe behaviour.* Radda Barnen/Swedish Save the Children, Stockholm.

Talbot, C. and Muigai, K. (1998). "Environmental education for refugees: guidelines, implementation and lessons learned", in G. Retamal and R. Aedo-Richmond (eds.). *Education as a humanitarian response.* Cassell, London/UNESCO International Bureau of Education, Geneva: 223–47.

Tawil, S. (2000). "International humanitarian law and basic education", *International Review of the Red Cross,* 82, 581–600.

Tefferi, H. (1999). *Psychosocial needs of children in armed conflict and displacement.* Radda Barnen/Swedish Save the Children, Stockholm.

Tilson, T. (1995). *The role for education: crisis prevention, response and development: report of meeting in February 1995.* RAPID-ED Rapid Response Education Programme, Academy for Educational Development, Washington, DC.

Tolfree, D. (1996). *Restoring playfulness: different approaches to assisting children who are psychologically affected by war or displacement.* Swedish Save the Children, Stockholm.

United Nations (1999a). *Consolidated Appeal for East Timor.* United Nations, New York/Geneva.

United Nations (2000a). *Children and armed conflict: report of the Secretary-General.* United Nations, New York.

United Nations (2000b). *Concept Paper for the UN Ten-Year Programme on Girls' Education.* Consultative Committee on Programme and Operational Questions 16th Session, United Nations, New York.

UNESCO (1999). *The right to education: an emergency strategy.* UNESCO, Paris.

UNESCO-PEER (2000). *UNESCO Regional Programme of Education for Emergencies, Communication and Culture of Peace: 1999 Annual Report.* UNESCO, Nairobi.

UNESCO-PEER and UNHCR (1999). *Environmental education pupil booklets and teacher guides, grades 1 to 8, for refugees in Ethiopia.* UNESCO-PEER, Nairobi/UNHCR, Geneva.

UNHCR (1994). *Refugee children: guidelines on protection and care.* UNHCR, Geneva.

UNHCR (1995a). *Revised (1995) guidelines for educational assistance to refugees.* UNHCR, Geneva.

UNHCR (1995b). *The State of the World's Refugees: In Search of Solutions.* UNHCR, Geneva.

UNHCR (1997a). *The State of the World's Refugees: A Humanitarian Agenda.* UNHCR, Geneva.

UNHCR (1997b). *Review of UNHCR's education activities.* Inspection and Evaluation Services, UNHCR, Geneva.

UNHCR (1997c). *Evaluation of UNHCR's efforts on behalf of children and adolescents.* Inspection and Evaluation Services, UNHCR, Geneva.

UNHCR (1999a). *Handbook for emergencies,* 2nd ed. UNHCR, Geneva.

UNHCR (1999b). *Tanzania Refugee Programme: Community Services and Education Annual Report for 1999.* UNHCR, Dar es Salaam.

UNHCR (2000a). *Briefing paper on the education sector in UNHCR's programmes.* UNHCR, Geneva.

UNHCR (2000b). *Refugees and others of concern to UNHCR: 1999 statistical overview.* UNHCR, Geneva.

UNHCR (2000c). *Summary update of Machel study follow-up activities in 1998/1999.* UNHCR, Geneva.

UNHCR (2000d). *Report of the inter-regional education coordination meeting, March 2000.* UNHCR, Dar es Salaam.

UNHCR (2000e). *Peace education resource pack.* UNHCR, Nairobi/Geneva.

UNHCR (2000f). *Global Appeal 2000: Strategies and Programmes.* UNHCR, Geneva.

UNHCR and SCA (2000). *Action for the Rights of the Child: resource materials to strengthen training and capacity-building.* UNHCR, Geneva/Save the Children Alliance, London.

UNICEF (1996). *The State of the World's Children.* UNICEF, New York.

UNICEF (1999a). *International guidelines for landmine and unexploded ordnance awareness education.* UNICEF, New York.

UNICEF (1999b). *Child-friendly spaces initiative.* UNICEF, Tirana.

Vargas-Baron, E. and McClure, M. (1998). "The new heroics of generational commitment: education in nations with chronic crises", in G. Retamal and R. Aedo-Richmond (eds.). *Education as a humanitarian response.* Cassell, London/UNESCO International Bureau of Education, Geneva: 271–88.

Williams, J. (2001). "On school quality and attainment", in Jeff Crisp, Christopher Talbot and Daiana B. Cipollone (eds.). *Learning for a Future: Refugee Education in Developing Countries,* UNHCR, Geneva.

World Education Forum (2000a). *Education for all 2000 assessment: framework for action.* International Consultative Forum on Education for All, UNESCO, Paris; see www.unesco.org

World Education Forum (2000b). *Thematic study: education in situations of emergency and crisis.* International Consultative Forum on Education for All, UNESCO, Paris.

World Education Forum (2000c). *Thematic Study: Community partnerships in education: dimensions, variations and implications.* International Consultative Forum on Education for All, UNESCO, Paris.

World Education Forum (2000d). *Girls' education.* International Consultative Forum on Education for All, UNESCO, Paris.

WHO (1999). *Partners in life skills education: conclusions from an inter-agency meeting.* Department of Mental Health, World Health Organization, Geneva.

WHO and UNESCO (1994). *School health education to prevent AIDS and STD: a resource package for curriculum planners.* World Health Organization, Geneva.

Zutt, J. (1994). *Children of war: wandering alone in southern Sudan.* UNICEF, New York.

Chapter 2
On School Quality and Attainment

James H. Williams

Summary

This paper looks at the research on attempts to improve the quality of schools in poor countries, which suggests four basic lessons for refugee education. First, educational quality is understood in different ways, reflecting the values and priorities of stakeholders. It is thus essential to clarify the important meaning(s) of quality to the relevant stakeholders. Second, improvements in educational quality do not necessarily require large investments of resources. Instead, many of these elements depend on the organization and management of inputs, and the participation of critical actors such as parents, teachers and principals, and so forth.

Third, school quality can be understood in several ways, including four interacting sets of factors such as the characteristics of the child, supporting inputs, enabling conditions, and the teaching-learning process. It also includes improvements in the capacities of learners, the supportiveness of learning environments, the appropriateness of content, the effectiveness of learning processes and the achievement of outcomes. Fourth, school improvement strategies are most effective when developed on site and in collaboration with stakeholders and implementers. To improve quality, the role of central authorities is less one of providing quality than of fostering environments that support site-based improvement. Innovations are less effectively "replicated" than promoted. Acting in these ways, however, requires different modes of operation than are common in many relief and development agencies.

Introduction

Most refugee camps and settlements of any duration provide access to some form of formal primary schooling.[1] However, the quality of such programmes varies widely, with great differences in the quality of inputs provided and the attainment of children, the extent of learning that takes place. While varying contexts necessitate differing approaches to education, refugee education lacks an adequate knowledge base that would inform programme planners on promising approaches to meeting refugee children's educational needs. Programmes vary greatly in goals as well as in their success in reaching those goals. There is little sharing of experience on which to build such a knowledge base.

1 This paper focuses on quality in the context of formal education, that is, schools. This is not intended to ignore or downplay the importance of non-formal or informal education or that of secondary and higher education. Instead, the paper highlights the critical importance of effective basic education programs.

At the same time, outside refugee education, efforts are underway in many contexts to improve quality and increase attainment. These efforts have led to identification of a number of factors, many under the control of school systems that can be changed to foster greater achievement. Given the priorities UNHCR places on both school quality and attainment (UNHCR, 1999), this research aims to provide policy makers and programme planners with the beginnings of such a knowledge base. This initial section outlines what is known about school quality and attainment in poor countries.

Multiple meanings of educational quality

Though often used in discourses about education, quality is a complex term, with multiple meanings reflecting the values and interpretations of different stakeholders.

Educational quality has received a great deal of attention in recent years, as educators and other stakeholders have recognized the need for improved quality in the wake of the tremendous growth of educational enrolments throughout the world in the 1950s-70s. Almost universally, there is agreement that quality needs to be improved: Government plans, international agency documents, officials regularly call attention to the need for improved quality, in poor and wealthy countries alike. Yet there appears to be little shared definition of what improved quality might concretely mean.

The research literature has identified seven common usages of quality: quality as reputation, quality as resources and inputs, quality as process, quality as content, quality as outputs and outcomes, quality as 'value-added' (Adams, 1997: 2-5), and quality as selectivity.

- ***Quality as reputation*** refers to a general consensus, rarely quantified, of high and low quality, most commonly used in reference to particular institutions of higher education that are "known" for their quality, or sometimes their lack thereof. In this sense, quality as reputation is less useful in refugee education.[2]

- ***Quality as inputs and resources*** is an extremely common usage of quality. In this sense high quality is seen in high levels of provision of resources such as buildings and other facilities, textbooks and instructional materials. Quality as inputs may also refer to the characteristics of pupils, or those of teachers and administrators, to their number or their levels of education and training. While resources are generally recognized as a necessary but insufficient condition for desirable outputs such as student achievement, the tangible, visible, and quantifiable nature of inputs makes this meaning of quality a common proxy for other, less easily measured aspects of education such as process and outcomes. Unfortunately, educational research has failed to identify in any very convincing and conclusive formulation the inputs most essential to desirable outcomes of education. Nor are the causal relationships between inputs, processes, and outcomes definitely specified or well understood. Subsequent discussion here provides an overview of the current state of understanding.

2 Though not commonly used in this way, *reputation among parents and community members* is an important dimension of quality in refugee education, where the attitudes of parents and community members toward schools plays an important role in determining the participation of children.

Education for women returnees in Myanmar. Ngar Khu Ya, Maungdaw District. UNHCR/01.1997/A. Hollmann

- ***Quality as process*** highlights the need to understand *the use of educational inputs*. Perception of this need is relatively new among policy-makers, who have traditionally focused on the inputs and, when possible, the outputs and outcomes of education systems. However, research has found that schools with similar levels of resources often produce quite different results. Infusions of resources often fail to lead to corresponding improvements in outcomes. As a result, attention turned to the processes within schools. Understandably, teachers and professional educators tend to focus on educational processes. Indeed, to those working in education, successful process may be sufficient: A teacher may feel his or her efforts are well-rewarded if students, for example, become more motivated to learn, regardless of the extent of learning that takes place. Unfortunately, much of the literature on educational processes is theoretical, prescriptive and descriptive in nature, with very little evidence of relative effectiveness. Thus, the empirical linkages between educational processes and educational outputs/outcomes are poorly defined. Nonetheless, a general consensus of the elements and processes of good schools can be described, and is summarized in the discussion below. Even so, the lack of knowledge and the complex and inherently subjective nature of good educational process have made conceptualization and measurement difficult.

- ***Quality as content*** refers to the knowledge, attitudes, and skills *intended* to be transmitted through the school curriculum. Quality as content "reflects the particular bias of a country, community, or institution to some body of knowledge, skills, or information" (Adams, 1997: 6) in such a way that some content is understood as being of higher quality than other.

- ***Quality as outputs or outcomes*** involves the consequences of education. "Outputs" refer to the short-term consequences of schooling, e.g., students' cognitive achievement, completion rates, certification, individual skills, attitudes, and behaviours, while "outcomes" refer to longer-term, often socially significant, consequences of education, e.g., employment, earnings, health, civic engagement, and the like, as well as social attitudes, behaviors, and skills. The importance of understanding quality in terms of the consequences of education is better understood than the ways of doing so. The difficulty of measuring outputs/outcomes validly and reliably on a large scale has meant that virtually no education systems know empirically whether their schools are achieving their goals and objectives.

- ***Quality as valued-added*** refers to the extent to which the school/system has improved, often in terms of students, sometimes larger groups or institutions. While related to processes, outputs and outcomes, a value-added focus considers the degree of change rather than the final state or the way in which the change came about.

- ***Quality as selectivity***, a final usage of quality not mentioned by Adams, refers to quality as a form of exclusiveness. In this view, the more exclusive, selective, or competitive a school or school system, i.e., the fewer who get or stay in, the higher the quality.

This discussion, summarized in Table 1, highlights the multiple meanings of quality, from which follow several propositions important to a discussion of quality and attainment in refugee education. Because of the several meanings of quality in use, agreement on the need to improve or address quality does not necessarily mean agreement on what improved quality might mean. Similarly, because of the multiple meanings, there is not a single way to improve quality; specification of strategies to improve quality depends on the particular meaning of quality. As a result, quality improvements from one perspective may not mean quality improvements to those holding a different view of quality. Moreover, an important step in improving quality is the negotiation of the meaning and priorities of quality, a process that necessarily involves the often conflicting goals, objectives and interests of important stakeholders.

Different meanings of quality do not necessarily correspond. While a minimum of inputs is certainly necessary for effective education, a high level of inputs – one definition of quality – does not necessarily mean higher quality measured in terms of outcomes or outputs, both of which require the *effective use* of inputs. Thus, increasing material resources alone may do little to improve quality. Financial cost may not be the primary constraint. Indeed, many quality improvements are not costly in financial terms. At the same time, improvements in quality may involve rather organizational or management costs that are not easily captured in budgetary terms.

A final point, elaborated in subsequent discussion, is that unless quality is judged solely in terms of inputs or resources, the quality improvement process is likely to be a complex and murky one, involving poorly-understood variables and relationships. Policy-makers typically work at the level of policy and resource provision. To the extent that quality requires more than the (relatively) simple provision of additional resources, educational leaders must shift their focus to the school and classroom. Research suggests that system-wide improvements in quality can rarely if ever be dictated from outside or above. Instead, strategies must be developed for engaging teachers, and often communities/parents, in the processes of improving quality. Little is known conclusively about these processes. However, a number of instructive models have been developed for improving the quality of schools in poor countries; several of them will be outlined here.

Table 1: Meanings of School Quality

MEANING OF "QUALITY"	MEASUREMENT & CONCEPTUALIZATION
Reputation	• Measured informally, socially • Difficult to quantify, despite general agreement
Inputs	• Measures include: number of teachers; education levels of teachers; class size; number and class of school buildings; background characteristics of students; numbers of textbooks, instructional materials; extent of laboratories, libraries and other facilities • Easy to conceptualize and quantify
Process	• Measures include: interactions of students and teachers; teaching and learning processes; 'Quality of life' of the program, school, or system • Difficult to conceptualize and quantify
Content	• Measures include: skills, attitudes, behaviors, and values to be transmitted through the intended curriculum • Easy to conceptualize and quantify formally espoused values; difficult to identify implicit values
Outputs	• Measures typically include: cognitive achievement; completion ratios; entrance ratios to next/higher level of education; acquisition of desired skills, attitudes, behaviors, values • Easy to conceptualize, more difficult to measure
Outcomes	• Typical measures include: income; employment; health; civic engagement; social cohesion; social levels of desirable attitudes, values, skills and behaviors • Some concepts easy to conceptualize, while others are more difficult, all are difficult to measure
Value-Added	• Measures extent of improvement • Relatively easy to conceptualize, depending on specifics, change is difficult to measure and requires baseline
Selectivity	• Measures include: percentages of children excluded, or failed • Easy to conceptualize, easy to measure

Source: Adams, 1997

UNICEF highlights a similar set of issues in a recent paper on educational quality in which it defines quality in terms of five dimensions:

- "Learners who are healthy, well-nourished, and ready to participate and learn, and supported in learning by families and communities;
- Environments that are safe, protective, and gender-sensitive, and provide adequate resources and facilities;
- Content that is reflected in relevant curricula and materials for the acquisition of basic skills, especially in the areas of literacy, numeracy, and skills for life, knowledge in such areas as gender, health, nutrition, HIV/AIDS prevention, and peace;
- Processes through which trained teachers use child-centred teaching approaches in well-managed classrooms and schools and skillful assessment to facilitate learning and reduce disparities;
- Outcomes that encompass knowledge, skills, and attitudes, and are linked to national goals for education and positive participation in society" (UNICEF, 2000: 1).

This five-fold formulation of learners, environments, content, processes, and outcomes well captures current thinking on the essential components of educational quality.

Factors associated with achievement

Researchers have focused on cognitive achievement, on the rationale that whatever else schools are intended to do, a basic function is to induce students to learn the content of the curriculum. Thus, a substantial body of research in high and low-income countries has examined factors associated with student's cognitive achievement.[3] This research fits well with this research's concern with attainment. While different schools of thought and methodologies have grown out of this research, a useful synthetic framework for understanding this research in the context of low income countries has been developed by Ward Heneveld, Helen Craig, and associates at The World Bank, a representation of which is shown in Figure 1. This model proposes four groups of factors affecting school quality, as measured by student outcomes:

- Individual (child) characteristics
- Supporting inputs
- Enabling conditions
- Teaching and learning processes

Individual (child) characteristics are what individual students bring with them to school. Though not under the school's control, they affect the child's work at school. School factors may interact with individual characteristics in a positive way to compensate for deficiencies the student brings to school or to enhance the child's capacities, or more negatively to further disadvantage the disadvantaged.

3 The research bases dealing with school effectiveness and school quality are quite large. One study of school quality and girls' education, for example, examined over 300 articles, reports, and books. This literature represents a broad range of research methodologies and strategies for understanding school quality and as well as strategies for bringing it about. A number of the primary references are listed in the bibliography.

Supporting inputs are those community or system-level factors determined outside the school yet which affect the work of the school. They include community support, policies, and material inputs.

Enabling conditions are characteristics of the school that facilitate effective teaching and learning. Enabling conditions include effective management and organization, including leadership, the teaching force, organization of instruction, curriculum, and time spent in school; as well as the climate of the school, the extent to which the school has created an atmosphere that fosters and values academic achievement.

Teaching and learning processes include classroom level factors that directly affect student learning, including learning time, teaching strategies, and student assessment.

This section attempts to summarize this body research on school quality and school effectiveness, drawing heavily on the work of Craig, but incorporating others' research as well. The research has led to greater understanding of the characteristics of effective schools. The resultant list of characteristics is better understood descriptively than prescriptively. The characteristics of effective schools might usefully serve as an information collection tool, to understand schools along a number of important dimensions rather than to prescribe what a good school should be.

Figure 1: Conceptual Framework: A Model of School Quality

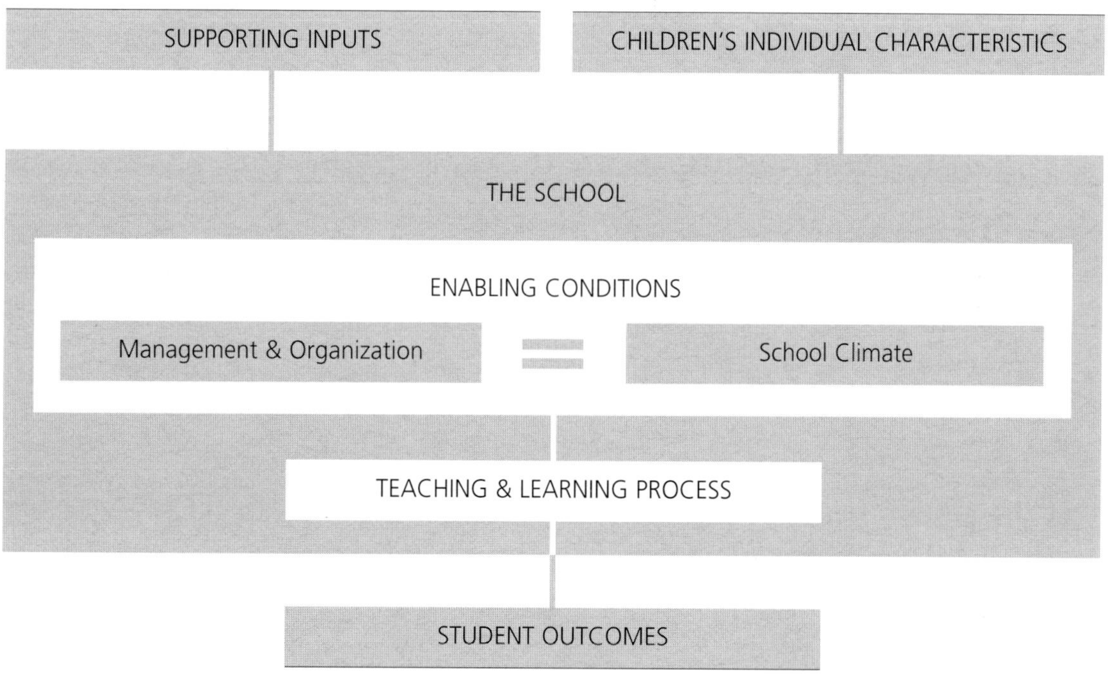

Children's individual characteristics

Perhaps obvious is the claim that children come to school with personal characteristics and individual histories that affect their persistence and attainment. In the general population, these characteristics include the child's health and nutritional status, gender, age, parents' or caregivers' attitudes, and experience with school, including early childhood development or pre-school programmes. In the case of refugee children, relevant factors are also likely to include any trauma the child has experienced as well as the nature and relative well-being or health of her or his "family." See Table 2.

Together, these characteristics affect the child's readiness to learn, which interacts, in turn, with school quality. A child with a high degree of readiness is better able to take advantage of high-quality learning resources, or to compensate for their lack. A child with low readiness is less able to capitalize on learning opportunities, and more vulnerable to deficient learning environments. However obvious these factors are, schools often do little to adapt their programmes to fit the characteristics of the child, especially children on the margin.

Refugee girls from Mali. M'Berra Camp School, Mauritania. UNHCR/11.1996/G. Matoso

Table 2: Individual Characteristics and Children's Individual Characteristics

FACTORS FROM RESEARCH	IMPLICATIONS FOR SCHOOL QUALITY & ATTAINMENT
Health and nutritional status – Research has documented a number of ways in which children's health and nutritional status affects their ability to attend school, concentrate, and learn. Children's attendance and persistence are related to their nutrition and health.	A number of health and nutritional problems can be remedied through low-cost community and school-based interventions, with consequent improvements in attendance, enrolment, persistence, learning, and overall attainment.
Gender – Virtually everywhere, girls are less likely to enroll and persist in school; often less likely to do well academically, especially in some fields such as science and mathematics; and less likely to pursue highly-skilled professional academic tracks.	Many aspects of school quality differ for girls and for boys. Almost all aspects of school quality have gender implications (Modi, Williams, and Winter, 1998).
Age – Under-age children may not be socially or developmentally ready for school. Over-age children may experience social difficulties unless accommodations are made. Family/community expectations for school children may change with adolescence. Similarly, children's attitudes toward school may shift with adolescence, as social and family expectations change, and income-generation and household responsibilities increase.	Techniques can be introduced through training, teachers' guides, pamphlets, etc. for working with under, or over-age children, or heterogeneous, multi-grade classes. Schools can vary school schedules to accommodate children's other responsibilities. Curriculum can include subjects of greater relevance.
Parental attitudes – Parent/caregiver expectations, positive or negative, toward school and the child's capacity, have a great impact on the child's enrolment, persistence, and attainment. The more positive the parent's attitudes toward education, the school, and the child's capacity, the more the child is likely to be able to take advantage of learning opportunities.	Steps can be taken to foster parental and community involvement in schools if needed. Awareness campaigns can be developed to work toward greater parental support.
Prior schooling, including early childhood/pre-school programmes – Prior educational experience will shape the child's response to schooling. High quality early childhood education is associated with greater academic success. The more positive the child's experience with school, the greater the child's readiness. Less academic educational activities such as organized recreation and extra-curricular activities are also likely to enhance the educational program.	Programmes may need to be adapted for work with children lacking prior education or positive educational experiences. Educational programmes need not be limited to academic work. In the refugee context, recreation and other activities may be essential.
Trauma – Children who have experienced trauma likely need services and support in addition to the standard academic offerings.	Additional programmes may need to be developed to provide support to children suffering from trauma or with weak family support.
Nature and "health" of family – Children with separated or traumatized families may also need additional support and services to supplement academic programs at school.	

Source: Craig, 1995

Supporting inputs

Supporting inputs refers to community or system-level factors that, while not under the control of the school, provide the school with essential support and, in a sense, the raw materials of education. Parents and communities provide the children, of course, and often, in emergency contexts, the schools as well (Sommers, 1999). In addition, parental and community attitudes and expectations promote or impede the work of the school (Modi, Williams & Winter, 1998: 24). Parents and communities may also provide the school with material inputs in cash or in kind and perhaps expertise in particular areas. The education system supports schools when it enacts appropriate educational policies, provides appropriate instructional and technical support, and supplies schools with sufficient and appropriate material inputs. Table 3 summarizes these inputs.

Child readiness and school inputs. To the extent that children's readiness for school is low, as described earlier, schools may need to compensate the standard offerings. Malnourished or hungry children, for example, need shorter lessons with more physical activities because of their shorter attention spans (Levinger, 1996: 45). Schools, in turn, may need assistance from the larger system to successfully adapt their programmes to meet the needs of such children.

Policy questions. In addition, a series of policy issues not highlighted by the school quality and effectiveness research but relevant to refugee contexts includes decisions about:

- **Language of instruction** – Whose language(s) should be used for instruction and for what grades?
- **Curriculum** – What curriculum should be used (that of the host country, that of the country of origin, or another curriculum)?
- **Purpose of education vis a vis refugee status** – Is education intended to integrate children into the economic and social life of the host country, or to prepare children for life in the country of origin?
- **Teacher qualifications** – What credentials should be required of teachers?
- **Credentials/articulation with existing system** – What credentials should graduates of different levels of refugee education receive, and how can these credentials be articulated with recognized credentials outside the refugee education system?
- **Second chances** – Do the school and system provide appropriate opportunities for children (and adults) to pursue schooling if they have missed out on opportunities at an earlier point?

Table 3: Supporting Inputs for School Effectiveness and Quality

CONCLUSIONS FROM RESEARCH	NAME OF INDICATOR
Parent and community support is effective when:	
• Children arrive at school healthy, ready to learn	• Health and learning readiness
• Parents and community provide schools with financial, in-kind, and/or psychic support, as able	• Community support for school
• School staff and parents communicate regularly	• School-parent communication
• Parents and community members assist with instruction, as they are able	• Parental assistance in instruction
• The community has a meaningful role in school governance	• Community role in school governance
Schools are effectively supported by the school system when:	
• The system communicates expectations clearly; expectations include high academic performance	• Clear academic expectations
• Schools are delegated with the authority and responsibility to improve themselves	• Delegated responsibility and authority
• The system provides schools with the technical and instructional support needed to achieve their objectives. Assistance is not limited to administrative matters and enforcement of rules	• Instructional support
• The system monitors and evaluates schools' academic performance, school improvement efforts	• Monitoring and evaluation
• The system helps schools adapt their programmes according to the needs/readiness of their children	• Adapting schools to children's readiness
The system provides schools with adequate material support when:	
• Schools have sufficient numbers of relevant textbooks and other reading material in an appropriate language for children to use	• Textbooks
• Teachers have guides for each subject that outline content and methods of instruction along with diagnostic and evaluatory material	• Teachers' guides
• Students have sufficient paper and writing implements to practice what is taught	• Paper and writing implements
• The school has enough classrooms to hold all students in reasonably sized classes	• Classrooms
• Classrooms have blackboards and chalk, desks for all children, and appropriate visual aids	• Classroom equipment
• Textbooks, instructional materials, and classrooms are appropriate to the readiness of children to learn	• Appropriateness of instructional inputs

Source: Craig, 1995

Enabling conditions

Research into successful schools found that the effects of inputs on teaching and learning are mediated by the leadership of the school head, the management and organization of the school and the school climate. When favorable, these "enabling conditions" provide a context in which inputs lead to effective teaching and learning. When unfavorable, these conditions reduce the effectiveness of teaching and learning.

Particularly important is the role of the school head in providing strong leadership and good school management. A good principal serves as a role model and guide, providing instructional leadership, setting a climate of high expectations, and mobilizing resources for the whole school (Lockheed & Verspoor, 1991: 43-44). In terms of quality, research has found the *instructional* leadership role especially critical.

Research has identified eight enabling conditions for high quality schools, discussed in more detail in Table 4:

- Effective school leadership
- Capable teaching force
- Autonomy in school decision-making
- Order and discipline
- Positive teacher attitudes
- An organized curriculum
- Incentives for academic success
- Maximized learning time in school

U.S. nun teaching Spanish to Guatemalan refugees. Keste Camp, Campeche, Mexico. UNHCR/06.1990/H.J. Davies

Table 4: Enabling Conditions for School Effectiveness and Quality

CONCLUSIONS FROM RESEARCH	NAME OF INDICATOR
School leadership is effective when the school head:	
• Works to ensure adequate resources are available to support teachers, provide learning materials, maintain an adequate learning facility	• Adequate resources
• Sets high academic standards for teachers and students	• High instructional standards
• Is visible and accessible; communicates regularly, effectively with parents, community, teachers	• Accessibility & communication
Teachers are capable when they:	
• Have mastered the material they teach	• Knowledge
• Can use the language of instruction	• Language of instruction
• Have several years of teaching experience	• Teaching experience
• Have worked together for several years	• Stability
Effective schools have enabling autonomy when they can:	
• Determine how school time and resources can best be used to improve academic performance	• Autonomy regarding time and resource use
• Seek resources from constituencies as needed	• Autonomy in external resources
Schools are effectively ordered and disciplined when they are:	
• Perceived as safe by students, teachers, parents	• Safety
• Well-organized (student and teacher attendance is high; classes begin on time, routines are smooth and efficient, noise levels are appropriate, etc.)	• Order
• Disciplined (student discipline is appropriate, fair)	• Discipline
Teachers have positive attitudes that enable high performance when they:	
• Have confidence in their teaching abilities	• Confidence
• Are committed to teaching and to students	• Commitment
• Cooperate with each other and school	• Cooperation
Curricula are effectively well-organized when:	
• Basic skills are emphasized (rather than ideal but unrealistic breadth of curriculum)	• Emphasis on basic skills
• Learning objectives are sequenced, integrated across grade levels, and matched to teaching strategies, available materials, and students' developmentally-appropriate needs	• Instructional design
• Organized in a way that permits teachers to adapt materials to students' needs and to produce local teaching materials and aids	• Locally adaptable
Effective schools reward academic performance (symbolically, ceremonially, publicly)	• Academic recognition
Schools are effective to the extent students spend time in school (days of year, hours in day)	• High time in school

Source: Craig, 1995

Teaching and learning processes

With teaching and learning at the core of education, quality improvements involve changes in the classroom interactions between teachers and pupils. Unlike supply of inputs and policy change, both of which can largely be managed from a central office, changes to the teaching and learning process require that teachers act differently, in ways that are poorly understood and difficult to bring about on a large scale, even in resource-rich countries such as the United States (Elmore, 1996: 2-3). See Table 5.

Refugee and returnee children and their teacher in a 'classroom'. Madhu, Sri Lanka. UNHCR/07.1999/M. Kobayashi

Nonetheless, some researchers feel that changing teaching practices may be the most promising quality intervention in poor countries. Research consistently finds that whole-class, teacher-centered instruction, lectures (frontal instruction), and rote memorization of abstract material are less effective in terms in fostering student learning than more participatory and varied teaching strategies. Effective teaching requires that students participate actively, and be allowed to practice and apply their lessons to their own experience (Tatto, 1999: 7-8). Teachers need to be able to modify their presentations based on student feedback, and use alternate instructional methods such as individual or small group instruction, cooperative learning, or group problem solving. Teachers need to be able to recognize students' differential learning needs and to match their instructional techniques accordingly.

Most studies agree that time on task or time teaching is an important condition for learning (Fuller, 1986: 86). In many schools, a great deal of classroom time is spent on discipline, waiting between activities, idle time or administrative matters. Another characteristic of high quality schools is the assigning and correcting of homework.

The appropriate use of assessment is an essential element of effective teaching and learning. It is useful to distinguish four types of assessment (Capper, 1996: 13-14): Regular classroom assessment provides the way to see whether students are acquiring and teachers teaching the desired curriculum. This kind of continuous feedback is essential to teachers and their supervisors working to improve instructional quality. Commonly, however, classroom assessment is used simply to grade students and not to improve instruction. Class examinations represent a second type of classroom-based assessment. Typically given at the end of a school term, class examinations assess the extent to which students have learned certain material. Such examinations tend to be used to grade students rather than to inform or change teaching practice. In many cases, the remaining two types of assessment are combined – standardized examinations given to students at different points in the school career, and selection examinations used to select students for higher levels of education. Selection examinations, because they hold the key to higher levels of education, are particularly likely to "drive" the curriculum and determine de facto teaching practice in the classroom.

A final characteristic of effective teaching and learning is the inclusiveness of teacher interactions with students. Research has documented systematic gender bias, for example in a number of countries, low and high income (Modi, Winter, & Williams, 1998). In some contexts, ethnic or linguistic groups may be systematically ignored or devalued in the classroom.

Table 5: Teaching and Learning Processes for School Effectiveness and Quality

CONCLUSIONS FROM RESEARCH	NAME OF INDICATOR
Teaching and learning is effective to the extent that:	
• Teachers use varied teaching techniques	• Varied instructional techniques
• Students are actively engaged in learning activities	• Student engagement
• Instructional time is maximized	• High learning time
• Homework is assigned frequently, and prompt feedback provided	• Homework
Student assessment is effective to the extent it:	
• Is regular and integrated into classroom, school, system	• Regular assessment
• Has as its primary purpose provision of diagnostic feedback to students, teachers, school leaders	• Diagnostic assessment
• Is fed back to students continuously	• Continuous feedback

Source: Craig, 1995

Student outputs

In addition to the preceding measures of inputs and process, school quality is demonstrated by high levels of participation and achievement. See Table 6.

Table 6: Participation and Achievement

CONCLUSIONS FROM RESEARCH	NAME OF INDICATOR
Effective schools have high participation when:	
• Attendance is high throughout the year for all groups of students	• Attendance
• The numbers of repeaters and dropouts are low	• Promotion
• The numbers of students continuing education is high	• Transition rate
• High proportions of children complete schooling	• Completion
High quality schools have high achievement in:	
• Reading and writing	• Literacy
• Mathematics	• Numeracy
• Core subjects	• Subject matter knowledge
• Other valued skills (e.g., problem-solving skills)	• For example, score on problem-solving test

Source: Craig, 1995

Quality in the context of refugee education

Though the primary purpose of this paper is to provide an overview of components and approaches to school quality, it is useful to highlight at least four ways in which school quality can be expected to vary in contexts of refugee education:

- In refugee contexts, learning readiness is likely to have been compromised by the traumas of refugee life. Similarly, families and communities may be less able to provide support to their children. Psycho-social interventions are likely necessary for students to be able to take part in academic activities.
- Teachers are also affected by the chaos and turmoil of refugee life, and may need psycho-social work in addition to more conventional pedagogical training.
- The provision of protected and safe learning environments is likely to assume greater importance in refugee contexts.
- Lacking the structures, resources, and social-economic networks of permanent communities, refugee children are likely to be in greater need of recreational opportunities as well as explicit instruction in skills that fall outside the narrower mandates of formal schooling. Such skills include income generation, peace education and conflict resolution, HIV/AIDS prevention, and the like.

Toward an approach to improving school quality

A description of the characteristics of high quality schools, of course, is not the same thing as a strategy for how to move from low to higher quality. Unfortunately, quality improvement strategies are much less well documented than the features of high quality schools, especially in poor country contexts, where resources are more tightly constrained and governance more centralized than in the U.S. or U.K., from which much of the literature from industrialized nations derives.

This review has suggested that the "quality" of inputs, while a common way of understanding school quality, is less useful than considering the *use* of inputs as seen in terms of desirable outputs and outcomes. The review has highlighted the multiple ways in which school quality is understood, hence the need for decisions about the type of quality to be enhanced. Finally, I have asserted, on the basis of considerable research that space does not permit me to discuss here, that quality improvements – because they reach into the classroom and involve changes in teacher practice – are more difficult to manage externally than changes that can be dictated from above.

It would be possible to derive a list of essential elements of quality. Such lists have been developed by researchers on school quality. Craig, for example, lists the following as likely to have the "greatest bearing on the quality of schooling" in the Pacific:

> ... the availability of books and other learning materials; Initial instruction in the mother tongue; capability of the teaching force; the autonomy, flexibility and accountability of educational management; instructional time available and use of that time; and the curriculum (the development of general education rather than vocational programs. (Craig, 1995: 5)

Outdoor classes for returnee children. Tajikabad, Shaartuz District, Tajikistan. UNHCR/05.1995/A. Hollmann

She cautions that quality improvements must be considered as a package because the factors are not independent of each other. Thus, for example, teacher training is unlikely to improve quality if appropriate textbooks and equipment are not available.

Lockheed and Vespoor, based on extensive review of project documents and empirical research, place the dimensions of school quality into the five categories of "promising avenues" and "blind alleys." See Table 7.

Table 7: Lockheed & Verspoor's View of Strategies to Improve Student Achievement

PROMISING AVENUES	BLIND ALLEYS
Curriculum: • Improving the implemented curriculum	• Adjusting the intended curriculum
Learning Materials: • Good textbooks and teacher guides	• Computers in the classroom
Teaching Quality: • In-service training • Interactive radio instruction (with pupils) • Programmed materials	• Lengthening pre-service pedagogical training
Teaching Time: • Setting and maintaining standards for instructional time: 25 hours of instruction per week for core subjects	• Lowering class size
Teachability: • Preschools (targeted at disadvantaged) • Nutritional interventions – school snacks/ breakfasts, micronutrients, treat parasites • Vision and auditory screening	• School lunches

Source: Lockheed and Verspoor, 1991

However useful such lists are heuristically, we take Sommers' cautionary notes seriously in thinking of such lists as prescriptions. Sommers cautions against the dangers of external agencies going in to refugee settlements with pre-existing solutions to refugees' educational needs (1999: 26).

Consistent with these recommendations, we suggest a collaborative, inquiry-guided approach to the improvement of school quality and attainment, building on what has gone on before the intervention. The following steps provide a rough overview of one possible approach:

Step 1. Understand first what's going on educationally in a particular settlement; assess what is wanted by the various stakeholders, especially the parents, children, community members, and teachers as well as NGO and UN advisors perceptions of educational needs and values.

Step 2. Develop a collaborative process for assessing the current and desired states of quality, and for designing plans to achieve the desired state. The process should include:

- Explicit, legitimate ways for all stakeholders to participate meaningfully, especially those who will be affected and those who will implement change;
- Facilitated methods to bring to the surface and come to agreement about the goals of education in the setting, the shared meanings of quality, and evocative descriptions of "high-quality" schools (descriptions that inspire action);

- Structured ways to collect, analyze and share – widely – information about the current status of educational efforts in the community, and the status of school quality and attainment. The approach should seek to include discussion of the relevance to the setting of findings and ideas from external research on school quality;
- Facilitated process for developing a school quality improvement plan, for understanding tradeoffs, developing buy-in, making commitments and decisions and developing plans to monitor implementation and make necessary mid-course corrections.

Step 3. Come to agreement about the goals of the system and objectives of the "reform," the meanings of quality and attainment to be utilized, and a rich description of the current system and the characteristics of a higher-quality system.

Step 4. Develop qualitative and/or quantitative measures of educational quality.

Step 5. Working with implementers, school staff, managers, and parents/community members, create a meaningful, i.e., achievable, list of minimum quality standards for the school, along with responsibilities and timetables for achieving those standards, and indicators of successful implementation. Such a list would likely include standards covering teachers, place, textbooks, teachers' guides, blackboards, paper and writing implements.

Step 6. Develop longer-range strategies for acquiring other necessary inputs, improving school governance, increasing external instructional support, developing school leadership, and promoting the ongoing professional development of teachers.

Examples of school improvement strategies

Two examples of comprehensive strategies to improve school quality may help to illustrate some of these points:

Fundamental Quality Level Indicators in Benin. Begun in the late 1980s and early 1990s in Benin, the Fundamental Quality Level Indicator (FQL) strategy attempted to engage community members, school teachers and directors, district and national Ministry of Education officials, and external funders in a process of defining minimum standards of quality which all schools were expected to achieve. Under the extremely tight resource constraints facing the country, it was felt that school quality improvement would not be feasible if high levels of "quality" inputs were required for all. Instead, the strategy focused on establishing minimum standards realistically achievable by all schools and felt necessary for effective teaching and learning to take place (Horn, 1992). The standards were discussed widely through an extensive series of meetings. Critically important, standards considered processes and outcomes as well as inputs. The existence of standards provided a way for Ministry officials to target schools needing inputs most urgently. The elaboration of standards of process provided ways for schools to improve quality independently of Ministry provision. The existence of standards provided parents and community members with concrete expectations for which schools could be held accountable. The negotiation and definition process provided a mechanism for stakeholders at all levels of the system to discuss educational issues related to quality.

Minimum standards were adapted to local needs and conditions, with certain national bottom line conditions set. Example criteria include:

- Pedagogic-Related Inputs
  There should be between 30 to 45 students per classroom and per teacher. At least one complete set of "approved" language and mathematics textbooks is available for the use of every three students (distributed to the pupils).
- Quality-Related Process
  Reports prepared by school inspectors or circuit officials indicate that classroom teachers report to school daily, and that head teachers or their deputies visit and observe in every classroom at least once per day. District reports indicate that a district or higher-level inspector observes in the school at least twice a year.
- Quality-Related Outcomes
  Over 75% of primary 1 entrants complete primary 6. At least 80% of primary 6 students attain specific performance standards in the areas of literacy and numeracy as measured by a criterion-referenced assessment.

  Source: Horn, 1992

Improving Educational Quality Project. Funded by USAID beginning in 1991, the Improving Educational Quality (IEQ) Project has evolved a strategy for working with school systems to improve educational quality in Ghana, Mali, Guatemala, Uganda, and South Africa. The strategy uses: "real information about what children are (or are not) learning; engages school staff and community members in reflection on how the school and home environments and day-to-day teaching affect children's learning; and uses this information and reflection to informal sectoral policy". (Hartwell, DeStefano, and Schubert, 1998: 2)

The process has three components, beginning with *assessment*. Measures of achievement, observations, and interviews provide data on individuals' and group experiences in schools. Meetings, dialogue, seminars, and conferences are used to *assimilate* the findings from the assessment phase. Data are presented to generate discussions about the quality of the education systems in terms of teacher training, for example, or policy, or textbook preparation, distribution, and use. Third is *action*, where decisions are taken on the basis of information and discussion to improve the system: policies are changed, for example, so that teachers are not held accountable for damage to textbooks (thus making teachers less likely to distribute textbooks to pupils); a community learning center is established to help pupils with school work, and so forth. Evolution of this strategy is guided by three fundamental principles:

1. "Meaningful discussion and action to improve the quality of education must include concrete information about pupils in the classroom, including instructional practice, pupil performance, and the classroom environment. All attempts to reform any aspect of education ultimately must reach the classroom. What happens there must be known and shared with diverse audiences.

2. "The priorities of the nation must guide the process of improving teaching and learning within a country. Findings and information gathered in one environment may not apply to others. Learning occurs in context, and it is the contextual knowledge about a nation's schools that opens the door to understanding how the system can be improved.

3. "Partners are united in the common purpose of improving the quality of education. The traditional technical assistance mode is replaced by a new spirit of collaboration whereby people learn from and teach one another. Host country researchers take the lead in their respective countries. Collaboration crosses hierarchical lines". (Hartwell, DeStefano, and Schubert, 1998: 5). In the context of refugee education, "nation" and "country" might be replaced with "community."

Next steps: assessing school quality – with stakeholders and implementers, on site

As an initial step in understanding issues of school quality in particular contexts, a series of questions could be developed from the material presented in this overview. To be most useful, such questions would best be generated collaboratively by researchers and beneficiaries on site.

To illustrate, questions could be generated from each of the sections above, as for example, the following questions from the "Children's individual characteristics" section:

- Are children suffering from health and nutritional problems? Can these problems be alleviated? Short-term hunger? Eyesight and hearing screening? Immunizations? Micro-nutrient deficiencies – Vitamin A, D, Iron, Iodine? Helminth infections? Protein-energy malnutrition?
- Do girls and boys enroll and persist at the same rates throughout school? At what grade level and age are the differences significant?
- Are there significant numbers of under- or over-age children in school? Are classes relatively homogenous in terms of age? Are adolescents enrolled at the same rates as younger children? Do the rates differ between boys and girls? How? What are the reasons different actors give for differences in participation for children at different ages and of different sexes?
- Who is not in school? How many out-of-school individuals are of school age? Beyond school age? Male and female?
- What kind of education do parents and community members want for their children? In general and for particular groups of children? How do parents and community members feel about the education their children are offered?
- Do a significant number of children suffer from trauma? What is the nature and degree of trauma? How intact are children's families? How "healthy" are those families?
- Have there been any adaptations to the organization of school, the curriculum, or teacher training in order to accommodate the special needs of refugee children?
- Has there been an assessment of the needs of refugee children?

Assessment tools such as these, developed collaboratively between educators in the community and educators with international experience, can be used to begin the process of quality improvement.

Conclusion

Research on attempts to improve the quality of schools in developing countries suggests four basic lessons for refugee education:

1. Educational quality is understood in different ways, reflecting the values and priorities of stakeholders. As a result, it is essential to clarify the important meaning(s) of quality to the relevant stakeholders in a particular context. Improvement strategies will vary, depending upon whether stakeholders are interested in improving quality as reputation, as inputs and resources, as process, as content, or as outputs/outcomes.

2. Improvements in educational quality do not necessarily require large investments of resources. A number of the elements of educational quality identified in the preceding discussion do not rely primarily on large outlays of resources. Instead, many of these elements depend on the organization and management of inputs, and the participation of critical actors such as parents, teachers and principals, and so forth. Thus, the primary constraint to quality improvement is not necessarily cost. However, quality improvements are likely to require more organizational capital than simple provision of inputs, and are more difficult to control from centralized authority or from afar.

3. School quality can be understood in several ways. One formulation involves four interacting sets of factors—the characteristics of the child, supporting inputs, enabling conditions, and the teaching-learning process. A school improvement strategy that ignores one or more of these factors risks missing an essential component of the whole. Another formulation sees quality in terms of five factors—the capacities of learners, the supportiveness of learning environments, the appropriateness of content, the effectiveness of learning processes, and the achievement of outcomes. Again, quality improvements must attend to all five dimensions.

4. School improvement strategies are most effective when developed on site and in collaboration with stakeholders and implementers. External assistance may be needed to provide a broader perspective on school quality as well as needed resources. Stakeholder-implementer buy-in and participation, however, are essential for the effort to be grounded in local realities and needs, especially when dealing with non-resource based aspects of quality. Careful attention to collaboration in the process by which problems are identified and solutions planned is essential for quality improvements to be sustained and to develop local capacity for ongoing implementation. To improve quality, the role of central authorities is less one of providing quality than of fostering environments that support site-based improvement. Innovations are less effectively "replicated" than promoted. Acting in these ways, however, requires different modes of operation than are common in many relief and development agencies.

References

Adams, Donald (1997). "Defining Educational Quality," *Educational Planning* 9(3): 3-18.

Bethke, Lynne (n.d.). *Topic 22—Education and Training, Conference Working Draft, for the Emergency Settlement Conference. Interworks:* Madison, Wisconsin.

Capper, Joanne (1996). *Testing to Learn ... Learning to Test.* Project ABEL, Academy for Educational Development: Washington, D.C.

Craig, Helen (1995). "School Effectiveness and School Improvement in the Pacific: Policy and Planning: Focus on the School." Paper presented at the annual meeting of the Comparative and International Education Society, Boston.

Elmore, Richard (1996). "Getting to Scale with Good Educational Practice," *Harvard Educational Review,* 66(1): pp. 1-27.

Floro, M. and Joyce Wolf (1990). *The Economic and Social Impacts of Girls' Primary Education in Developing Countries.* Creative Associates International, Inc.: Washington, D.C.

Fuller, Bruce (1986). *Raising School Quality in Developing Countries: What investments boost learning? World Bank Discussion Papers No. 2.* The World Bank: Washington, D.C.

Fuller, B. and P. Clarke (1994). "Raising School Effects While Ignoring Culture? Local Conditions and the Influence of Classroom Tools, Rules, and Pedagogy," *Review of Educational Research,* 64(1): 119-157.

Ginsburg, Mark & Jane Schubert (2000). "Choices in Improving Educational Quality in Developing Countries: A Conceptual Framework," (unpublished draft manuscript). Improving Educational Quality Project, Center for International Research, American Institutes of Research: Washington, D.C.

Hartwell, Alfred & Emily Vargas-Baron (1998). "Learning for All: Policy Dialogue for Achieving Educational Quality." Paper prepared for the International Working Group on Education, Munich, June 23-26, 1998.

Hartwell, Alfred, Joseph DeStefano & Jane Schubert (1998). "Learning and Educational Quality," (unpublished manuscript). Improving Educational Quality Project, Center for International Research, American Institutes of Research: Washington, D.C.

Heneveld, Edward and Helen Craig (1995). *Schools Count: World Bank Project Designs and the Quality of Education in Sub-Saharan Africa.* The World Bank: Washington, D.C.

Horn, Robin (1992). "The Fundamental Quality Level Indicator System for Primary School," (draft memorandum). USAID: Washington, D.C.

Levinger, Beryl (1996). *Nutrition, Health and Education for All.* United Nations Development Programme: New York.

Lockheed, Marlaine & Adriaan Verspoor (1991). *Improving Primary Education in Developing Countries: A review of policy options.* Oxford University Press: London.

Modi, Manisha, James H. Williams, and Carolyn Winter (1998). *School Quality and Girls: What We Know, What We Don't Know, and What to Do Next?* (unpublished manuscript prepared for The World Bank). Washington, D.C.

Odaga, Adhiambo (1995). *Girls and Schools in Sub-Saharan Africa: From Analysis to Action.* The World Bank: Washington, D.C.

Purkey, Stewart C. & Marshall S. Smith (1983). "Effective Schools: A Review," *The Elementary School Journal,* 83(4):427-452.

Ross, Kenneth N. & Lars Mahlck (1990). *Planning the Quality of Education: The Collection and Use of Data for Informed Decision-making.* International Institute of Educational Planning, UNESCO: Paris.

Sommers, Marc (1999). *Emergency Education for Children.* Women's Commission for Refugee Women and Children: New York.

Tatto, Maria Teresa (1999). "Conceptualizing and Studying Teacher Education across World Regions: An Overview," (Background paper prepared for the Conference on Teachers in Latin America: New Perspectives on their Development and Performance, San Jose, Costa Rica, June 28-30, 1999). World Bank: Washington D.C.

Tietjen, Karen, et. al. (1991). *Educating Girls: Strategies to Increase Access, Persistence, and Achievement.* USAID Office of Education, Office of Women in Development: Washington, D.C.

UNHCR (2000). *Briefing Paper on the Education Sector – Present Activities and Future Plans.* Geneva.

UNHCR (1999). *Refugee Education in the 1990s and Issues for the Next Decade* (unpublished). Geneva.

UNICEF (2000). "Defining Quality," (Paper presented at the International Working Group on Education meeting, Florence, Italy, June).

Windham, Douglas (1987). *Indicators of Educational Effectiveness and Efficiency.* Improving the Efficiency of Educational Systems Project: Tallahassee, Florida.

Chapter 3
Improving Quality and Attainment in Refugee Schools: The Case of the Bhutanese Refugees in Nepal

Timothy Brown

Summary[1]

In the context of UNHCR's current funding crisis and the generally low standards of refugee education world-wide, a substantive case study of the Bhutanese refugee education programme in Nepal is presented. The Bhutanese example was chosen because of its comparatively high-quality education. Using the lessons learned from the Bhutanese case study and elsewhere, do-able solutions for improving the quality of education and the attainment of refugee students are sought which could be applicable to refugee situations in other parts of the developing world.

A conceptual framework is set up in which the various components of quality are examined – actors, tools, environment and outcomes. The actors are further divided into a pyramidal framework with the refugee community at the base, the pupils and teachers in the middle and the programme managers at the apex. Environment is isolated as a separate category because of the unique situation which refugees suffer. It is necessary to look at the broad picture – classroom, school, camp, programme, context – because recommendations are needed for the programme managers so that they can help to improve the quality of education for refugee children in the classroom and raise the educational attainments of refugees.

It is found that the strengths of the Bhutanese programme, such as positive attitudes, the importance given to the teacher and good organization, are often under the control of the various local actors involved, whereas the weaknesses, such as the refugee situation itself, decreasing funding and the lack of further education opportunities, are more likely to be beyond their control. This points a way to improving quality realistically – the local actors should focus on strengths rather than weaknesses and maximize the use of available resources.

It is suggested that actors in other refugee localities learn from the Bhutanese case study by building on such strengths as motivation and cooperation, teacher training and support, and cost-effective approaches. To achieve this end, recommendations for refugee education managers are proposed.

1 The author is indebted to all those friends and colleagues who have contributed to his experience and knowledge of refugee education during the eight years he has been working with UNHCR. Special thanks go to Brother Mike Foley, Myriam Houtart, Susanne Kindler-Adam, Helmut Langschwert, Sister Maureen Lohrey, Sister Lolin Menendez, Sarah Norton-Staal, Barry Sesnan, Robin Shawyer, Margaret Sinclair, Chris Talbot and Hans Thoolen. He is grateful to the Bhutanese Refugee Education Programme and Field Director Fr P. S. Amalraj for their assistance and cooperation during his field trip in Nepal, without which he could not have produced this paper. Most especially, he is grateful to all the refugees he has worked with, in both Uganda and Nepal, for their inspiring example.

In particular, it is suggested that UNHCR field offices should foster cooperation and motivation among all actors involved – ensuring that appropriate training is given to managers and teachers, monitoring the programme efficiently and providing opportunities for refugees to advance themselves through further education and participation in camp activities.

At headquarters level, it is suggested that UNHCR should encourage the development of effective reporting procedures, develop guidelines and training tools, and seek the collaboration of other partners who have expertise in education and resources of their own. Further research should be promoted on more specific issues of quality, especially at the classroom level, to find practical ways of dealing with the reality of enormous refugee schools and large classes in situations of stress and limited funding.

Refugee children from Bhutan. Sanischare Camp, Nepal. UNHCR/12.1997/H.J. Davies

Prologue

The generally low standards in refugee education

This work was planned as part of a series of papers on refugee education. Sinclair (2001) has considered emergency education with special focus on early emergencies, which characterize the situation at the beginning of a refugee crisis. Naumowicz Gustafson (2000) has considered education for repatriation, which represents the situation at the end of a refugee crisis.

The present paper considers education in those indefinite situations in between, which can go on for many years and where "formal" schools are set up in the refugee camps or settlements. These schools are normally run by the refugees themselves on limited budgets, with the help of outside organizations often funded by UNHCR. Such chronic refugee situations can easily be forgotten by donors. The present study is restricted to developing countries (where governments can barely afford education for their own citizens, let alone for refugees). The quality of education given to refugees in these circumstances is often very deficient, with resulting poor standards achieved.

> The results for the 1998 Burundian National Examination were received during the reporting period. Out of 1,233 students [from Tanzanian camps] only 46 pupils (3.7 per cent) passed with marks above 50 per cent. The general performance of the primary schools was very poor due to lack of textbooks and qualified teachers. Other problems reported were poor conditions of the schools, the environment and funding. (UNHCR, 1999)

> Over the years, refugee enrolment and retention [in Balochistan, Pakistan] has taken on a pyramidal shape whereby only a few students (mainly boys) are to be found in the higher grades. Both quality and quantity are on diminishing scales, as most camp schools are unattractive to trained teachers, and conditions for economic survival of students are diminished. (UNHCR, 2000a)

Indeed, a review of refugee education activities by the UNHCR Inspection and Evaluation Service has concluded: "Many refugee schools encounter problems maintaining an acceptable level of performance." (UNHCR, 1997: 15)

The lack of adequate funding

In the last few years, UNHCR has been undergoing a financial crisis. Lack of adequate funding is a major reason for poor quality in refugee education. It can even lead to schools closing down.

A UNHCR official working in the Democratic Republic of Congo commented in December 2000:

> Assistance provided to education is very much lower than the minimum standards recommended by UNHCR, due to limited funding. From the funding available, we hardly succeed to supply the programme with teaching and learning materials, uniforms and furniture. Nobody will believe that refugee children in Aru have never seen a globe of the earth.

Refugees International reported the impact of funding cuts on education for Liberian refugees in 2000:

> Assistance for 100–120,000 Liberians remaining in Guinea will end in July when the schools close and organized repatriation ends. Unless the international community provides the funds to integrate Liberians into the Guinean school system, more than 10,000 Liberian children and adolescents will be without any educational prospects after next month (Refugees International, 2000).

Even in areas where the refugee education programmes have been fairly well resourced in the past, such as in Nepal and Uganda, they are beginning to feel the pinch.

A senior UNHCR official wrote concerning Nepal in May 2000:

> On the issue of education, we were informed by UNHCR Sub-Office in Jhapa that CARITAS-Germany had stopped funding secondary education since the beginning of the year and that UNHCR was facing difficulties in financing it. This was presented to the High Commissioner as one of their programming concerns. Needless to say, the ongoing prioritization exercise has also an impact on the programme.

The Jesuit Refugee Service described similar problems for education in Uganda in November 2000:

> It seems that the funding crisis that has affected and is actually affecting UNHCR and its partners is getting worse … It seems that in the most optimistic way there will not be enough money to pay the teachers for the months of November and December.[2] This is very bad since the examinations of the primary pupils are at the end of this month and a possible teacher strike could create big problems for the exercise.

A poor prognosis

The situation is not expected to get any better in 2001 because all UNHCR programmes have been told to cut their budgets by 20 per cent. UNHCR and NGO staff all over the world are reporting that many activities have been cut from their 2001 education budgets. This typically includes co-curricular activities, environmental education programmes, sports activities and special campaigns to boost girls' education, as well as the reduction in teaching staff.

For example, in Kenya, the UNHCR Community Services Officer has indicated the following negative consequences of the budget cuts: low-quality education due to lack of classroom supplies; non-completion of construction of classrooms; lack of teacher training; inadequate desks due to lack of resources; lack of sporting materials; laying-off of teachers (UNHCR, 2000b).

The problem of low funding has lately been compounded by UNHCR's new system of "unified budgets", which makes it difficult for a UNHCR country programme to absorb special earmarked funds. In each country of operation, the UNHCR Representative is supposed to stick to the ceiling of the overall budget, which is agreed with UNHCR Headquarters on a yearly basis. When the US government (through UNHCR's Refugee Children Unit) recently offered US$1.8 million to bail out the Uganda education programme, UNHCR Uganda was unable to accommodate it. Acceptance would have meant that they would have had to reduce spending in other vital sectors (such as health and sanitation) to compensate.

2 A UNHCR officer in Uganda later informed the author (January 2001) that the salary problem for the primary school teachers had been sorted out, although severe problems remained for refugee secondary education.

In response to the grave funding situation, the Sudanese refugee teachers in North Uganda wrote a memorandum (13 November 2000) to UNHCR. They asked the following questions. "Does UNHCR expect quality education if the staff reduction, scholastic materials and co-curricular activities are reduced from the budget? Is the teacher the least important person in the list of UNHCR supported staff? Without quality education, what does UNHCR think shall be the side effects on the refugee communities and the host country?"

Learning from the good practice of the Bhutanese refugees

This paper is not, however, about lack of funding, which is only one cause of poor-quality education. Rather, it is about the way in which the Bhutanese programme in Nepal has succeeded in producing comparatively high-quality education for its refugees in spite of the ever-present financial constraints. It is hoped that the lessons learned from this good practice will help other refugee operations throughout the world to produce good-quality education programmes in situations of tight funding.

Why the Bhutanese? When Sadako Ogata, the then High Commissioner for Refugees, visited a Bhutanese refugee camp in early 2000, she was "very impressed and even thought that it was one of the best refugee camps in the world". Susanne Kindler-Adam, UNHCR Education Officer, also went on mission to Nepal in 2000. She was "impressed by the quality and commitment of the Bhutanese refugees and CARITAS-Nepal to make the Bhutanese Refugee Education Programme a unique success story ... I would guess that, in fact, BREP is our best education programme world-wide" (Kindler-Adam, personal communication).

The author of this present report spent two weeks in eastern Nepal (in Sept-Oct 2000), visiting the Bhutanese schools. Formerly, he was in Uganda for about eight years as UNHCR Education Adviser. This work is a case study of the Bhutanese Refugee Education Programme in Nepal, enriched by reference to the experience of Uganda for further insights into the identification of sound management practice of refugee education programmes.

Introduction

Birth of a refugee school

The following is an account of how the Sudanese refugee schools in Moyo district, north Uganda, were formed in the early 1990s. It is fairly typical of the formation of refugee schools elsewhere.[3]

The refugee situation starts with a mass movement of people across a border due to gross violations of human rights, massive insecurity or war in their home country. When the refugees have reached safety in a new country, their first priority is to find shelter and enough food and water to survive. After these basic needs have been attended to and the initial shock of displacement has subsided, the refugees begin to turn their minds to the future. Education for their children then becomes a top priority.[4]

3 For other examples with details on the initial development of refugee schools, see: Smawfield (1998: 32–33) for Mozambican refugees in Malawi; Lange (1998: 8–9) for Liberian refugees in Guinea; McDonogh (1996: 8–9) for Bhutanese refugees in Nepal.

4 In a teachers' memorandum to the Head of UNHCR Sub-Office Pakele dated 13 November 2000, the Sudanese refugees recommended that "UNHCR should consider education as a top priority and put more funds on it". Note also that Sudanese are not alone in their strong desire for education: "Education has been a clear priority for both Sierra Leonean and Liberian refugees in exile" (UNHCR/IRC, 2000: 1); "Education is high on the list of priorities for the [Burundian, Rwandan and Congolese] refugee community" (UNHCR, 2000c).

An outdoor classroom for refugee women from Bhutan. Beldangi Camp, Nepal. UNHCR/12.1992/A. Hollmann

Refugee leaders organize the children into age-groups and find suitable volunteers from the community to look after them. These volunteers are often young people themselves, who have not completed their own education. Suitable "classrooms" are identified, frequently outside under the shade of a big tree, and the volunteers start teaching the children. This is the beginning of a refugee school.[5]

5 Sesnan (1990) describes a refugee school as a "series of shadows circulating around trees. The density of the children sitting on the ground is at its greatest when the shadow is at its smallest".

As the refugee situation continues, the community starts to develop these rudimentary schools, often with the help of the surrounding host community and outside organizations such as UNHCR and NGOs. Refugees clear sites, gather building materials and offer free labour in the construction of temporary or semi-permanent classroom blocks. Teachers try to "beg, borrow or steal" basic textbooks and stationery for their lessons, while the leaders might raise funds from the community to buy essential materials and pay minimal incentives to the teachers. Teacher and parent committees manage the schools and evaluate their achievements.

Strengths and weaknesses

The above account reveals major characteristics, good and bad, of a refugee school. It also hints at possible differences between schools inside and outside camps in developing countries. It is often found that the major strengths of a refugee school are the motivation, commitment and social organization of the entire refugee community. These strengths are frequently lacking in local schools outside the camps, which are often in the poorest and bleakest areas of an under-developed country.[6]

For their own self-esteem, refugees need to show to the rest of the world that they are not completely hopeless. They may have lost most things in life but knowledge and skills once acquired can never be taken away. Education is therefore a priceless commodity for refugees to cling on to. Indeed, it holds the future of their very existence – for the individual and the community as a whole.[7]

Many refugee parents are prepared to sacrifice their time, labour and even money to set up schools for their children. Refugee teachers are often willing to give their services for little or no pay. Refugee pupils can work extra hard under difficult circumstances because they thirst for education and realise that it is their only hope. They can even perform better than nationals in nearby local schools, as in Uganda and Nepal. Motivation is therefore a major driving force which should be harnessed, whenever possible, to improve the quality of education in refugee schools.

On the other hand, a great weakness in refugee camps can be the lack of trained, qualified and experienced teachers.[8] Volunteer "teachers" recruited at the beginning of a refugee emergency are "unleashed" on the children even though they are often under-educated, untrained and inexperienced. Their only qualifications are motivation and commitment.

A major job of UNHCR and NGO partners is to help refugees improve the quality of volunteer teachers by filling in gaps in their education and providing them with appropriate in-service training. This contrasts with the official situation in many developing and developed countries, where teachers should normally be qualified, trained and registered before they can start teaching.

---

6 National teachers in Nepal are "generally poorly motivated – a consequence of low salaries, limited career development and poor supervision and monitoring" (UN, 1999: 45). On the subject of poorly motivated local teachers, a Jesuit Refugee Service education manager noted in November 2000: "I would mention how unsatisfactory the education programme in Ndungu [northern Democratic Republic of Congo] turned out, mostly as a result of using local teachers for the education programme for Sudanese refugees. It seemed to be impossible to motivate these teachers to take a serious interest in the programme. "

7 "Our only hope is if our children can go to school. The children are our future" (Refugees International, 2000).

8 Even when qualified teachers are available, some of them can be attracted away from education by the relatively high salaries offered by NGOs for camp management in other sectors.

In this study, we will be considering how quality can be improved in a refugee school. The camp schools in eastern Nepal will provide a case study from which we hope to draw general conclusions applicable to other refugee situations throughout the world. Much research has already been done on the quality of education in developing countries (see, for example: UNICEF, 2000; Williams, 2001). However, little is officially known about educational quality and attainment in refugee camps. As Appadu and Retamal (1998: 57) have stated, "there is definitely a need for more research and case studies to be done in the area of refugee education".

External constraints

Clearly, quality ought to be improved if we increase the inputs and resources.[9] More books and desks, additional classrooms and facilities, lower pupil–teacher ratios and higher teachers' salaries should all contribute to a higher standard of education. But UNHCR does not have unlimited resources at its disposal. In these days of economic constraint, UNHCR is struggling to find enough funds to cover its routine care and maintenance activities and the day-to-day necessities of refugee populations. In many country programmes, refugee education is severely under-funded, especially when refugees have other, life-sustaining, needs to be met.

In 1997 there was a comprehensive evaluation of refugee education (by the UNHCR Inspection and Evaluation Service), and various minimum standards were recommended as an outcome of the appraisal (UNHCR, 1997: Annex V). This was followed up in a global UNHCR workshop in Dar es Salaam, Tanzania, in which the recommendations were endorsed by Community Services and Education officers. There was an assumption that UNHCR would succeed in raising funds to cover the implementation of the recommendations in all refugee programmes throughout the world. Since that time, UNHCR has experienced a continual succession of donor cuts, a trend which shows no signs of reversal up to this day. These minimum standards therefore exist only on paper, and resourcing of refugee education programmes in some countries falls far below the recommendations (see the first section of this paper).

Besides, UNHCR should not be giving privileged treatment to refugees, in total disregard of their surrounding circumstances. A fundamental principle of UNHCR is that it should aim for parity when comparing standards of assistance to refugees with standards in their country of origin or country of asylum. Anything else would be unfair and likely to cause friction and resentment in the short and long terms. Disparities in educational standards can even give rise to a "pull factor".[10]

Getting real

The example of the Bhutanese refugees in Nepal shows how comparatively high-quality education can be achieved at a relatively low cost to UNHCR. The cost-effectiveness is due to many reasons – not least, the participation of the refugees themselves, who are offered very low financial incentives. The teachers and headteachers are all refugees, as are most of the managers running the education programme.

9 Williams (2001) states, however: "While a minimum of inputs is certainly necessary for effective education, a high level of inputs … does not necessarily mean higher quality measured in terms of outcomes or outputs, both of which require the effective use of inputs".

10 In November 2000, Brother Mike Foley of JRS commented: "There is little doubt that educational opportunities are what attract many Sudanese to seek refuge in Uganda. Yet no one seems to be willing to officially admit this, probably because seeking education is not a legitimate reason for seeking/granting refugee status".

It is hoped that the lessons learned from Nepal will help other refugee education programmes to improve in quality. In this study, we will not be so concerned with questions like "what are the minimum requirements?" or "how much more money do we need?" We will be more interested in questions like "what resources are actually available? or "how do we maximise the use of these existing resources?"

The refugee situation is not an ideal circumstance. We cannot expect refugee schools to be the best in the world. We hope they are only temporary. But however low the baseline is, improvements should always be sought and made. In many situations, quality can be increased substantially with only a small material input, such as the provision of one textbook to a teacher when there are no other books, as an extreme example.[11]

Contents of this paper

In the next section, the methodology of the field work in Nepal is described in some detail and a conceptual framework is set up. The activities undertaken are specified together with the constraints found. The rationale behind the chosen framework will be explained. How the framework evolved during the course of the research will also be discussed.

This is followed by a substantive case study of the education programme for the Bhutanese refugees in eastern Nepal. The study is divided into sections according to the adopted conceptual framework. The topics highlighted are on refugee background, resources and facilities, the early history of the programme, the present management structure, the refugee schools, the school curriculum and curriculum development, training of teachers and managers, teaching methods and assessment, monitoring and evaluation, and outcomes.

Next, the findings of the research are discussed and analysed. First the quality of the education programme is considered from the refugees' perspective. Then the strengths and weaknesses of the Bhutanese refugee education programme are identified and discussed in the light of the conceptual framework, which gives some indications as to how the quality of other education programmes might be improved.

The study ends with a discussion of the priorities which managers of refugee education programmes world-wide might consider for improving the quality of their refugee schools. The paper concludes with specific recommendations for UNHCR Field Offices and UNHCR Headquarters.

11 Williams (2001) states that "improvements in quality need not necessarily be costly in financial terms".

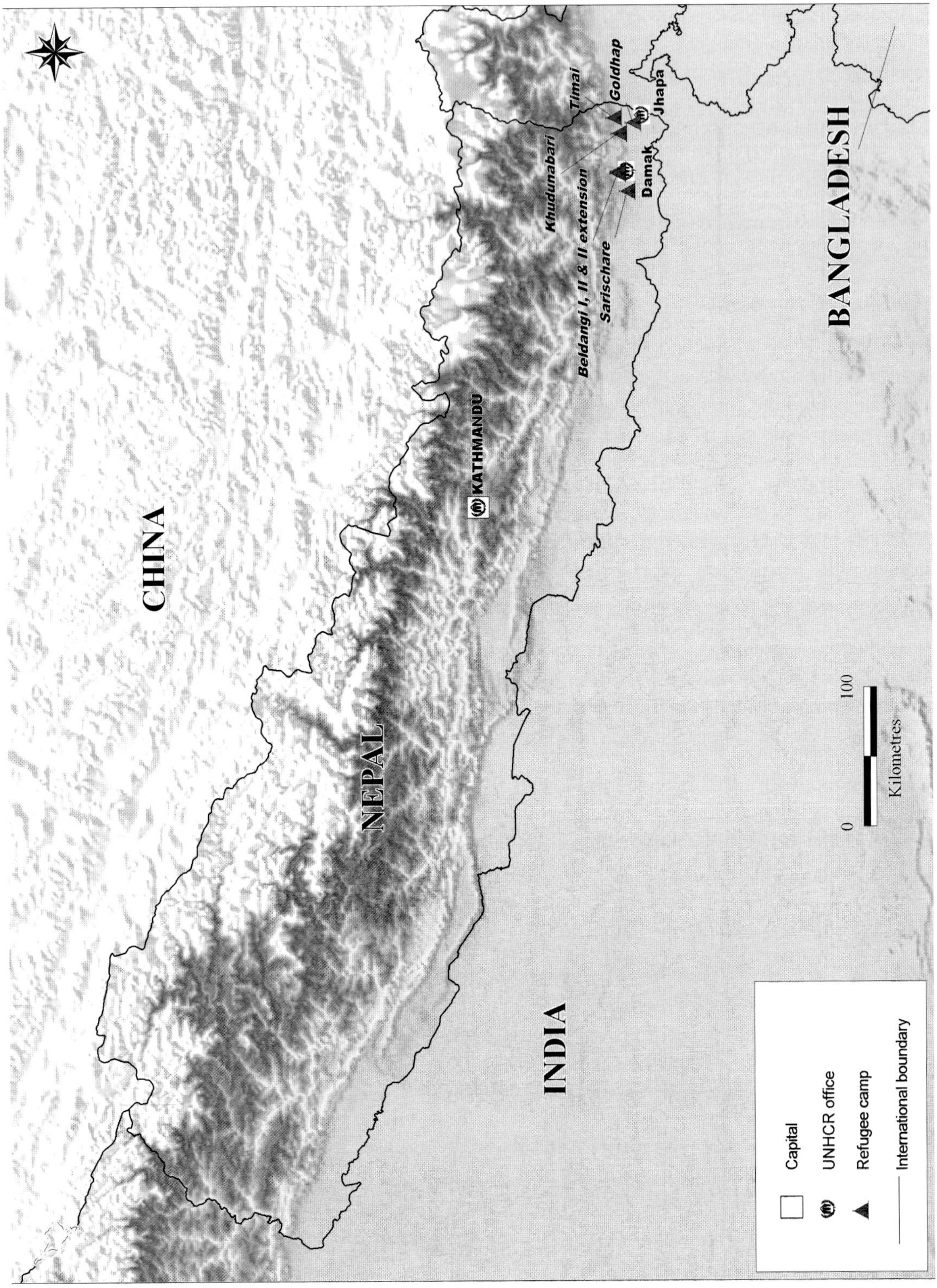

PGDS/GIMU - October 2001

Research methodology

Conceptual framework

The possible factors affecting quality of education and attainment in developing countries have been discussed in the literature. UNICEF (2000), for example, defines quality around the five dimensions of learners, environments, content, processes and outcomes. Heneveld and Craig (1995) propose a model of four groups of factors affecting school quality, as measured by student outcomes: child characteristics, supporting inputs, enabling conditions, teaching and learning process.

For analysis in a refugee context, the author has found it convenient and logical to group the factors in the following four categories: *actors, tools, environment and outcomes* (see Figure 1).

The rationale for the choice of this grouping is explained as follows. The **actors** are:

- Refugee community
- Refugee learners
- Refugee teachers
- Refugee school managers
- Programme managers (implementing NGOs and UNHCR)

The actors can be regarded as "change agents" who can make improvements in the quality of refugee education.

The **tools** are the "instruments" which the actors can use to bring about the desired changes in education quality. Commonly used tools can be summarized as:

- Curriculum and curriculum development
- Training of teachers and managers
- Teaching methods and assessment
- Monitoring and evaluation

The author defines **environment** here as the following:

- Refugee context (refugee history, future prospects)
- Camp background
- Available funding from international community
- Resources and facilities
- Host community (attitudes, government regulations and policy)[12]

Refugees suffer a unique situation and therefore "environment" has been isolated as a separate category. An enabling environment provides the surroundings and circumstances in which positive changes in quality can take place.

Finally, the **outcomes** are attainments. They give an indication of the degree of quality achieved. Important examples of outcomes are:

- Examination results
- Literacy and numeracy levels
- Further education, employment and self-reliance
- Skills, attitudes and behaviour in the camps
- Enrolment and persistence at school, including gender balance

12 When refugees are being integrated into the host population, as in Uganda, it would be more relevant to categorize the host community as an "actor". However, in most refugee situations the camps are separated from the local population, in which case the host community is probably better categorized as "environment".

Figure 1: Conceptual Framework for Refugee School Quality

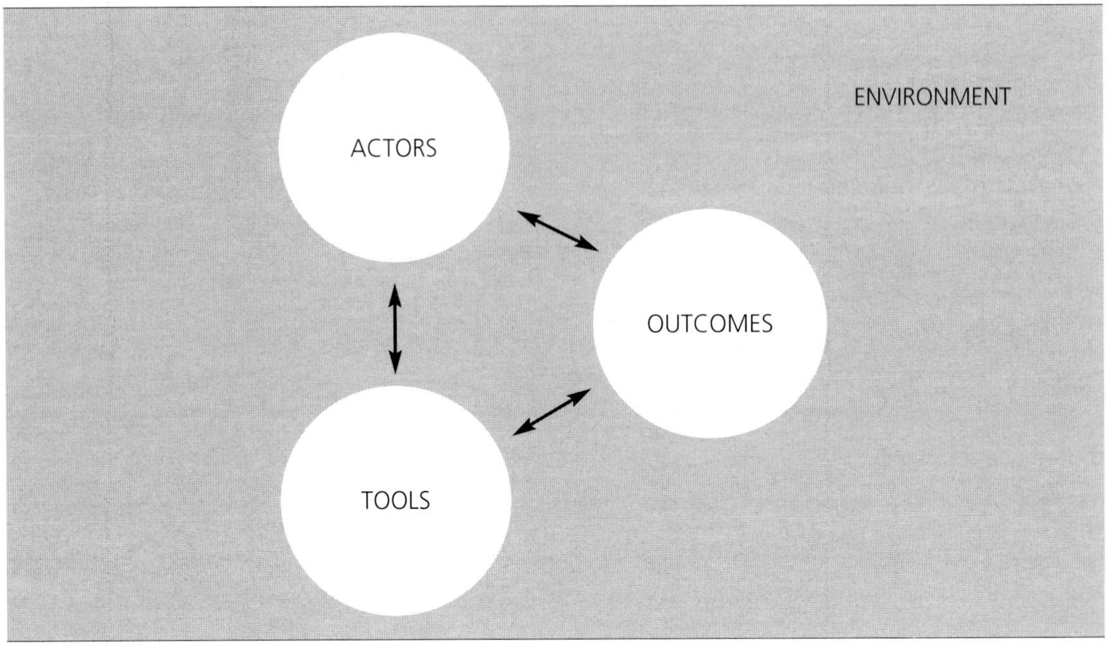

Interviews[13]

One objective of the research was to find out from the different actors their opinions on quality, since *they* are the beneficiaries and the ones responsible for making any changes. To guide the research, a set of preliminary questions for each type of actor was formulated. The author did not wish to pre-empt the answers with any of his own pre-conceived ideas. It was therefore important that the questions should not be "loaded" or closed, but should be open-ended as much as possible so that the interviewees could be given a free rein to their thoughts. The interviews were only semi-structured, so that the prepared questions were not rigidly adhered to. Some typical questions asked by the author for each of the actor groups are indicated below.

Refugee community – Why do you send your children to school? Are you happy with the school? How do parents contribute to their children's education? Do you learn from your children? How does the community use the school for its activities?

Learners – Do you enjoy school? Why do you go to school? How do you find the standards? What are your problems? How can the school be improved? What do the boys do at school? What do the girls do? What do you do at home?

Teachers – What makes a good teacher? Why is school important? How much training and experience have you had? How do you assess your lessons? What are your problems? What problems do pupils have? What are the solutions?

13 The appendix gives a list summarizing the categories of people interviewed and places visited by the author during the field work in Nepal.

At the camp's secondary school, refugee children from Bhutan are taught both Buthanese and Nepalese. Sanischare Camp, Morgang District, Nepal. UNHCR/12.1997/H.J. Davies

School managers – What do you understand by quality? What is the purpose of education? How is your school managed? What school records do you keep? How do you deal with disabled children? What problems does your school have?

Programme managers – What are the main strengths of your programme? How do you measure quality? How do you achieve cost-effectiveness? What improvements have you made? What are the gender issues and how do you deal with them?

Interviews in the field were carried out in English except for those with the parents, the Focal Person for Women and the Women's Group. In these cases, interviews were conducted in Nepalese, or a mixture of Nepalese and English, with the help of an interpreter. English was the medium of instruction in the schools and it was therefore widely spoken. When the need arose, it was never difficult to find an interpreter willing to assist.

Interviews were sometimes held individually, especially with the key informants, and at other times in groups. The groups could be formal or informal, depending on the circumstances. Sometimes, for example, the headteacher would arrange a formal meeting so that the author could meet all the staff together. But most of the time the author would talk with a small group of teachers informally.

Observations, documents and meetings

In the camps, when the author visited the schools, his investigations included the headteacher's office, the staffroom, stores, the resource room, the library, the laboratory, classrooms, the school compound and latrines. He also looked round the camp to see the facilities and general environment. He entered a few refugee huts and visited one teacher's home for lunch.

The author tried to observe as many lessons as possible, sometimes two half-lessons in one period, usually in the presence of a resource teacher and/or an in-school resource teacher (defined in next section). During the lessons, the author would sit at the back of the class as inconspicuously as possible. He looked for indicators of quality such as evidence of lesson planning, use of teaching and learning aids, learner activity and assessment. After the lessons, he observed how the in-school resource teachers guided the teachers and how the resource teachers advised the in-school resource teachers.

Various school records were examined, such as registers, admission lists, school statistics, examination results, reports, inventories and school files. Documents were also collected from both UNHCR and CARITAS on such topics as camp school guidelines, job descriptions, monthly situation reports, sub-project monitoring reports, case studies, the country operation plan and briefing notes on the country programme.

At the CARITAS office in Damak, the author attended some of the regular staff meetings, such as for the office administrative staff, the education planners (coordinators and resource teachers) and the headteachers. These occasions provided a captive audience, and as such were sometimes also used by the author to hold his own mini-workshops in which he discussed his research progress and findings and asked for feedback.

Time was a major constraint.[14] If time had allowed, the author would have met staff of partner agencies operating in the camps to find out how their various activities affected the education programme. With more time, the author would also have been able to meet members of the surrounding Nepalese community and visit their schools, especially since many of the refugees were studying or teaching at these schools. These additional activities would have helped to build up a broader picture.

Another constraint was the effect of the author's presence on the outcomes. On visiting a school, the author was often treated like a distinguished visitor and this detracted from his objective of "merging into the scenery" and seeing the real situation.

Looking at the broad picture

A large refugee education programme, such as that in Nepal, has many levels of organization and activities which are structured somewhat like a pyramid (see Figure 2), from UNHCR at the apex down to the refugee community at the base. Each level has its own actors who play a role in the delivery of quality education.

14 For various reasons beyond the control of the author, such as prior commitments of key field personnel and the occurrence of public holidays, the field research was limited to only 13 days.

At the apex, UNHCR is often responsible for raising funds from the donors and distributing them to implementing agencies. It plans, coordinates and monitors the performance of these agencies. The implementing agency for education in Nepal is CARITAS-Nepal, which is rather like a miniature Ministry of Education, because it is involved in many of the same operations as a ministry, using the funds provided by UNHCR. It procures books for the schools, pays teachers their salaries (incentives), oversees examinations, organizes training for the teachers and monitors standards.

Further down the pyramid there are many schools, each of which is managed by a headteacher with the assistance of deputies, senior teachers, subject heads and other staff. Near the bottom of the pyramid, at classroom level where the actual learning of the children takes place, some hundreds of refugee teachers are interacting with many thousands of refugee pupils in schools scattered over the whole refugee area. At the base of the pyramid is the refugee community, providing additional support to the schools.

Figure 2: Pyramid of Levels in Refugee Education

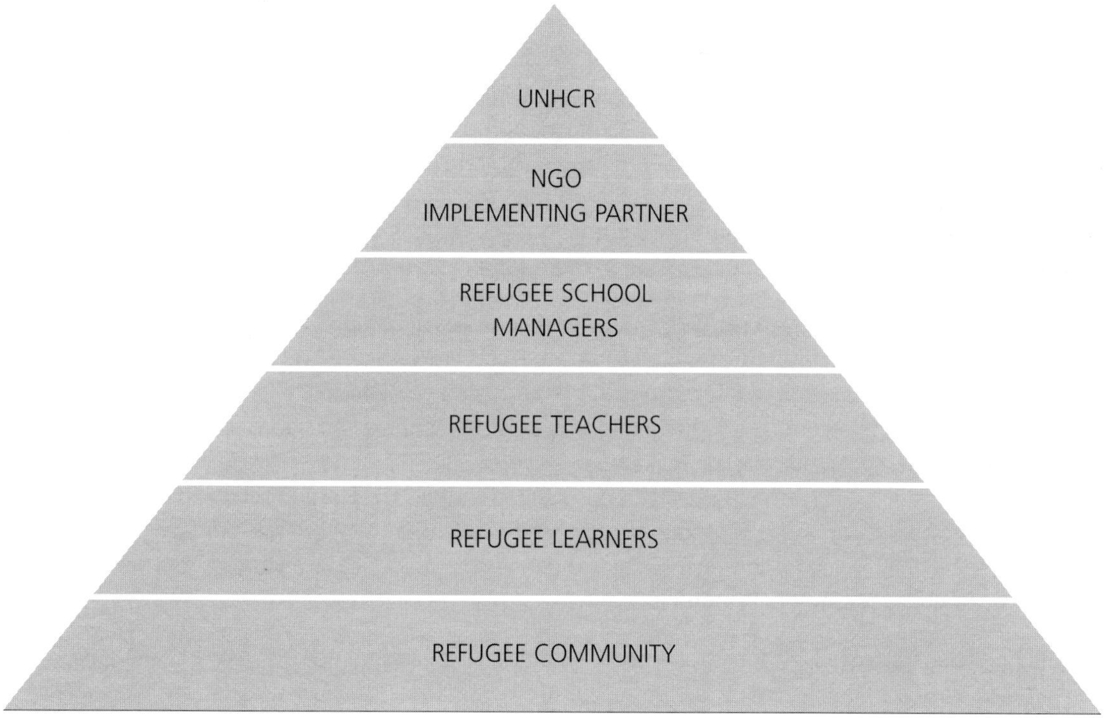

The main objective of this work is to find out how UNHCR and other programme managers can help to improve the quality of education for refugees in the classroom. It is therefore necessary to look at the system in its entirety, the whole pyramid, and examine the roles of each level and how they interact.

In view of the scope of the present work and the current scarcity of published information on refugee education overall, the author believes that the broad picture approach is justified in this case. Indeed, in the final section the author takes the pyramid as the fundamental framework on which to pin the discussion. In particular, recommendations are given for the actors at the top end of the pyramid which should benefit the actors at the bottom end in the delivery of quality education to refugees.

Bhutanese refugee education programme in Nepal[15]

> The commitment and sacrifice of the Bhutanese refugee staff is inspiring and calls for admiration. The Bhutanese Refugee Education Programme stands as one of the models to be imitated and emulated. (UNHCR/CARITAS-Nepal, 1998)

In this section a case study of the Bhutanese Refugee Education Programme (BREP) is presented using the suggested conceptual framework. We start with "environment", which describes the refugee context, the camp background, the attitudes of the host community and the resources and facilities. Next we consider the "actors", both in the early history of the programme and at the present time. We continue with some "tools" of quality, namely: school curriculum and curriculum development, training of teachers and managers, teaching methods and assessment, and monitoring and evaluation. Finally, we discuss the "outcomes" of the Bhutanese programme.

Environment[16]

The Bhutanese refugees began to arrive in eastern Nepal at the end of 1990. They are mostly of Nepalese ethnic origin and come from southern Bhutan. Many of them claim that they were compelled to leave their homeland due to the Bhutanese government's introduction of discriminatory and sometimes persecutory measures against the Nepalese-speaking southerners. The refugees are desperately wanting to go back home as they wait and hope for a positive outcome to the ongoing negotiations between Nepal and Bhutan, which could pave the way for their repatriation. The refugee situation in Nepal has become long-drawn-out, however, with many refugees staying there for almost ten years.

Refugee camps. There are seven camps giving shelter to almost 100,000 refugees, about half of whom are located in Beldangi where there are three camps (I, II and II-Extension). The camps are situated on the plains of east Nepal, spanning two districts (Jhapa and Morang) which are among the most heavily populated in Nepal. The security is good, although hazards such as fires and floods are potential threats to the safety of the refugees due to the makeshift nature of their bamboo huts. No land is available to refugees for cultivation, apart from a small plot around each hut (in the fire prevention line) on which they grow a few vegetables for home consumption. Life in the camps is therefore not preparing the younger generation for a farming life back home. There is a danger that reliance on hand-outs and free food can lead to the dependency syndrome setting in.

Basic food rations provided by the World Food Programme are distributed through the refugee camp committees. The basic ration, which is assessed yearly, consists of rice, pulses, vegetable oil, sugar and salt. In addition, UNHCR provides vegetables to ensure that minimum dietary needs are met. Vulnerable groups, such as under-nourished expectant mothers and sick or severely malnourished children, are given supplementary food rations. No meals are provided at school. The health situation in the camps is generally satisfactory. Every two huts share one latrine. UNHCR has put emphasis on preventive health care and health

15 Much of the background and factual information in this section is based on personal observation, corroborated by information from the following reports: UNHCR (2000d), UNHCR (2000e), UNHCR (2000f), UNHCR/CARITAS-Nepal (1998), CARITAS-Nepal (1999), CARITAS-Nepal/UNHCR (undated). Accuracy has been verified by refugees Bala Sharma and Loknath Pokhrel, education coordinators, who have been with BREP since its inception.

16 For the definition of "environment" see the explanation of the Conceptual framework in the previous section.

Basic food rations of rice, pulses, vegetable oil, sugar and salt are provided by the World Food Programme. Refugees from Bhutan, Beldangi I Camp, Jhapa District, Nepal. UNHCR/12.1992/A. Hollmann

education programmes. As a result, the rates for population growth, under-5 mortality and malnutrition are all significantly lower than the corresponding national figures for Nepal. Moreover, the incidence of common infections and diseases is not high in comparison with the local situation outside the camps.

Host community. The policy of the government in Nepal is that refugees should remain inside the camps. Both entrance to and exit from the camps require official permission from the government representatives (the camp supervisors). In practice, however, the camps are open, and the government estimates that an additional 15,000 Bhutanese are settled in Nepal outside the camps without UNHCR assistance. It is quite easy for the Nepalese-speaking refugees to mingle with the surrounding Nepalese population and vice versa. Indeed, some refugees go outside the camps to work for Nepalese citizens on farms or building sites. Because this is not officially allowed, the refugees are somewhat exploited by the citizens in that they receive wages below the national rates. Similarly, some refugee teachers, after receiving training and experience in the camp schools, are attracted to the private schools outside.

Although the private schools pay salaries less than the national rates, the refugees still receive more than the incentives they were getting in the camps. The educational standards of the refugee teachers are relatively high and so the private-school headteachers and parents are normally happy to accept them. However, problems do arise when citizens cannot find employment after jobs have been taken up by refugees. In some such cases, refugees have been arrested and imprisoned for a few days before being returned to the camps. Such occurrences are the main cause of tension between locals and refugees, otherwise their relations are generally harmonious. To help improve relations, UNHCR is assisting the local population with basic infrastructure such as schools, health posts and road maintenance under the Refugee-Affected Area Rehabilitation Programme.

Resources and facilities. There is a total of nine main schools. In the big camps of Beldangi (I, II, II-Extension) and Sanischare, the schools are divided into sub-campuses known as sectors or extensions, in addition to the main campus. The sector schools are for the infant classes (pre-primary up to Grade 3) and correspond to the administrative sectors of the camp. This ensures that the younger children do not have to walk far to school. The extension schools are normally for the Grade 4 children (sometimes grades 5 and 6) and relieve pressure on the main school, which is used for the higher classes. In Beldangi II there is also a special secondary school for grades 9 and 10 only, for all children in the Beldangi camps. In the other camps, these secondary grades (9–10) are incorporated into the respective main schools.

Most of the schoolrooms are temporary structures made of bamboo and grass. Many of the lower classes do not have desks and the children are sitting on jute mats which have been manufactured in the camps by vulnerable groups as income-generating activities. However, all classrooms are provided with a table and chair for the teacher. The blackboards are portable with an easel. Each school has a large open space where assemblies can take place.

Each main school has a headteacher's office, staffroom, store, resource centre, library, counselling room and laboratory. The store contains the classroom and office supplies sent by the central CARITAS office. The resource centre, where reference books and teaching aids are kept, is an office for the in-school resource teachers. Teachers meet here for preparation of their lessons and discussions with the in-school resource teachers. It is also a place for preparing teaching aids with materials found locally or sent by the central office. The libraries contain a few hundred textbooks and reference books. The school is supplied with limited amounts of manila paper and marker pens so that teachers can make their own visual aids. The counselling rooms are used by specialist teachers to counsel students and others with problems. These teachers have received special training to do this. The "laboratories" are basically stores where a few pieces of equipment and chemicals are kept, to be brought out by teachers for demonstration purposes only.

All pupils are supplied with textbooks and stationery, the amounts of which depend on their grade. Supplementary reading materials, however, are limited. In the higher grades (4 and above), the pupils receive individual copies of textbooks for each subject. Pupils can take these books home to do homework, but they must return the books in good condition at the end of the academic year. A book is expected to last for three years. If a pupil spoils a book, appropriate sanctions (such as fines) are applied. In the lower grades, only Nepalese textbooks are given. There are also workbooks for the pupils to fill in. Many of the books have been written and produced by the programme itself for pre-primary up to Grade 8, and there is constant updating and re-writing of materials, especially when there is a change in curriculum, as there was recently in Nepal. Some of the textbooks used in Nepal schools, or in Bhutan, have also been modified and updated by the refugees. Moreover, teachers are provided with manuals and guides, produced by the office, to help them carry out their lessons effectively.

A temporary school made of bamboo for Bhutanese children refugees. Sanskrit class, Timai Camp, Jhapa District, Nepal. UNHCR/12.1992/A. Hollmann

Actors[17]

Many of the refugees are farmers, coming from a traditional rural background, but some of them were officials or civil servants with the government prior to their departure from Bhutan. When they first arrived, illiteracy was rife, particularly among the women and the older generation, but literacy has improved in the camps due to the efforts of the refugees themselves in non-formal adult education programmes. Almost half of the population are children under 18 years of age. There is not much evidence of traumatization among children although some refugees allege harsh treatment and disproportionate punishment by authorities prior to their departure from Bhutan.

The camps are well organized and maintained by the refugees themselves through the elected camp management committees with help from the government of Nepal, UNHCR and its implementing partners. There is good cooperation between agencies working in the camps. An inter-agency meeting takes place each month between the government, UNHCR and the partner agencies responsible for specific sector activities. Some agencies fund projects from their own resources for activities not covered by UNHCR. The cost-effectiveness of the programme is largely due to the high level of participation of the refugees. Around 1,700 refugees receive minimal "salaries", or incentives, for work performed in the camps, mainly as teachers or health workers. Another 3,000 refugee workers are volunteers.

Early history of the Bhutanese Refugee Education Programme.[18] The Student Union of Bhutan (SUB) initiated the education programme in November 1991. There was a large influx of refugees the following year and as new camps were formed, SUB organized the education in each one. In the same year (1992), UNHCR and CARITAS-Nepal came in with funding to support the programme, at the request of the refugee community.

There were a few trained teachers among the refugees and, encouraged by UNHCR and SUB, they formed the Bhutanese Refugee Education Coordinating Centre (BRECC), which later became an independent refugee education body taking over the management of the schools. It was guided by an advisory committee and consisted of representatives from each camp including headteachers and refugee education specialists.

At this point, CARITAS-Nepal was very small and did not have the expertise to support BRECC professionally. Its role was merely of funder – paying teachers a token incentive and purchasing educational and building materials for the schools. In 1993, at the request of UNHCR, BRECC was effectively disbanded and became part of CARITAS, the large majority of whose staff remain refugees, albeit not at the top levels of Director and Assistant Director. Also in 1993, CARITAS agreed to take on five expatriate volunteers recruited by the Agency for Personnel Service Overseas (APSO). These Irish volunteers were education experts, one coordinator and four teacher trainers, and their secondment filled a gap in the CARITAS team. APSO was chosen because of its earlier successful experience in Bhutan, where it helped to introduce the New Approach to Primary Education (NAPE) programme, a pupil-centred methodology for the lower primary school.

> In this venture of CARITAS in BREP there is the stamp of long experience and expertise of its partners of education. (Bhutanese refugee resource teacher)

17 For the definition of "actors" see the Conceptual framework in the previous section.

18 Much of the information in this section on the history of BREP has been obtained from McDonogh (1996).

During the next few years, the APSO personnel worked with the refugees on a curriculum for the lower primary school (pre-primary through to Grade 3), producing a number of manuals to be used by the teachers. Prescriptive lesson plans were written out so that they could be immediately used by the untrained teachers. The teacher trainers were known as resource teachers, and they spent much of their time visiting the schools, advising and supporting the refugee teachers.

The resource teachers also identified suitable Bhutanese teachers who had the potential to become resource teachers inside the schools. These refugee teachers were formally appointed as in-school resource teachers. The APSO resource teachers then worked mainly with the in-school resource teachers when they visited the schools, holding fortnightly meetings with them to discuss their work and any problems. This was the period during which the refugees gradually took over the responsibility for curriculum development and in-service training. More responsibility was given to the in-school resource teachers who were expected to guide and train the teachers independently, by planning and conducting their own workshops, for example. The in-school resource teachers concentrated on child-centred learning methods at the lower primary level, which is the most formative stage of a child's learning.

As there was also a growing need to cater for the higher levels, qualified resource teachers among refugees were identified and appointed. They took care of the upper primary and secondary levels and were responsible for curriculum development and in-service training. In addition, some in-school resource teachers were appointed for middle primary level.

The support from both UNHCR and CARITAS-Nepal has continued up to this day. The assistance of APSO ended in 1997 but the Jesuit Refugee Service (JRS) has been providing CARITAS with expatriate volunteers on a continuing basis.

Present management structure of the refugee education programme. At the UNHCR level, there are no staff dealing specifically with education. There used to be a Social Services officer but that post no longer exists. The programme section at UNHCR in Jhapa, under the head of Sub-Office, is presently responsible for all sectors of the programme, including education, and participates in the annual review for education. UNHCR staff are involved in the tender process in which school materials are purchased, and they monitor the financial accounts. A UNHCR officer visits schools on special occasions such as prize giving. Day-to-day monitoring is carried out by the two UNHCR field assistants, who are local staff otherwise known as project monitoring officers (PMOs). Their educational duties, which are a fraction of their total work, normally focus on hardware such as infrastructure, classrooms and school supplies. They attend meetings in the camps for sensitization of the community on topics such as drop-outs and parents' cooperation. They are sometimes called to the schools when there are specific problems to solve, such as disputes between parents and teachers.

At the implementing agency level, there are 41 staff members working at the CARITAS central office in Damak under BREP. These include six expatriate volunteers from India provided by the Jesuit Refugee Service. They are well-qualified education experts and two of them occupy the top two management positions – those of Field Director and Assistant Field Director. A few of the posts are held by Nepalese nationals, in particular the positions of Finance Officer and Personnel Officer. Most of the other staff of CARITAS are refugees. The refugee staff in Damak are paid on the same incentive scale as that operating in the camps but with an additional daily living allowance. The work of the office is organized in eight sections: education, personnel, finance, logistics, procurement, technical, computer and scholarships. The management (section heads) meet every week and there is a meeting with all the headteachers once a month.

The biggest section of the central office is that of education, and it is spearheaded by the two education coordinators – the "lower" one for pre-primary to Grade 5 and the "upper" one for Grade 6 and above. The main functions of the coordinators are planning the programme for the whole year and supervising the implementation of the plans. Their work involves preparation of budgets, report writing, the finalization of books and examinations, attending meetings and the recruitment of teachers. Under the coordinators are several resource teachers who are responsible for curriculum development, the compilation of textbooks, teacher observation and training, and the supervision of examinations. The "lower" coordinator is supervising four general resource teachers and three specialist resource teachers, respectively for Nepalese (mother tongue), value education and special needs. The "upper" coordinator has six resource teachers, responsible for the main subjects of English (two), Dzongkha (the native language of Bhutan), mathematics, science and social studies. One of the main activities of the resource teachers is updating manuals, workbooks and textbooks.

The computer section is responsible for getting the in-house books ready for printing. It produces updated guidelines for the schools and any handouts needed for various workshops and training programmes. The office also procures commercial textbooks and school supplies through a tendering process and distributes the items to the schools. Due to theft in a camp school store, most of the classroom supplies are now stored in a central warehouse in Damak from where the materials are sent out to the schools on a monthly basis. The procurement section conducts regular checks at the schools to ascertain the quality and use of the materials.

Refugee schools. There are nine refugee schools with a total of 964 teachers, 138 non-teaching staff and 40,204 students (figures valid as of 31 August 2000). Of the teachers, 735 (76 per cent) are male and 229 (24 per cent) are female. Of the pupils, 21,034 (52 per cent) are male and 19,170 (48 per cent) are female. The average size of a school is more than 4,000, which is enormous; the school at Beldangi II has almost 8,000 pupils, spread into smaller sub-campuses.

Over 40 per cent of the refugee population are attending the camp schools, not to mention those refugees who are attending school outside the camps. This gives an overall gross enrolment ratio exceeding 100 per cent, indicating the refugees' strong desire for education. The anomalous enrolment ratio is explained by the fact that there are many over-aged refugees attending school. The schools in southern Bhutan were closed down in 1990, so that when the refugees reached Nepal they rejoined school to catch up on their earlier missed education. At the lower level (pre-primary to Grade 5), CARITAS claim that the net enrolment is almost 100 per cent, implying that virtually all refugees of primary school age, girls and boys, are going to school. At the upper level (grades 6 to 10), the enrolment level is somewhat lower and there are more boys (8,344) attending than girls (6,077).

The overall pupil–teacher ratio is 42: 1, but in reality the classes are much bigger than this because teachers don't teach all the time. They have free periods in which they plan and prepare their lessons and do corrections. (Each teacher is time-tabled for 32 periods per week.) Some of the specialist teachers, such as the in-school resource teachers, are given very few periods, if any at all. The number of pupils per class therefore averages around 60 to 65. This has increased over the years from about 40, due to the constant reduction in funding and the increasing number of students. The author even observed a few lower classes with over 100 students, caused by a merging of two classes when one teacher was away sick.

Since the education in the camp schools has been recognized by the government of Nepal, they follow the academic calendar of the district education office from July to June. Children start school at the age of 5–6 years. There are 66 days per term with two month-long holidays per year and a few short holidays for religious and national festivals. The camp schools run from Monday to Friday with a half-day on Saturday. The lowest classes (pre-primary and Grade 1) operate on a shift system so that there can be two sessions per day, thus economising on classroom space. From grades 2 to 10, the number of lessons per day varies from seven to eight, each period lasting for 40 minutes. (A shift system operated formerly for the higher grades, but was unsuccessful because it was very tiring for the teachers.)

The schools are well organized, as evidenced by the extensive range of files kept in the headteachers' offices. Discipline is good and corporal punishment is officially banned. Each school has a headteacher, assistant head and those in charge of the sub-campuses. There are also seven in-school resource teachers – two each for the lower school, upper school and Nepalese language, and one for special needs. Moreover, staff from the central CARITAS office visit the schools regularly to encourage the teachers and give them advice. The schools have set up various committees to assist their functioning on various matters, including admission, discipline, welfare, maintenance and examinations.

Tools[19]

The school curriculum and curriculum development. The Bhutanese refugees are using English as the language of instruction in their schools, following the same pattern as in Bhutan.[20] This contrasts with the government schools in Nepal, which use the Nepalese language (only the private schools, reputedly better than the government schools, use English as a medium). The refugees are following a mixed system, combining elements of both Bhutanese and Nepalese curricula, so that they can be prepared for the eventuality either of returning back home or of settling in the host country. A generation of children have been born outside Bhutan, who need to learn about their home country.

In the lowest grades, from pre-primary to Grade 3, the refugees basically follow the Bhutanese syllabus (NAPE) plus Nepalese language. There are no subject teachers, except for Nepalese language, so that the children are taught by one class teacher for most of the time. The syllabus is child-centred and activity-based, and is meant to reflect Bhutanese traditional values and culture.

In the middle years (grades 4 to 8) the refugees are following a mixture of the Bhutanese and Nepalese curriculums. The refugees study the four core subjects of the Nepalese curriculum (English, Nepalese, mathematics and science), as prescribed by the Nepalese Ministry of Education, and in addition they take the optional subjects of English II, social studies, Dzongkha (the national language of Bhutan) and value education, covering environment and population. The teachers specialize in two or three subjects.

19 See Conceptual framework in previous section for definition of "tools".

20 There are three languages in the Bhutanese refugee picture. The mother tongue is Nepalese, which is also the national language of Nepal, the country of asylum. The national language in Bhutan, the country of origin, is Dzongkha. Yet the refugees prefer to study in English, as is done in Bhutan. They feel that an international language provides a better-quality education, which is therefore more motivating for them.

Children learn both Bhutanese and Nepalese at the secondary school to be prepared for the eventuality of returning home. Sanischare Camp, Morang District, Nepal. UNHCR/12.1997/H.J. Davies

The refugees feel that there is a need to strengthen their knowledge of Dzongkha, in particular, to prepare them for repatriation. Special workshops are conducted to expose the teachers to methods of teaching Dzongkha. The programme staff, the resource teachers and in-school resource teachers, have produced syllabuses and textbooks for all these optional subjects.

For the top years (grades 9 to 10), the refugees adhere completely to the Nepalese curriculum and sit the national School Leaving Certificate examination. Each teacher is responsible for between one and three subjects. CARITAS arranges for the translation into English of the relevant Nepalese-language school textbooks. The programme also provides supporting curricular material and teacher training notes.

The Bhutanese refugee education programme attaches great importance to those aspects of education learned outside the classroom – the "hidden curriculum". Pupils do 10 minutes' "social work" each day before assembly (and 30 minutes on Saturday mornings). The work involves cleaning the classrooms and keeping the school compound tidy. Students also take it in turns to make speeches during assembly. This gives them an opportunity to improve their confidence. It also instils positive feelings, both towards schoolwork and to their home country. There is a house system which implants a spirit of both cooperation and competition. Various games, sports, literary and cultural activities are organized in the schools. There are annual sports, and inter-class, inter-house and inter-school football and volleyball tournaments.

The schools also organize quizzes and debates, and have competitions in extempore speech, general knowledge, essay writing, singing and dancing. The refugee schools participate in athletics tournaments organized by the district education officer for all schools in the district. Many of the refugees win prizes and some are selected to represent the district in zonal athletics gatherings.

There has been continuous curriculum development in the refugee schools, with each section of the programme developing materials and corresponding teacher training notes. The refugees have recently added a new subject, value education, from Grade 4 upwards, with the purpose of making children aware of the values held by the Bhutanese community. There is a danger that the refugees may lose touch with their traditional culture when exposed to the negative effects of camp life. In these classes, the refugees learn about their responsibilities, respect for their elders and how to make a positive contribution to their community. They also learn how values can change for the better, for example the community's changing attitude towards the education of girls. [21] Teachers handling this new subject are given special orientation programmes.

The curriculum has become inclusive in the sense that children with special needs are now integrated into the classrooms. An objective of the programme is for disabled children to have equal educational opportunities, with full participation and the necessary support. There are 1,085 children with various disabilities in the camps, of whom about 30 per cent are hearing-impaired. These children are admitted into school at the same time as the normal children, although some flexibility in age is allowed. Only one type of disabled child is put in any one class and the children are normally seated in the front row for easy access to the teacher. Awareness programmes have been given to the community and all teachers. Each school has a special needs support teacher. The special needs support teachers receive training from the central office, after which they train the schoolteachers in how to deal with disabled children in their classes. The special needs support teacher also provides support and guidance to the disabled pupils. Where necessary, remedial classes are given to the disabled children after school hours. The special needs support teachers visit the homes to guide and train the parents so that they can assist their disabled children and monitor their progress. The students with special needs are encouraged to participate in co-curricular activities. Guidebooks have been written by CARITAS for teachers to help them to deal with children with special needs.[22] Contacts have been made with donors who have offered hearing aids or spectacles to the children after they have been tested physically.

In terms of personality development, some older children have themselves received training. In particular, class 10 students have benefited from a workshop on leadership skills. The objectives were to help the students learn about themselves, their peers and the environment, and to develop critical thinking. Moreover, the older girls (class 8 and 9) have been given self-awareness training to help them cope with the problems of growing up. An objective of this programme is a reduction in the number of early marriages and elopements during the girls' studies. Results so far have proved positive.

Training of teachers and managers. Suitably qualified teachers are recruited from the refugee population. Ideally, they should already have teacher training certificates or degrees but in practice the majority of them have just come out of school with higher secondary (Grade 12) certificates or just school leaving certificates (Grade 10). Candidates are interviewed for suitability by a panel of staff from the central

---

21 According to one informant, the community had previously considered that girls' education was a curse.

22 See, for example, Meera (1999; undated).

office. During the interview, the candidate presents a "lesson" on a chosen subject to demonstrate his or her communication skills. The panel makes its selection according to this performance, also taking qualifications, work experience and community service into consideration.

There is an extensive system of in-service teacher training. The duration and frequency of the courses vary according to the category of training. Newly appointed teachers have a three-day workshop in which they are given the basics in lesson planning and delivery. This includes demonstration and practice lessons, after which they have some confidence to enter the classroom. All primary teachers have a meeting every week with the in-school resource teachers (on Saturday mornings), when they plan for the following week's lessons. During the week, the in-school resource teachers observe the teachers and support them with further ongoing guidance and advice, especially those who are newly appointed. Workshops on particular subjects are arranged by the resource teachers, as and when necessary, taking place at the central office in Damak. Earlier, CARITAS used to give out certificates to all teachers attending workshops. Although these certificates are not recognized by the governments in either Nepal or Bhutan, they can help refugees to secure employment in the private schools in Nepal. As part of the measures to curtail the "brain-drain", CARITAS has now stopped issuing certificates after workshops. However, they continue to award experience certificates to refugee teachers.

During the year, central workshops are arranged for office-based staff, in-school resource teachers, headteachers and sector in-charges, ranging from three to five days according to the availability of external facilitators. The topics are chosen to help these personnel to keep abreast of the latest ideas and become more effective.

The content of the various types of training obviously depends on the category of the trainee. The primary teachers are given basic classroom management and child psychology, for example. The in-school resource teachers and subject-based teachers are trained in subject matter and development of alternative learning resources. The headteachers receive training in counselling, alternative ways of disciplining students, children's rights, and leadership and managerial skills, and the central office staff are trained in management, training of trainers and conflict resolution.

Teaching methods and assessment. Child-centred methods are encouraged during training, but teachers often find them difficult to carry out in the classroom. Traditionally in Bhutan, culture and religion have been strongly intertwined in the lives of these people, and education has assumed a kind of religious significance. The learning process is venerated, and the teachers, often called gurus, are respected like religious leaders. Schools are revered as temples, and as such are looked after and treasured by the community.[23] The culture tends to favour the "lecture method" of instruction by teachers,[24] and the author observed that the pupils listened to their teachers, respectfully and often unquestioningly, without much active participation, exacerbated by large class size and shortage of teaching materials.[25] As an illustration of this point, the author noticed a hand-written poster on a classroom wall which included the following sentence: "A good student is one who talks less in class. "

23 On several occasions, the author was told by Bhutanese refugees (parents, teachers and pupils) that a school was like a temple.

24 The tendency towards "lecture method" has been noticed by the author in other developing countries, such as Sudan, Uganda and Kenya.

25 "The students are encouraged to ask questions and the system is building up gradually, though the pupils are very hesitant." Personal communication with Bala Sharma and Loknath Pokhrel, the refugee education coordinators of BREP.

In the general context of this region of the world, educational process is assumed to be one of give and take – knowledge given by the guru and taken by the *shishya* (student/disciple). However, such a situation is not to be taken as absolute. In many concrete situations one can observe elements of the Western/modern/secular approach. (Bhutanese refugee resource teacher)

In Grade 4 and above, the pupils sit for examinations at the end of each term. In the lower classes, examinations are given at the end of each "block" of work. Although some assignments and tests are done throughout the term, they don't carry any weight in the final assessment, except in Grade 8. Prizes are given to the highest-ranking pupils as well as to those who have excelled in general school life, such as school captains and winners of various literary, cultural and sports competitions. Students who fail to achieve an average of a pass over their three termly examinations have to repeat the year. They might do so more than once; disabled students are treated more leniently. Each school sets its own examinations, apart from the District Common Board Examinations (end of grades 5 and 8) and the National School Leaving Certificate Examinations (end of Grade 10). In the Common Board Examinations, the schools contribute their own internal assessment marks.

The district recognizes the education of the refugee pupils and allows them to sit for the Common Board Examinations. Moreover, CARITAS has been authorized to set additional papers especially for the refugees in the camps. This was achieved after much representation to the district authorities, to the great credit of the CARITAS management. The additional papers added for Grade 5 are in English II, Dzongkha and Bhutan social studies. The additional papers for Grade 8 are English II, Dzongkha, and Bhutan history, geography and value education. The rationale for introducing new papers is twofold: the refugees want to maintain their high standards of education and at the same time they want to preserve their identity with Bhutan. CARITAS is fully involved in these board examinations, which it has now taken on as an additional responsibility. CARITAS has created a separate examinations section in their programme, to deal specifically with matters such as liaising with the district education office. Functions of this section include registering students, paying their fees, setting the questions, distributing the stationery, supervising the examinations, evaluating the answer sheets and tabulating the results. CARITAS is one of the members of the district examination board.

The Grade 10 students have to sit for a qualifying ("sent-up") examination, set by the district, before they can enter for the School Leaving Certificate, which is a national examination. The certificates obtained by the refugees at the grades 5, 8 and 10 levels are all officially recognized by the government of Nepal.

Monitoring and evaluation. The refugee programme monitors and assesses itself through regular meetings with its administrative and education staff, headteachers, sector in-charges, in-school resource teachers, special needs support teachers and store in-charges. Future plans, current problems and suggested solutions are considered in detail at these meetings. Every six months, to satisfy UNHCR's monitoring requirements, each department writes a report, which is collated and presented for discussion at a general staff meeting. Before the end of the academic year there is a three-day review for all CARITAS staff to which UNHCR officials and outside experts are also invited. Achievements and non-achievements are thoroughly debated, and in the light of this, plans are made for the following year. The teachers are given the chance to make suggestions for curriculum changes, new courses, teacher training or any other improvement for the running of the schools. They make their opinions known to the in-school resource teachers who channel them to the appropriate authorities (headteachers or resource teachers).

Outcomes[26]

In a recent monitoring report submitted by CARITAS to UNHCR (CARITAS-Nepal, 1999: 5–8), it was stated that over 90 per cent of the refugee students who sat the district and national examinations were successful. More specifically, the overall refugee pass rates for the official Grade 5, Grade 8 and Grade 10 examinations were 94.7 per cent, 96.6 per cent and 91.5 per cent respectively. It is clear that the Bhutanese refugees are maintaining an excellent academic standard.

Classroom tests and government examinations are not the only way that the programme measures attainment of the refugee students. Behaviour and attitudes are considered to be very important. When the author asked the headteachers how they measured children's attainment, they gave the following additional answers: vocabulary used in writing and speech; performance in debates and essay competitions; student participation in co-curricular activities and sports; discipline; attendance; confidence; behaviour towards the community; social participation; effort; help to other students; leadership roles. Teachers observe their pupils both inside and outside the classroom to obtain a broad picture of attainment.

Table 1: Overall Student Attendance at Camp Schools, Grades 9 and 10.

YEAR	GRADE 9	GRADE 10	TOTAL
1992	92	11	103
1993	119	59	178
1994	240	119	359
1995	356	221	577
1996	373	312	685
1997	436	346	782
1998	635	432	1,067
1999	1,085	583	1,668
2000	1,294	1,040	2,334

Source: Amalraj, 2000

Table 2: Attendance by Girls at Camp Schools, Grades 9 and 10.

YEAR	GRADE 9	GRADE 10	TOTAL
1995	93	44	137
1996	90	84	174
1997	120	108	228
1998	189	124	313
1999	369	170	539
2000	438	337	775

Source: Amalraj, 2000

26 See Conceptual framework in previous section for definition of "outcomes".

Although the total refugee population has remained fairly constant since the influx of 1992, enrolment and persistence at school have been improving steadily during the period of the refugees' exile, as can be seen in Table 1, which covers the two highest grades in the camp schools. More specifically, the same report indicates that the enrolment and persistence of girls have also multiplied, as shown in Table 2.

Literacy levels have increased in the camps, as mentioned earlier. Some teachers and older students help the community by giving adult education classes at the schools in the evenings.

Although employment prospects are low, the education which refugees receive in the camp schools does give some boost to their chances. Many refugees who successfully complete their education in the camps start teaching in the refugee schools. Some move on to schools outside the camps.[27] The little money they earn is often used for further education.

The skills, attitudes and behaviour which refugees learn at school can contribute to the overall good management and wellbeing of the camps. This is an important outcome which a quality refugee education programme should achieve. "Already we have good administration in the camps. This will be better and best when more and more educated youth participate in camp management" (Amalraj, 2000).

The education the refugees receive is good because they achieve higher percentage results than the nationals. (Deputy Director of the Refugee Coordination Unit, Government of Nepal)

Most refugees were farmers and didn't know the value of education. But this is now improving. The school has played a role by bringing in parents for meetings and discussions. (Bhutanese refugee headteacher)

We know the value of education and we motivate our children to attend school. (Bhutanese refugee parent)

Quite a few of the teachers who have acquired some degree of competence of a few years' teaching and in-service training, are attracted by the offers from outside. This lure becomes all the more irresistible in the case of a people who have been languishing for years in the camps and thus rendered passive and bereft of hope of repatriation and brighter prospects. (Bhutanese refugee resource teacher).

There isn't much conflict in the camps. (Bhutanese refugee leader).

We are able to maintain the camp so well and so peacefully because of education in the camp schools. Managing 41,000 students has greatly contributed to the peaceful atmosphere of our seven camps. (Field Director, CARITAS-Nepal)

Education is an important "occupational therapy", keeping refugees busy and preventing anti-social activities. The level of crime and misbehaviour in the Bhutanese camps is very low. Time is a huge resource that the refugees possess as they wait in the camps for many years, hoping for their situation to end. It is important that this resource is harnessed for positive rather than negative use.

27 It has been noted earlier that private schools in Nepal are frequently willing to accept Bhutanese refugee teachers in view of the relatively high educational standards of the refugees.

Findings

> Quality is a complex term, with multiple meanings reflecting the values and interpretations of different stakeholders. (Williams, 2001)

In this section, the author will first look at quality from the Bhutanese refugees' viewpoint. What do they consider to be quality education and has it been achieved in the Nepalese camps? The author will then go on to present his own findings, by identifying what he perceives as the main strengths and weaknesses of the Bhutanese refugee programme. Finally, these will be discussed in relation to the conceptual framework, throwing some light on how other refugee programmes might address quality education issues.

Refugees' perspective

Many schools in Southern Bhutan were closed down in September 1990 before the refugees fled. The schooling of the students had therefore been seriously disrupted and from the beginning of their exile, the Bhutanese refugees have appreciated the importance of quality education, both for the individual and for the community. The Bhutanese refugees regard education as their only wealth in exile and their key to the future. It is the hope of almost every refugee that they will return to their homeland. "Quality education empowers people to contribute to the building of their nation and to enhance their dignity as individuals" (UNHCR/CARITAS-Nepal, 1999).

The education facilities provided by CARITAS are good. In Bhutan, we were deprived. (Bhutanese refugee headteacher)

We need to know our identity. Who are we, where are we and what are our responsibilities? (Bhutanese refugee leader)

We are happy with the schools because our children are benefiting. They will be able to serve the nation when they go back. (Bhutanese refugee parent)

Elopement has reduced. There is more awareness now. (Bhutanese refugee women's leader)

Girls are growing more confident, and some speak better than the boys during assembly. (Bhutanese refugee headteacher)

We learn how to talk to elders and respect them. (Bhutanese refugee student)

School is good because there are no disputes or misunderstandings among teachers and students. (Bhutanese refugee student)

Frequently the first thing that the Bhutanese refugees told the author was that they wanted to go home. Repatriation is their chief objective and this dream seems to dominate their thoughts. Education is regarded as an important weapon to help them prepare to go back home. They want to contribute to nation building, compete for leadership and fight for justice. They believe that education will help them do this. And education for repatriation does not just involve the drawing up of a syllabus similar to the one in

Bhutan. It is also a process of developing a desire in the pupils to go back to their homeland. Many of the children were born in the camps, and even the older ones are too young to remember what life was like in Bhutan before they fled. Education is therefore a chance for the children to know who they are and build their identity. Every morning during assembly, a few refugee pupils stand up on the raised-earth stage and speak to the other pupils and teachers. Their speeches not only urge the audience to work harder at school but they also instil patriotic feelings and the yearning to go home.

Education is not only a vehicle in which the values and behaviour of the community are passed on to the children. It is also an agent for bringing about positive change. Since they became refugees, the Bhutanese community has a better understanding of the value of girls' education and, as a result, almost all refugee girls are now going to school. The caste system has also grown to be less significant, helped by the fact that the refugees have become united in their suffering together in the camps. Young people are now beginning to be more open, and this should lead to more critical thinking and questioning in class in the future.

Generally, the interaction between the teachers and pupils was excellent, with each group showing respect for the other. This is an indicator of the quality of the Bhutanese refugee education programme.

The author also received negative comments from refugees concerning the quality of the education programme, including the following:

- Although student numbers are increasing, the facilities have decreased. (Bhutanese refugee parent)
- We lack furniture and have to share some books. We haven't had a geometry set for three years. (Bhutanese refugee student)
- Girls are poor at mathematics. (Bhutanese refugee female teacher)
- Computer education should be provided. Without it, we will not be able to compete with others. (Bhutanese refugee teacher)
- Our children receive only minimum help for grades 11 and 12. There is no scope after Grade 12. (Bhutanese refugee parent)

Strengths of the Bhutanese refugee education programme

The author identifies the following main strengths which have contributed to the quality of the programme.

Refugee participation. The education programme was initiated by the refugees themselves and continues to be run predominantly by them. Clearly, among their greatest resources are the human resources provided by themselves. The parents provide their labour without charge in the construction and maintenance of the school buildings. Teachers provide their services for very low pay. Their participation promotes cost-effectiveness and sustainability. By having the responsibility of teaching their own children, the refugees are motivated to do a better job. Being refugees themselves, the teachers can more easily understand the problems of the refugee pupils. They can counsel the pupils and teach them more relevant subject matter. They realise that whatever is done now is an investment whose value will be evident after they repatriate. Moreover, the involvement of refugees in the schools ensures that there will be a cadre of educators and teachers who will be experienced and trained to continue or set up schools on repatriation.

Motivation. The refugee pupils, teachers and community are highly motivated and committed towards education. They understand the value of education and are always eager to learn. School enrolment is very high and absenteeism, among both teachers and pupils, is low. Any visitor to the camps during school hours will see few children outside school. Instead, inside any school, the visitor can't fail to be impressed by row after row of bamboo classrooms full of well-behaved children working hard and concentrating on their lessons. Many young teachers view their jobs as an opportunity to further their own knowledge and skills and they are therefore willing to handle different classes and subjects each year. On top of that, most teachers are studying for additional qualifications on their own, following distance education programmes from Nepal or India to further their careers. Parents also help. They construct new classrooms and facilities, and encourage their children to go to school, giving them space in their huts to do homework in the evenings. The refugees are united in their goal of education for repatriation.

Cooperation. There is a good spirit in the camps because the attitudes of the "actors" involved are very supportive towards the main objective of improving life for the refugees. Cooperation, sharing and teamwork are evident at all levels of the programme. The refugees themselves are willing to share their limited resources and learn from each other. At camp management level, the various agencies meet regularly, both formally and informally, to assist each other in solving their mutual problems. The health NGO might be asked to deal with the illness of a student, for example, or the construction NGO might be asked to repair school furniture. At local government level, the district education officer has rendered much assistance to the refugees, not least by giving official recognition to their examinations. The assistance is reciprocated by the CARITAS office, whenever possible, such as by lending vehicles to the district education officer during the busy examination periods.

Orderliness. The programme is well organized. Everywhere the author went, he found people working in an orderly manner – knowing what to do and getting on with it. Two extensive documents have been produced by the refugees to guide the running of the programme. One document (CARITAS-Nepal, 2000) on office procedure and personnel policy specifies detailed job descriptions of all central office posts, from field director down to office attendant. All sections have a section head and there are well-defined lines of duty. Organization is enhanced by meetings and training workshops for office administrators and school heads. These take place on a regular basis and are planned many months in advance. The other document (UNHCR/CARITAS-Nepal, 1999) comprises the camp school guidelines in which school rules and job descriptions have been well laid down, having been agreed by the refugees and camp management. This document includes procedures on disciplining students and teachers, admission of students, appointment of heads, school committees and examinations. The refugees themselves are organized and well disciplined. They understand the importance of rules, and are able and willing to carry out the procedures specified in the guidelines.

Management. Much of what the refugees have achieved has been due to the support and assistance received from the programme management. The support has taken many forms – financial, human resources, educational and moral. UNHCR has realised the importance of education since the very beginning of the emergency, and has continued to support the programme with necessary funds and guidance. CARITAS-Nepal has also been bringing in its expertise and has seconded volunteer staff who are highly qualified and motivated. Moreover, it has provided additional financial resources to improve the primary education programme (mainly funded by UNHCR) and has entirely funded the secondary education programme. The leadership of CARITAS has been promoting positive attitudes among the refugees,

If given the opportunity, refugee women show a keen interest in acquiring new skills. The adult education classes held in this camp were immediately over-enrolled, despite the lack of facilities. Goldhap Camp, Jhapa District, Nepal. UNHCR/12.1992/A. Hollmann

the host government, UNHCR and other NGOs. This has greatly helped to create an atmosphere of cooperation, trust and mutual support – an enabling environment for the smooth and successful management of the programme. At school level, programme management has ensured that the schools are administered by experienced, qualified and trained headteachers who have been a good influence on the teachers and have helped to promote stability and a quality education.

Curriculum development. The programme is always on the lookout for ways of improving the refugee curriculum, either by modification or the addition of new components. This ongoing curriculum development process is a major strength of the programme, since it allows the teaching/learning process in the schools to respond positively to the evolving circumstances and surrounding conditions, such as a change in the external Nepalese curriculum or the growing needs of the refugee community. This enables the curriculum to be more relevant. A number of additional subjects have been added recently, such as value education, leadership training and the environment, promoting a comprehensive and rounded curriculum. Moreover, the curriculum has become inclusive, children with disabilities having been encouraged to join school, their needs catered for with the help of special needs support teachers. All teachers are trained in dealing with disabled students and the rest of the pupils gain by sharing the class with their disabled colleagues, accepting them and learning from them in the broadest sense.

Children are doing well. Schools are there and they get materials. (Bhutanese refugee mother)

There is a need for in-school resource teachers because teachers are not qualified and they require constant help. (JRS resource teacher)

Teacher training and support. The ongoing curriculum development requires a constant provision of teacher training and support. The innovative system of resource teachers (resource teachers and in-school resource teachers), which was introduced early on in the programme, is a great strength which has permitted the continuation of a high level of quality. To have in-school resource teachers in all schools is an effective method of reaching all teachers. Teachers benefit from this support, since they have daily access to the advice and guidance of the in-school resource teachers, and on Saturday mornings they are given hints on planning lessons and developing teaching materials for the following week. Moreover, since many teachers are leaving the schools for more highly paid jobs or further education, they are constantly being replaced by young refugees who have mostly just finished school. The ongoing teacher training and support that is provided for these new, inexperienced teachers is essential for building up their confidence and providing them with the skills necessary for effective teaching.

Examinations. The examinations sat in the refugee schools are now recognized by the government of Nepal. This ensures that the students passing these examinations are considered to have attained a satisfactory level of achievement. The certificates acquired, moreover, provide satisfaction to the successful students in that their achievements have been duly recognized. This gives the student confidence and self-esteem, important for building up even higher achievements, which is a great motivating force for other students to follow. When examination results are officially certified, the qualifications become portable and can be used to obtain employment or further education in the host country, country of origin or in a third country of resettlement.

Records and reporting. Extensive records are kept in both the central office and the schools. Minutes are written for meetings. The records examined by the author seemed thorough, accurate and up-to-date, and he noted the large number of files kept in the headteachers' offices. Registers of attendance are scrutinised by the headteachers each day, and if any teacher is absent the head makes efforts to find a temporary replacement from the pool of unoccupied teachers. Examination results are compiled by each teacher and double checked by the in-school resource teachers before they are sent out to the parents. Each school sends a regular monthly situation report to the CARITAS central office. The reports include details on pupil enrolment and dropping out, teacher data, school events, training activities, problems, staff movements, stores and supplies, school construction and maintenance. The reports are consolidated by the computer section of the central office and sent off to UNHCR in the monthly situation report for monitoring and evaluation purposes.

Textbooks. Most of the primary school textbooks (and some of the higher-level books) given to the students are produced by the programme itself, and this ensures that the books are comparatively cost-effective and relevant. Indeed, it was estimated that the books produced in this way cost about two thirds of the price of a commercial book. It was claimed, moreover, that they contained fewer mistakes. The refugees are very creative in the ways in which they make books. They sometimes write their own materials; they compile materials from various sources; they do straight translations of commercial texts; or perform any combination of the three methods. All students are normally given individual copies of the main texts. This promotes quality, since children can take books home for their individual study. Many of the refugees have a remarkable thirst for education and a desire to study on their own out of school. If students have books to take away, not only do they get the thrill of owning a book but they can also read it flexibly in their own time. This is especially important for girls who have to fit in many household chores as well. Another advantage of having a personal copy of a book is that, through reading it, students may be able to discover and compensate for any mistakes made by an incorrect or inexperienced teacher. (Of course, this does not apply to the younger children at the lower primary level.)

Satellite schools. The policy to decentralise the schools as they increase in size is one of the strengths of the programme. Where feasible, sector schools have been constructed for the lower classes (Pre-primary to Grade 3). This not only reduces the massive size of the main school but, more crucially, it gives importance to the lower primary classes whose children are at their most decisive time of development. The sector schools have their own teachers and head (sector in-charge). Previously, the lower classes were neglected and had large pupil-teacher ratios with few materials. Under the system of sector schools, more attention can be given to the individual pupils and the schools can be handled more easily. Moreover, pupils have shorter distances to walk to school and they are separated from the older students, making them less prone to bullying or harassment.

Problems in the Bhutanese refugee education programme

The author identifies the following main problems and weaknesses which have hindered the delivery of quality education.

The refugee situation. The protracted refugee situation has given the refugees an uncertain future. This can lead to frustration and a drop in motivation and morale, which might eventually result in poor performance by refugee teachers and pupils. Furthermore, the longer the refugees subsist on donated food and handouts, the greater the danger that the dependency syndrome could set in. Although the health and nutritional status of the refugees is generally satisfactory, congestion in the camps can lead to various health and social problems.

Decreasing funding. Due to the awareness campaigns in the camps and the increasing number of school-age children, the number of students enrolled in school has increased over the years. Coupled with diminishing funding, this has led to a deterioration of standards, evidenced in reduced quantities of classroom supplies, supplementary reading materials, furniture and science equipment. In particular, the average number of pupils per teacher has increased from 40 to about 65.

Lack of opportunities for further education. At present, UNHCR is funding the primary education programme in the camps (pre-primary to Grade 8) while CARITAS is funding the secondary education programme (grades 9 and 10). But for upper secondary education (grades 11 and 12) the refugees have to go outside the camps to study on nearby government or private campuses. CARITAS gives only limited support to these students. At university level, the situation is worse. It has been decided by UNHCR that there will be no new beneficiaries in the future and so the German-sponsored DAFI (Deutsche Akademische Flüchtlingsinitiative) programme in Nepal has been frozen.[28] This could have adverse effects on the motivation of the refugee community, particularly the students. The problems accumulate as the years go

28 The decision was taken because UNHCR was expecting imminent repatriation of the Bhutanese refugees. The decision may have to be reviewed in the light of current circumstances.

by because of the successful primary education programme. More and more children are reaching secondary level, especially girls, but it is becoming increasingly difficult to accommodate them all at secondary school, and beyond, due to lack of funds.

Low incentives. People will always ask for higher salaries, and refugees are no exception. The Bhutanese refugees are paid a small incentive, ranging from about $10–20 per month, depending on their position. They are not paid full salaries because they benefit from food and non-food items. However, the incentive rate has hardly risen over the last few years and falls well behind inflation. The teachers say that they need the extra money to buy decent clothes and set a good example to the pupils. If it were a fair world then the teachers would certainly receive a higher wage because they deserve it for the amount and quality of work they do. The unfortunate reality is that funds are not enough.

Unrecognized teacher training. Teachers are unable to obtain a recognized teacher qualification. Although refugee teachers work hard, gain valuable experience and receive a lot of non-formal training in the camps, they end up with no official qualification. The district education officer now recognizes the examinations sat by the refugee students but does not yet officially recognize the training received by the refugee teachers. CARITAS is presently trying to work out a solution to this problem.

Teacher absenteeism. Since most teachers are very motivated this is not a huge problem, but there are instances when teachers are unable to attend school for such reasons as ill- health or family problems. The headteacher tries to find other teachers to substitute but this is not always possible (due to limited capacity). In some cases, classes are merged to produce an enormous class of over 100 children. In other cases, the class is left without a teacher or, rarely, the children have to go home.

The standard has gone down. Trained teachers have left and class size has gone up to 65. (JRS resource teacher)

We need higher incentives to maintain our tidy look. It is important to be an exemplary figure. (Bhutanese refugee teacher)

Every year about one third of the teachers go away and their place is taken up by a new set of untrained teachers. It is becoming more and more difficult even to find people with the barest requirement of qualification/ability. (Bhutanese refugee resource teacher)

A girl's job is to cook and wash the plates. (Bhutanese refugee boy student)

Boys don't do any housework. (Bhutanese refugee girl student)

Weakness in science. Performance in science subjects is generally weak. The science laboratory in each refugee school is basically a cupboard containing a few chemicals and pieces of apparatus. There is no running water, gas or electricity in the schools. The few experiments performed are done by the teacher in front of the students. Lack of practical work is an obvious reason for poor performance. Another reason is the lack of qualified teachers. It is a vicious circle. Although many teachers are furthering their studies through distance education courses in Nepal and India, they are only pursuing arts courses because science courses require practical work and laboratory facilities.

Temporary classroom structures. The classrooms, being made of only of bamboo and grass, are in frequent need of repair, requiring funds and much labour. In particular, the roofs can leak during the rainy season, causing the children to suffer and sometimes preventing lessons from taking place at all. Moreover, the water can spoil the desks and mats, shortening their effective lives. Semi-permanent structures would probably be more cost-effective but the Nepalese government does not permit their use.

Teacher turnover. There is a high turnover of teachers, locally referred to as the "brain-drain". Throughout the year many teachers leave to further their education or to seek higher-paid jobs in the private schools outside the camps. This has a doubly adverse effect in the refugee schools: there is a constant need to select and train new teachers; and learning is disrupted each time a teacher leaves – one class had five different teachers in a single year. This has been going on for many years, despite various attempts to halt it.

Gender imbalance. Although the number of girls persisting at school is increasing each year, they are not performing as well as the boys. The society tends to favour males, and the girls are often very shy. There are few female teachers, and no female headteachers or deputies. The author attended a special assembly in one of the schools and was asked to award prizes to the top performing students. There were about fifteen winners who were, embarrassingly, all boys.[29]

Lower primary classes. Many problems still exist in the lower primary classes. The untrained teachers find the new NAPE pupil-centred methods demanding, especially as the younger children are more difficult to handle. The classes tend to be bigger, and the teacher is required to spend a lot of time planning the lessons and preparing the materials for the children's activities. Moreover, teaching in the lower primary classes is generally held in less esteem, and many teachers try to move up to the higher classes as soon as they can. Some classes are therefore faced with a continual change in young and inexperienced teachers.

Analysis of strengths and weaknesses

In the previous sections, the author has identified major strengths and weaknesses of the Bhutanese refugee education programme. Quality will be improved if we can build on these strengths and minimise the weaknesses.

In terms of the conceptual framework, the first five strengths enumerated can be classified under "actors" and the next four strengths under "tools", while the last two strengths fall under "environment". See Table 3.

On the other hand, the first eight problems or weaknesses can all be classified under "environment" and the next two problems under "actors", while the final weakness (lower primary classes) fits better under "tools", since it is mainly concerned with teaching methods. See Table 4.

In summary, it can be seen that the strengths of the Bhutanese Refugee Education Programme are mainly to be found in the actors and tools, whereas the weaknesses are mainly located in the environment. This is, perhaps, not surprising. Quality improvements require an "enabling" environment. A refugee situation would more honestly be described as a "disabling" one.

29 During the presentation, the author asked the headteacher to identify the girl with the highest examination mark. An impromptu prize was awarded to her by the author.

Table 3: Strengths of the BREP in Terms of the Conceptual Framework

Actors	• Refugee participation • Motivation • Cooperation • Orderliness • Management
Tools	• Curriculum development • Teacher training and support • Examinations • Records and reporting (monitoring)
Environment	• Textbooks • Satellite schools

Table 4: Weaknesses of BREP in Terms of the Conceptual Framework

Environment	• Refugee situation • Decreasing funding • Lack of opportunities for further education • Low incentives • Unrecognized teacher training • Teacher absenteeism • Weakness in science • Temporary classroom structures
Actors	• Teacher turnover • Gender imbalance
Tools	• Lower primary classes (teaching methods)

This points a way to improving quality. We should build on the strengths, which focus on the actors and tools. And we should minimise the weaknesses, which focus on the environment. But parts of the refugee environment can be impossible or difficult to change. For example, refugee history cannot be altered. Rape and torture cannot be undone. Moreover, the laws of the host country, the prospects of refugee repatriation or the amount of funds donated by the international community are well beyond the control of the actors in our simple pyramid of refugees and programme managers.[30]

Williams (2001) states that "Because of the multiple meanings, there is not a single way to improve quality". In the final section, we will be focusing on those ways which are realistic and under the control

30 Weaknesses can be difficult to overcome when operating on a tight budget with little room to manoeuvre. Some of the problems in the Bhutanese programme are simply due to lack of resources, where the only obvious way to solve them is with an injection of funds.

of the actors in our pyramid. In particular, the author suggests recommendations for the programme managers (at the top end of the pyramid) which, if implemented, would ultimately benefit the refugees (at the base) in the delivery of quality education.

Priorities and recommendations

There are many factors which can influence the quality of education. Although much research has been done elsewhere on quality in developing countries, which should have general relevance to refugees, it is the intention in this work to highlight and focus on those factors which are specifically relevant to the management of longer-term refugee situations. The author has found it important to look at the whole picture – schools, camps, programme, context – and not just what goes on in the classroom. The broad picture approach is necessary because the major objective of this research is to come up with some practical recommendations for UNHCR and other programme managers which will have an impact on refugee children and the refugee community as a whole.

In this final section we will be considering what lessons can be learned from Nepal. In particular, how did the Bhutanese Refugee Education Programme achieve and maintain good quality? How did it improve and overcome its problems? And what additional steps could be taken to improve it further? We will also make recommendations as to how the quality of refugee education can be improved generally, for the wider refugee world.

Priorities

The main strengths of the Bhutanese programme as perceived by the author are summarized in the following three qualities:[31]

- Positive attitudes
- Recognition of the importance of the teacher
- Good organization

Cooperation and motivation have been persistently promoted and developed for advancing the refugee education cause. Ongoing teacher training and support have greatly contributed to the continued success of the programme. Sound management and cost-effectiveness through stringent monitoring and sheer thrift have enabled the Bhutanese refugee education programme to achieve outstanding results with a minimum of inputs.[32] These are strengths which can be further built on to maintain and improve the quality of the programme even when financial inputs and other resources are diminishing.

31 The same three qualities were found to be important in the education programme for the Sudanese refugees in Uganda (see Introduction, above).

32 Using data supplied by the BREP Field Director, the author calculated that the primary education programme which CARITAS currently implements costs UNHCR only $12 per pupil per year. This is indeed value for money. It is a remarkably small amount considering the quality of the education provided. About 41 per cent of the budget goes into teachers' incentives (an ordinary teacher is paid about $13 per month), 18 per cent on books (an average book costs about $1) and 16 per cent on classroom supplies.

In the following paragraphs we shall be considering three important factors in more detail: motivating refugees, training refugee teachers and finding cost-effective approaches. There are general recommendations for programme managers or implementing partners. The section ends with specific suggestions for UNHCR's possible role in linking the various factors and coordinating improvements in the quality of education given to refugees.

Motivating refugees[33]

> It is the commitment, determination and self-sacrifice of the [Bhutanese] refugee staff that has made the quality education possible. (Amalraj, 2000)

After the initial trauma of displacement has passed, refugees want to get on with their lives and build some kind of future. We have seen that refugees can be highly motivated, enabling them to achieve many objectives in spite of the odds.[34] However, this intrinsic motivation cannot always be guaranteed. Indeed, as the refugee situation shows no signs of ending, refugees can become frustrated and start to lose hope. Their motivation and morale will almost certainly drop. An important function of programme managers is to provide "extrinsic" motivation to the refugees which will reinforce or raise the refugees' own "intrinsic" motivation.

There are various ways of motivating people (Everard and Morris, 1990: 31). Important elements for refugees can be summarized as *responsibility, achievement, recognition and advancement.* Refugees should be encouraged to participate fully in their education programmes, including the planning, monitoring and evaluation phases. If they are given this responsibility, they can often rise to the challenge. A sense of achievement can be very satisfying especially when working against the odds. It can motivate refugees to carry on achieving more. Satisfaction can be enhanced when achievements are recognized by others. It is therefore very important for programme managers and outsiders to recognize and duly acknowledge the accomplishments of the refugees. Refugees also need to satisfy their hopes that there can be a future. They would like advancement and personal development during their time in the camps.

In the case of teachers, refugees should be given responsibility to plan and assess their own lessons, and make suggestions for improving the programme such as changes to the curriculum. They need continued training and support, and their achievements should be recognized, for example, by provision of a certificate. Recognition by their fellow teachers can be encouraged by displaying evidence of good performance, such as putting teacher-made artefacts in the school resource centre. This might also encourage the other teachers to make their own aids. It is important that teachers are also respected by the larger community, and efforts should be made, if necessary, to sensitise the community to the value of education.

---

33 When the author recently asked Brother Mike Foley of JRS what he considered to be the most important factors contributing to the quality of refugee education, his reply was "teacher training and teacher motivation". By "motivation", he meant salaries or "incentives". Although the author entirely agrees that this is a very crucial issue, the monetary aspect of "motivation" is deliberately avoided in this section, in line with the spirit of the present research, where low cost solutions are being sought. (Teacher incentives normally constitute the major part of any UNHCR education budget.) In the same vein, however, the following statement is taken from a report by Ethel Nhleko, Senior Community Services Officer, UNHCR, Kigoma, Tanzania (Nhleko, 2000: 9): "Secondary school teachers should be paid incentives in order to boost their morale which will lead to improved performance."

34 It has been reported in Guinea that, in the normal situation, the Liberian and Sierra Leonean refugees were de-traumatized and highly motivated to undertake school projects, whereas in the new emergency situation, the refugees became re-traumatized and unmotivated (UNHCR/IRC, 2000: 3).

Teachers also need to advance in their professional development. Training should be provided as well as opportunities for career development within the school. Successful teachers can be rewarded with senior positions such as subject heads. It is important to have gender balance among the teachers. Senior female teachers, such as a female headteacher, provide powerful role models for getting more girls to perform well at school. Teachers should be helped, wherever possible, to pursue distance education courses to further their own education ("earn and learn"). Teachers who provide good service over a long period of time should be rewarded for their loyalty by promotion to the next level on the refugee incentive scale, that is, seniority should be recognized as a legitimate qualification.

It is also important to provide good working conditions for the teachers. They should be provided with tables and chairs in both staffroom and classroom. Tea provided during the day is an added bonus for keeping up spirits and welcoming visitors. Refugees appreciate outside visitors; they want to learn from them and at the same time they want the visitor to learn about their plight and perhaps spread the information to the wider world.

Refugee pupils should be motivated at school in the same ways as other children. Lessons should be varied; children need to be challenged; teachers should be competent; there should be regular work with prompt feedback; praise; work should be displayed in classroom; counselling should be available when needed; there should be a loving and caring atmosphere in the classroom; the environment should be clean and safe; special care should be provided for children with disabilities; there should be cooperative group work; tests and examinations should take place; house spirit and rivalry should be fostered in inter-house competitions; there should be co-curricular activities, art, music and sports. Refugee children often have greater needs than ordinary children because of the trauma they have been through. But there is clearly much scope for a good refugee programme to motivate refugee children using the above-mentioned methods.

On special school occasions, prizes can be awarded to children in front of their parents.[35] This is a good opportunity to motivate the whole community. The monetary value of the prize may be minuscule, but that doesn't matter, since the honour of winning it is more important. Prizes should be awarded to the best girl students, not only to the boys, because this will encourage more girls to improve and will send appropriate gender messages to the boys and community at large. Refugee girls frequently perform less well at school simply because they are given additional household duties at home. Several Bhutanese boys told the author that "household duties are a girl's job".

We have seen that the Sudanese and Bhutanese refugee communities have played an immense role in both the establishment and on-going management of the refugee education programmes in Uganda and Nepal respectively. The Liberian and Sierra Leonean refugees in Guinea provide another example: "The programme's history is an inspiring example of success, particularly through well-supported refugee community self-help efforts" (UNHCR/IRC, 2000: 1). In Tanzania, moreover, "the refugee communities have persuaded primary school teachers, social workers and other refugees working for different NGOs to give up some of their incentives in order to pay post-primary school teachers" (UNHCR, 2000c). Sharing incentives is a shining example of refugee cooperation.

35 "14 December has been declared as an Education Day. The programme of activities will include prize-giving to refugees who will be selected by the committee as best student, best teacher, best headteacher" (Ethel Nhleko, UNHCR Tanzania, 8 December 2000, personal communication).

But community support cannot always be guaranteed. It may need to be cultivated, as illustrated in the following example from Pakistan.

> The main challenge will be to request a reasonable community participation without affecting the quality of education that greatly contributed to the improved access and retention ratios during the last years. Therefore a cautious approach will be necessary as in the case of Balochistan, a province which is already disadvantaged, where to convince and motivate refugees regarding the importance of education took a long time. Asking the community to pay for their children's fees, when they are already paying a huge amount to manage their water supply schemes as well as for health services (fees and drugs), could have an adverse effect, as the drop-out rates in higher grades are already high due to the poor economic situation. But it does not mean no community participation. Participation of the community could be obtained to repair schools and provide labour. This can be achieved through a higher level of community mobilization and outreach programmes. (Van De Casteele, 2000)

Girls get motivated by female teachers. (Bhutanese refugee female teacher)

The newly selected teachers are given at first some sort of a hurried basic training at the beginning of the academic year. Later they are sustained through follow-up and supervision by the in-school resource teachers who in turn are trained by the office-based resource teachers. This built-in revival/renewal system of BREP is at the very core of the educational programme. (Bhutanese refugee resource teacher)

Training refugee teachers

The teacher is the most important element for quality education in refugee schools (Sister Carmel Louis, JRS resource teacher, Damak, Nepal, September 2000).

The same is true in Uganda. In the chapter on quality of education in *Education in the refugee-affected areas of Northern Uganda* (Sesnan, Brown and Kabba, 1995: 37–43), the section on teachers is the first and by far the largest.

Other refugee programmes have also found teachers to be the most important factor for quality. At an inter-regional education coordination meeting in Ngara, Tanzania (UNHCR, 2000g), strategies to improve education quality were discussed. Nine problems were highlighted of which four were concerned with lack of resources (classrooms, furniture, water and teaching materials). The other five problems were all related to teachers (lack of skill using new book, difficulties in teaching French and mathematics, lack of discipline among some teachers, poor attendance of female teachers during pregnancy and heavy workload of teachers).

Moreover, in the Somali refugee education programme in Yemen, the following lesson has been learned: "The experience of this programme confirms that although various teaching aids and physical school facilities are of great value, well-trained, dedicated and hard-working teachers are much more important to the success of an education programme" (Gezelius, 1998: 117).

The training and support of refugee teachers is therefore of paramount importance for quality education. "It is important in all cases to build in-service teacher training into refugee school programmes" (Sinclair, 1998: 268).

One of the income generating schemes run by the British aid agency, OXFAM, is to produce chalk for Nepalese schools. Goldhap Camp, Jhapa District, Nepal. UNHCR/12.1997/H.J. Davies

In a project concept note submitted to the Refugee Education Trust, Robin Shawyer stated:

> The quality of primary and secondary education available to refugees in east Africa and the Horn is often poor, in large part because of the lack of qualified teachers. Many primary and secondary school teachers in schools attended by refugees need access to training to improve their performance, to reduce the high turnover of teachers, to motivate teachers and students and to develop the skills within the refugee community to meet the continuing educational needs. The lack of trained teachers has an effect on the capacity of the community to develop the skills to become self-reliant (Shawyer, 2000).

The importance of teacher training for refugees in east Africa and the Horn has been further confirmed by Sarah Norton-Staal, the Senior Regional Adviser for Refugee Children (7 August 2000, personal communication):

> I understand that suggestions for proposals are rather urgently requested. I would like to propose, under the priority category of Education, "Enhancing quality of education through teacher training" as a possible project. I feel that this has been recognized as a critical need in our area. Lack of female teachers is often noted as a problem and thus females could also be targeted in a teacher training programme. Training of teachers is a critical issue for repatriation and successful reintegration.

Teacher training is an effective way of harnessing existing resources efficiently. Trained teachers should be able to communicate their knowledge in child-friendly ways and make maximum use of standard resources such as textbooks and blackboards. They should also know how to be creative and make innovative teaching aids out of locally available materials. Many refugees are recruited into teaching straight from school. They are young and inexperienced. Training is essential if education quality is to be achieved.

Training of refugee teachers can be classified into three categories. First, full-time training in an official institution leads to a recognized qualification. The disadvantages of this method are that it is the most expensive and that the refugee might be away from the camp school for a long period (two years) with no guarantee of return after graduation. Second is distance education, in which the refugee teacher studies for a recognized qualification partly through correspondence. It takes longer but allows the refugee to stay teaching in the camp schools, receiving incentives, throughout the training period. This is probably the most appropriate method, although it demands a lot of the refugee teacher. Third is non-formal training, the usual form of training in a refugee camp, organized by the implementing agency, normally in the camp schools. It doesn't normally lead to any recognized qualification but it is very effective because it is cheap and can cover all the teachers, giving them relevant information and skills on the spot.[36] Workshops lasting from half a day to a couple of weeks (during the school holidays) can be given on specific topics according to needs. The content of the training varies for each workshop, but the initial ones normally include the basics such as lesson planning, the use of the blackboard and other resources, and classroom management. Many refugee teachers have had a deficient education themselves, so that it is also important to include lesson subject matter in the training seminars as well.

Although the blackboard is probably the most important teaching aid, teachers should be taught how to make and use their own visual aids. Moreover, tangible objects are normally more effective in lessons than drawings, so that teachers should be encouraged to make them, using locally available materials.[37] The use of teaching aids can help to make lessons more interesting; teachers need to be taught how to keep children active and interested. Children themselves can also be used as "teaching aids" by the teacher.

Refugee teachers in developing countries often follow the traditional system of teaching, when they tend to lecture and have little interaction with the pupils. They often ask rhetorical questions like "Do you understand?" after which the class replies "Yes, sir!" in chorus. Children should be encouraged to both answer and ask questions. Teachers should be trained in questioning techniques so that the pupils can participate more fully in the lessons and be encouraged to think more critically.

In Nepal, the in-school resource teachers gave advice to the Bhutanese teachers after they had observed a lesson. The author was present on some occasions and was impressed by the expertise of the in-school resource teachers as they critically analysed the lessons. They would first enumerate the positive points and then go on to any negative points. But one essential aspect was usually missing. The teachers themselves were not asked first to assess their own lessons. For sustainability, it is important that teachers reflect on their lessons, trying to identify what went right and wrong, and thinking how they might improve next time. Although it is difficult for inexperienced teachers, if they don't acquire this habit they will never be

36 In Guinea, however, the teacher training that IRC gives to Liberian refugees is officially recognized in Liberia (Nordstrand, 2000: 8). UNHCR should advocate this good practice in other places.

37 The author observed one refugee teacher drawing stones on the blackboard. It would have been better to use real stones, perhaps collected by the children themselves.

able to improve on their own. The in-school resource teachers should therefore encourage a teacher to speak *first* in the after-analysis of a lesson. Refugee teachers can be made less dependent on the advice of the in-school resource teachers by appropriate training in self-evaluation skills. One way of encouraging this is for teachers to insert a "remarks" column in their lesson plans which they fill up with their own comments after each lesson. Another way is for teachers to give a practice lesson to their peers in micro-teaching sessions, after which there is critical analysis among the fellow teachers in a group discussion.[38]

Finding cost-effective approaches

In the preceding sections we have seen that motivation and teacher training are excellent ways of improving quality which do not necessarily need a large input of funds. In this section we will be considering other cost-effective approaches which have been used, or might be used, in the Bhutanese refugee programme. The author suggests that they might be tried in other refugee programmes world-wide, so that money saved might then be used to improve quality in other ways, such as buying more books or paying more teachers.

In-school resource teachers. Refugee participation brings down the costs, especially when all the teacher trainers (in-school resource teachers) are refugees. The system of in-school resource teachers is an economical and sustainable way of providing regular training to the teachers, especially those most in need of it. In cases where classes are merged due to the absence of a teacher, one teacher may have to deal with a class of over 100 pupils. This could be an opportunity for an in-school resource teacher to step in and take over the teaching of the big class, the other teacher assisting and observing.

Screening new teachers. High teacher turnover is wasteful in terms of the loss of investment in training and the need to start selection and training all over again. Initial teacher interviews should include screening for motivation. Where possible, older teachers should be appointed, especially women, since they are likely to have families and be more settled.

In-kind incentives. To combat low financial incentives, teachers could be paid a contribution in-kind. In particular, they could be helped with further studies through distance education programmes. Examples of assistance include provision of a book allowance, granting of examination leave or a contribution towards their tuition fees. An extended programme would ensure that the teacher stays in school over a number of years, while a better-educated teacher benefits the whole class. The offer of clothes could be another help, if the camp receives a bulk donation.

Certificates. A certificate is just a piece of paper and is very cheap to produce. Yet, because of what it represents, it can have an enormous effect on the recipient, in terms of self-esteem, motivation and hope for the future regarding job prospects. Efforts should be made in getting the education of refugee students and the training of refugee teachers recognized by the host government. If these efforts are unsuccessful, the programme managers should take the initiative and award their own certificates, for example, to teachers attending training workshops and for teachers with long-serving experience.[39]

---

38 For more information on self-evaluation, see "Some problems in refugee teacher education and how to overcome them", presented by the author at the International Conference on Education and Training for Refugees and Displaced People in Kampala (Brown, 1995).

39 "All the pupils who have passed the national and the inter-regional examination will be awarded UNHCR/UNICEF certificates on 14 December 2000 which has been declared an Education Day in the Tanzania camps, in commemoration of the 50th anniversary of UNHCR" (Nhleko, 2000: 9).

Books produced in-house. Textbooks actually produced by the programme management can be cheaper and more appropriate than books produced elsewhere. They are heavily used if all the children have their own copies which they can take home. Books should be budgeted to be replaced every three years, but management should always be on the lookout for cost-cutting measures. If some pages of a book are spoiled, the good pages can be kept and combined with the good pages from another spoiled book to make a composite "new" book. When books have finally "died" the paper might be recycled, either in the camp dispensaries for wrapping up medicine or by being sold off to a local paper factory.

The character and success (whatever be the norms to gauge them) of a refugee education programme depend to a large extent on the implementing agency. (Bhutanese refugee resource teacher)

Camp-manufactured items. Various education-related items might be made in the camps and their use should be encouraged, since they would be cheap and appropriate. Their purchase would also benefit the camp economy. Examples are chalk, school bags, whose use can prolong the life of the books, and jute mats, to prevent children sitting on the bare floor where there aren't classroom desks.

Sharing resources. Resources should be shared wherever possible so that maximum use can be obtained from them. Supplementary reading materials and reference books such as dictionaries and atlases are not distributed individually, and must be shared; cooperation of the teachers and pupils is a necessary prerequisite. Teachers are also encouraged to share the teaching aids they make, and good examples of teaching aids should be kept in the school resource centres. Operating a shift system (morning/afternoon) is another way of sharing resources. Although it is not an ideal situation, shifts can work adequately for infant classes which have a shorter day.

High-impact items. To reduce costs, programmes should look for items which are relatively inexpensive but can have a big impact on the quality of education. Blackboard paint is a prime example of this: the quality of a blackboard can greatly contribute to the quality of a lesson, and the application of a coat of blackboard paint can often make a big difference. Newspapers can also have a big impact on refugee motivation and learning. Supplying two or three different newspapers to each school is a cheap way of providing relevant and politically balanced information to refugees. Newspapers also make excellent teaching aids and can have many other uses. Another high-impact example might be a metal trunk to protect valuables from thieves and rats.[40] A further example is a megaphone. Assemblies often take place outside, with enormous numbers of children; use of a megaphone could help many more to hear the proceedings clearly.

Sensitization. Parents may need to be made aware of the importance of education for their children. In particular, there should be awareness programmes to sensitize refugees on the importance of looking after books and materials. Items should be used properly, handled with care and adequately stored. Waste-reducing and recycling methods should be applied wherever possible. If items are not well looked after and are spoiled because of children's negligence, appropriate punishments or sanctions should be administered.

40 When an in-school resource teacher from Beldangi II camp was showing the author some demonstration models of teaching aids which had been produced by the teachers, some of the aids were discovered to have been destroyed by rats.

Monitoring and evaluation. Strict monitoring and thorough record keeping are necessary to hold the programme on track. Corruption, theft and misuse of materials are common in developing countries, especially in chaotic refugee situations where people may be trying to take advantage and turn a quick profit. The situation can be kept in check by close monitoring and necessary follow-up action. Longer-term evaluation is also necessary to ensure that funds are being used in the most cost-effective ways.

Recommendations for UNHCR field offices

Selection of implementing partner. In view of the importance of education and the fact that a substantial portion of UNHCR's budget is often devoted to the education sector, UNHCR should try to appoint an implementing partner which is a specialist in education and has its own independent source of funds. This will ensure that due priority is given to education with the necessary expertise and backup. *Volunteer* international staff would be an added advantage because they are cost-effective and are likely to be more motivated, strengthening the refugees' own motivation.

Monitoring visits to schools. UNHCR field staff should visit schools regularly, but mainly on a random basis to avoid schools making "preparations" for the visit which could hide the true picture. The visits need not be lengthy, but long enough to talk to the headteacher and a few other teachers and students. Some records can be checked and classrooms visited. Quality aspects should be monitored as well as the facilities (school buildings). Although the main purpose of the visit would be for routine monitoring (which should be done in a friendly and non-threatening manner), the field staff should show interest in the school, encouraging the refugees and boosting their morale at every opportunity.

Speech days. UNHCR officers should also visit schools, when invited, on special occasions such as prize-giving days and school celebrations. In their speeches to the whole assembly, which would include parents, they should not forget to recognize and congratulate the excellent hard work and achievements of the refugee community, in particular the teachers and pupils. They should further use this opportunity to sensitize the community on the importance of education and to convey any other vital educational messages.

Training of UNHCR staff. There are very few UNHCR staff who are specialists in education, and most education monitoring which takes place concentrates on fiscal matters and hardware. The generalist staff should receive some training in education so that they are able to plan and monitor the 'soft" quality aspects of an education programme. This will ensure that the relatively substantial funds allocated to the education sector are used for maximum benefit and are not wasted.

Training of refugee teachers. Teacher incentives, school supplies and textbooks usually take up the lion's share of a UNHCR education budget, and the teacher training component can easily be neglected. Non-formal training is not expensive. UNHCR should ensure that appropriate refugee training is included in the annual education plans and budgets of the implementing agencies.

Incentives for refugee teachers. For motivating the refugees, UNHCR should have some kind of graduated incentive scale for the teachers so that those with more qualifications and experience are paid at a higher rate. In particular, the extra work done by heads and teachers with special responsibilities should be recognized.

Headteachers. For the successful running of a school, it is important that the headteachers of the refugee schools are qualified and experienced and have the appropriate leadership qualities. Headteachers or their representatives should be invited to attend general management meetings in the camps, especially when education is on the agenda. UNHCR staff should also try to attend crucial school meetings when requested by the headteacher.

Opportunities for further studies. UNHCR should advocate more scholarship places for further studies, since this would motivate refugees still in school. UNHCR should ensure that a balanced quota of girls are awarded scholarships so that they can carry on with their education and become role models for other girls. Sensitization programmes on gender issues should be continued in the camps.

Inter-agency cooperation. UNHCR should encourage cooperation with all partner agencies so that relevant resources can be shared. In particular, collaboration with the district education officer should be sought. UNHCR could pay a monthly incentive in recognition of the extra workload caused by the presence of the refugees, a move which might ensure cooperation when needed.[41]

Certificates. By contacts and advocacy with the host government, UNHCR should help its implementing agency to get refugee examination results officially recognized. If the host government does not endorse the refugee certificates, UNHCR and implementing partners might consider doing it themselves, in conjunction with other organizations such as UNICEF and UNESCO, where possible.

Recommendations for UNHCR Headquarters

Advocacy for more education funding. In long-term refugee situations, when refugee schools get established, refugee education can fall between two stools, with neither humanitarian nor development donors taking responsibility. UNHCR should advocate more funds so that education programmes can be adequately resourced. UNHCR, with support from UNICEF and UNESCO, might approach development donors, such as the World Bank and governments of developed countries, trying to convince them of the need and of their responsibility to donate to longer-term refugee education.

Education database. Donors are more likely to part with their funds if they can be given hard evidence of the shortage of teachers, classrooms and materials in the refugee camps. It would therefore be useful if UNHCR headquarters could improve the existing reporting procedures for collecting and saving the most essential information and education statistics from country programmes world-wide. This would also promote a uniformity of standards and could help Headquarters identify where the greatest educational needs are. With assistance from the field, a more effective reporting format should be developed and, to ensure sustainability, incorporated into the general UNHCR programming procedures.

Roster of specialist NGOs. UNHCR should keep a roster of specialist NGOs who would be willing to implement education programmes in various parts of the world. These NGOs would preferably have access to resources of their own. UNHCR field offices tend to choose implementing partners who are already on the ground but have no specific expertise in education. The roster would allow a wider choice for the field offices.

41 Wherever possible, UNHCR should provide assistance to the host population so that positive attitudes of the host community towards the refugees would be promoted.

Voluntary organizations. UNHCR should also foster close relationships with voluntary organizations, and encourage the recruitment of volunteers, which can be a very cost-effective mechanism. Many volunteers would welcome the challenge of serving in a far away place, and refugees are often motivated by the presence of foreign experts.

Education guidelines. The standards of UNHCR education programmes across the world vary. This is partly due to the fact that budget allocations are decided by the particular UNHCR country offices. Some UNHCR offices may attach more importance than others to education, depending on the attitudes of the individual staff members. In these cases, relatively more funds may be allocated to education programmes. But education should not be left to the whims of particular individuals. UNHCR headquarters should sensitize its field offices to the importance of education by issuing circulars, guidelines and training materials. In particular, the current education guidelines (UNHCR, 1995) should be updated.

Development of training tools. There are very few specialist education officers on UNHCR's staff. Most education programmes are currently monitored by other specialist staff, such as community services officers, or general staff, such as field officers and programme officers. Headquarters should therefore consider producing a straightforward tool to help the field staff monitor their education programmes. This tool could be in the form of simple guidance notes and an indicator checklist, and would be initially developed with assistance from the field, based on the experiences and recommendations of ongoing programmes. Guidance tools should be given to implementing partner staff as well, especially as many of these agencies are managing multi-sectoral programmes and may have no particular expertise, or even experience, in running education programmes.

Inter-agency collaboration on certification. UNHCR should actively collaborate with other agencies such as UNICEF and UNESCO to find ways of solving the certification problem, which is common in many situations of emergency and crisis throughout the world.[42]

Further research. UNHCR should continue to promote research in vital aspects of refugee education and best practices, establishing links with universities and other key personnel and institutions. The present paper has dealt with the broad picture of refugee education. Further detailed research on specific issues of quality, especially at the classroom level, might lead to fruitful results. Refugee camps are characterized by massive concentrations of people. This congestion often leads to over-sized schools and other problems. Research is needed to find cost-effective approaches and the best ways of dealing with the reality of enormous schools and large classes, in situations of stress and limited resources. The divide between the ivory towers of academia and the real world of refugees also needs to be bridged. UNHCR could encourage the involvement of practitioners from the field and refugee scholars themselves in identifying and carrying out appropriate research projects in refugee education.

42 "An issue that is connected to quality is that of certification, both of pupils and of teachers. Without proper certificates, how can serious training be done?" (Sister Lolin Menendez, JRS, 21 September 2000, personal communication).

Conclusion

Although UNHCR is experiencing a financial crisis, with drastic consequences for refugee education, improvements in the quality of education in refugee schools are achievable and need not cost much money. Lessons learned from the refugee programme in Nepal and elsewhere have shown that the following factors are important for quality education: positive attitudes such as motivation and cooperation; teacher training and support; and cost-effective approaches. Managers of refugee education programmes throughout the world are advised to address these factors and learn from the Bhutanese case study in their efforts to find affordable and economical solutions for improving the quality of refugee education in their own localities.

Appendix

The following list summarizes the categories of people interviewed and the places visited in Nepal, including those people whom the author contacted while in Geneva prior to his field trip.

- UNHCR Headquarters, Geneva, Switzerland: many officers, including those on the Nepal Desk, staff members formerly serving in Nepal, officers in the Education, Community Services and Refugee Children units, and other experts.
- UNHCR Branch Office, Kathmandu, Nepal: Representative, Deputy Representative and Protection Officer.
- UNHCR Sub-Office, Jhapa, Nepal: Head of Sub-Office, Programme Assistant and Programme Monitoring Officers.
- Representatives of the government of Nepal in Jhapa: District Education Officer, Deputy Director of the Refugee Coordination Unit, Beldangi I Camp Supervisor.
- CARITAS Office, Damak: Field Director, Assistant Field Director, Education Coordinators, Resource Teachers, Procurement Officer and other staff.
- Refugee schools in Beldangi (I, II and II-Extension), Sanischare, Goldhap, Timai and Khudunabari: headteachers, assistant heads, extension and sector in-charges, in-school resource teachers, special needs support teachers, store in-charges, counsellors, teachers and pupils.
- Refugee leaders: camp secretaries and Beldangi I Focal Person for Women.
- Refugee community: parents, women's group, students and vocational training group for the disabled in Beldangi I.
- Local community: headteacher and teachers of Siddhartha Boarding Higher Secondary School, programme coordinator of vocational training centre.

References

Amalraj, P. S. (2000). *An appeal to the Refugee Education Trust.* Damak: CARITAS-Nepal.

Appadu, K. and Retamal, G. (1998). "Education for Eritrean and Ethiopian refugees in Sudan", in G. Retamal and R. Aedo-Richmond (eds.). *Education as a humanitarian response.* London: Cassell and Geneva: UNESCO International Bureau of Education: 45–58.

Brown, T. (1995). "Some problems in refugee teacher education and how to overcome them", paper presented at the International Conference on Education and Training for Refugees and Displaced People, Kampala.

CARITAS-Nepal (1999). *Final sub-project monitoring report (SPMR). Part II.* Kathmandu: UNHCR.

CARITAS-Nepal (2000). *Office procedures, job descriptions and personnel policy.* Damak: CARITAS-Nepal.

CARITAS-Nepal/UNHCR (n.d.). *Bhutanese Refugee Education Programme (BREP).* Kathmandu: UNHCR.

Everard, B. and Morris, G. (1990). *Effective School Management.* London: Paul Chapman Publishing.

Gezelius, H. (1998). "The Somali refugee primary school in the Republic of Yemen", in G. Retamal and R. Aedo-Richmond (eds.). *Education as a humanitarian response.* London: Cassell, and Geneva: UNESCO International Bureau of Education: 106–18.

Heneveld, E. and Craig, H. (1995). *Schools count: World Bank project designs and the quality of education in Sub-Saharan Africa.* Washington, DC: World Bank.

Lange, E. (1998). *The IRC education programme for refugees in Guinea, 1991–1998: a best practice study.* Geneva: UNHCR.

McDonogh, O. (1996). *Review of APSO's involvement in the Bhutanese primary education programme.* Dublin: APSO.

Meera, R. A. (1999). *Integrated education for the special needs children.* Damak: CARITAS-Nepal.

Meera, R. A. (n.d.). *Tips for teachers of special needs children in integrated education.* Damak: CARITAS-Nepal.

Naumowicz Gustafson, D. (2000). "Education for repatriation in Bosnia and Herzegovina", (unpublished draft).

Nhleko, E. (2000). *Education programme in the refugee camps in Kigoma and Kagera regions of Tanzania: report on primary and post-primary examinations in the year 2000.* Dar es Salaam: UNHCR.

Nordstrand, M. (2000). *End of assignment report: education.* Monrovia: UNHCR.

Refugees International (2000). "Liberian refugees plead for their children's education", *Refugees International Bulletin,* 22 June.

Sesnan, B. (1990). *Education for Sudanese refugees in Uganda.* Kampala: EPSR.

Sesnan, B., Brown, T. and Kabba, M. G. (1995). *Education in the refugee-affected areas of northern Uganda.* Kampala: UNHCR.

Shawyer, R. (2000). *Project concept note: teacher training for refugees in eastern Africa and the Horn.* Geneva: UNHCR.

Sinclair, M. (1998). "Refugee education in the mid–1990s", in G. Retamal and R. Aedo-Richmond (eds.). *Education as a humanitarian response.* London: Cassell, and Geneva: UNESCO International Bureau of Education: 262–70.

Sinclair, M. (2001). "Education in emergencies", in Jeff Crisp, Christopher Talbot and Daiana B. Cipollone (eds.). *Learning for a Future: Refugee Education in Developing Countries,* UNHCR, Geneva.

Smawfield, D. (1998). "Refugee education in an international perspective: the education of Mozambican refugees in Malawi, 1987–1993", in G. Retamal and R. Aedo-Richmond (eds.). *Education as a humanitarian response.* London: Cassell, and Geneva: UNESCO International Bureau of Education: 27–44.

UN (1999). *Common country assessment.* Nepal: UN.

UNHCR (1995). *Revised (1995) Guidelines for Educational Assistance to Refugees.* Geneva: UNHCR.

UNHCR (1997). *Review of UNHCR's refugee education activities.* Geneva: UNHCR.

UNHCR (1999). *Situation Report, June 1999, Kigoma, Tanzania.* Dar es Salaam: UNHCR.

UNHCR (2000a). *Refugee education for Afghani refugees in Balochistan – Pakistan.* Quetta: UNHCR.

UNHCR (2000b). *Community services monthly report – November 2000.* Nairobi: UNHCR.

UNHCR (2000c). *Proposal for funding of post-primary education.* Kigoma: UNHCR.

UNHCR (2000d). *Briefing note on country programme.* Kathmandu: UNHCR.

UNHCR (2000e). *Country operation plan.* Kathmandu: UNHCR.

UNHCR (2000f). *Bhutanese refugees in Nepal.* Kathmandu: UNHCR.

UNHCR (2000g). *Inter-regional education coordination meeting, Ngara, 15–16 March 2000.* Dar es Salaam: UNHCR.

UNHCR/CARITAS-Nepal (1998). *Bhutanese refugee education programme.* Geneva: UNHCR,PTSS.

UNHCR/CARITAS-Nepal (1999). *Camp school guidelines.* CARITAS-Nepal, Damak.

UNHCR/IRC (2000). "Country presentation: refugee school system in Guinea" (paper presented at the Inter-Agency Consultation on Education in Situations of Emergency and Crisis, Geneva, October).

UNICEF (2000). "Defining quality" (paper presented at the International Working Group on Education meeting, Florence, June).

Van De Casteele, G. (2000). *Community participation in the education sector.* Islamabad: UNHCR.

Williams, J. (2001). "On school quality and attainment", in Jeff Crisp, Christopher Talbot and Daiana B. Cipollone (eds.). *Learning for a Future: Refugee Education in Developing Countries,* UNHCR, Geneva.

Chapter 4
Peace Education and Refugee Youth

Marc Sommers

Prologue

The challenge of peace and the power of Rambo[1]

Why do people need to be educated on how to be peaceful? Are human beings inherently violent and divisive? The challenge of peace is an ancient concern, one that has preoccupied religions across the world for millennia.[2] The results of their efforts have been decidedly mixed. John Ferguson has observed that "Of the great religions Christianity and Buddhism have been the most clearly pacifist in their origins and essence". Yet Ferguson also notes that even these religions "have been deeply involved with militarism from a fairly early stage in their history" (1978: 157). Such gaps between words and action have led some towards despair, among them religious studies expert Raimon Panikkar, who has concluded that "religions have contributed precious little to the keeping of peace" (1999: 187).

The quest for peace nonetheless continues. It has spawned, among other developments, a cottage industry of recent literature, manuals and initiatives, both secular and religious, designed to promote peaceful behaviour and resolve conflicts. But such efforts have been regularly confronted by more violence, in addition to waves of powerful messages of heroism and redemption through war and violence. In popular culture, just wars and righteous warriors are much more prevalent than peace and pacifists. As Joanna Bourke has commented, "Long before any prospect of real combat, boys and girls, men and women, [create] narratives of pleasure around acts of killing", concluding that "it is not difficult to see the attraction of combat literature and films" (1999: 4–5).

But if "martial combat has become an integral part of the modern imagination" (ibid.), its impact on youth has proved particularly strong. Reflecting on African youth, Ali El-Kenz explains that, in the globalized modern world, "the frustration of the young is aggravated by imaginations which feed on television, radio and cinema". He lists "Bruce Lee, Rambo and an infinite succession of James Bonds" as among their most

---

1 The author wishes to acknowledge the assistance of Mwachofi Singo, who served as a Field Researcher during fieldwork in Kenya, and Betsy Mull and Alberta P. Addison, who both served as Research Assistants during the archival research phase. Mr Singo is a Lecturer with the Department of Government and Public Administration and Associate at the Centre for Refugee Studies, Moi University. Ms Mull is a graduate of the Graduate School of Education and Human Development at George Washington University and now teaches in the Washington, DC area. Ms Addison, is a graduate student in Boston University's School of Education. Special thanks are also due to the UNHCR staff in Uganda and Kenya, the Jesuit Refugee Service staff in Adjumani, Uganda, DED staff at Imvepi Refugee Camp near Arua, Uganda, and Sue Mulcock, Professional Assistant, Evaluation and Policy Analysis Unit, UNHCR.

2 It appears to have been a much more recent philosophical concern. Howard P. Kainz has noted that "elaborate and detailed philosophical thinking about peace comes to the fore primarily in the last five centuries". He adds that, "It is probably no accident that the last five centuries have also witnessed the emergence to pre-eminence of that peculiar institution, the nation state" (1987: x).

popular icons (1996: 55). The Sierra Leone case, Paul Richards notes, documents the peculiar power of Rambo. There, youths have interpreted the movie character from the initial First Blood movie as "a trickster figure in the classic West African mould" (1996: 59) caught up in a conflict that "serves to wake up society at large to the neglected cleverness of youth" (ibid: 58). Richards further notes that Liberian and Sierra Leonean rebel leaders, "alert to the political potential of the Rambo message" (ibid.), regularly screened *First Blood* for their young captives.

In a world where attempts at cultivating cultures of peace are confronted by the fact that "it is a small step from the culture of violence to its actual practice" (El-Kenz, 1996: 55), refugees and other forced migrants, most of them victims of violence, struggle to re-establish peaceful lives. It is not an easy task, particularly for youth, who are frequently drawn into violent activities. Many aid agencies have responded by offering peace education programming. Examining some of these initiatives and considering the context of violence in refugee youth lives will be the subject of this report.

Senegalese refugees at the Nouakchott site, Mauritania. UNHCR/09.1989/A. Billard

Introduction

This report will examine peace education concepts, assumptions and programmes for refugee populations that are being conducted by international humanitarian agencies. It will also investigate the lives of a primary peace education target group in refugee populations – refugee youth – to understand the violence they confront and their responses to it.

Since refugees constitute one of many groups involved with peace education activities, the report will review literature and knowledge about peace education to situate refugee experiences in a broader context. It will also examine literature and knowledge about refugee and other youth involved in violence.

Refugee youth have been highlighted as "the most explosive segment" of a population in conflict-related situations (Retamal and Devadoss, 1998: 87). In the highly influential report prepared by Graça Machel on children in armed conflict, education for forced migrant adolescents is recognized as "particularly effective in assisting [their] psychosocial wellbeing" and "keeping them out of military service" (Machel, 1996: 56). In addition to military recruitment, this population is also considered "at high risk of prostitution, indoctrination ... and criminality" (UNHCR, 1997: 18).

One of the central problems involving refugee youth is the wide variety of ways in which they are defined. Lowicki (2000) notes, for example, that the World Health Organization defines them as people between 10 and 24 years old. The Lutheran World Foundation in the Kakuma refugee camps in Kenya states that they range from ages 7 to 40. In some cultures a youth is anyone who is unmarried. For purposes of clarity, in this report "youth" will refer to people between the ages of 12 and 30. Although this definition is no less arbitrary than many others, it is an attempt reasonably to integrate the ideas of adolescence and young adults into one category.

A central component of this report will be findings drawn from a case study of an emerging peace education programme for refugees in Kenya and Uganda, most of whom were from Somalia and Sudan. This programme is run by UNHCR, whose experts have not only supervised implementing partners carrying out the programme, a role that UNHCR typically plays, but also spearheaded its development and execution, something UNHCR does not often do. Field research with peace education implementers and participants will be examined, together with findings drawn from interviews with refugee youth, women's groups, religious congregations and leaders. Analysis of interviews with UNHCR officials about peace education, and with a selection of officials from other aid agencies involved with peace education, will also be included.

Among the primary target audiences for this report is UNHCR and its partners who are engaged in peace education activities. Accordingly, this report is designed to provide an enhanced understanding of critical issues surrounding peace education efforts and a primary target group, refugee youth. It will review lessons that can be drawn from present refugee and agency experience, recommend policy options for future action, and, additionally, consider how the report's findings can be used to inform UNHCR's educational policy and guidelines relating to peace education and related activities mentioned in UNHCR's *Revised (1995) Guidelines for Educational Assistance to Refugees.* The guidelines state that "education for peace, cooperation, conflict resolution and reconciliation" are all "prerequisites for the durable solution of voluntary repatriation and reconstruction" whose promotion can "avoid repetition of conflict by a new generation" (UNHCR, 1995: 53).

One caveat, however, requires mention. The breadth of peace education as field of endeavour has created an overlap between peace education and conflict resolution initiatives. Both address the themes of peace, cooperation and reconciliation, and train people in problem-solving skills. The terms "conflict resolution" and "peacemaking" can also be seen as complimentary if not interchangeable.[3] But significant differences emerge at the operational level. Peace education initiatives tend to teach about how to prevent conflicts before they take place. Its teachers often present overarching peace-related themes to a wide range of students, from school-age children in formal schools to adults in non-formal settings. Conflict resolution initiatives, on the other hand, typically address specific, context-based issues about conflicts that already exist. Adults are the primary target audience. This distinction will be used to separate the focus of this report – peace education – from conflict resolution and conflict mediation-based programmes.

The report will first review some of the literature on peace education concepts and programmes, as well as those pertaining to refugee youth and violent youth more generally. It will then turn to the objectives, methods and findings drawn from the field research conducted in Kenya and Uganda. Interviews with officials at UNHCR's headquarters office in Geneva, Switzerland, and with peace education experts will also be incorporated into this discussion. The report will close with a review of conclusions and recommendations relating to peace education and refugee youth.

The peace education world

"Peace" is a broad concept with spiritual and practical connotations. It can imply a state of inner calm or the end of a conflict. As Lincoln P. Bloomfield notes, "Peace is what you think it is (or want it to be)" (Bloomfield, 1986: 237). This expansive quality has led to misunderstandings about peace education. Some observers consider it vague, preachy, insubstantial and perhaps even a waste of time. This was certainly the impression of a number of humanitarian agency officials interviewed in east Africa. Many of those not directly involved with peace education programming displayed a poor grasp of its content and objectives. As a result, some were sceptical and even suspicious of it. One emergency education expert noted that this sort of reaction has fuelled an inherent tension over peace education programming for refugees. While many aid agency officials question the utility of peace education, "refugee communities like it, and the donors do, too".

Donor support is, in fact, constrained by the hesitation of some donor agencies to support any education initiatives during humanitarian emergencies. One donor official explained that her agency did not "fund education because it's not relief. It's [a] development activity".[4] The tendency for relief agencies more generally to "see education as a development activity" (Foster, 1995: 20) is underscored by its absence from the areas covered by the Sphere Project. This groundbreaking initiative is spearheaded by a diverse array of humanitarian organizations, led by the humanitarian consortia (sometimes described as alliances or coalitions) Steering Committee for Humanitarian Response (SCHR) and InterAction, with support from VOICE, the International Council of Voluntary Associations (ICVA) and the International Committee of the Red Cross (ICRC). The Sphere Project aims to provide "minimum acceptable levels" (Sphere Project,

3 See, for example, Aline M. Stomfay-Stitz' characterization of "the concept of teaching conflict-resolution or peacemaking skills to children and young people" (1993: 297).

4 This issue is detailed in the author's "Emergency Education for Children" (Sommers, 1999).

1998: 2) of humanitarian assistance in five categories: water supply and sanitation, nutrition, food aid, shelter and site planning, and health services. The authors emphasize that these minimum standards "of what people have a right to expect from humanitarian assistance" (ibid.) are also "linked explicitly to fundamental human rights and humanitarian principles" (ibid: 1).

Two officials involved in the Sphere Project stated that education was considered as a potential category by Sphere's authors but ultimately dropped because a majority of committee members did not view it as an essential emergency provision. Education's exclusion highlights a widespread view of education as a secondary humanitarian concern. As one official who helped develop the Sphere standards observed, "Essentially we were looking at what had to be done in the first few weeks of an emergency to save lives". But education may in fact be as vital to the preservation of human life as the five assistance categories addressed by the Sphere Project, as it has been widely cited as a basic protection tool for victims of humanitarian emergencies.[5]

Access to education, moreover, has also been identified as a fundamental human right. Article 28 of the United Nations' 1989 Convention on the Rights of the Child (CRC) states that "Each child has the right to education" (CRC, 1989). Refugee children are covered by this treaty, since "all CRC rights are to be granted to all persons under 18 years of age (Art. 1) without discrimination of any kind (Art. 2)". The Machel report notes that denying education to refugee children "clearly contravenes" Article 22 of the 1951 Convention relating to the Status of Refugees (which states that refugees should receive "the same treatment as is accorded to nationals with respect to elementary education") in addition to Article 28 of the CRC, and urges that agencies and governments "ensure that education services are part of both relief and immediate reconstruction activities" (Machel, 1996: 57).

Peace education is a component of a child's right to education. Section 1(d) of Article 29 of the 1989 Convention on the Rights of the Child addresses one aim of education that specifically applies to the subject of this report:

> The preparation of the child for responsible life in a free society, in the spirit of understanding, peace, tolerance, equality of sexes, and friendship among all peoples, ethnic, national and religious groups and persons of indigenous origin.

Peace education, then, can be interpreted not only as an essential component of a child's educational experience but an instrument for the promotion of peaceful, responsible, tolerant, equitable, friendly and free societies. The connection between teaching schoolchildren about peace and the cultivation of peaceful societies suggested here is one of the central assumptions of peace education, and will be among the assumptions considered here.

5 See, for example, Boyden and Ryder, 1996; Foster, 1995; Retamal and Aedo-Richmond, 1998; and UNHCR, 1994.

Thinking about peace and peace education

A split in approaches among peace researchers has created two concepts of significance to peace education: positive and negative peace. David Hicks explained the evolution of this divide in chronological terms. He noted that, beginning in the 1950s, "the initial emphasis in peace research was on direct (personal) violence" such as "assault, torture, terrorism, or war" (1988: 6). He further noted that the emphasis on conflict led peace to be defined "as merely the absence of war", or negative peace (ibid.). By the late 1960s and early 1970s, however, definitions of peace emphasized violence that was indirect and structural in nature. This shift was directly influenced by Johan Galtung's conception of "structural violence" (Galtung, 1969).

Galtung's expansion of the definition of violence led to a changed definition of peace and non-violence. Accordingly, many peace researchers argued that the movement towards peace involved not simply eradicating war but "cooperation and non-violent social change, aimed at creating more equitable and just structures in a society" (Hicks, 1988: 6). Hicks termed this second approach positive peace. His diagram illuminates the difference between negative and positive peace (Figure 1).

Negative and positive peace, two concepts that were once thought to be in opposition to each other, are increasingly seen as complimentary. Kenneth Boulding, whom Betty A. Reardon identifies as a "leading opponent" of the positive peace–negative peace separation (Reardon, 1988: 11), attempted to unify these two concepts. Boulding's idea, which he called "stable peace", borrowed the notion of the absence of war from negative peace. Stable peace, he explained, "can be defined as a situation between two independent

Somali refugees at a peace education lesson in Abdulaziz Primary School, Ifo Camp, Kenya. UNHCR/07.1999/B. Press

nations in which neither has any significant plans to go to war with the other" (Boulding, 1991: 108). But Boulding also drew from the positive peace concept. Research on stable peace, he said, entailed exploring how social systems such as "religion or ideology" and economic behaviour "diminish or increase the chances of movement towards stable peace" (ibid: 111). The accent of his research is on education itself, for "the development of stable peace is fundamentally a learning process" (ibid.). Boulding also admits that the process itself remains largely unknown.

Figure 1: "Defining Peace"

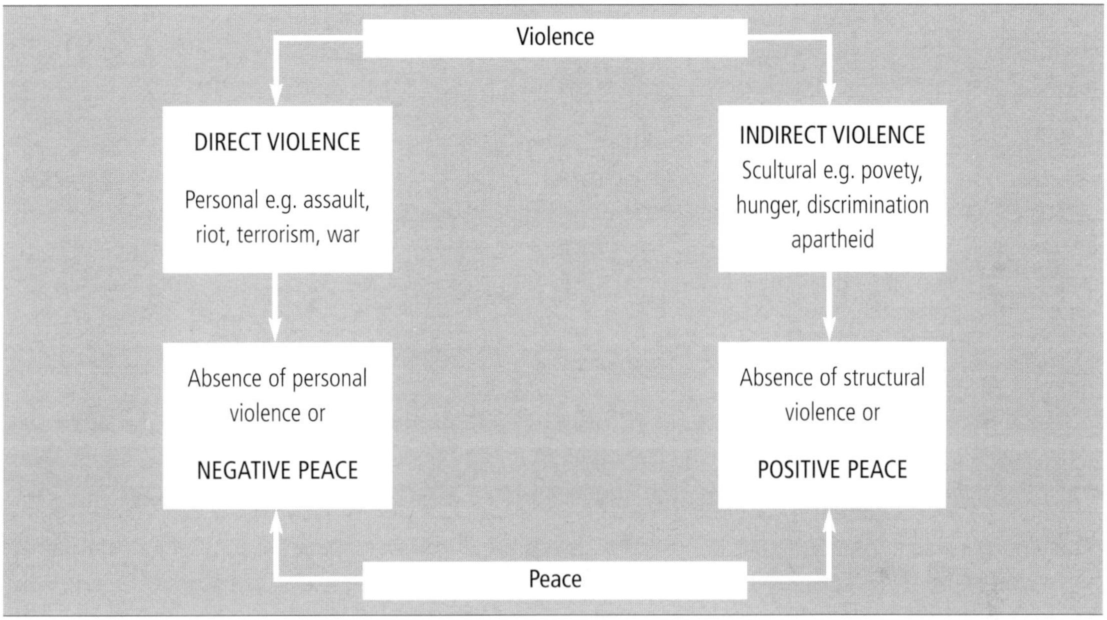

Source: Hicks, 1988

Galtung takes a different approach. Where Boulding focuses his gaze on places where peace already exists, Galtung examines situations where it does not. Conflict is his starting point. In Galtung's view, conflict is always present and cannot be permanently "(re)solved" (1996: 265). As a result, peace cannot be achieved by attempting to eradicate conflict. Conflict must be turned into a non-violent activity. As Galtung states, "Peace is what we have when creative conflict transformation takes place non-violently" (ibid.).

Here, Galtung seems to be a researcher from the negative peace fold. Conflict is a fact of social life. Peace is defined by the absence of violence. Yet his research approach crosses directly into areas Hicks identified as positive peace. He argues that the transformation from violent to non-violent conflict "should be peaceful in itself, meaning low on structural and cultural violence" (ibid.).

While the ideas of Boulding and Galtung suggest that the positive–negative peace dichotomy may ultimately be a false one, Reardon observed that many peace educators continued to emphasize the idea of negative peace because it was comparatively easy to teach. Most peace education teaching, she said, still "focused on negative peace – that is, on reducing the likelihood of war" (1988: 14). Positive peace, on the other hand, was still "not conceptually clear enough for curriculum-planning purposes" (ibid: 13).

The peace education field is still evolving. Many of the programmes to be reviewed here suggest that, like Boulding and Galtung, peace education is increasingly incorporating positive and negative peace components together, mixing, for example, discussions about values and rights connected to peace with the identification of factors that can lead to violence. One such approach is encompassed in an emerging field known as futures education, which, as one expert observed, focuses "on children's dark or hopeful visions of the future". Many futures educationalists, indeed, emphasize the need to bolster optimism and empowerment in children. Frank Hutchinson, for example, argues that "In too many cases, children's hopes and fears are put at a severe discount, with a failure to address their concerns responsibly and in empowering ways" (1998: 133). A central question in futures education is how to "foster learning environments likely to enhance outcomes that actually benefit young people and empower them to change their situations" (ibid: 142). Implicit in this argument is that, should this occur, young people would steer clear of violence and direct themselves towards a peaceful and satisfying path of action.

If conceptual issues in the peace education field seem to be coming together, however, at least one important difference still divides the field. Peace education can be taught as an explicit course or module, such as the peace education package (PEP) developed for Somalia and described in Aguilar and Retamal's UN discussion document (1998). It can also be infused into existing courses, which Hicks describes as "the creation of a dimension across the curriculum" (1988: 11) which incorporates skills (empathy, cooperation) and attitudes (a commitment to justice, respect for others and oneself) with knowledge (about conflict, peace, power). Some educators have further noted that the pedagogical approaches of teachers do not promote values relating to peace and non-violence. Under the section heading "Teaching as violence", Barsh and Marlor argue that "authoritarian instruction is a form of domination, and implicitly legitimizes domination". Moreover, they contend that being taught about "how 'they' think and act, not how 'I' think and act ... denigrates the students' own lives and experiences" (2000: 33).

Peace education as a formal subject, it must be said, has arisen primarily in the Western world. This hardly means that peace education was cultivated only in the West. But it does mean that the mainstream peace education field has cultivated assumptions that are grounded in Western traditions. Here are some prominent examples. First, most peace education approaches centre on schoolchildren. Yet in most poor, non-Western countries, significant numbers of children drop out of school, often early in the formal education process. Second, though it may be assumed that teaching methods are authoritarian, classrooms are often not as authoritarian as the work environments that school drop-outs face. Third, a number of peace education approaches highlight the significance of training teachers to teach differently. But teachers, whom Reardon, among many others, believes constitute "the very heart of the educational process" (1997: 56), are already, in many non-Western countries, poorly trained in the subjects they teach. Changing the way in which teachers are trained, particularly in resource-poor countries where training opportunities are already limited, may be viewed as unreasonable or practically impossible.

In addition to these realities, there is the challenge of national and regional examinations. In the many countries where examination results are used to gauge educational quality, any expansion of subjects (to include peace education), revision of existing curricula (to instil peace education themes, values and concepts into existing subjects) or reforms in pedagogy (to change the way in which teachers teach) might not only call for increased investment levels that in many countries are unattainable but directly conflict with existing educational priorities. Decreasing classroom periods reserved for exam subjects, even in the cause of peace education, would no doubt cause some educators, students and, not least, parents, considerable concern.

Peace education critiques

The tone in most peace education literature is buoyant. Stomfay-Stitz, for example, observes that the development of peace education in the United States has been "embodied in a philosophy of hope in the future" in which "education is an instrument of [peaceful] change" (1993: 335). Such optimism is also central to the educational philosophy of Peace Education International, a US-based NGO. "Peace Education", one article on their website states, "is the holistic umbrella that encompasses learning how to be a peacemaker and a peace builder based on the theories of non-violence and human behaviour."[6]

The emphasis on transforming the behaviour and attitudes of individuals is widely mentioned as a central objective of peace education and the peace-building process.[7] Boyden and Ryder consider it the primary underlying assumption of peace education, which they state as follows:

> That conflicts are the result of learned attitudes and learned behaviour and that it is possible to change both attitudes and behaviour through educational interventions. (1996: 51)

This characteristic of peace education has attracted two primary criticisms which will now be examined. The first points out peace education's generally poor evaluation record. The second calls into question the tendency of peace education programming to focus on children.

The implicit overarching goal of peace education – to replace violence with peace – is obviously a broad and daunting challenge. Violence is a component of human experience. For some observers, this turns the task of evaluating peace education into an unreasonable expectation. Consider former UNICEF staff member Anna Obura's response to the following question:

> Is there any way of measuring the outcome of Peace Education? My own answer would be in the negative ... Just as Education cannot solve the problems of unemployment – that is the business of economic planners in a nation – so Peace Education cannot be expected to prevent war. (1996: 5)

Obura's explanation underscores the lofty goals of many peace education programmes, making the success of any programme difficult to determine and hard to measure. As Aguilar and Retamal note, "no systematic evaluation has been carried out in order to assess the relevance of [peace education] experiences and the impact of their methodological approaches" (1998: 41). This state of affairs has created the same potential hazard that UNICEF's Mary Joy Pigozzi warns has already arisen for emergency education: the fact that, without sufficient evaluation, "we ... run the risk of promoting activities that are not, in the long run, in a child's best interest" (1999: 19).

6 Peace Education International (1997–98), see www.kidspeacenet.com

7 Behavioural and attitudinal transformations are central to the thesis of Johan Galtung (1996), for example. Another example is UNICEF's peace education approach, which "promotes the development of values as the basis for behavioural change, and views behaviour as an indicator of an individual's or group's values" (Fountain, 1999: 4).

The question of children's best interests, and those of the communities they belong to, lies at the core of the second peace education critique. Psychologist Ed Cairns has observed that "adults continue to pursue conflictive relations" while peace educators focus on changing the behaviour of children (Boyden and Ryder, 1996: 55). Peace education thus positions itself between schoolchildren and adults in the same community, making it "virtually impossible for education to inculcate peaceful values in children when adult role models are built on conflict". In fact, cultivating a disjunction between values promoted at home and in school may cause "anxiety and distress in children" rather than optimism and peacebuilding (ibid.: 55–6).

This is a serious charge. If it is true, then educating school children about peace is counterproductive, as it serves to increase the distance between peace education's work and its goals. But instead of addressing this criticism directly, peace educators tend to emphasize the universally commendable principles inherent in their work and the paramount importance of addressing children's needs. To most, educating children about peace seems a manifestly logical starting place for cultivating peaceful change in society. Many, moreover, cite the fact that access to education, and, somewhat indirectly, peace education, are the rights of all children guaranteed by internationally sanctioned instruments.

As a result, the inspiring and hard-to-reach mission of peace education has led its implementers to view their methodologies uncritically: if peace is good then peace education must be good. The outcome can be fairly sentimental. At the end of her book on peace education, Stomfay-Stitz notes that "there is one common dream that could unite all – concern for children". She adds that "children and young people should be the heart and core of peace education" (1993: 343–44). The introduction to a peace education manual for schools in Bosnia-Herzegovina is justified in a still more expansive fashion: "It is only by placing the struggle to understand the complexities of what it means to be a human being ... alongside the struggle to understand the world in which we all live, that people can begin to examine the separate strands that contribute towards existence" (Dulic and Chamberlain, 1998: v).

Good intentions, of course, do not guarantee good results. Patience and faith that positive outcomes will eventually arrive are ultimately insufficient. Galtung suggests that the connection between children and peace faces a fundamental challenge:

> If *peace* and war are, above all, [about] relations among states, and if peace *education* is something that takes place, above all, among teachers and pupils at school, then how are these pupils going to make use of what they have learnt? (1983: 282)

Boyden and Ryder go still further, calling the entire peace education approach into question:

> Since it is group identity and group behaviour, rather than inter-personal behaviour, that are determinant in armed conflict it is suggested that many of the premises upon which peace education and similar approaches are built are false. (1996: 56)

At the core of Boyden and Ryder's criticism is peace education's tendency to concentrate not simply on children but individuals instead of groups. This emphasis on individuals is an issue considered by An-Na'im in his analysis of international human rights. In both fields, individuals are the primary focus: the target for behaviour and attitude change in most peace education programmes and the primary optic of international human rights instruments. But the strong emphasis on the individual, An-Na'im argues, is primarily based on a Western conception. In the case of human rights, Western elites have asserted their claim to "an exclusive right to prescribe the essential concept and normative content of human rights for all societies to implement" (1998: 8). An-Na'im considers the heavy influence of "Western civil liberties theory and practice" over the definition of human rights for all people to be inappropriate not simply because of an implicit power imbalance between Western and non-Western societies. The emphasis on the individual has also resulted in "the conceptual exclusion of collective rights as human rights" which are "essential for the majority of human societies and communities around the world"(ibid: 10–11).

This critique could be applied to many if not most peace education programmes. Paul Lederach supplies a response to An-Na'im's concern over Western centrism, in this case regarding the conflict resolution field (a field related to peace education). Lederach argues that "we should not operate on the supposed, self-evident basis that conflict resolution, as we understand it in North America, is a good thing worthy of wide dissemination" (1995: 119). Culture (and non-Western cultures in particular) "should not be understood ... as a challenge to be mastered and overcome", but instead should be "approached as a seedbed" that can be "excited, probed, and fed" (ibid: 120).

Many peace educators, together with experts in related fields, struggle to adapt their work to the cultural contexts in foreign settings. What role, if any, should cultural context play in a peace education programme and its evaluation? Will other cultures and their adherents ultimately turn out to be seedbeds for peace-building, or do peace education's assumed universal principles ultimately transcend the values inherent in specific cultures?

The responses to these questions remain insufficient. Indeed, peace educators have yet adequately to address the most serious criticisms about their work. The field has yet to be adequately evaluated. The logic of targeting schoolchildren or individuals instead of adults or communities, respectively, remains largely unsupported, although, as will soon be discussed, changes in this approach are surfacing. And, as just mentioned, there is also the problem of the cultural relevance and appropriateness of peace education programming. Given these challenges to peace education, what has peace education accomplished thus far? Does it work?

While these questions will be explored shortly, here are two observations on the road that peace education has travelled thus far. First, there is the connection between women and peacemaking. Reardon admits that "most peace education is humanistic, and much of it claims to have as its goal the transformation of the human condition". But she also maintains that feminism is the key, as it is "the most fully human current perspective on peace and peace education" (1988: 9–10). Stomfay-Stitz highlights the leading roles that women have played in the development of peace education in the United States.

Second, there is the suggestion that, if peace education aims lower, setting before itself smaller and more reachable goals, it can achieve more. As one peace education expert noted, peace education will work "depending on what you want it to do. Can peace education students improve their understanding of conflict, negotiation and mediation issues? Yes, if they've gone through a skill-based, problem-solving course".

Peace education in the religious world

The criticism that peace education targets individuals instead of groups loses strength when it is applied to peace education programming conducted by religious organizations. In fact, the targeting of communities to receive peace education is one of the central strengths of religion-based programmes. For many religions, such tendencies emerge as natural applications of their philosophies. Consider the following comment about Islam: "In Muslim thought man is always a member of society, and thought of in relation to the community" (Ferguson, 1978: 129). Peace is also a vital spiritual concept in all the world's great religions. As Appleby has noted, "Deep formation in the peaceable heart of a religious tradition is fundamental to the religious militancy that can serve conflict transformation" (2000: 286).

The dominance of the idea of peace in the religious world should not imply that religious people share similar approaches to it. Differences in perspective are widespread, such as the tension between the "just war" doctrine and pacifism in the Christian tradition, which is examined in more detail in the Appendix. Consider, for example, the following two Catholic viewpoints of peace and violence. In a book published by the Catholic Foreign Mission Society of America (Maryknoll), John Dear states that "Non-violence ... offers a way to fight against injustice and war without using violence" (1994: 10). Alternatively, Smith noted that a number of Latin American Catholics who were "committed to revolution" concluded that "non-violent revolution, although morally preferable, does not work" (1971: 260). This led many to consider "violent action to overthrow tyranny" as a legitimate option against intractable cases of violence and injustice (ibid: 262).

Although such philosophical debates attract considerable attention among communities of believers, they may not spill into peace education work. There, issues of appropriate expressions of violence are sublimated to concerns about peace and justice. Religious approaches to peace education also tend to be holistic and targeted primarily at their own religious communities. Two Catholic examples illuminate this. "Confronting a culture of violence", a US Catholic Bishops' pastoral message (1994), provides American Catholics with an outline for action. The outline incorporates a number of activities, including: the significance of worship and preaching on peace-related themes; an emphasis on Catholic schools, where "basic values and conflict resolution" are taught; young adult and adult education programmes taking place in parishes where skills training on parenting and conflict resolution mixes with "spiritual development"; family and youth "ministry", where programmes are offered on a range of issues, among them peaceful relationships and sports; and outreach with local Catholic charities.

Dwyer's comments on peacemaking and education in the Catholic context combine themes similar to the bishops' pastoral message with many found in secular peace education programming. In addition to mentioning a familiar peace education emphasis on reaching individuals ("The responsibility to foster peace ... entails a conversion within each human heart"), Dwyer's attention turns to families and parish communities, describing the latter as "an important locus in which creative peace education can take place" (1999: 157). This she defines as a combination of a number of elements, among them "encourag[ing] the congregation to think about justice [as] the foundation of a true peace" and central to their spiritual lives, and providing workshops on non-violent conflict resolution. Finally, in another theme resonating through peace education literature, Dwyer emphasizes teaching in formal schools about an array of peace-related topics: peace, war, global interdependence, non-violent dispute resolutionand an encompassing reverence for life that includes "the ecological wellbeing of the planet" (ibid.).

The peace education programming of religious groups does not often intersect with their secular-based counterparts. This disconnect is particularly notable in post-war situations. Prior research with religious groups in Rwandan refugee camps, for example, illuminated how Christian churches and Muslim mosques were at the forefront of peacemaking activities in camp communities even while their connections to humanitarian agencies in the camps were limited (Sommers, 1998). Such lack of interaction and coordination between religious and humanitarian worlds is not exceptional. But the distance between the two can limit or even undermine peace education's effectiveness with forced migrants, as the two may create conflicting messages about peace and how to prevent or mediate conflicts. In such cases, it is quite possible that religion-based programmes and their messages will prove more influential among forced migrants, especially forced migrant children. After all, children go to churches, temples or mosques in addition to schools. And when they do, they join a community of believers who frequently learn about peace in an environment that can powerfully influence their ideas and behaviour.

A review of selected peace education programmes

Peace education programming takes many different forms in the humanitarian and development worlds. Some, like UNESCO's Culture of Peace and the many peace education-related initiatives at UNICEF, are expansive and ambitious. Others, like the human rights-oriented programming of the Norwegian Refugee Council, are more targeted. These three programmes will here serve as examples of current peace education programme approaches.

UNESCO. UNESCO's "Transdisciplinary Project" for a "Culture of Peace" is undoubtedly one of most ambitious secular peace initiatives ever attempted. Based on the Declaration on a Culture of Peace adopted by the UN General Assembly on 13 September 1999,[8] the UNESCO-led effort aims to foster and promote a culture of peace involving, among other things, education, economic and social development, respect for human rights, gender equity and democratic participation.

The declaration itself defines the "Culture of Peace" in fairly comprehensive terms: as a "set of values, attitudes, traditions and modes of behaviour and ways of life" based on a number of elements, including a set of principles (such as freedom, justice, solidarity existing "at all levels of society and among nations"), respect for life and the promotion of a variety of basic human rights. Five Culture of Peace projects are to be started in 2000–01. They will take place in the Russian Federation, Mali, Cambodia, the Dominican Republic and a selection of Arab states.

Given the lofty goals of the Culture of Peace initiative, it is perhaps not surprising that it "has often been criticized for its inability to move from concept to the concretization of the concept and to palpable and concrete actions" (UNESCO-PEER, 1999: 35). UNESCO's Programme of Education for Emergencies and Reconstruction (PEER) has adopted the Culture of Peace framework to its work in the Great Lakes and the Horn of Africa. This work includes a "Culture of Peace Network", a regular series of conflict resolution workshops involving "nearly 80 organizations working with problems of conflict resolution through peaceful dialogue" (ibid: 36) and a variety of country-specific activities.

8 Noted as "A/53/243, Fifty-Third Session, Agenda Item 31, Culture of Peace".

The peace education package, or PEP, is one such activity.[9] This "self-contained package" comprises "all the software and the hardware" required to provide 40 schoolchildren with a year's worth of activities (UNESCO-PEER n.d.: 2). Among the materials provided is an activity book which, like so many peace education approaches, focuses "on the role of the individual in bringing about peace" (Aguilar and Retamal, 1998: 44). There is also a songbook which, together with the activity book, address broad, peace-related themes. The book of stories, on the other hand, features Somali characters and concerns more directly.

UNICEF. UNICEF's peace education work is actively world-wide in scope and shares many of the inclusive values and expansive goals expressed within UNESCO's Culture of Peace initiative. UNICEF argues that "peace education is an essential component of quality basic education" (Fountain, 1999: 1). The organization contends that peace education provides "another lens or perspective through which to examine how peace can be 'mainstreamed' in basic education" (ibid: 7). Among the other lenses or perspectives are: children's rights/human rights education; education for development; gender training; global education; life skills education; landmine awareness; and psychosocial rehabilitation. Taken together, this is a broad educational arc, but UNICEF is pushing still further. A UNICEF education official explained that "an issue we are pursuing is to get recognition that peace education is (among other things) a curriculum issue – not just for post-conflict societies, but for every education system". Officials are also developing ways to evaluate peace education more effectively.

Within the realm of peace education, UNICEF differentiates between two kinds of settings for peace education (within schools and outside them) and develops country-specific programmes that are "highly responsive to local circumstances" (Fountain, 1999: 15). Although direct coordination between country programmes appears to be limited, different country programmes may share a number of general themes. The programmes may include the creation of interventions aimed at "improving the school environment so that it becomes a microcosm of the more peaceful and just society that is the objective of peace education" (ibid.); curriculum development, which usually consists of "activities around themes such as communication, cooperation, and problem solving" (ibid: 16); and teacher training that promotes interactive and participatory teaching methods and may address issues such as children's rights and conflict resolution skills.

UNICEF's peace education programming that takes place outside schools is diverse. It sponsors national peace campaigns, youth camps, groups and clubs, sports and recreation programmes, training and workshops for community leaders and parents, and a variety of youth public awareness and advocacy initiatives. Although it is not always clear how UNICEF's school- and out-of-school-based programmes are connected, a UNICEF education official notes that efforts are under way to link "peace education in schools and peace building in the community" more directly.

The Norwegian Refugee Council (NRC). The Norwegian Refugee Council has centred its peace education efforts within the realm of human rights education in the Caucasus. An NRC document notes that human rights education programming shares most of the same topics with peace and civic education programmes, such as "elements of tolerance and respect, conflict resolution or management, and reconciliation, rights and responsibilities" (Midttun and Brochmann, 1998: 2). The implication here is that conceptual differences between such programmes are minimal.

9 Also known as the Peace Education Package for Somalia, or PEPS.

The emphasis on students and the school environment, common to most peace education programmes, is also present here. The two main target groups for NRC's programme are teachers (and teacher trainers) and primary school students. The parents of students are informed of, but do not directly participate in, the programme. As one NRC education official observed, "We emphasize the involvement of the parents and brief them about the programme". The programme is also developing an information brochure for parents.

Educating students and teachers about human rights is a process involving instruction about universal human rights instruments, a demonstration of "how individuals can take part in the realization of human rights ideals" and the development of skills to promote peaceful conflict management and the protection of human rights (ibid: 3). There is also an effort to train teachers to teach differently. NRC officials have found that, as one observed, "children do learn better if they're not afraid". As a result, the programme instructs teachers on how to curb the authoritarian tendencies present in their teaching methods.

The refugee youth challenge

Boyden and Ryder deliver a word of caution to those who consider education the most important remedy for youth problems:

> Education delays participation in the world of adults and lengthens childhood dependence. This is bitterly resented by many youth. When it does not guarantee employment, education can also raise false expectations among young people. (1996: 12)

As field research for this report illustrates, youth resentments and false expectations often find expression through frustration and violence, and it does not seem to matter whether the youth are relatively well educated or not. But it is with this understanding of particular and frequently predominant youth difficulties that the following peace education programmes for youth should be examined.

Although youth who are not in school are often out of luck when target groups for peace education are considered, a number of youth programmes have been developed for them. Two will be briefly mentioned here. The first is a set of programmes sponsored by the Office of Juvenile Justice and Delinquency Prevention in the US government's Department of Justice. Among the initiatives is a Program for Young Negotiators (PYN) which targets troubled youth, together with their teachers and administrators, and "aims to teach individuals how to achieve their goals without violence" by using a "means of goal achievement and dispute resolution that has at its heart the practice of principled negotiation" (Crawford and Bodine, 1996: 15).

The second is the "Youth Peace Training Manual" developed by the All Africa Conference of Churches (AACC) in Nairobi, Kenya. With a range of tools and training modules, the programme aims to help youth "transform themselves from objects and subjects of war into agents of peace". It expresses deep concern for the "culture of war" prevalent in Africa, and calls for "a change in the approach and content of peace building". The training manual provides what it considers a new approach, one which is "deeply rooted in our African culture and guided by the Gospel" (AACC, 1999: xi-xii).

The UNHCR Peace Education Programme

The previous section reviewed the current state of the peace education field. This section will examine one peace education programme in detail. It will investigate how members of one implementing organization, UNHCR, view their agency's peace education programme and consider the programme's content and approach. It will also describe key contextual issues involving peace and violence in refugee communities in Uganda and Kenya, especially issues relating to refugee youth, and review the peace education programme's implementation in both countries. Before turning to these concerns, however, a description of research methods is required.

Sudanese refugees playing "The Wheel of Education" board game developed by UNHCR Ethiopia. Bonga Camp, Gambella Region, Ethiopia. UNHCR/02.2001/B. Neeleman

Research methodology

Field research in Geneva (Switzerland), Kenya and Uganda in June 2000 was targeted at two interrelated concerns. First, it aimed to gather an understanding of the concepts, assumptions and methods of the UNHCR Peace Education Programme by investigating programme documents and interviewing participants, teachers and officials involved with the initiative. Second, it investigated the context of this programme through interviews with refugees and local government officials, with emphasis accorded to the perspectives and experiences of peace and violence among refugee youth. Findings about these two concerns were then used to develop an understanding of the Peace Education Programme's perceived and potential impact by contrasting programme goals and actions with the challenges of peace confronting refugee communities in general and refugee youth in particular.

The field research was not intended as an evaluation of UNHCR's programme. The programme was instead used as an example of peace education programming for refugees.

The research team consisted of four people: the author, who was the principal investigator and team leader; Mwachofi Singo, a field researcher, who assisted in carrying out interviews in the refugee camps in Kenya; and two research assistants, Betsy Mull and Alberta Addison, who carried out archival research and collected relevant peace education documents from libraries, organizations and the internet.

Over the course of more than three weeks of field research, the author visited Geneva, Uganda and Kenya to carry out interviews with more than 100 individuals and conducted group interviews with nearly 600 refugees. Mwachofi Singo conducted mainly group interviews with an additional 183 refugees. Both researchers also observed several peace education workshops and school classes in the refugee camps. Among those interviewed were: UNHCR officials in Headquarters (Geneva) and in branch offices and sub-offices in Kenya and Uganda; peace education experts; officials from the governments of Kenya and Uganda; and officials from local and international NGOs and UN agencies. Those interviewed from the refugee population centred on: peace education teachers, facilitators and programme participants; primary school teachers and headmasters; settlement, clan and religious leaders; and members of church congregations, an array of youth groups, women's groups and in-school and out-of-school youth. The author also carried out telephone interviews with peace education experts.

Interviews with organization officials concentrated on their understanding and views of UNHCR's and other peace education programmes and their perceptions of peace and violence within refugee populations. Interviews with refugees and non-refugees directly involved in UNHCR's Peace Education Programme attempted to gather a broad understanding of how the programme worked and what its impact might be. Interviews with refugee leaders (camp, clan, religious, women's) focused on how refugees solved their own problems and promoted peaceful relations within refugee societies, and on what factors, UNHCR's Peace Education Programme among them, affected their work and the climate of peace and violence in the refugee camps. Interviews with refugee youth aimed at investigating the range of activities they were involved in, the kinds of frustrations and difficulties they confronted, how they sought to address major frustrations and difficulties, and what role, if any, peace education played in their lives.

Most of the field research took place in refugee camps in northern Kenya and northern Uganda. The Kenya sites were chosen because they comprise the initial sites where the UNHCR-led peace education project was first piloted. The peace education programme in Ugandan refugee camps began more recently and is still in the formative stage. Together, these two sets of refugee camps – one where peace education activities are established and one where they are getting started – provided a comparative framework for analyzing the peace education programme and key peace and violence issues in different refugee camp populations.

UNHCR and peace education programming

Peace education programming is at once popular and controversial. Most would agree that the objectives of promoting peace to prevent violence and of empowering people to solve conflicts peacefully are laudable. But promoting peace and preventing conflict are difficult to do. Expectations of programme success can be unreasonably high. Transforming uplifting ideals into concrete action is complicated. And, of course, measuring the success of peace education has proved a difficult, long-term process.

Somali refugee women at a primary school, Ifo Camp, Kenya. UNHCR/06.1994/B. Press

As a result of these factors (in addition to a handful of bureaucratic and personality concerns), many UNHCR staff members were sceptical about their agency's new peace education programme. Some of the questions raised were fundamental. One staff member wondered, for example, why agencies should "teach peace to victims of aggression and not to their aggressors", since refugees are, by definition, victims of violence and justifiably fearful of persecution.

Others wondered about the cultural context and applicability of peace education. "Africans commonly refer to themselves with the pronoun 'we' instead of 'I'", one official commented. Another added that there was a disjunction between Westerners, who spearheaded the development of the programme and whose culture "focuses on nuclear families", and Africans, whose culture "focuses on extended families". A third official emphasized how "keeping people busy can keep them out of trouble", a perspective suggesting that other ways of promoting peace exist besides peace education.

Still others focused on results, something that was particularly true of personnel in the field offices, who are responsible for reporting to donors and colleagues on the effectiveness of their activities. This was also a concern of local government officials, including one Ugandan official who remarked that "human and financial resources are scarce, so the question is how should they be used?" "Don't assume that peace education needs to be done," he added.

One peace education expert responded to this tendency towards scepticism over peace education by asserting that those refugees involved with peace education programming usually liked it, and that the real problem lay with two sets of "enemies of peace education" in the humanitarian world. The first set are officials who contend that peace education distracts agencies from the challenge of providing basic education to refugee children. The second set are those officials who believe that focusing only on the refugees' essential needs (food, clothing, shelter and protection, but not education) is both sufficient and appropriate.

One of the primary problems about UNHCR's Peace Education Programme centred on its name. Including "peace" in the title implied that "peace" was the programme's goal. This either raised expectations that the programme would lead directly, and perhaps fairly quickly, towards peace or that the programme seemed so idealistic that any impact would ultimately prove inconsequential.

Even those directly involved in the programme considered the title misleading. The programme, one of its developers remarked, is "skill-based and cross-cultural" in approach and has a problem-solving framework with an orientation towards conflict prevention. The programme, another added, "doesn't really look at violence but at conflict with a small 'c'". It brings a practical orientation to the adult workshops and school classrooms where it operates, and it does not provide psychosocial training or sports activities like other, more holistic peace education programmes.

Were there better titles available, such as Life Skills, Basic Skills, Coping Skills or perhaps Tolerance Education? Perhaps. But in the end, it was decided that Peace Education, given the title's popularity with programme donors and refugees, should be maintained.

The Peace Education Programme began in Kenya as a pilot project, starting simultaneously in two refugee camps in Kakuma, in the north-western part of the country, and expanding to three refugee camps in Dadaab, located in north-eastern Kenya near the border with Somalia. Preliminary research began in 1997 in both Dadaab and Kakuma with the purpose of initiating a peace education programme for primary school students. The intention, one official noted, was to "meet with every [refugee] group that there was to see what they needed in peace education". Those refugees who were consulted included community, women, religious and youth leaders, refugees who worked for NGOs and nationality and ethnic groups, all of whom indicated that they should receive peace education training in addition to refugee school children.

From the outset, the programme developers accorded cultural relevance a high priority:

> After initial review of existing materials it was felt that these were not necessarily culturally appropriate. Indeed it could not be assumed that even the concept areas are universal. For example, most [peace education] programmes start with self-esteem; but "self" as a core concept belongs to those societies that are individualistic – this is not valid for many traditional societies and it is not generally valid for many groups for whom the project is designed. In addition, the programmes investigated were not adequately cross-cultural. (Baxter, 1998: 20)

Here, it is suggested that the Western orientation towards individuals, a common feature in peace education programming, should be sublimated to local, and therefore non-Western, cultural priorities. The resulting focus on collective and not individual concerns is a prominent feature of UNHCR's programme.

From these early stages, other important programme features surfaced.

- The emphasis on refugee "ownership" of the programme and a high degree of refugee involvement aligned with the elicitive, culturally sensitive approach endorsed by Lederach and An-Na'im. But it also had the indirect outcome of limiting the participation of humanitarian agency officials. As a result, a finding arising in the programme's preliminary research phase was frequently noted during the field research for this report: that refugees, while learning problem-solving skills in the peace education programme, consistently mentioned problems between refugees and UNHCR, its NGO implementing partners and the local government that they could not resolve.
- The assumption, widely held in the international humanitarian community, that refugee leaders adequately represent the views of nearly all refugees and are reasonably efficient at accurately communicating messages to the larger refugee community, also applied to the UNHCR's Peace Education Programme, although to a greater extent in Uganda than Kenya. The refugee leaders played an important role in the development and guidance of the programme.
- The initial emphasis on starting peace education programming for primary school students led the programme to be, as one UNHCR official observed, "skewed toward conflict prevention"; this was a fairly logical approach for children. Conflict resolution (or transformation) thus became a secondary programme concern. This was particularly true for the programme in Kenya.
- Peace education materials are currently written in English, the language of educated refugees. Programme materials have recently been translated into French and Swahili.

The number of UNHCR staff directly involved in the programme never expanded beyond six (in 1998). The current staff level is three, none of whom is working in Uganda. The number of refugees involved in the programme, however, is much higher. They include:

- Peace education teachers, who are refugee school teachers working in camp primary schools who have been trained to teach peace education to their students 1–2 times a week;
- Facilitators, who have been trained to lead peace education workshops designed as twelve half-day sessions;
- Translator/assistants, who translate facilitator instructions and participant responses during workshop sessions.

The Uganda programme differed from the Kenya programme in fairly significant ways. First, two of UNHCR's NGO implementing partners play significant roles in the Uganda programme, which is not the case in Kenya. Second, unlike the programme in Kenya, where scarcely any Kenyans are involved, Ugandan nationals are directly involved in the programme as facilitators, participants and programme staff. This is a reflection of the generally closer relations between refugees and host populations in Uganda. Third, and as noted above, the Uganda programme does not yet have a primary school component. This originally arose in part because, as one UNHCR official noted, community leaders "can be very demanding". The programme thus "focused on people who have a specific role in the community first". Among those trained were refugees and Ugandan nationals who work for NGOs. It was felt that workers who regularly dealt with refugees and their problems would be able to put the skills learned in the peace education workshops to immediate and good use.

Finally, there is also a noticeable accent on transformation in the Uganda programme which was not as prominent in the Kenya programme and is not a feature of the programme's overall design. But signs of its presence are nonetheless notable in the refugee camps near Pakelle and Adjumani, where the Jesuit Refugee Service (JRS) serves as the NGO implementing partner. This sort of transformation does not refer to changing violent into non-violent conflicts, as Galtung suggests. Instead, the focus is on transforming communities and, by extension, their cultures. As one peace education official in Pakelle/Adjumani observed, "We try to give them values and attitudes so they can accept where they are wrong."

Programme materials

Among the findings from the preliminary research in Kenya was the identification of the following ambitious list of programme objectives:

- Skills

  Communication:

  - better listening
  - understanding perceptions and misperceptions
  - understanding emotions and their effect on communication
  - understanding the other person (empathy)
  - being fair to all sides
  - understanding of bias
  - understanding of stereotypes, discrimination, prejudice

  Appropriate assertiveness:

  - understanding of self
  - understanding of others
  - similarities and differences
  - assertion, aggression and submission

  Cooperation:

  - understanding of own and others' strengths and weaknesses
  - trust

  Critical thinking:

  - analysis
  - fact vs. opinion (impartiality and bias)
  - problem solving

  Conflict resolution:

  - negotiation
  - mediation

- Knowledge

  Understanding of:

  - peace and conflict
  - justice
  - human rights and responsibilities
  - gender issues
  - interdependence

- Values and attitudes

  Promotion of:

  - self-respect and respect of others
  - trust
  - social responsibility
  - open-mindedness
  - tolerance

  Source: Baxter, 1998

"Once these areas were defined", an early report noted, "a series of support materials were developed for the different components of the programme" (ibid: 6).

While the range of materials for classroom teachers and their students and community workshop facilitators and their participants, respectively, is too wide to give in detail in this report, here are some general observations:

- One of the main developers of the UNHCR programme emphasized that it "is extremely structured because of the training limitations of the teachers and facilitators". It is also "extremely pragmatic and tells [teachers and facilitators] how to put the [information] into action".
- For the most part, refugees (and, in Uganda, some Ugandan nationals) served as peace education teachers and workshop facilitators. In both Kenya and Uganda, expatriate UNHCR and partner NGO staff led the introductory and teacher training sessions during the early programme stages.
- There is a clear awareness of the limited training that most teachers and facilitators have previously received. In addition, teachers and facilitators were being asked to use new teaching methods. The most significant of these new methods was leading discussions on questions that have no precise answer instead of providing factual information through lectures.
- The breadth and detail of materials is impressive. The teacher activity book, for example, contains lesson plans for all eight primary school grade levels. There are a number of other detailed training and curriculum materials (such as a training manual and resource notes for primary school teachers and a lesson plan guide and training manual for community workshop facilitators) in addition to several supplementary materials, provided for use as "discussion starters", role plays and content-related singing.

- The materials were developed by UNHCR peace education experts, but in collaboration with the teachers and facilitators who used the books.

- Some of the supplementary materials are potentially powerful learning tools, not only for refugees involved in the courses but for those working with refugees as well. The poetry book, for example, contains poems written by workshop participants that are revealing of refugees' thoughts and lives. In one poem, entitled "Life in War" (UNHCR, 2000: 29–32), a 20-year-old youth (Majok Peter from Kakuma refugee camp in Kenya) describes how he learned to be "independent of mind" and able to cook, clothe, shelter and defend himself after becoming an orphaned refugee at the age of six. The survivor ethic described here ("so learn to be men and women in war or in peace!") is not necessarily attached to peaceful behaviour but is a portrait worthy of reflection and discussion.

More specific commentary on primary, workshop and evaluation materials will now follow.

Primary school materials. The central curriculum concern for the primary school component is that it is cyclic, which is defined as teaching "the same concepts ... year by year through different activities so that the children develop the concept for themselves" (Baxter, 2000b: 4). This idea of cultivating conditions where students can develop an understanding of difficult concepts (such as empathy, analysis, conflict resolution, negotiation and mediation) and be able to use them underscores the focus on empowerment in the overall course. It also sheds light on the tall task that the programme has set before it.

The instructions to teachers illuminate an approach that is envisaged as conducive to learning about peace education. "Peace education", the teacher activity book reminds teachers, "is an attempt to change attitudes and behaviour and to develop constructive attitudes and behaviour for use in everyday life" (Baxter, 2000b: 7). It thus reminds teachers to replace rote learning methods with more open-ended discussion about complex ideas. The implicit power relations between teacher and student are also addressed. "Do not use a stick, cane or pointer", the activity book instructs. "These are weapons ... [and] if the only motivation is fear, the children will learn nothing about what peace really is" (ibid: 5). Positive reinforcement should also replace criticism or punishments. Finally, teachers are asked to recognize that becoming a peace education teacher transforms them into role models who must demonstrate good listening, communication, observation and other skills taught in the course.

The course employs several teaching methods, all of which were found to be outside the everyday methods that teachers normally employed at the primary schools visited. Instead of providing detailed lectures to students, teachers were encouraged to stimulate group discussions and facilitate dramatic role-plays and games among students.

Community workshop materials. The peace education workshops were designed as "empowerment course[s]" (Baxter, 2000a: 2). Far more than the expectations of primary school teachers, the workshop facilitators were expected to be role models before their adult peers, and even directly connect "the skills of a good teacher, trainer or facilitator" to those of a "peace maker" (ibid.). The implicit idea that facilitators, and sometimes even workshop participants, may be seen as community "peacemakers" was in evidence in the refugee camps, particularly in Kenya.

The Community Workshop materials, intended for adults (most of whom were literate), were significantly more complex than those designed for primary school teachers and students. Facilitators were taught about developmental psychology (including Maslow's "Hierarchy of needs"), education theory, and peace and conflict theory. The Community Workshop Manual is dense with detail. There are complicated concepts – such as the idea that assertive behaviour is "functional" while aggressive and submissive behaviour are both "dysfunctional" – which call for a considerable degree of instruction and explanation from the facilitators. Group discussions, however, are also part of every lesson.

Evaluation materials. As with most peace education programmes, the programme's self-evaluation tools were weak because what was evaluated was the peace education course itself rather than whether or how effectively the course's objectives were practised.

Workshop participants were the primary evaluators. They completed questionnaires that were routinely provided at the end of each workshop course. These questionnaires produced overwhelmingly positive responses about the courses they participated in (such as: "All workshop participants said the course was interesting and useful"). While this is not, of course, an insignificant finding, it cannot be seen as an adequate measure of a peace education programme's effectiveness.

The insular evaluation focus has produced one significant and positive outcome. Course materials have been regularly evaluated and revised. This has been the product of observations of course presentations and of discussions between UNHCR and NGO implementing partner officials and the peace education teachers and workshop facilitators. There has also been a detailed analysis of the *Teacher Activity Book* by an outside evaluator which recommended, among other things, either revision or deletion of the 23 per cent of the school lessons that were difficult to teach (Robinson 2000). Many of the recommendations have been accepted, and the *Teacher Activity Book* has recently been revised.[10]

Field research: The Kenya programme

There were significant differences between the Kenya and Uganda programmes. Differences also existed within each country, particularly between the refugee camp areas of Kakuma and Dadaab, in Kenya. Findings from Kenya will first be described because it was the initial site of the Peace Education Programme.

The situations for of Dadaab and Kakuma are similar in a number of important ways. They are both located in resource-poor desert areas where potable water is a perennial problem. Situated near the borders across which most refugees have fled but far from concentrated population areas, the camps in both locations serve simultaneously to isolate refugees from Kenyans while facilitating cross-border communication and travel between refugee camps and the refugees' countries of origin.

The Kakuma and Dadaab refugee camps are also true encampments: refugees are not allowed to farm inside the camps, and the Kenyan government does not permit refugees to leave them (one important exception exists for Dadaab, where refugees are permitted to collect firewood outside the camps, an issue which will be examined below). Children are allowed to attend primary school, but they can only learn the

10 It is also expected that an impact evaluation of the Kenya programme will take place in the future.

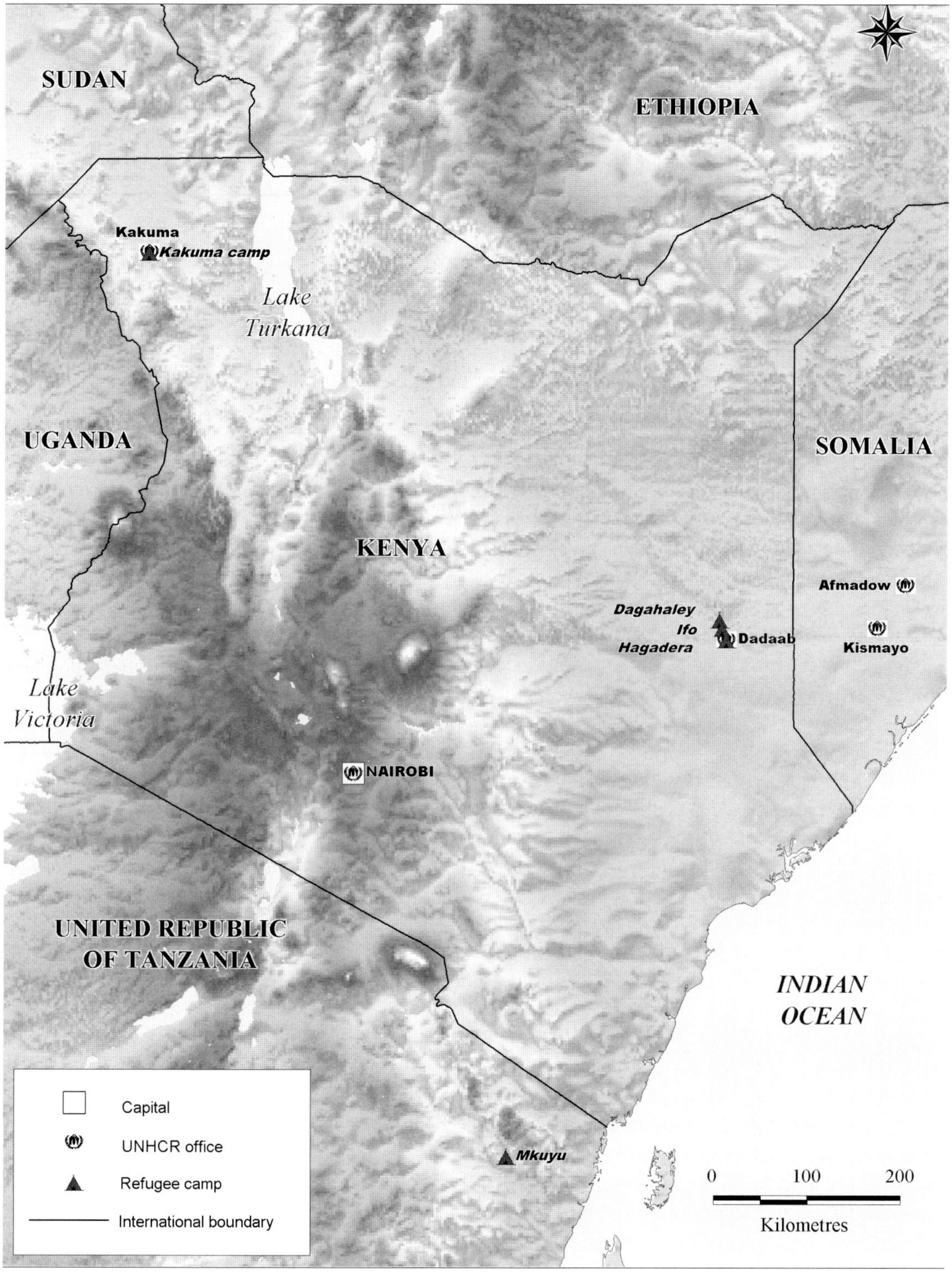

PGDS/GIMU - October 2001

Kenyan curriculum. Geography classes consequently teach students about the Rift Valley and other notable Kenyan features. Students learn about the Kenyan political system and Kenyan history, and so on. Primary school, in short, provides young refugees with a foundation for host country integration, which they are strictly forbidden to practise.

Security is the dominant concern for refugees in both areas, and one which Jeff Crisp elaborates in chilling detail:

> The refugees are obliged to remain in areas which have traditionally been insecure, where the rule of law is weak and where the perpetrators of violence can act with a high degree of impunity. The refugees themselves are obliged to live in very trying circumstances – circumstances which increase their propensity and vulnerability to violence. Originating from countries which have experienced protracted and very brutal forms of armed conflict, they find themselves without freedom of movement, with few economic or educational opportunities, and with almost no immediate prospect of finding a solution to their plight. (1999: 2–3)

The camps in Dadaab and Kakuma are multinational, but the security issues primarily arise from within the main nationality group in each set of camps. The three Dadaab camps largely contain Somali refugees, while Sudanese refugees predominate in the three Kakuma camps. The configuration of the main conflicts, however, differs. The Kakuma camps are plagued by fighting mainly between various combinations of Dinka and Nuer sub-groups and ethnic groups from Equatoria Province in southern Sudan. The central problem in the Dadaab camps is violence between Somali refugees and Somalis who are Kenyan nationals. But violence within the Dadaab camps is thought to be particularly significant, and security restrictions are numerous and strict. Humanitarian aid and Kenyan officials move between the camps in heavily armed convoys and can only visit refugee housing areas under escort. These two restrictions made Dadaab the most challenging field site for this research.

The dependence of refugees on humanitarian aid is another vexing and seemingly intractable problem for aid officials and a subject of considerable debate between refugees and officials. Refugees freely admit that they depend on aid agencies for a variety of basic needs. They also regularly complain about the type and amount of water, food rations and a host of other supplies and services (including the insufficiency of peace education programming). In both areas, but especially in Kakuma, even firewood is a regular component of refugee rations.

Kakuma

The refugee camps of Kakuma (Kakuma I was established in 1992, Kakuma II in late 1997 and Kakuma III in early 1999) are, without a doubt, unique. Where refugee camps are usually dominated by women and children, most refugees in Kakuma are male youth. While most refugee camps offer at least some formal primary schooling, Kakuma offers youth a wide range of educational opportunities, most of which are entirely free. Kakuma also has extraordinary diversity in the refugee population: refugees come from nine countries (Burundi, Democratic Republic of Congo, Eritrea, Ethiopia, "Kenya/Stateless", Rwanda, Somalia and Uganda, in addition to Sudan) and more than 20 ethnic groups. Almost three-quarters of the overall population (73.6 per cent) are from Sudan. The majority of each national population is male (the Sudanese contingent is nearly 60 per cent male).

The camps' orientation to refugee male youth and their needs is directly connected to the presence of some of Kakuma's first residents. The famous "lost boys of Sudan" whom Refugees International has described as "a unique phenomenon in the world", comprised some 17,000 boys who in 1987 began fleeing the fighting in southern Sudan and entered Ethiopia. In 1991, however, the Ethiopian government closed the refugee camps, forcing the "lost boys" back towards the battle zone in their own country. Some 10,500 of this original group eventually arrived in Kakuma the following year (Refugees International, 1998: 1).

Inspired by this initial, and much publicized, male youth influx into Kakuma, youth programming is remarkable and extensive (the definition of a refugee youth in Kakuma, it should be noted, is all refugees between the ages of 7 and 40). UNHCR reports that 28 per cent of the total refugee population – more than 25,000 out of a total population of nearly 93,000 – attend schools in the camps. In addition to primary school, there are pre-school, secondary and vocational schools. Youth (of whom there are nearly 65,000) comprise 70 per cent of the total population; more than 19,000 (29 per cent) of them are part of a Youth and Culture Programme led by the Lutheran World Federation that provides organized activities such as fine arts, drama, music, cultural dances, debate, leadership training, exchange visits and educational tours. Ninety per cent of all youth involved in these programmes, according to one UNHCR official, speak English. There are 700 refugee youth sports teams in Kakuma. As for the original "lost boys", preparations are being made to resettle them in the United States.

Blind class for refugee students reading Braille. The teacher is also blind. Multi-purpose centre run by IRC, Kakuma, Kenya. UNHCR/07.1999/B. Press

Peace education programming. UNHCR's Peace Education Programme was first piloted in, and received the most enthusiastic support from, the UNHCR Sub-Office in Kakuma. All pilot programmes benefit from favourable conditions, and all of these elements contributed to the successful launch of the peace education programme in Kakuma. As one UNHCR official proudly commented, "the famous euphoria of Peace Education started here".

The euphoria he referred to was not within UNHCR, its implementing partners or host government officials but within refugee communities. As in Dadaab and Uganda, the Peace Education Programme officially closed down for a number of months (that is, no UNHCR peace education staff and limited or no funding was present), and the Kakuma programme was officially frozen for eight months beginning in mid-1999. However, again as in the other two sites, this did not stop refugees involved in the programme from continuing it. Strong, enthusiastic refugee support for the programme remains one of the most important existing indicators of peace education's impact.

Early in the pilot process, which began in 1997, there was an attempt within UNHCR to attach the Peace Education Programme to the Protection Unit instead of to the Community Services Unit. This was a novel and intriguing idea, and there were at least two important reasons for considering this. First, as one UNHCR official explained, in the Protection Unit "we implement protection", while Community Services monitors but does not implement programming. Second, "peace education teaches the core principles of UNHCR", the official continued. Refugees should "know their rights and obligations", and this could be integrated into the peace education curriculum.

A powerful logic supports this argument – peace, problem-solving and refugee rights and obligations all support protection concerns and potentially counteract violence and lack of refugee protection. But institutionally the argument was considered weak. Peace education is seen predominantly as an education programme within UNHCR. The idea of directly linking peace education to the Protection Unit was ultimately dropped.

Among the first refugees associated with the Peace Education Programme was a group of church leaders who were involved in resolving a violent conflict involving Sudanese Dinka and Nuer youth. Members of this group (who originally received support from the Jesuit Refugee Service) were some of the first refugees to be trained as facilitators and teachers during the pilot phase. A member of this original church-based group continues to associate the Peace Education Programme with Christian values. "I like this programme very much," he said,

> because I'm a Christian ... We see a world full of conflict, especially in Africa. So to live together and solve problems peacefully is the only way [we Africans] can solve our problems on our own.

The inclusion of religious leaders in the peace education facilitator and teacher faculty seemed an appropriate and even natural fit to many of those involved. For them, and for so many other refugees in Kakuma, Dadaab and northern Uganda, the Peace Education Programme aligned and supported the values and mission of churches and mosques, whose leaders are regularly called on to help resolve outbreaks of violence between refugees.

Four implications of this alignment between religious leaders and the Peace Education Programme will be noted here:

First, the training represented a form of enhanced recognition and empowerment for facilitators, teachers and adult participants alike. Although this was most pronounced in Dadaab, where the sense that those involved in the Peace Education Programme became "peacemakers" was widespread, it was also present in Kakuma as well as northern Uganda. At all three sites workshop graduates and some primary school students routinely formed peace education groups and many peace education teachers, but especially facilitators, were called on to help refugee community leaders and elders attempt to resolve conflicts. The results of this impact, it should be noted, are not necessarily positive, but may well be. In any event, this constitutes an important indicator of impact that the programme itself has yet to monitor, document and evaluate systematically.

Second, the attention paid to religious leaders is among the factors limiting the involvement of women refugees. "Some peace education workshops have no girls at all," one male youth graduate of a peace education workshop observed. He was a member of "The Peace Education Union", a self-styled male youth group organized by workshop graduates. A Peace Education Programme official acknowledged the lack of many women teachers, facilitators and participants to be a deficiency that is now being addressed.

Third, at all three peace education sites (Kakuma, Dadaab and Uganda), far more men than women know English. This is not an impediment to access to peace education in primary schools, but is for the adult workshops. Religious and other leaders, as well as other well-educated refugees, naturally become candidates for peace education programming, and most of these people are men. This is also the case with refugee youth, since, as one refugee involved in the Peace Education Programme noted, "most girls don't know English".

Fourth, although this was not true for all teachers and facilitators, there were strong indications that, in Kakuma and elsewhere, the "natural" connection between peace education and religious values affected the way in which peace education was taught. This was particularly evident with primary school teachers, when the method of instruction sometimes resembled sermons. "Let us bring peace to the society here, so we can plant peace", one teacher exhorted his students. Another reminded his students that they "should not exclude [others]. As God is our creator, don't discriminate by tribe, nationality, colour, race or geographic location". A third explained that "the peace education approach to peace is related to the religious [approach] in many ways". This final implication, it should be remembered, must be taken in context. Peace Education Programme training has been limited (some teachers reported having been trained for a month), but the training that most refugee teachers had received to become teachers was also limited.

Refugee youth. Despite the wealth of youth activities and the availability of free education, many refugee youth in Kakuma drop out of school and participate in few or no youth activities. These marginalized youth lack representation in the larger refugee community, a fact repeatedly made clear by refugee leaders, who were often called to resolve violent conflicts involving marginalized refugee youth. Many leaders confessed that they do not understand the youth known as "Drop-outs", who routinely ignore their advice.

If marginalized youth (most of them allegedly male) in Kakuma ignore refugee leaders – a tendency also found in Dadaab and northern Uganda – what does this say about the influence of refugee leaders and the institutions, such as UNHCR and host government officials, who work with refugee leaders? Regarding the Peace Education Programme, the implication is fairly clear: apart from the primary school component, only those refugees who are already peaceful (and influential) tend to become involved in the programme. Those refugees who are not peaceful do not.[11]

The problem that "Drop-outs" represent is a matter of general concern in the Kakuma camps. They are perceived as being difficult, quarrelsome outcasts. "These Drop-outs", an educated youth explained:

> They do nothing, they don't have jobs, they are idle without anything. They are frustrated. Drop-outs can be robbers, in breweries. They are never allowed into [our] traditional dances. Peace education is for the most peaceful youth, not the Drop-outs, who are in the majority.

According to this youth, Drop-outs are not entitled to receive peace education training. This may add to the frustration that already characterizes the lives of Drop-outs, who are also often living on their own. Young men become Drop-outs, another youth commented, "due to frustration. Without food at home, with hunger, they can't understand what they've learned [in school]". There is also the issue of trauma. "Some people do not understand [Drop-outs]," another youth explained. "They are not well because they saw killing, looting, and so on during war, so they're still disturbed."

Frustration was a characteristic of the lives of nearly every refugee youth interviewed for this report. For refugees from Sudan and Somalia – the refugee majority in Kakuma, Dadaab and northern Uganda – peace in and repatriation to their countries of origin seemed a long way off. War and instability had lasted for years and was showing few signs of letting up. In this situation, even education was thought to be only a temporary relief from idleness. Many thought it would be useful one day, but employment opportunities for primary, secondary and vocational school graduates were severely limited in both countries. As a result, as one Sudanese youth related, "there's no way to use our education".

Given the fact that education does not necessarily facilitate advancement and the time required to meet essential needs, education became, for many youths, an optional activity or perhaps simply a diversion. One Sudanese male youth explained that there were "two kinds of boys: those who like to attend school and the people who don't like to attend school". Another youth explained his fate in the following way: "I've failed education and I've failed getting a job. I'm just idle." In such a circumstance, beer is useful: "If I stay two days without food, beer becomes a medicine and you forget about hunger."

Few female refugee youth in Kakuma were involved in the Peace Education Programme or, in fact, most other programmes. Sudanese girls are reportedly routinely driven out of school in the higher primary grades, often by male students in their grades who do not want girls receiving higher examination grades than they do. Others were married, often not by choice and frequently to older men. These circumstances – girls leaving school early and marrying early – were commonplace in Sudan as well. But in Kakuma, it was also commonplace for male and female youth to mix with people of other countries. This could lead to violence, but did not necessarily do so. As a women's group leader observed, "the youth mix between cultures, but elders rarely do. Youth are more dynamic and outgoing". "These 'youth outside of society'," another women's group member added, "still have their own peer groups." Collectively, the membership of these youth peer groups may well comprise the majority of all refugees in Kakuma I, II and III.

11 The attraction to training and working with refugee leaders is not specific to the Peace Education Programme, and will be addressed in the Uganda section below.

Wooden boards carrying Koranic verses are often the only educational material accessible to the children. Bardera Camp, Gedo Region, Somalia. UNHCR/01.1994/B. Press

Dadaab

There are more than 120,000 refugees in the three refugee camps in the Dadaab area, which began to host refugees in 1991. By June 2000, Ifo camp had nearly 45,000 refugees, Hagadera 44,408 and Dagahaley 33,455. The camps are overwhelmingly Somali in composition, ranging from 96 per cent (in Ifo camp) to 99.5 per cent in Hagadera camp. Small numbers of Sudanese and Ethiopians also reside in the camps, with still smaller numbers of Congolese, Ugandans and Eritreans.

The Dadaab refugee camps are hot, dry, remote, grim, confining and, above all, dangerous. The dominant problem for refugees in Dadaab is rape. "Of the main two issues in Dadaab", one UNHCR official commented, "the problem of sexual violence is the highest priority" (the other priority problem was banditry). During the month prior to the field visit (May 2000), for example, there were ten reported rapes, or about one every three days. The number of unreported rapes may have been significantly higher, since "if a rape is reported by a woman, the rapist is likely to cause more problems" for his victim. The problem has had a profound cumulative effect on Somali refugee women: members of the Anti-Rape Committee asserted that "if six of seven women go to fetch firewood, maybe five have [already] been raped" at least once.

Somali women also tend to view rape, and fear of rape, as the predominant problem in the camps. They must collect firewood outside the camps almost daily, where they regularly confront ethnic Somali "bandits". Somali men generally refuse to collect firewood for their families. The role is considered part of the women's domain, even by many women, and "a part of our culture". There is also a widely held view that "women will get raped but men will get killed" if they confront bandits. Given the choice, in other words, rape is preferable to death. A component of this debate, however, was the fact that Somali men regularly ventured into the "bush" surrounding the camps with donkey carts to cut firewood for sale. But during interviews with Somali men, it was clear that they were not prepared to budge from their position of not accompanying Somali women into the bush. It was also clear that they had become accustomed to discussing the firewood issue with foreign researchers.

Somali men and women both maintained that the "bandits" who carried out these crimes (with virtual impunity) were Kenyans of Somali ethnicity who were members of rival clans or sub-clans. Members of the Somali leadership (all men) reported that all the violence in or near the camps was caused exclusively by these "bandits". Aid agency and Kenyan security officials felt that refugees were also involved in criminal activity in the camps.[12] Many refugees supported the officials' view. One woman, for example, explained that, in the camps,

> There are four kinds of Somali refugees: [those from the] Harwiye and Darod clans, minorities (Afars, Issas, Madibau, Tumal, Midgan, Boon, and so on), and Somali Bantu. The Harwiye and Darod are dominant. The Somali Bantu can't marry [members of] the other three groups, so they rape women from those three groups. The minority groups can't marry [Harwiye and Darod], so they rape their women. I [also] suspect that Somali clan members are raping the unmarried [virgin women] of other clans to prevent them from marrying. In the refugee camps, [Somali men] rape. This is their chance for revenge.

All in all, given the situation, it was not surprising to hear one Somali woman conclude that, "Somali men are the source of all [Somali women's] problems".

The Dadaab camps, unlike Kakuma, were not dramatically skewed towards males over females. The proportion of refugees who were youth appeared to be statistically very significant, however, something the aid officials and refugees alike supported. Precise numbers were unavailable both because the definition of youth varies across (and sometimes within) cultures and UNHCR's statistical age categories split what many would think of the youth population into two larger age groups (refugees aged 5–17 years and those aged 18–59). A smaller proportion of refugees participated in educational activities in the Dadaab camps than in Kakuma, but it was still a considerable proportion: 23 per cent of the population participated in pre-school, primary school, secondary school, vocational school, special education and adult literacy classes. What follows are key findings and analysis arising from the fieldwork.

Peace education programming. A meeting with community and religious leaders in Ifo camp revealed how the peace education programme related to traditional methods of problem solving. Somali elders described a collaborative internal framework. "We use four problem-solving groups," one leader explained.

> First, religious leaders solve problems through Sharia [Islamic] law. Second, clan leaders solve problems according to their culture. Third, youth group leaders also participate in finding solutions for problems. Fourth, Peace Education Programme facilitators contribute.

12 Some officials also wondered whether some Somali women were reporting rapes that didn't occur in order to receive consideration for third country resettlement or increased firewood rations.

The integration of refugee facilitators into the problem-solving mix indicates the degree of acceptance accorded the Peace Education Programme. A second Somali elder explained why the programme had been so widely accepted.

> The first time people entered the programme, they were confused. But when [programme] teachers and facilitators taught us, we realized that these are the same skills which our ancestors were using. Before, we were only taught to solve problems through our brainwork. But now, there is the paperwork approach of peace education. So we've appreciated the UNHCR approach.

A significant proportion of Somalis interviewed indicated that the "modern" techniques inherent in the UNHCR Peace Education Programme approach – men as well as women, older adults in addition to youth – were thought to complement traditional problem-solving approaches. One elder noted that:

> In the old days, the first guns had only one bullet. Nowadays, people can be bombed. So, although our ancestors had ways to solve problems, peace education is also connected to the modern world.

A group of refugee youth supported this view. One male youth commented that "the advanced people in the world are the peaceful people. So we want to be like them". For this group of youth, and for many other graduates of peace education workshops in Dadaab, building on their programme training seemed like a good starting place for connecting to the "advanced" or "modern" world.

It is hard to underestimate the enthusiasm of refugees in Dadaab for UNHCR's Peace Education Programme. Refugees who had participated in the programme clamoured for more training and support while others sought access to the training. Youth graduates from the workshops formed large peace education groups that regularly circulated in their neighbourhoods, calling themselves "peacemakers" and "professors of peace".

It should also be noted, however, that meetings with refugee leaders and peace education participants revealed how equity was more often defined in terms of refugee nationality than gender (this finding applied to Kakuma as well). This was demonstrated in the participation levels at peace education workshops. While many nationalities were regularly represented, there were relatively few female participants.

Gender equity, it must be said, is frequently difficult to achieve. The problem is specific neither to refugee camps nor to the Peace Education Programme. But the Peace Education Programme does instruct refugees on such issues as bias, empathy and perceptions. Given the daily threat of rape, the disjunction between what peace education taught and the predominance of male participation in training was not lost on Somali women. Members of the Anti-Rape Group were particularly frustrated over their treatment:

> People like you come and listen to our problems and then leave, with no help for us. What will come of your report?

They also associated peace education, as a UNHCR programme, with their criticisms of UNHCR more broadly. As one woman said, "UNHCR talks of human rights but they don't practise it. UNHCR is biased [since] women being raped are not being assisted". Even seemingly small steps, some women indicated, would be beneficial, such as balancing attendance ratios to peace education workshops, so that, as one woman suggested, "Somali men and women could go to the Peace Education Programme together".

Refugee youth. Just about every young refugee man interviewed expressed tremendous frustration about his living situation. As in Kakuma, marriage opportunities for many young men were, at best, distant. Tensions over limited opportunities for employment or productive activities generally were high. "Persuade the Kenyans to let us integrate," one refugee youth implored. Often male youth violence exploded as they waited in line for water or food. Some responded to the situation by chewing the bark and leaves of a plant known as chat or miraa. This fairly mild narcotic is popular with many Somali men and some women. Crisp notes that chat addiction among Somali men is connected to domestic violence (Crisp, 1999: 23). The broader issue of male youth frustration is also connected to rape. One youth stated, "If I don't have a wife, I have to rape". Another explained how access to peace education courses helped to relieve the tensions that young men endured. "If you have the knowledge of peace", he said, "it helps. Without it, you begin raping someone because you are frustrated".

The combination of violence, boredom and tremendous tension had led some to seek out new ways to solve their problems. Some described the significance of "video parlours" – small theatres in the camp run by refugee entrepreneurs – in their lives. The most popular videos address the two themes that haunt male youth lives: sex and violence. Videos with live war action seemed particularly popular – two examples were news videotapes of Gulf War bombing and the war in Kosovo. But young refugees didn't just attend the video parlours (also popular with boys and young men in Kakuma). They studied them carefully. Detective films, one youth explained, "help us understand how to identify and solve problems".

Field research: The Uganda programme

More than 150,000 Sudanese refugees occupy a series of refugee settlements in the northern Ugandan districts of Adjumani, Moyo and Arua (Adjumani district hosts more than 70,000 refugees, Arua more than 50,000 and Moyo more than 35,000). The refugee settlements in these districts are somewhat different. The settlements in Adjumani and Moyo are small and numerous, particularly in Adjumani, where there are 22 different refugee settlements.[13] Arua district, in contrast, has two: Rhino camp and Imvepi. Many thousands more Sudanese refugees are spontaneously settled in the area, and particularly in Arua district, which is by far the most urban and densely populated of the three.

In most respects the refugee situation in these Ugandan districts differs dramatically from those in Dadaab and Kakuma in Kenya. The Sudanese refugees in northern Uganda are surrounded by a host population that is not only friendly but, in the case of many, speak the same language and may even be related. Familiarity between the host population and the refugees in Uganda was enhanced by the fact that people living near the northern Uganda–southern Sudan border have either become or received refugees, or both, for decades. Merkx notes that refugee movements across the border began in 1955. As many as 250,000 Ugandans fled to southern Sudan in 1979–83 (Merkx, 1999). Many Ugandans, back in their homeland, proudly state that they have not forgotten the hospitality they received from the Sudanese. Some of those who were refugees in Sudan are now members of the Ugandan government.

---

13 The places where refugees live are called settlements instead of camps because "the refugee programme has evolved from emergency assistance to local settlement" (UNHCR Uganda and the Office of the Prime Minister, Government of Uganda, 1999: 8).

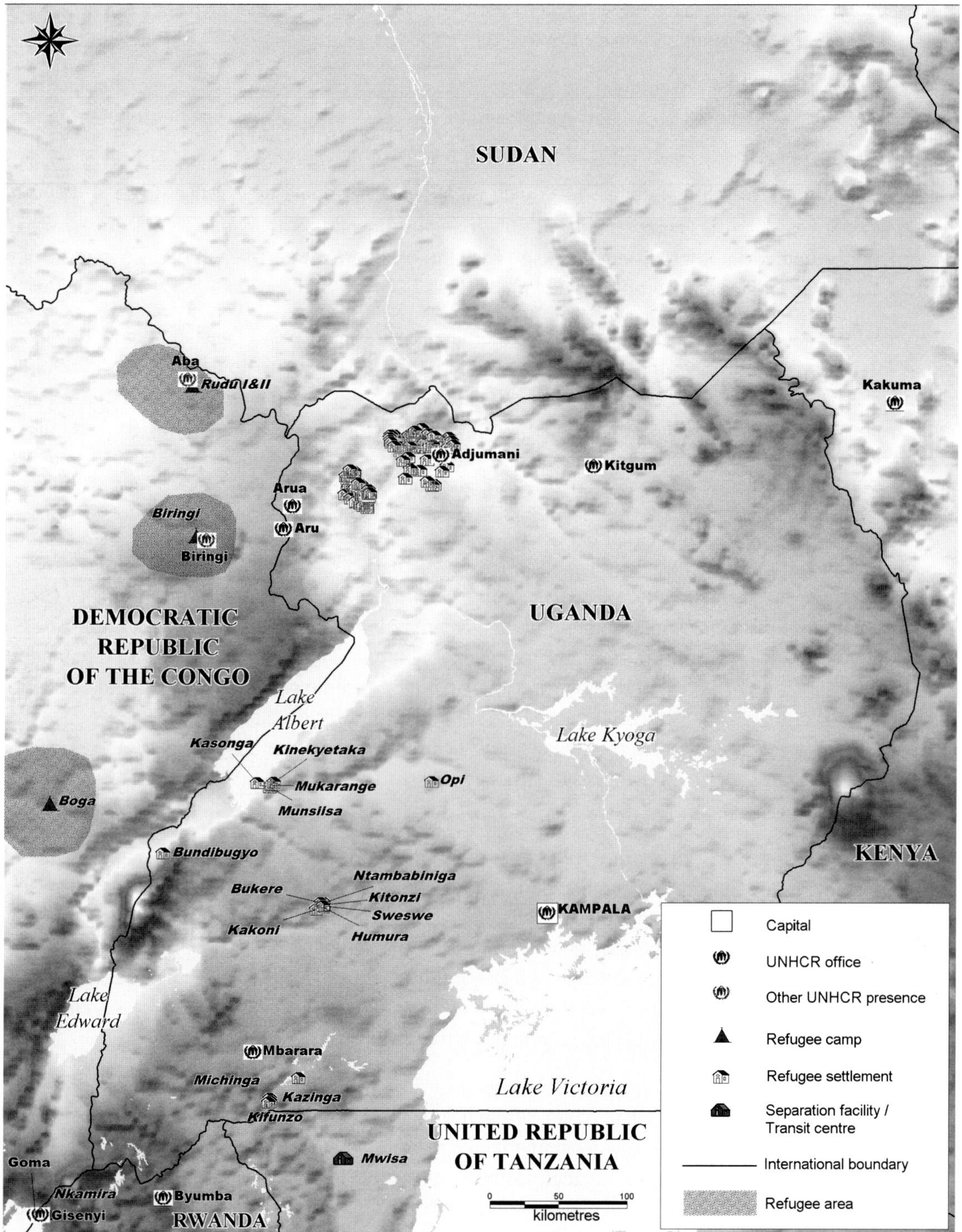

PGDS/GIMU - October 2001

The Ugandan response to the Sudanese refugees has been unusually charitable, and serves as a striking contrast to the Kenyan government policy towards refugees:

> It is remarkable that the government of Uganda was willing to allow refugees to occupy large areas of the north. The land itself was made available to the refugees by local communities, represented by elders and the local councils. (Merkx, 1999: 18)

Merkx also notes, however, that the Ugandans, while obviously generous, opened up farmland to refugees in a somewhat calculated fashion: "Land was still abundant [in northern Uganda] and in many areas the local population was not interested in settling [on land offered to Sudanese refugees] because of its isolation and because of security problems" (Ibid.).

The settlements themselves are not nearly as dangerous as the Kakuma and Dadaab camps. However, serious insecurity problems near the settlements began in 1996 and regularly threaten host and refugee populations. The West Nile Liberation Front rebel group attacked some refugee settlements. More recently, banditry and abductions of children by members of the notorious Lord's Resistance Army (LRA) regularly plague the area. Based to the east and south of the settlements, the LRA remain dangerous for refugees and Ugandans alike, particularly those residing in Adjumani and Moyo districts.

The relationships between refugees and Ugandan nationals, but especially between refugees and both humanitarian agencies (UNHCR in particular) and the Ugandan government, are changing. This is by intention. The Self-Reliance Strategy (SRS) was adopted by UNHCR and the Ugandan government's Office of the Prime Minister in 1998 and is entering an implementation phase scheduled to last through 2003. Reduced donor funding, concerns over refugee dependency on humanitarian assistance while repatriation to Sudan remains a distant goal, and enhancing the Ugandan government's authority over all residents in the northern districts appear to be the chief motivating factors for developing the SRS. Merkx, who was "directly involved" in developing the SRS, explains the overall reasoning of the strategy in the following terms: "by targeting assistance programmes to refugee hosting areas the impact could be more sustainable" (1999: 22–23).

The overall goal of the SRS – "to improve the standard of living of the people in Moyo, Arua and Adjumani districts, including the refugees" – is embodied in two objectives. The first is to "empower refugees and nationals in the area to the extent that they will be able to support themselves". The second is to "establish mechanisms which will ensure integration of services for the refugees with those for the nationals" (UNHCR Uganda and the Office of the Prime Minister, Government of Uganda, 1999: 8). The formulators of the strategy envisage that refugees will soon be able "grow or buy their own food, access and pay for basic services and maintain self-sustaining community structures" (ibid.).

Refugees themselves are far less confident about the outcome of this strategy. They feel abandoned by UNHCR (although the agency will retain a presence and limited mission in the area) and unsure about their future relationship with the Ugandan government, whose officials will, under the SRS, assume greatly enhanced responsibilities for refugees in their districts. While this issue will be returned to below, two comments are given here. First, the Sudanese refugees in Kakuma are far more dependent on outside assistance than their comrades in Uganda, and their dependence on UNHCR shows no indications of waning. Much of this is unavoidable, given the Kenyan government's policy to contain refugees inside camps, but it is an issue not lost on Sudanese refugees in Uganda. Second, it should be noted that UNHCR's Peace

Education Programme, especially the adult workshop course that aims to enhance the problem-solving skills of its participants and is regularly offered to refugee leaders, is not a featured component of the Self-Reliance Strategy, even though refugees and local Ugandans (residents and officials alike) might all benefit from programme training workshops, given that they will be working together more closely from now on. What follows are key findings and analysis arising from the fieldwork.

Peace education programming. UNHCR's Peace Education Programme in Uganda started later than the Kenya programme (in mid-1999) and is far less developed. There is no primary school component, although some UNHCR officials connected to peace education stated that this was a future intention. UNICEF officials, who are currently developing a peace education programme for Ugandan primary schools with the Ugandan government, were not aware of UNHCR's activities or of its interest in providing peace education programming for refugee students. One UNICEF official commented, however, that this was not unusual, since "the nature of the business is not to coordinate peace education work".[14]

The process of programme development included seven five-day awareness workshops to introduce refugees to the course. This was followed by three "training of trainers" workshops (one each in Arua, Adjumani and Moyo districts). These trainers were then expected to lead workshops for refugees and Ugandans working with refugees (trainers in the Uganda programme were known as facilitators in the Kenya programme). Peace education was thus designed "to enhance the community's awareness about elements of peace, through the existing structure of community workers" (Freeman, 2000: 1). The intention, in other words, was to equip existing community workers (many of whom were refugees and Ugandans working for UNHCR's NGO implementing partners and Ugandan government offices) with peace education skills so that they could serve the community's needs more effectively.

There has been additional training of trainers since this initial set of workshops. One of the workshop organizers related that "most of those trained were Ugandan local government officials who are responsible for both refugees and Ugandans". Some of those trained were also from southern Sudan and would return there following the training.

A number of constraints have hampered programme development. "The greatest hurdle now", one NGO official stated with regard to the programme, "is the problem of trainees focusing on food instead of the training". Issues of trainer incentives and provisions of food and per diems to workshop participants plague the programme. This might be expected, given the uneven history of programme management. UNHCR hired a consultant to start up the programme beginning in mid-1999. Problems involving contract extensions ensued in early 2000 and the consultant was only able briefly to visit the northern Ugandan districts during that time. The consultant's contract was not renewed.

Working with limited direction from UNHCR, NGO implementing partners in northern Uganda nonetheless kept the programme going. The peace education programme is popular with refugees and Ugandans, but it is especially popular during the "hungry season" when food supplies run low. Food, indeed, was a main issue of discussion for most refugees interviewed in Uganda, since the SRS policy had begun to reduce food rations. Refugees were supposed to supplement rations with crops they grew on their settlement farms.

14 The recollections of UNHCR officials suggested otherwise. They explained that peace education workshops and meetings were held with UNICEF and officials at Uganda's Ministry of Education, and samples of UNHCR's materials were shared. Due to interruptions in staffing at UNHCR, however, no follow-up ensued.

The programme remains a small-scale endeavour. The workshops themselves are well attended, but they last half the time of workshops in Kenya (three full days instead of twelve half-days). The budget allocated to the Jesuit Refugee Service for peace education for the year 2000 is US$13,000. UNHCR's support for the programme is weak. As one UNHCR official observed, "Peace education is always the first thing to be cut in the budget".

There is also the problem of overlap and poor coordination with other workshop-based programmes. "I believe in peace education", one UNHCR official explained. "But my problem is we have so many peace-related activities already going on." The official listed some examples of workshops that have taken place in refugee settlements in recent months: children's rights, gender awareness, girls' education, leadership and domestic violence. "And the same refugees go to all of the workshops", the official added.

Refugees who might be considered leaders or community workers – officials in the refugee settlement structure, those working with NGOs, teachers and other educated professionals – confirmed that members of this elite refugee group attended the varieties of workshops periodically offered to them. Some admitted that while many of the workshops addressed similar issues – the one most often mentioned was communication – they sometimes did so in conflicting ways.

One set of leaders, however, was not considered part of this elite group: clan leaders. "What is happening now", one refugee clan leader explained, "it that most problems are tackled according to the judiciary, the laws" by refugee community leaders (who are part of an official organized refugee structure containing Welfare Council, Block and Cluster leaders) and Ugandan authorities. "The religious leaders settle other issues in a religious way." Clan leaders are under attack ("the religious leaders say that our traditional ways are sinful").

Significantly, however, a number of refugees who were involved with the Peace Education Programme believed that the problem-solving methods they learned in the programme resembled the clan leaders' approach, which tends to focus on reconciling the parties in conflict. One participant said that, whereas the refugee Welfare Council, Block and Cluster leaders "act like government officials" and decided who was right and who was at fault, "the clan leaders want to decide problems peacefully". The idea here, another participant who was also a refugee religious leader explained, was that "sometimes we decide things too administratively", like the Welfare Council, Block and Cluster leaders. But like the clan leaders' methods, peace education "helps us to listen to each side" in a conflict "to know how the conflict started".

Refugee youth. Officials with the Office of the Prime Minister, which is largely responsible for refugee affairs in the Ugandan government, described how as many as "70–75 per cent of all [Sudanese] refugee youth go to secondary school". A corrective to this statistic was suggested by a UNHCR education official, who estimated that 20 per cent of Sudanese refugee youth attend secondary school, provided "you define youth as [aged] 13–18". The official also surmised that the far higher figure provided by government officials may be a result of three factors: the fact that although a high number of refugee youth are in school, most attend primary schools; that many refugee youth not in school leave the settlements for lengthy periods; and that perhaps two-thirds of all refugees who qualify for secondary school subsequently attend one.

Government and aid agency officials share the same perspective about Sudanese attitudes to education. As one government official observed, "The Sudanese like education so much." In the districts hosting refugees, the official added, "more refugees than Ugandans are in secondary school". This fact should not imply, however, that the citizens of northern Uganda are uninterested in school. Sudanese refugees may

Sudanese refugees at an outdoor classroom. Fugnido Camp, Gambella Region, Ethiopia. UNHCR/02.2001/B. Neeleman

have a zest for education, but their fees are also subsidized, although not as much as are those of refugees in Kenya's Kakuma camps. Ugandan students, by comparison, receive no such support. This arrangement is due to change once the SRS is fully implemented.

Many male Sudanese refugee youth make a connection between the ready availability of secondary school education in Uganda and the porous border between Uganda and Sudan. That some Sudanese refugee youth return to Sudan after receiving their education is common knowledge. Some reportedly commute to the camps when food rations are handed out. Others use the education they received in Ugandan settlements to search for work either with international humanitarian agencies working in southern Sudan or with the Sudanese Peoples Liberation Army (SPLA) as military officers. As one youth observed, "If you have education, you can go and fight".

Not all male youth are so mobile. As with youth in Kakuma and Dadaab, frustration and idleness are common themes in their lives. A number of refugees and officials working with refugees mention the incidence of refugee youth suicides. The rate of actual and attempted suicides was seen to be on the increase. In interviews, Sudanese refugees spoke often of the night-time "disco dances" that refugee youth regularly attended. These involve not only dancing but drinking alcohol and, frequently, violent clashes. Some female youth told of rapes that took place near discos. "Our parents don't want us to go to the discos," one refugee youth explained, "but for us, it's one of the only refreshing and entertaining things to do. At discos we can make friends with our brother and sister [youth]."

For female youth, the connection between education and marriage was strong. At all times, the girls are reminded to stay away from the "Drop-out" boys. Male youth who have left school early often seek to marry soon afterwards. Some of these boys, one teenage schoolgirl remarked, "rape us when we are alone with them". They also regularly harass their female peers who have remained in school. The girls understand that the best way to avoid an early marriage to these "Drop-outs" is to attend secondary school. Secondary school fees, however, although subsidized, are still prohibitive. Some girls (as well as boys) consequently work as day labourers during school vacations to save money for school fees. If they are unable to save enough money, and if their families cannot provide sufficient support, they may be unable to continue their schooling. Refugee teachers and parents explained that when this occurred, the likelihood of early marriage for the girls dramatically increased.

Conclusion

"Peace," a Sierra Leonean refugee once explained to me, "is a dangerous idea in my country." His brother had participated in demonstrations calling for a peaceful resolution to the current civil war in Sierra Leone. Many had interpreted this support for peace as an endorsement and acceptance of the rebel forces, whose combination of child exploitation and atrocities had made them profoundly unpopular and militarily successful. "My brother was killed for supporting peace," he said.

Peace is an idea with a wealth of different interpretations, some of which are reflected in the unwieldy subject known as peace education. Certain general aspects of the peace education field, however, are apparent. It is popular but hard to define. Its values are widely embraced but its implementation inspires scepticism. It espouses universal ideals that are often interpreted according to Western cultural notions of universality. It preaches acceptance, communication and inclusion, while programmes relating to it may actively resist collaboration and coordination with each other. Its programmes are usually targeted at people who are already peaceful. And peace educators strongly endorse its expansion while claiming that its results cannot be easily assessed.

Peace education, in short, is a field that does not at first appear to take itself very seriously. This is not the case. Many peace educators are dedicated to enhancing the prospects of peace: the Somali refugee youth "professors of peace" in Dadaab are but one example of such dedication. And while the major criticisms of peace education are valid and important, it is also true that few in any field succeed at turning violent conflict into non-violent conflict.

Peace educators address an important need when they address issues of peace, particularly for people plagued by violence. At the same time, the weaknesses in peace education's approach are considerable and are not being sufficiently addressed. It is necessary to examine peace education's successes and shortcomings in more detail by commenting in particular on UNHCR's Peace Education Programme.

The strengths of the UNHCR Peace Education Programme are many. It promotes refugee empowerment and self-sufficiency. It appears to have been reasonably successful in bridging cultural gaps in Kakuma and Dadaab by means of carrying out its initial research and development phase. Its practical orientation and objectives naturally and appropriately connect to the objectives and values inherent in refugee protection and education. It takes significant strides in translating its materials into other languages. The problem-solving skills it teaches have the potential to support both peaceful refugee repatriation and stable resettlement. It is also popular with refugees: a measure of its success lies in the fact that refugees in the programme not only continued but sometimes even expanded the programme during periods when UNHCR peace education personnel were not present. Finally, it is cost-effective.

Such inherent programme potential makes the consternation over the Peace Education Programme within UNHCR unfortunate and troubling. Peace education seems a bother to many officials, and scepticism about the programme appears to be widespread. A degree of this attitude towards peace education can be explained. Officials in field offices need to know what a programme can do and how it can provide them with tangible results that they can report to their superiors. As with any new programme, peace education's success will partly depend on addressing adequately this institutional preoccupation.

The argument that peace education is primarily an education programme and therefore should not be expected to provide regular indicators of its effectiveness is not a sufficient argument against evaluation. Evaluation in the peace education field is generally poor, partly because it is scarcely attempted and partly because the goals of peace education programmes are often unreachable. If Boulding is correct in stating that we are not sure of just how peace is achieved and maintained, then how can peace educators reasonably claim that their work contributes to peace?

Nonetheless, it is possible if not probable that the sort of tangible results UNHCR and other institutions normally require of programming can, to some degree, be achieved for peace education programming – provided that the programmes have tangible, concrete aims. One possible evaluation approach is briefly outlined in the 'Recommendations' section below.

The following programme weaknesses considered here are not specific to UNHCR's programme but are reflections of weaknesses in the broader field:

1. Training leaders (in this case, refugee leaders) to solve problems, while useful, is an inadequate means of addressing issues of serious violence. Since refugee leaders in most cases do not represent refugees directly involved in violence, their ability to promote peace may be severely constrained. This problem is particularly applicable to the Uganda programme, where the focus is on training community workers and leaders. But in Kenya as well, while the programme is not restricted to refugee leaders, they comprise an important component of the peace education trainee group. In Kakuma, refugee leaders lack the credibility, and perhaps even the access, to the primary perpetrators of violence: marginalized male youth. And in Dadaab, the problem of rape is so divisive and serious, and the indications that refugee leaders are not working purposefully to address it so apparent, that targeting leaders for peace education might even prove counter-productive.

2. Training is a form of empowerment. Targeting refugee elites – most of whom are male and educated – instead of the most vulnerable and violent may strengthen the existing power structure and contribute to the frustrations, and perhaps the violence, of the marginalized.

3. Peace education, like the concept of peace, is inherently symbolic. For UNHCR's Peace Education Programme, the symbolism of the language of instruction was powerful because it often limited access rather than demonstrated the importance of inclusion. English was the language of refugee elites in Uganda and Kenya. This was a logical starting point for the two programmes. But expanding access to the programme requires translation of all peace education materials into local languages, an effort that is well under way for UNHCR's programme in Kenya. Carrying out this slow and complicated task will be an important programme advance because it can ensure that the meanings of critical peace education concepts (bias, empathy, etc.) are preserved following translation, something that is difficult to do now in the simultaneous translations that may take place during the workshops themselves.

   Expanding a programme's credibility would also be demonstrated by coordinating programmes in both conceptual and regional terms. An opportunity exists to act on peace education principles in east Africa, for example, where UNICEF and UNESCO are working on peace education alongside UNHCR. The coordination is limited. Coordination appears to be equally limited within UNHCR regarding the many workshops and courses provided for refugees. Workshop training could ultimately prove counterproductive if it addresses similar issues in different ways while regularly targeting the same refugees.

4. The real and perceived threat of violence in the refugee camps blurs the distinction between conceptions of conflict prevention and conflict resolution in peace education work. A more important distinction is prioritizing those who could make the best use of peace education training. Clearly, the limited participation of marginalized "Drop-out" youth in the programme limits the programme's potential to transfer needed problem-solving skills to refugees who could benefit from the experience. The "Drop-outs" are marked by frustration and a tendency towards involvement in violent activities, and peace education alone cannot solve these significant problems. These youth need jobs and the sort of productive activities that very few seem to be receiving. But peace education may help.

5. The proportion of female youth in the programme is alarmingly small. Their problems and frustrations are as significant as those of their male counterparts, although their lives are quieter. The regular threats of rape and other forms of violence offered to this population are alarming, particularly in Dadaab. These young women are not often targeted for programme participation, and they should be.

6. The possibility of peace education becoming counter-productive when it is taught to children and not to their parents or guardians is a serious consideration that peace education programmes must address more forcefully. The UNHCR programme in Kenya has taken the important first step of inviting parents and guardians to workshops, but more should be done to incorporate parents and guardians into programme activities.

Recommendations

If peace education is to become an effective tool for peace, it will have to address the important criticisms of its detractors head-on. It will have to consider the impact of targeting schoolchildren for peace education highlighted by Boyden and Ryder, particularly those children whose homes are plagued by domestic violence or whose lives are surrounded by actual or potential violence. School-based activities should thus become but one component of community-based programming that includes in the educational process the students' parents and guardians.

With this in mind, the concept of community, and the implications of crossing cultures with peace education concepts, must also be carefully considered. If the existing programme emphasizes individual concerns and the culture within which it will be taught emphasizes community concerns, then the programme should be adjusted accordingly. UNHCR's programme demonstrated that this sort of adjustment is attainable and appropriate.

At the same time, since the impact of conflicts is regional, peace education programming in conflict and post-conflict zones should also aim to be regional. Such an approach will never be feasible until coordination between peace education programmes in a given region is accorded a high priority. Steps should be taken, by the relevant implementing organizations in addition to donor and local governments, to ensure that appropriate and similar programming is being provided by different organizations working with related populations (refugees and internally displaced persons of the same nationality, for example). As one NGO education expert observed, "effective programmes that deal with conflict have to be regional, not community by community".

Addressing the problem of evaluation will require investments of time, money and, not least, patience.[15] In order to be able actually to measure the impact of peace education, programmes must focus on practically applicable concepts and skills that students can absorb and use. Measuring the impact of programming must begin before peace education takes place. Case studies could be developed to examine

15 A UNICEF education consultant observed: "Possibly the greatest obstacle to doing the kinds of evaluations of peace education projects that are currently needed is the fact that behaviour change of this complexity takes time; and project officers report that many of these projects are donor-driven. If donors want to see significant results within a relatively short time span, perhaps six months to a year, that is not long enough to do a meaningful evaluation study. Some good 'education' of donors on behaviour change processes in peace education is needed in order to obtain support for longer-term studies of how these projects impact behaviour, and whether those changes are sustainable."

how people struggle to solve problems before and after they receive the training.[16] The role of peace education personnel who become conflict mediators should, without question, also be evaluated.

The tendency for peace education programmes to target already peaceful people is a significant weakness of the field. While reinforcing the skills of already peaceful people is a valid programme objective. Particularly, as a starting place for a programme, the fact remains that those people who need the peace education skills and understandings most – marginalized refugee youth and rape victims in Kenya and Uganda, for example – rarely receive the training, and they should.

UNHCR's Peace Education Programme in Kenya has a strong foundation. The programme in Uganda does not. Both are under-supported, under-utilized and should be carefully expanded. In addition to considering application of the general recommendations mentioned above, here are some specific, UNHCR programme-related recommendations:

1. Calls by refugees for two levels of peace education courses should be heeded. This would allow for a review of the existing material, which is challenging and requires more teaching and discussion time to be absorbed and used by refugees.

2. A far greater selection of refugees should be trained. Survey research is needed to determine who would most benefit from the adult workshops and what measures need to be taken to ensure their attendance. In the refugee camps and settlements of Kenya and Uganda, this will be a long list. But certain groups could certainly be targeted for training now, such as victims of rape (including the Anti-Rape Committee in Dadaab), "Drop-outs" (male and female), women's groups such as the Girls' and Women's Support Group of Kakuma, the parents, guardians and companions of schoolchildren (especially in homes where severe domestic violence is present), and so on.

3. To reach those most in need of peace education in refugee communities, the issue of the language of instruction is critical. The Peace Education Programme's steps in translating materials should be supported. Indeed, materials translation should be steadily expanded to address within reason the language needs of all refugees where the programme is operating. This will take careful planning to ensure that the original concepts and pedagogy are consistently preserved and culturally appropriate following translation. It will also require the increased involvement of refugee (and national) staff in evaluation.

4. Appropriate peace education programming necessarily incorporates both protection and education concerns. Accordingly, institutional and curriculum revision measures should be explored to ensure that the programme is not only coordinated between but connected to the Protection and Community Services Units of UNHCR.

5. Since UNHCR's Peace Education Programme is a problem-solving training and education programme, it should regularly be applied to help solve pressing problems. One example of possible application would be developing workshops where the misunderstandings and fears of refugees in Ugandan regarding the Self-Reliance Strategy, when refugees and Ugandan government, UNHCR and NGO officials could jointly participate. Another would be to address Somali responses to rape in Dadaab.

16 UNHCR's Peace Education Programme, it should be noted, did carry out baseline studies in Kenya and Uganda in advance of their work, but did not conduct case studies that were monitored over time.

Sudanese refugees in a class for deaf children, using sign alphabet. Kakuma Camp, Kenya. UNHCR/07.1999/B. Press

The comments of too many young refugee men about rape were alarming, and the victimization of too many refugee women, young women in particular, to sexual violence was equally troubling. Such population groups could be targeted for peace education training. A third would be to engage youth involved in specific violent events or facing potentially explosive situations, such as the thousands of frustrated Sudanese refugee youth who have been encamped in the Mirieye transit camp in Adjumani District, Uganda for years. And so on.

6. Coordinating with other peace education programmes in the region should be given a high priority. Refugees in Kenya and Uganda should know when peace education is also being offered in their countries of origin. Expanding existing coordination between UNHCR, UNESCO and UNICEF should be enhanced, particularly when the agencies are working with people of the same nationality. Partnerships should be considered with relevant peace education NGOs (such as CECORE in Uganda). Coordination between religious groups involved in peacemaking and peace education programmes should also be undertaken whenever appropriate. Additionally, lessons learned from programming for disadvantaged and violent youth in non-refugee settings should be researched and applied to refugee programmes.

7. Coordination should also take place within UNHCR to ensure that the various workshops (such as Life Skills, Communication Skills, Gender, etc.) on peace education-related issues work well together. These workshops should also be used to target the most appropriate refugee groups, and evaluations should be conducted to determine the impact of the various kinds of training on refugee lives.

8. The wealth of "peace groups", particularly those involving youth in the Dadaab camps, that have arisen among those who have received the peace education training is a welcome indicator of peace education's acceptance in communities. Very small requests for support for these emerging groups have been made. They should be supported.

9. The issue of incentives, meals and per diems, which were mentioned in every field site visited (but particularly in northern Uganda), is a complicated one. Teachers and facilitators in the programme are being expected to provide professional (and important) services. Recognizing their work by means of increased incentives seems reasonable and appropriate, provided that it does not upset the existing incentive scales. In Uganda, the question of food and per diems is a particularly sensitive issue, because the programme is still so new and it arrived while reductions in food rations were sending shockwaves through refugee communities. It is also sensitive with aid agency officials. But the potential significance of the workshops themselves calls for the food and per diem issue to be appropriately addressed.

10. The Uganda programme is lurching ahead. It has limited and unenthusiastic support from UNHCR. Its workshops are too short and probably should not be run as all-day training. While current efforts by NGO implementing partners are generally commendable, particularly given the small budget allotments they receive, UNHCR's programme management in different districts is uncoordinated; the overall Uganda and Kenya programmes are also uncoordinated. The accent on cultural transformation should be avoided, as should expansion into primary schools, unless they are carried out in collaboration with UNICEF and the Ugandan government, which are already involved in peace education in the primary schools. The programme should be restarted from within UNHCR and connected with the Kenya programme more directly, so that lessons learned from the Kenya programme's pilot phase can be better applied to the Ugandan context.

Peace education, finally, should be accorded a specific set of stand-alone guidelines for educational assistance to refugees by UNHCR. These should state that peace education should build on and adapt the existing model it has already developed in Kenya; that new initiatives should be carefully researched and managed, initially as pilot projects to ensure that they are applied in culturally relevant ways and only when the refugee communities are receptive to it; that it should focus on practically applicable skills and concepts; that it should be targeted at communities in a way that promotes the involvement of the marginalized as well as the leadership; that the curriculum and management be coordinated with both the Community Services and the Protection Units; and that evaluation and monitoring procedures should start at the outset of the pilot phase.

Appendix

Just War Doctrine and Pacifism in the Christian Tradition: A Brief Overview

Although learning about and practising peace in a religious context is a subject reaching well beyond the scope of this report, some consideration of the religious world of peace education is useful. The example of Christian thought and action on the issues of peace, violence and justice will thus be briefly reviewed here.

Peace, Gilligan reminds us, is a central tenet in Christian thought: "Jesus explicitly rejected violence and urged his disciples to turn the other cheek, to return good for evil, to bless their enemies and persecutors rather than curse them" (1990: 16).

Following Jesus' death, Ferguson notes, "the simple fact is that for something like a century and a half after the ministry of Jesus, Christians would not touch military service" (1978: 103). In fact, for nearly three centuries the early Christians were "regarded as unfit for military duty because of their exotic attitudes toward violence and warfare" (Gilligan, 1990: 16).

In AD 313, Christianity's relationship with the state dramatically changed. Instead of its continuing as an outcast religion, the emperor Constantine, a Christian convert, declared that Christianity would be the Roman Empire's official religion. The resulting "Constantinian bargain" was clear: "the Church received the protection and patronage of the emperor, and in return [Constantine's] military campaigns and designs were pronounced in advance to be part of the divine plan for the triumph of justice" (ibid: 17).

From that point onwards, Christians were faced with "the problem of reconciling the teachings of the Prince of Peace with the perceived need for the use of armed force" (Gilligan, 1990: 17). Additionally, as Ferguson observed, "the fortunes of the Church were now tied up with the fortunes of the state" (1978: 105).

Over time, a theory or doctrine of Just War arose, which accepted violence if it was carried out in the pursuit of justice: "The undergirding notion [of Just War] is that while violence against one's fellow human beings is reprehensible, it is essential that justice prevail in human society lest the weak and the innocent suffer at the hands of the violent" (Gilligan, 1990: 17).

Ferguson points out two central problems with Just War doctrine. First, "no objective tribunal" exists that can "declare a cause just". This gives the doctrine "a veneer of self-justification but not an atom of legality". Second, "it seems to have very little to do with the Christian faith" itself, since, in Ferguson's view, "the arguments of Augustine and Aquinas [two leading contributors to the development of Just War doctrine] are a replacement of the teaching of the New Testament by Greek philosophy or Roman law" (1978: 111).

Tensions arising in the Christian tradition regarding peace and violence surfaced not only in the development of pacifist churches such as the Mennonites, Friends and Amish. It also sparked successions of debates between members of various Christian denominations. This tendency was particularly notable when wars took place. As Johnson observed, "wartime tends to divide the ranks of the proponents of peace" between those supporting a war as appropriate and necessary and others who oppose all wars (1987: 226).

References

Aguilar, Pilar and Gonzalo Retamal (1998). *Educational Response in Complex Emergencies: A discussion document.* Geneva: International Bureau of Education.

All Africa Conference of Churches (AACC) (1999). *Youth Peace Training Manual*. Nairobi: AACC Publications.

An-Na'im, Abdullahi A (1998). "Human Rights and the Challenge of Relevance: The Case of Collective Rights", in Monique Castermans-Holleman, Fried van Hoof and Jacqueline Smith, (eds.). *The Role of the Nation-State in the 21st Century: Human Rights, International Organizations and Foreign Policy: Essays in Honor of Peter Baehr.* The Hague and Boston: Kluwer Law International, pp. 3–16.

Appleby, R. Scott (2000). *The Ambivalence of the Sacred: Religion, Violence, and Reconciliation.* Lanham, MD: Rowman & Littlefield.

Barsh, Russel Lawrence and Chantelle Marlor (2000). "Grounded, Experiential Teaching about Violence". *The HFG Review*, 4 (1): 27–38.

Baxter, Pamela (1998). *Refugee Education for Peace Project: Progress Report, 1997–1998*. Geneva: UNHCR Programme and Technical Support Section, Kenya.

Baxter, Pamela (2000a). *Facilitators Resource Notes.* Nairobi: UNHCR Peace Education Programme.

Baxter, Pamela (2000b). *Teacher Activity Book*. Nairobi: UNHCR Peace Education Programme.

Bloomfield, Lincoln P. (1986). "Imagination and Responsibility: Dilemmas in Translating Creative Ideas into Action", in Earl W. Foell and Richard A. Nenneman, (eds.). *How Peace Came to the World.* Cambridge, MA and London: MIT Press, pp. 237–250.

Boulding, Kenneth E. (1991). "Stable Peace Among Nations: A Learning Process", in Elise Boulding, Clovis Brigagao and Kevin Clements, (eds.). *Peace, Culture and Society: Transnational Research and Dialogue.* Boulder, CO, San Francisco and Oxford: Westview Press, pp. 108–14.

Bourke, Joanna (1999). *An Intimate History of Killing: Face-to-Face in Twentieth Century Warfare*. New York: Basic Books.

Boyden, Jo, with Paul Ryder (1996). "The Provision of Education to Children Affected by Armed Conflict". (unpublished paper), Refugee Studies Centre, Oxford.

Convention on the Rights of the Child (1989). Adopted by UN General Assembly 20 November 1989, entered into force 2 September 1990. Geneva and New York: Centre for Human Rights, United Nations Office, and UNICEF.

Crawford, Donna and Richard Bodine (1996). *Conflict Resolution Education: A Guide to Implementing Programs in Schools, Youth-Serving Organizations, and Community and Juvenile Justice Settings: Programme Report.* Washington, DC: Office of Juvenile Justice and Delinquency Prevention, US Dept. of Justice/Office of Elementary and Secondary Education, US Dept. of Education.

Crisp, Jeff (1999). "A State of Insecurity: The Political Economy of Violence in Refugee-Populated Areas of Kenya". *New Issues in Refugee Research*, Working Paper No. 16. Geneva: UNHCR.

Dear, John (1994). *The God of Peace: Toward a Theology of Nonviolence*. Maryknoll: Obis.

Dulic, Sead and Roger Chamberlain (1998). "Peace-building in an educational context", in Tag McEntegart, (ed.). *In the Garden of the Imagination: Sowing the seeds of a peaceful future.* Bosnia-Herzegovina: Centre for Drama-in-Education, pp. iv-v.

Dwyer, Judith A. (1999). "The Evolving Teaching on Peace Within Roman Catholic Hierarchical Thought", in Judith A. Dwyer, (ed.). *Vision and Values: Ethical Viewpoints in the Catholic Tradition,* Washington, DC: Georgetown University Press, pp. 149–61.

El-Kenz, Ali (1996). "Youth and Violence", in Stephen Ellis, (ed.). *Africa Now: People, Policies and Institutions.* London: James Currey, and Portsmouth, NH: Heinemann, in association with the Ministry of Foreign Affairs (DGIS), The Hague, pp. 42–57.

Ferguson, John (1978). *War and Peace in the World's Religions.* Oxford and New York: Oxford University Press.

Foster, Annie (1995). *From Emergency to Empowerment: The Role of Education in Refugee Communities.* Washington, DC: Academy for Educational Development.

Fountain, Susan (1999). *Peace Education in UNICEF*, Working Paper Series, Programme Division, Education Section. New York: UNICEF.

Freeman, Marnie (2000). "Peace Education Programme: End of Consultancy Report", (unpublished), UNHCR, Uganda.

Galtung, Johan (1969). "Violence, Peace, and Peace Research". *Journal of Peace Research*, 6 (1): 167–91.

Galtung, Johan (1983). "Peace education: learning to hate war, love peace and to do something about it". *International Review of Education*, 29 (3): 281–7.

Galtung, Johan (1996). *Peace by Peaceful Means: Peace and Conflict, Development and Civilization.* Oslo: International Peace Research Institute; London: Thousand Oaks; New Delhi: Sage.

Gilligan, John J. (1990). "Teaching Peace in a Christian Context", in Leroy S. Rouner, (ed.). *Celebrating Peace.* Notre Dame, IN: University of Notre Dame Press, pp. 15–32.

Hicks, David (1988). "Understanding the field", in David Hicks, (ed.). *Education for Peace: Issues, Principles, and Practice in the Classroom.* London and New York: Routledge, pp. 3–19.

Hutchinson, Frank (1998). "Young people's hopes and fears for the future", in David Hicks and Richard Slaughter, (eds.). *World Yearbook of Education: Futures Education*, London: Kogan Page, pp. 133–47.

Johnson, James Turner (1987). *The Quest for Peace: Three Moral Traditions in Western Cultural History.* Princeton: Princeton University Press.

Kainz, Howard P. (1987). "Introduction", in Howard P. Kainz, (ed.). *Philosophical Perspectives on Peace: An Anthology of Classical and Modern Sources,* Athens, OH: Ohio University Press, p. x.

Lederach, John Paul (1995). *Preparing for Peace: Conflict Transformation Across Cultures.* Syracuse: Syracuse University Press.

Lowicki, Jane (2000). *Untapped Potential: Adolescents affected by armed conflict: A review of programs and policies.* New York: Women's Commission for Refugee Women and Children.

Machel, Graça (1996). *The Impact of Armed Conflict on Children*. New York: United Nations.

Merkx, Jozef (1999). "Refugee Identities and Relief in an African Borderland: A Case Study of Northern Uganda and Southern Sudan". Draft working paper, Refugee Studies Programme, Oxford.

Midttun, Eldrid K., and Helge Brochmann (1998). "Background, Concept and Process of Human Rights Education for the School Systems in the Caucasus", (unpublished), Norwegian Refugee Council, Oslo.

Obura, Anna (1996). "Peace Education: A Lesson Observed", (unpublished), Nairobi.

Panikkar, Raimon (1999). "Religions and the Culture of Peace", in Leroy S. Rouner, (ed.). *Religion, Politics, and Peace.* Notre Dame, IN: University of Notre Dame Press, pp. 185–204.

Pigozzi, Mary Joy (1999). *Education in Emergencies and Reconstruction: A Developmental Approach.* Working Paper Series, Programme Division, Education Section. New York: UNICEF.

Reardon, Betty A. (1988). *Comprehensive Peace Education: Educating for Global Responsibility.* New York and London: Teachers College Press (Columbia University).

Reardon, Betty A. (1997). *Tolerance – The Threshold of Peace: Unit 1: Teacher-Training Resource Unit.* Paris: UNESCO (The Teacher's Library).

Refugees International (1998). *The Lost Boys of Sudan.* Washington: Refugees International.

Retamal, Gonzalo and Mudiappasamy Devadoss (1998). "Education in a Nation with Chronic Crisis: The Case of Somalia", in Gonzalo Retamal and Ruth Aedo-Richmond, (eds.). *Education as a Humanitarian Response.* London: Cassell, pp. 74–93.

Retamal, Gonzalo and Ruth Aedo-Richmond, (eds.) (1998). *Education as a Humanitarian Response.* London/Cassell, UNESCO International Bureau of Education, Geneva.

Richards, Paul (1996). *Fighting for the Rain Forest: War, Youth and Resources in Sierra Leone.* Oxford: James Currey, and Portsmouth, NH: Heinemann, in association with the International African Institute.

Robinson, Phillip (2000). "Analysis of the UNHCR Peace Education Teacher Activity Book: The Kenyan Pilot Project", (unpublished), Nairobi.

Smith, Donald Eugene (1971). *Religion, Politics, and Social Change in the Third World: A Sourcebook*. New York: Free Press, and London: Collier-Macmillan.

Sommers, Marc (1998). "Reconciliation and Religion: Refugee Churches in the Rwandan Camps". Occasional paper, Life and Peace Institute, Uppsala, Sweden.

Sommers, Marc (1999). "Emergency Education for Children". Working paper published by the Inter-University Committee on International Migration and the Mellon-MIT Inter-University Program on Non-Governmental Organizations (NGOs) and Forced Migration. Cambridge, MA: Center for International Studies, MIT.

Sphere Project (1998). "Introduction", *Humanitarian Charter and Minimum Standards in Disaster Response.* Geneva: Sphere Project.

Stomfay-Stitz, Aline M (1993). *Peace Education in America, 1828–1990: Sourcebook for Education and Research.* Metuchen, NJ and London: Scarecrow Press.

UNESCO-PEER (1999). *1999 Annual Report.* Nairobi: UNESCO-PEER.

UNESCO-PEER (n.d.). *Peace Building Practices in Somalia.* Nairobi: UNESCO-PEER.

UNHCR (1994). *Refugee Children: Guidelines on Protection and Care.* Geneva: UNHCR.

UNHCR (1995). *Revised (1995) Guidelines for Educational Assistance to Refugees.* Geneva: UNHCR/PTSS.

UNHCR (1997). *Review of UNHCR's Refugee Education Activities.* Geneva: UNHCR (Inspection and Evaluation Service).

UNHCR (2000). *Poetry Book.* Nairobi: UNHCR Peace Education Programme.

UNHCR Uganda and the Office of the Prime Minister, Government of Uganda (1999). "Self-Reliance for Refugee Hosting Areas in Moyo, Arua and Adjumani Districts, 1999–2003: Actual state of affairs and strategy for implementation". Strategy paper. Kampala: UNHCR Uganda and Office of the Prime Minister.

US Catholic Bishops (1994). "Confronting a Culture of Violence: A Catholic Framework for Action". United States Catholic Conference, Washington, DC.

Additional reading

Alfred, Taiaike (1999). *Peace, Power, Righteousness: An Indigenous Manifest.* Don Mills, Ont.: Oxford University Press.

Appleby, R. Scott (2000). *The Ambivalence of the Sacred: Religion, Violence, and Reconciliation.* Lanham, MD: Rowman & Littlefield Publishers.

Berman, Sheldon (1997). *Children's Social Consciousness and the Development of Social Responsibility.* Albany: State University of New York Press.

Bey, Theresa M., and Turner, Gwendolyn Y. (1996). *Making School a Place of Peace.* Thousand Oaks, CA: Corwin Press.

Bodine, Richard J., Crawford, Donna K. and Schrumpf, Fred (1994). *Creating the Peaceable School: A Comprehensive Program for Teaching Conflict Resolution: Student Manual.* Champaign, IL: Research Press.

Bodine, Richard J., and Crawford, Donna K. (1998). *The Handbook of Conflict Resolution Education: A Guide to Building Quality Programs in Schools.* San Francisco, CA: Jossey-Bass Publishers.

Braybrooke, Marcus (1992). *Stepping Stones to a Global Ethic.* London: SCM Press.

Byrne, Sean, and Irvin, Cynthia (2000). *Reconcilable Differences: Turning Points in Ethnopolitical Conflict.* West Hartford, CT: Kumarian Press.

Catholic Association for International Peace (U.S.). Peace Education Committee (1934). *Peace Education in the Curriculum of the Schools.* Washington, DC: The Catholic Association for the International Peace.

Dobb, Leonard (1981). *The Pursuit of Peace.* Westport, CT: Greenwood Press.

Elias, Robert and Turpin, Jennifer (1994). *Rethinking Peace.* Boulder, CO: Lynne Rienner Publishers.

Ferdman, Bernardo, M., Weber, Rose-Marie, and Ramirez, Arnulfo (1994). *Literacy Across Languages and Cultures. Albany: State University of New York Press.*

Foell, Earl W. and Nenneman, Richard A. (1986). *How Peace Came to the World.* Cambridge, MA: MIT Press.

Garner, Howard G. (1995). *Teamwork Models and Experience in Education.* Boston, MA: Allyn and Bacon.

Goleman, Daniel (1995). *Emotional Intelligence.* New York: Bantam Books.

Grossi, Verdiana (1998). *Report of the International Peace Education Conference of Geneva: November 26-–29, 1998.* International Peace Bureau: UNESCO 2000, Hague Appeal for Peace.

Hansen, Holger Bernt, and Twaddle, Michael, (eds.) (1995). *Religion and Politics in East Africa: The Period Since Independence.* London: James Curry; Athens, OH: Ohio University Press.

Haynes, Jeff (1995). *Religion, Globalization and Political Culture in the Third World.* Houndmills, Basingstoke: Macmillan; New York: St. Martin's Press.

Heater, Derek (1984). *Peace through Education: The Contribution of the Council for Education in World Citizenship.* London and New York: Falmer Press.

Hicks, David and Richard Slaughter, (eds.) (1998). *World Yearbook of Education: Futures Education.* London, Stirling: Kogan Page.

Hutchison, Francis P. (1996). *Educating Beyond Violent Futures.* London, New York: Routledge.

Jacobs, Ida T., and DeBoer, John J. (1940). *Educating for Peace: A Report of the Committee on International Relations of the National Council of Teachers of English.* New York, London: D. Appleton-Century.

Kreidler, William J. (1984). *Creative Conflict Resolution: More than 200 Activities for Keeping Peace in the Classroom.* Glenview, IL: Scott, Foresman.

Kung, Hans (1998). *A Global Ethic for Global Politics and Economics.* New York: Oxford University Press.

Kung, Hans (1996). *Yes to a Global Ethic: Voices from Religion and Politics.* New York: Oxford University Press.

Long, Edward LeRoy, Jr. (1983). *Peace Thinking in a Warring World.* Philadelphia: Philadelphia, Westminster Press.

Nieuwmeijer, Louise and Oliver, Johan (1996). *Conflict and Peace Research: South African Realities and Challenge.* Pretoria: HSRC Publishers.

Powers, Gerard F., Christiansen, Drew, SJ, and Hennemeyer, Robert T. (1994). *Peacemaking: Moral and Policy Challenges for a New World.* Washington, DC: United States Catholic Conference.

Read, Herbert (1949). *Education for Peace.* New York: C. Scribner's Sons.

Reardon, Betty A. (1997). *Tolerance – The Threshold of Peace: Primary-School Resource Unit.* Washington, DC: UNESCO Publishing.

Schaffner, Christina and Wenden, Anita (1995). *Language and Peace.* Aldershot and Brookfield, VT: Dartmouth.

Smith, Donald Eugene (1971). *Religion, Politics, and Social Change in the Third World.* New York: Free Press.

Stassen, Glen H. (1992). *Just Peacemaking. Transforming Initiatives for Justice and Peace.* Louisville, KY: Westminster/John Knox Press.

United States Department of Education (1998). *Early Warning Timely Response. A Guide to Safe Schools.* Washington DC: United States Department of Education.

UNICEF (2000). "Curriculum Report Card". Working Paper Series, Education Section, Program Division, New York.

US Catholic Conference Inc. (1995). "Confronting a Culture of Violence: A Catholic Framework for Action: A Pastoral Message of the US Catholic Bishops". Washington, DC.

Van Loan, Anna Fitzgerald (1925). *Peace Lessons for Schools.* New York: Fleming H. Revell.

Wollman, Nell, *Working for Peace. A Handbook of Practical Psychology and Other Tools.* San Luis Obispo, CA: Impact Publishers, 1985.

Articles and journals

Abu-Nimer, Mohammed (2000). "Peace Building in Postsettlement Challenges for Israeli and Palestinian Peace Educators". *Peace and Conflict: Journal of Peace Psychology,* 6 (1), January 21.

Bush, Robert (1999). "Book Review: Proclaim Peace: Christian Pacifism from Unexpected Quarters". *Peace and Change: A Journal of Peace and Research,* 24 (2), April: 255–7.

D'Andrea, Micheal and Daniels, Judy (1996). "Promoting Peace in Our Schools: Developmental, Preventive, and Multicultural Considerations". *The School Counselor.* 44, September: 55–64.

Farrell, Michael J. (1993). "The Military Mystique". *National Catholic Reporter,* February 19.

Forcey, Linda Rennie and Rainforth, Beverly (1998). "Team Teaching 'Conflict Resolution in Educational and Community Settings': An Experiment in Collaboration and Conflict Resolution". *Peace and Change: A Journal of Peace Research,* 23 (3), July: 373–85.

Hart, Julie and Gunty, Mark (1997). "The Impact of a Peer Mediation Program on an Elementary School Environment". *Peace and Change. A Journal of Peace Research,* 22, 1, January: 77–93.

Knoll, Erwin (1991). "Not a Just War, Just a War". *The Progressive,* June.

McCarthy, Colman (1987). "The Class of Nonviolence". *Washington Post,* September 21.

McCarthy, Colman (1998). "Peaceful Conflict Resolution Teachable: Nine Steps Provide the Key to Resolving Disputes Peacefully", *Sun,* March 15.

McCarthy, Colman (1992). "Peace Education: The Time Is Now". *Washington Post,* December 29.

McCarthy, Colman (1999). "Peace Studies: One Student's Victory". *Washington Post,* September 28.

Mendelsohn, Michaela and Straker, Gill (1998). "Child Soldiers: Psychosocial Implications of the Graça Machel/UN Study". *Peace and Conflict: Journal of Peace Psychology,* 4 (4): 399–413.

Nelson, Linden, Van Slyck, Michael R., and Cardella, Lucille A. (1999). "Curricula for Teaching Adolescents about Peace and Conflict". *Peace and Conflict: Journal of Peace Psychology,* 5 (2): 169–76.

Peace and Change: A Journal of Peace Research, 25 (2), April 2000: 149–51, 166–87, 208–25, 288–9.

PeaceTimes, Center for Teaching Peace, Washington DC, September 1999.

Zeiger, Susan. "Teaching Peace: Lessons from a Peace Studies Curriculum of the Progressive Era". *Peace and Change: A Journal of Peace Research,* 25, (1), January 2000: 53-68.

Selected Websites on Peace Education

AED publications:	www.aed.org/publications
Balkan Flowers:	www.balkanflowers.org
CARE:	www.care.org
Character counts:	www.charactercounts.org
Community of Caring:	www.communityofcaring.org
Conflict Web/USAID:	www.usaid.gov/regions/afr/conflictweb
Cooperation and Tolerance:	www.peacesite.org
Facing History and Facing Ourselves:	www.facinghistory.org
GINIE (Global Information Networks in Education):	www.ginie.org
International Youth Foundation:	www.iyfet.org
Justice and Peace Studies/Links/ Georgetown University:	www.georgetown.edu/departments.pjp/programs
Lutheran Immigration & Refugee Service:	www.lirs.org
National Council of Teachers of English:	www.ncte.org/chronicle/ttolstorMay1999.html
Oregon Peaceworks Fund:	www.teleport.com/~opw/frontdoor.html
Peace Work:	www.afsc.org/peacewrk.html
ProMotion Alliance for Justice:	www.afj.org
Co/Motion Project:	www.comotionmakers.org
Refugee Youth Summer Enrichment:	www.hcs.harvard.edu/~ryse/
Sites on Re-thinking Conflict:	www.relationshipjourney.org, www.newciv.org, www.pattern.com, www.worldtrans.org
Refugee Project:	www.refugeeproject.org
UNESCO/Culture of Peace:	www.UNESCO.org
United Nations Development Fund for Women:	www.unifem.undp.org
EmpowermentResources.com: weblinks:	www.empowermentresources.com
Youthlink.org:	www.youthlink.org

Chapter 5
Vocational Training for Refugees: A Case Study from Tanzania

Erik Lyby

Prologue

Work banishes those three great evils: Boredom, Vice, and Poverty. (Voltaire, Candide)

When a Turkish peasant farmer gave these words of wisdom to Candide, their logical consequence was explained to be that, in order to avoid the three great evils, a man should cultivate his garden. When doing so, he would spend his time in a useful way rather than falling into idleness and vice; he would watch the crops grow and avoid boredom; and he would escape poverty and hunger through the fruits of his work.

The three great evils coincide in the refugee camps for Burundians in western Tanzania, and the solution to work one's garden is not obvious – farmland is in very short supply.

Providing employable skills to the youths, enabling them to work and earn, is one way to combat the evils. But, with 10,000 young Burundian refugees entering adulthood each year in the camps, the scope for boredom, vice and misdemeanour is also ample and a case for concern.

Vocational skills training can help prepare some of the young people for a productive life once they return to their country. However, it is not everybody who is suitable for, or interested in, such training. The present paper tries to look at both sides of the problem – on the one hand, the transfer of skills that will be useful upon repatriation – and on the other, ways and means to keep young people busy and out of trouble.

Summary

UNHCR currently provides protection and assistance to some 350,000 Burundian refugees distributed in 10 camps in the Kigoma and Kagera regions in western Tanzania. The assistance includes activities such as support for primary and secondary education, as well as formal and non-formal vocational training. Formal vocational education and training is supported through a scholarship programme implemented by the Southern Africa Extension Unit (SAEU), whereas non-formal training is carried out in the refugee camps by other NGOs tasked with education and community services there.

The paper concerns the evaluation of ongoing skills training programmes, with a view to expanding them into a wider programme based in the refugee camps. The proposed training programme would be based on the concept of *education for repatriation*, with the aim of extending skills that will be of use on return to Burundi. The evaluation used qualitative interviews with key informants, supplemented by a questionnaire survey.

As of mid-October 2000, approximately 90,000 new refugees had registered with UNHCR in Tanzania. The vast majority originate from Burundi with a smaller number from DRC and Rwanda. Ngara Camp, Tanzania. UNHCR/08.2000/L. Boscardi

The evaluation

The *formal* training on offer to the refugees, which is supported by scholarships, only reaches very few, mostly those who have been in Tanzania for a long time, and who have an English-language capability. The courses they attend are accredited by the Tanzanian Vocational Education and Training Authority (VETA).

As for the *informal* training in the refugee camps, the evaluation found that overall the programmes are relevant to the situation, as well as cost-efficient. At least 2,500 people have received training, in addition to those involved in income-generating activities, which also often include a training component. However, the management of the programmes is somewhat loose, with no clearly formulated objectives and plans. There was a mix of economic and social objectives – on the one hand to transfer employable skills, and on the other to occupy the many out-of-school youths with little to do in the camps. As a consequence of the lack of consistent design, monitoring is limited to basic reporting and accounting of the spending of funds.

All training is carried out by skilled refugees, in the form of group training. The trainers receive no compensation for their work; it is considered to be a service to the community. However, this is a problem, since many trainers could find alternative ways to use their time and skills. Many skilled people do not participate in the training but go about their own small businesses instead. These micro-entrepreneurs represent a potential resource for a larger training programme if offered the right incentives.

The training is predominantly practical, which is a good thing. However, the quality of what is produced is often rather low, and more attention and resources allocated to theoretical instruction, including an upgrading of the skills of the trainers, could help to achieve a higher quality of products.

Vocational training has not had the highest priority among a range of activities competing for the time of the implementing NGO staff. A common and more consistent approach by the NGOs in the planning, coordination, selection of trainees, monitoring and evaluation could have led to the achievement of greater impact in the form of employment and economic activity, as well as of sustainability. Better targeting through the formulation of clear objectives and the definition of target groups would facilitate this process.

Proposals for a wider skills training programme

It is assumed here that large-scale repatriation will only occur in the medium or longer term, and that an expanded skills training programme is therefore relevant and necessary. The programme takes as its point of departure the fact that there are both economic and social objectives that are valid but not easy to accommodate within a single vocational training programme. It is therefore proposed that the programme consist of two main parts:

- Vocational training, aimed at the provision of skills for (self)employment – the economic objective;
- Non-vocational activities, aimed at occupying youths not interested in vocational skills training with positive activities for the body and mind – the social objective.

The main modalities should be a continuation of the ongoing group-based training (GBT), supplemented by enterprise-based training (EBT). Incentives to group trainers should be offered at the same level as existing incentives to other eligible refugees. Micro-entrepreneurs should be supported with tools and materials in return for taking in apprentices in enterprise-based training. A training centre should be established in each camp to strengthen theoretical instruction, as well as to offer upgrading courses to craftsmen in areas such as quality control and business skills.

Horticulture should be organized as training rather than as an income-generating activity and extended to as many refugees as possible. NGOs involved in practical logistical or construction work in the refugee camps should be approached in order to identify new training opportunities. New environment-friendly technologies should be tested in order to support training in building work, for example.

Non-vocational activities aimed at achieving the social objective are proposed to include the establishment of sports clubs, the organizing of competitions, and the inclusion of ball games in primary schools. Taking a different course, it is proposed to establish Internet cafés in the main camps, as well as in the nearby Tanzanian towns.

A management structure to coordinate the programme is also proposed. It should be headed by UNHCR and include representatives of all NGOs involved in training. Summary Terms of Reference for the Coordination Group are included in the proposals. In order to ensure a strong link to Burundi, the Group would be assisted by the Centre de Formation et de Perfectionnement Professionel (CFPP) from Bujumbura, as well as by local consultants. It is recommended that a programme review take place early in 2002.

Introduction

UNHCR currently provides protection and assistance to some 350,000 Burundian refugees distributed in 10 camps in the Kigoma and Kagera regions in western Tanzania. The assistance is extended in close cooperation with the World Food Programme (WFP) and UNICEF, as well as a number of international and local NGOs which act as implementing partners of specified activities. In addition to shelter, food, water and sanitation, the assistance includes activities classified under Education and Community Services, such as support to primary and (to a lesser degree) secondary education, as well as formal and non-formal vocational training.

Formal vocational education and training is supported through a scholarship programme implemented by the Southern Africa Extension Unit (SAEU), whereas non-formal training is carried out in the refugee camps by other NGOs tasked with education and community services there. In view of the small numbers benefiting from the above-mentioned scholarship scheme (project no. 404), a wider, community-based vocational training programme is being conceived to replace it, as a proposition mainly for out-of-school youths with an interest in learning skills that can help them in their future life.

Although the political situation in Burundi remains unsettled, there are hopes that an orderly and voluntary repatriation can start in 2001. It is in this light that the proposed training programme would be based on the concept of *education for repatriation*, with the aim of extending skills that will be of use on return to Burundi.

The present paper is the result of an evaluation of the current training activities with a view to making proposals for a wider programme. The study was funded by a grant from Danida.

The mission

According to its terms of reference, the evaluation exercise has as its objective to "reorient vocational training activities implemented by partner agencies in Tanzania in such a way that they provide the majority of young refugees with meaningful skills and a future orientation, match with required skills in Burundi, and with those skills suitable and conducive to the socioeconomic reintegration of returnees in Burundi."

Four main aspects are to be covered:

- The review of existing skills training and income generation programmes in terms of their effectiveness, impact and target group orientation, and the identification of gaps in the provision of training;
- The exploration of existing and planned structures and facilities for vocational training in Burundi by contacting relevant government departments, UN developmental agencies, and NGOs specialized in vocational training;
- The redesigning of training programmes in such a manner that they provide effective and reintegration-oriented skills training for refugees relevant for their possible repatriation to Burundi;
- The proposal for a mechanism for coordination between programme implementation in Tanzania and relevant agencies in Burundi.

The mission took place between 28 August and 20 September 2000. Visits were made to UNHCR Branch Offices in Dar es Salaam and Bujumbura, sub-offices in Kigoma and Ngara, field offices in Kasulu and Kibondo, and the refugee camps Mtabila 1 and 2, Muyovosi, Nduta, Mtendeli, Kanembwa, Karago and Lukole A and B. In Bujumbura, there were meetings with three ministries (Education, Youth, and Reconstruction), as well as with the World Bank office, NGOs and public and private training institutions.

A debriefing note was prepared during the mission and presented at the UNHCR Sub-Office in Ngara, the Branch Office in Dar es Salaam, and at Headquarters in Geneva. The debriefings resulted in a range of reflections and ideas being raised, which altogether contributed to the final result.

The paper

The paper is divided into three main sections. The first section is on the actual evaluation of past and present training activities, organized according to an established evaluation structure. The next section is on the situation in Burundi, and the prospects for repatriation as seen by the author. This is followed by a section proposing an extended training programme, with a discussion of the options, modalities and most promising activities. Following these three parts a coordination structure, with elements of a monitoring and evaluation system, is proposed.

In spite of the many contributions from people during the mission, the conclusions and recommendations are of course those of the author and do not necessarily reflect any official views of UNHCR or the Tanzanian or Burundian authorities.

Evaluation

The evaluation methodology included the use of qualitative interviews with key informants as well as a small questionnaire survey.

Key informants were the responsible UNHCR staff, NGO field staff and refugees. Among the latter, the trainers and local craftsmen were particularly important with regard to obtaining information on the market situations, their own backgrounds from the training they received in Burundi before becoming refugees, and their assessment of the feasibility of a number of training activities under consideration.

The questionnaire survey was more directed towards obtaining quantitative information on numbers trained, costs and so on. It was addressed to the NGOs concerned, which were asked to give the numbers and gender of people trained in each course since 1997. They were also asked how many of those trained in 1999 they estimated were still able to use their new skills on a regular basis.

Secondly, the NGOs were asked about the income-generating activities they sponsored, in terms of numbers of groups and individuals, and how many of the groups were still in existence.

Thirdly, they were asked to account separately for the kind of assistance given both to training and to income-generating activities, as well as its costing in Tanzania shillings. This should make it possible to arrive at the cost per trainee, and the cost per participant in income-generating activities.

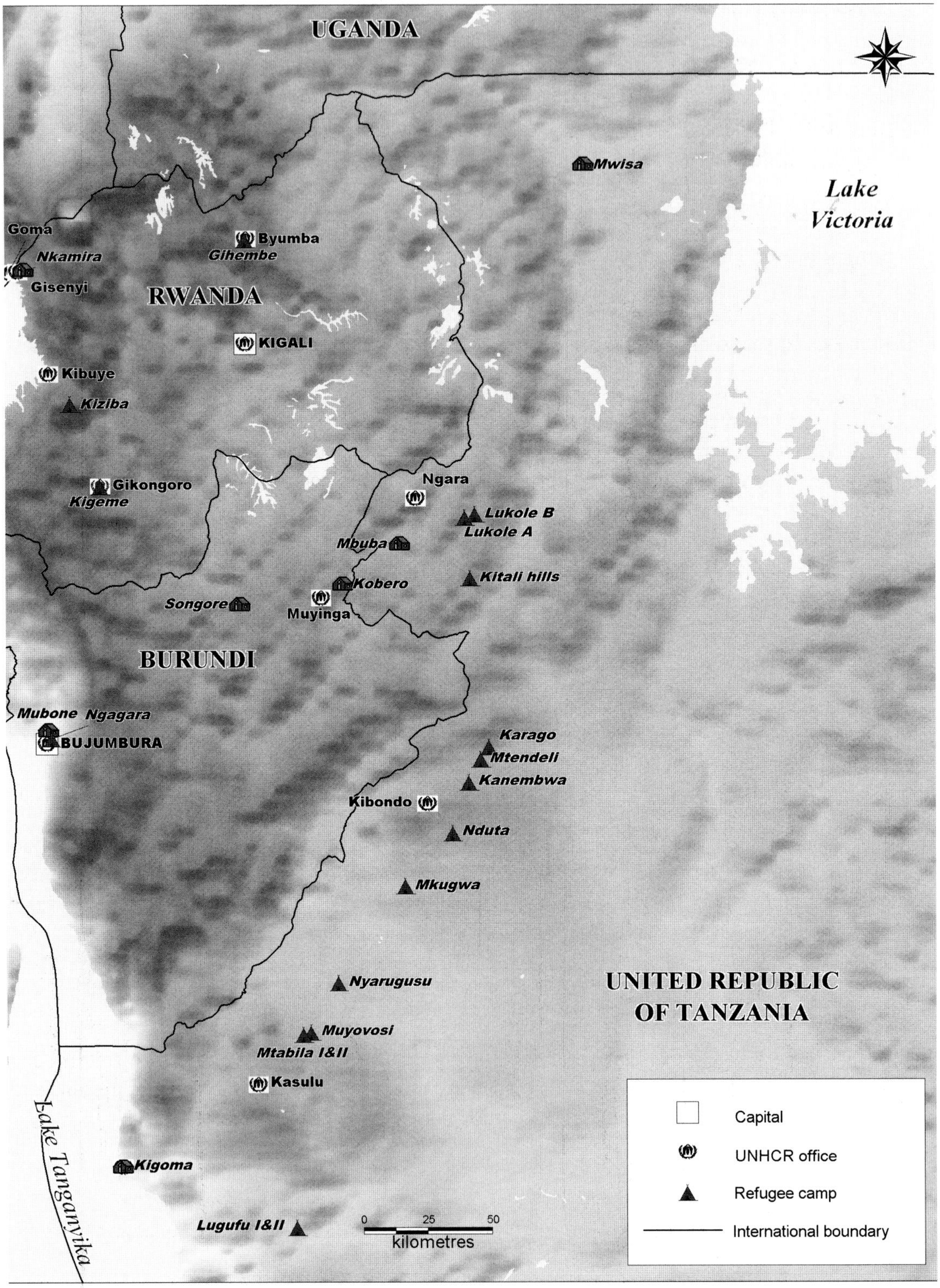

PGDS/GIMU - October 2001

This section is structured according to the following questions:

- ***Relevance*** – is the training relevant to the needs of those receiving it?
- ***Preparation and design*** – are the training interventions well designed, that is, do the objectives correspond to the efforts (activities) in a way that is likely to bring about the desired results?
- ***Efficiency*** – three types of efficiency are examined: (i) financial efficiency – do the results justify the costs? (ii) efficiency of approach – is the work best organized to achieve the desired results? (iii) and management efficiency – do the NGOs have sufficient capacity to coordinate and deliver training at the level required?
- ***Effectiveness*** – are the objectives in effect being achieved?
- ***Impact*** – what impact does the training programme have?
- ***Sustainability*** – to what extent are the benefits of the training likely to be sustained over time?

Context. Given the slow pace of the Burundi peace talks and the ongoing hostilities, UNHCR Tanzania foresaw a continuing influx of refugees during 2000 (100,000 persons), with some repatriation movements to Burundi in the second half of 2000 (50,000), and large-scale repatriation in 2001 (150,000), leaving a residual caseload of 200,000 at end–2001. The main assumption underpinning this scenario was that the Burundi peace talks, facilitated by former South African president Nelson Mandela, would be successfully concluded during 2000. However, the Arusha Peace Accord, signed on the 28 August by most parties, did not include provision for a ceasefire. It is understood that, in spite of very considerable pressure being put on the parties to sign, two of the political factions declined to do so. Meanwhile, the refugees maintained a wait-and-see position, and at the time of the evaluation, repatriation had not started. On the contrary, violence continued in Burundi and new refugees arrived daily at the UNHCR centres.

This continuing uncertainty regarding the future of Burundi creates a difficult environment for securing the Tanzanian government's agreement on crucial points of refugee policy, in particular those involving greater refugee participation, self-reliance and freedom. An area of particular concern is the restriction imposed on the movement of refugees – according to which they are not allowed to move beyond a 4 -km limit around their camp.

While a substantial number of children of school age are now, through concerted efforts of the involved organizations and the refugee communities themselves, attending primary school, the options for school-leavers and drop-outs are very few indeed, and the risk of widespread youth delinquency is imminent. The age group 15–25 years is estimated to make up about 100,000 out of the total Burundian refugee population of 350,000. Around 10,000 youths enter this age group every year (while 10,000 leave it to move into the next age group).

Assessment. The relevance of giving support to vocational training is evident from the numbers mentioned above. The 10,000 new adolescents per year represent at the same time much talent and energy that should be harnessed for the development of the individuals, their families and the community, but also a huge potential for trouble.

The scholarship programme implemented by SAEU sponsors, inter alia, vocational training in formal Tanzanian institutions under the VETA system. Students must sufficiently master the English language to be able to benefit

Medical care is provided by the Tanzanian Red Cross, MSF and other non-governmental agencies. Benaco Camp, Ngara, Tanzania. UNHCR/05.1994/B. Press

from this training. The VETA system is developing more flexible training modalities, which are considered to be more relevant to current labour market needs than the previous training dispensation in Tanzania.

The English-language requirement probably bars many of the post-1994 refugees from getting scholarships, since those who speak a language other than Kirundi are likely to speak French. Apparently the scholarship programme has to a large extent benefited the early refugees, who arrived in the 1970s, of whom many of the young were actually born in Tanzania and are used to Kiswahili and English.

The composition of the training activities in the camps is overall relevant. This is to a high degree due to most NGOs being sensitive to the signals sent by the refugees and trying to support community initiatives. The range of activities is fairly standard, but a certain focus on agriculture and construction is observable; this should be relevant in a repatriation situation.

Preparation and design

A brief project description in the UNHCR format exists for the SAEU scholarship project. However, vocational education is here defined so as to include teacher and nurse education, which is normally not considered part of vocational education and training. In addition, vocational education and training is lumped together with secondary school education, hence making it difficult to distinguish between the different categories. The project description makes little direct reference to vocational education and training.

As for the non-formal training carried out in the camps, there is no specific project description at all. It has been understood as being one element in a large package of community services, and has developed in response to community demand.

No consistent problem analysis, which could have led to the formulation of common and agreed objectives, has been carried out, with the result that there is considerable variation between the approaches of different NGOs.

Two main objectives can be deduced from the training programmes:

- To enable target groups to earn a living through the transfer of "meaningful" skills - predominantly an economic objective;
- To occupy out-of-school youths who have otherwise very little to do - predominantly a social objective.

While both objectives are valid, they can be difficult to reconcile. Where should the emphasis be – on giving those with the highest potential skills which can lead to their gainful employment (objective 1), or on keeping as many as possible occupied and out of trouble (objective 2)? Or should the assistance be focused on vulnerable groups, likewise for social rather than economic reasons?

The answers to these questions would normally decide the nature, composition and cost of the training. Since they were not explicitly asked, the NGOs have felt free to go ahead with what seemed to be appropriate in the local situation. Target groups were sometimes defined as youths, sometimes women, or sometimes various categories of vulnerables.

The project design is sketchy at best. However, the NGOs should not be blamed for this. Activities arose from the situation and, overall, they did follow the requests from the refugee communities. However, the training programmes could have benefited from better guidance with regard to common objectives, definition of target groups, and the expected, measurable outputs of each training activity, as well as the uniform use of inputs (the level of assistance in the form of tools, materials, etc.).

Efficiency

Efficiency is concerned with the transformation of means into ends. Financial efficiency deals with the relationship between financial costs and the achieved outputs. Methodological efficiency refers to the approach that is applied in the delivery of training programmes. Management efficiency concerns the way in which training programmes are organized. And in the same context, there are the monitoring and evaluation systems, which should allow for an assessment of the different types of efficiency.

Financial efficiency

The Scholarship Programme. The Deutsche Akademische Flüchtlinge Initiativ (DAFI) scholarship programme sponsors training of refugees at Tanzanian training institutions. The programme supports students in a variety of fields, most of which are not normally categorised as vocational training. Table 1 organizes the scholarships into five categories: technical and vocational education and training (TVET); teacher education; agriculture and fisheries; health; and "others", which include inter alia business schools, journalism and community development.

Table 1 indicates that out of 97 students who have completed their course, or who will be doing so before the end of 2000, the TVET category accounts for 25, against 27 teachers, 17 within agriculture and fisheries, seven health professionals/ paramedics, and 21 in other subjects. The average costs per trainee per year are also indicated, with TVET and "others" being twice as high as the teacher training colleges and the other categories falling somewhere in between.

Table 1: Scholarships by Sector and Cost

Completed 2000	Number of students	Cost per year per trainee	
Category		Tanzanian shillings	US$
TVET	25	983,600	1'230
Teacher training college	27	418,500	523
Agriculture and fisheries	17	640,000	800
Health	7	680,000	850
Others	21	1,000,000	1'250
Total	**97**		

The relatively high cost of TVET is linked to the need for equipment and training materials, which is highest at technician level. Table 2 gives a breakdown between the five TVET institutions receiving students with DAFI scholarships.

Table 2: TVET Scholarships

Training institutions	No. of students attending in 2000				Duration of course	No. of students completing course		Cost per trainee each year (Tz. shillings)
	Year 1	Year 2	Year 3&4	Total		2000	1999	
Vocational Training College (Mpanda, Ulyankulu, Mbeya)	1	9	–	10	2 Years	9	2	316,500
Vocational Teacher Training College (Morogoro)	1	–	–	1	1 Year	1	–	992,250
Dar es Salaam Institute of Technology (DIT)	5	5	3	13	3 Years	–	–	1,276,500
Technical College (Mbeya; Arusha)	2	2	1	5	3 Years	2	4	1,671,500
National Institute of Transport (NIT)	2	1	–	3	2 Years	1	3	1,567,000

Standard vocational training stands at only 316,500 shillings per year – which is not much and probably a reflection of the poor state of the vocational training centres, which tend to be seriously starved of resources. A vocational training course of two years' duration at a vocational training centre costs the equivalent of US$800, while a three-year technician course in Arusha costs US$6,300.

None of these costs are worrying, but there could be reason for concern about the quality of the courses, especially at vocational level. However, according to SAEU, most of the institutions receiving supported students have some industrial attachment included in their courses, normally two to three months.

Many of the vocational education and training graduates are from the early waves of Burundian refugees in the 1970s. This means that most candidates aged 18–20 years were actually born in Tanzania, but are still regarded as refugees.

SAEU goes through a selection procedure for candidates, which tries to assess their suitability, mostly based on secondary school performance. A preference is given to females and post-1993 refugees. The courses to be supported are chosen based on their cost and on the employment potential for the graduates.

Camp-based vocational training. The exact numbers of those who have received training are difficult to establish, since the links between training and income-generating activities or micro-projects tend to obscure the picture (some training within the micro-project context may escape the count, while other cases may be double-counted).

According to the information provided by the NGOs in the questionnaire survey, the total number of trained people is 2,154. However, some known training courses are not reported on, such as shoemaking in Lukole and Kanembwa, and horticulture in Mtabila, the latter classified as an income-generating activity but consisting of 171 groups with 1,700 female and 800 male members. Leaving income-generating activities aside, an educated guess would be that at least 2,500 people have received instruction under the heading of vocational training. The numbers given by the NGOs indicate that there are 380 groups with a total of 3,884 members who have received assistance to start income-generating activities. Adding the horticulture project in Mtabila brings this number up to 550 groups with 6,400 members.

The reported cost per trainee varies a lot, probably due both to different practices by NGOs as well as to under-reporting by some. In addition, many of those who receive assistance for income-generating activities do so after having completed a training course, which means that the assistance they receive is higher than is indicated by the training costs alone. And, if the total economic costs were to be calculated, they should include a proportion of the running costs of the NGOs, for salaries, transport, equipment, incentives to refugee assistants, and so on. These overheads probably make up more than the direct training costs and income-generating activities support, as can be deduced from the size of sector P (agency operational support) of UNHCR's Financial Management Information System, which overall is by far the highest item in projects 270 (Kagera) and 271 (Kigoma).

The mission saw women groups training in the handicrafts which form part of a strong Burundian tradition, and in tailoring, carpentry, typing, embroidery, bicycle repair, sandal-making and shoe repair, baking, and cassava bread-making. Bricklaying was only found in one case, since the firing of bricks is being discouraged for environmental reasons. Agricultural and horticultural activities were classified as income-generating activities, although they are important training grounds (particularly impressive in this respect is the horticulture and pisciculture project in Mtabila, which has been receiving seeds from FAO).

According to the questionnaire responses, the costs are highest for tailoring and typing, due to the need for sewing machines and typewriters, followed by carpentry (Table 3).

Table 3: Costs of Training and Income-Generating Activities by Subject

Activity	Training costs (US$)	Income-generating activities support (US$)
Tailoring	73	40
Carpentry	43	42
Handicrafts	13	39
Bicycle repair	8	14
Typing	72	–
Hairdressing	4	35
Horticulture	?	12
Restaurant	–	23
Baking	–	44
Soap-making	–	4
Guitar-making	–	19

Assessment. As can be seen, the training in the camps is run on very low-cost budgets. The cost per trainee varies with the investment needed and the length of the course, from short handicraft courses to a 12-month course in carpentry. These direct costs are inexpensive by any standard. If the overheads were included, they would probably increase the cost by 100–200 per cent – which would still be quite acceptable. While it is not possible to calculate a rate of return within the limits of this study, it may be mentioned, as a comparison, that enterprise-based training projects run by local NGOs in India and Egypt stand between US$120 and US$200 per training, which is also considered very cost-efficient. The camp-based training is not more expensive.

The material assistance is limited to the provision of hand tools to supplement those already owned by the trainers and some training materials. Where possible, the NGOs try to negotiate economical solutions. This must be generally commended, but it should also be recognized that there could be a lower limit beneath which the quality of training can suffer.

The quality of many products is in fact quite low. The trainers can only impart skills to the same level that they themselves master, conditions are not the best for high-quality production, and customers apparently accept what they get. The programmes could benefit from a more systematic focus on quality control, together with an offer of upgrading of skills of the trainers. Overall, however, the programmes are considered to be cost-effective.

Efficiency of approach

Group training. The common approach to training by the NGOs is group training. All the training is conducted by Burundians previously trained in their own country. The NGOs give support but emphasize that the initiatives must come from the communities themselves. For practical reasons the training is generally done in groups composed of trainers and trainees working together. The duration of courses varies between three and 12 months. The trainers do not receive any remuneration for their work – it is "voluntary". This leads to many complaints from the trainers, who could otherwise spend their time and skills on activities which could bring in some income. On the other hand, the items produced by a group belong to it and can be sold – the NGOs and other agencies being major clients.

Group training is sometimes targeted at any *mixed group* of applicants (which may include people with disabilities), and sometimes at *specific groups*, such as the physically handicapped, or unaccompanied minors or elderly people. Where the first category represents a mainstream training focus, the second one is targeted at vulnerable people who are considered to be able to benefit more from being trained together in a group.

Many skilled artisans do *not* participate in the training programmes but carry out their own business as micro-entrepreneurs, often with a young person taken on in a traditional apprenticeship – by far the most common mode of skills acquisition in Africa. This choice is perfectly understandable. However, this category represents an important potential resource for training on a wider scale. Overall, there are ample human resources available in the refugee community that could, under the right circumstances, be deployed for a variety of activities.

The training is overwhelmingly practical, mostly due to a lack of facilities for theoretical classes. While the practical orientation is basically good, it could be improved if supplemented with standard theoretical courses.

Many groups keep simple records of purchases and sales but do not have the capacity to carry out costing and pricing. Some of the group trainers reported that they had attended a one-day course in keeping books and said it had been interesting but too short. Upgrading trainers, particularly in quality control and business skills, could be very useful. In addition to enhancing their effectiveness as trainers, such offers of upgrading would certainly serve as an incentive to them.

A tale of two tailors

In the main market place in Kanembwa camp, Mr A. is sitting with his sewing machine. He is 60 years old and learned his trade in four years of traditional apprenticeship in Burundi in 1958–62. He had his own workshop and was sewing for people; most of the time he had one or two apprentices.

After the outbreak of violence he fled the country, and he has taken up trade in the Kanembwa market, mostly doing repairs. He lost most of his belongings, his clothes are tattered and he does not wear shoes. The sewing machine is rented from another refugee and it is not in good order. Nonetheless, although business could be better, he has enough to do to keep an apprentice, a man of about 30 years of age.

In Nduta camp Mr B. has his workshop in his house. Like most houses in the camp, it does not look much from the outside, but inside the tailoring workshop is impeccable – clean and with everything in its place. Mr B. learned tailoring up to an advanced level in Burundi, where he achieved an A3 diploma. He is now making suits of a quality that compares very well with what is being produced in capital cities in Africa or Europe. His customers come to him from afar, for example from Kigoma. He keeps a young girl as his apprentice.

When asked whether they could take in more than one apprentice, both Mr A. and Mr B. say that they could do so if they had the necessary tools and materials to support the training.

Some refugees manage to make a small income by using their skills in tailoring or textile printing. Rwandese refugees in Inera Camp, Bukavu Region, South Kivu. UNHCR/12.1994/A. Hollmann

Income generation. Training courses are often linked to income-generating activities. After completion of the course, a group may be eligible for further assistance in the form of a micro-project or other support, in an attempt to give opportunities to apply the newly acquired skills and make some money. Such a link can influence the motivation for somebody to apply for a training course, so that the course is perceived merely as a means of receiving further assistance in the short term. While this is understandable, it is also unfortunate, and an improved effort in the selection of candidates for training could help to identify those with more long-term ambitions.

Micro-finance. In Nduta and Mtendeli, the assistance for micro-projects is given under the name of micro-*credit*. However, the repayment rates are very low, for various reasons. First, no savings scheme is organized which could help borrowers develop the habit of saving and lending within a group; second, no credit training is provided; third, the NGO has insufficient experience in handling credit in a professional way; fourth, the perceived possibility of repatriation may make some borrowers hesitate to pay back their loan. The result is that the NGO spends a disproportionate amount of time trying to recover bad debt. This is a waste of time and is not effective in accustoming people to handle credit. Micro-credit is a highly specialized field that is best left to professionals, and it should be discouraged in the refugee camps.

Management efficiency

The Community Services and Education sectors in the UNHCR classification system were merged in Tanzania and from February 1999 were coordinated as one unit. The new unit is faced with a very long agenda, combining a wide range of areas. Formal vocational education falls under tertiary education (under the DAFI scholarships implemented by SAEU), while the camp-based training activities are lumped together with pre-school, post-primary, and distance education, under the heading of non-formal education. The micro-projects and other income-generating activities, which are often closely linked to vocational training, fall under community services.

Close consultation and the coordination of primary education activities across the camps have facilitated contacts with the Burundian Ministry of Education, leading to students sitting primary school examinations following the Burundian curriculum and certification system.

Unlike other education areas, there is no regular coordination of the training activities carried out by the NGOs. There is currently talk of introducing common standards (syllabi), and a workshop was organized to initiate this. Such a harmonization would be useful, but other areas such as exchanging experiences, introducing new activities and evaluating programme effectiveness would also benefit from being coordinated between the NGOs.

All NGOs have attached a number of refugees to them according to various activities – gender, education, non-formal education, health, and so on – offering as an incentive 14–20,000 shillings per month. This arrangement expands very considerably and at low cost the number of people involved in the organization of activities. In addition, it builds upon the local human resources in the community and serves as an encouragement to the refugees.

The overall level of commitment of the NGOs seems to be high – working under stressful conditions, they try to be responsive and assist within the means available. However, in the absence of coordination, the level of management efficiency varies considerably.

UNHCR invests large amounts in building the capacity of implementing NGOs, including providing them with vehicles, office infrastructure, salaries and training. This seems justified and necessary for the operations to succeed.

In the case of formal education, an assessment of the impact of SAEU from 1999 found that SAEU had the capacity to become the single coordinator of all post-primary activities. However, in the case of SAEU as well as of other NGOs their capacity needs to be strengthened.

Monitoring and evaluation

The NGOs produce monthly reports that supply the numbers of current participants in each training course or income-generating activity.

Some NGOs try to monitor the degree of success of the income-generating activities. However, being in the position of provider, NGOs can have difficulties in obtaining accurate information from refugees, who see the interview as an opportunity to present their problems and needs. There certainly seems to be under-reporting as far as incomes are concerned, and there is need for a special study to look into this matter.

Assistance is given on the basis of apparent merit, and the level of assistance varies from activity to activity and from camp to camp. The monthly reports do not allow for an analysis of the financial (or economic) costs per trainee for each activity.

The response given by NGOs to the evaluation questionnaire was characterized by being incomplete, which indicates weak monitoring. A wider training programme would need to have this information available, together with more reliable information on markets and incomes.

Effectiveness

Employment. Effectiveness is concerned with the extent to which a project does actually achieve its objectives. In the absence of any real project designs, it is assumed that there are two objectives, as mentioned above, namely a predominantly economic and a predominantly social one.

The prime indicator of having achieved the economic objective is that graduates from training courses come into gainful employment, either as wage-workers or as self-employed. However, there is little solid information on the extent to which the graduates from the training are in fact able to apply their skills; unless ex-trainees continue with an income-generating activity, their whereabouts are generally not being monitored.

The questionnaire survey used as an indicator of effectiveness the number of people trained in 1999 who were continuing to use the acquired skills on a regular basis. Again, there was considerable variation from camp to camp, which may be an indication that the estimates made by the NGOs range from very optimistic to rather disillusioned. Table 4 summarizes the information received by trade across the camps.

Table 4: Continuing Use of New Skills

Skills category	Percentage
Carpentry	52
Masonry	100
Tailoring	23
Handicraft	74
Hairdressing	85
Bicycle repair	97
Agriculture	71
Home management	59
Livestock	100

From the information submitted in the questionnaires it emerges that in Kanembwa, of the 107 people who received training in 1999, 90 – 85 per cent – are estimated as still applying their skills on a regular basis. Corresponding figures for other camps are: Muyovosi 70 per cent, Mtendeli (Dutch Relief and Rehabilitation Agency – DRA) 60 per cent, Mtabila 55 per cent, Nduta (DRA) 39 per cent, Lukole 18 per cent.

However, a survey by the International Rescue Committee (IRC) of 110 ex-trainees in Mtendeli and Nduta indicated that only 22 per cent utilized the skills they had been taught on a regular basis, while 78 per cent did not. However, 88 per cent found the skills "useful". There can be different explanations for this relatively low rate of entry into gainful economic activity.

The quality of training could be one reason: in this particular case, all courses were of maximum three months' duration. This is very short time in which to expect someone to become a qualified carpenter or tailor.

Motivation could be another reason. It appears that the majority of youths, as well as their parents, would prefer secondary education rather than vocational training. If a training course is chosen as a last resort, the motivation is likely to be low and the learning may be ineffective. The selection of candidates for training courses also seems in most cases to be rather mechanical, only standard criteria such as the ability to read and write being applied. Thus a partial explanation for low scores on employment resulting from the training could be linked to the nature of the selection of candidates.

Market constraints resulting from the restriction of movement beyond 4 km from the camp, and the low level of purchasing power (exacerbated by a recent cut in food rations), are other important impediments to production and trade that limit the extent to which ex-trainees can find employment.

While the target of employment should be above the 22 per cent found in the IRC survey, it should not be expected that the training could ever achieve a 100 per cent score. The overall score from the present questionnaire survey, which includes the low figures from IRC, still comes to 36 per cent – which is not altogether bad. A better selection, and a strengthened market analysis could help to bring up the success rate. A future programme should aim at 50–60 per cent employment after a year, and the monitoring of this aspect should be considerably strengthened.

A man is what he can do

In Kanembwa camp, Mr C. is sitting under his shed repairing shoes. He is physically handicapped after a traffic accident in Burundi, and his right leg cannot support him so he walks on crutches. In the camp, he attended a six-month training course for the handicapped, where he learned to mend shoes. His tools are few but enough – they can be carried in a small bag. His business is doing alright – the money is not much, but there are many customers who need his services.

Mr C. has got himself a new identity by being a craftsman. He expresses it when he says: "A man *is* what he can *do*!"

Target groups. It appeared that a large proportion of trainees or recipients of income-generating activities support were adults rather than youths. This is normal for income-generating activities but somewhat surprising for training, which should to a large extent be an offer to out-of-school adolescents.

As far as gender equity is concerned, the distribution follows traditional patterns: carpentry, building and bicycle repair are for men; hair-*cutting* is done by men while hair-*dressing* is for women. Handicraft, home management and baking are done in women's groups; and tailoring and typing have both male and female participants. An effort to widen the choice of access for women should be made.

Haircutting and barbering run by refugees. Kakuma Camp, Kenya. UNHCR/07.1999/B. Press

Impact

Impact assessment is invariably the most intricate part of evaluation. In the absence of clearly defined targets, baseline information and assessments based on monitoring, only a few spontaneous observations can be made.

At least 2,500 people have participated in training since the start of the programmes. Their access to markets varies with the trades, as do the levels of income derived. Information on incomes is particularly shaky – while carpenters and tailors said that the market was for their services was satisfactory, the incomes they report are very low. This could be because they don't want to disclose the true facts, or that they do produce with lower profits than their Tanzanian competitors.

The general picture seems to be that ex-trainees appreciate the training they received (cf. the IRC-study mentioned in the previous section). Many were found to be busy with different kinds of production, which is an indication that they find the work to be worth their while. In some other cases, typically with handicrafts carried out by women's groups, the economic returns seemed to be very small, and the benefits were mostly social ones arising from belonging to a group.

Sustainability

A project is considered sustainable when the benefits derived from it can be expected to continue beyond the project assistance. The benefits are in this case the newly acquired skills.

The sustainability of the training programmes can be looked at from two angles: from the point of view either of an impending repatriation or of a prolonged (in fact open-ended) stay in the camps.

The skills learnt on the training courses in the camps represent a broad range of trades and occupations, most of which should be useful in the event of early repatriation. This is particularly so for the agricultural activities and the construction trades, but also for smaller manufacturing and community services.

In the case where repatriation does not take place in the near future, the loss of skills from their not being practised will be greater. However, the longer-established camps do take on a certain atmosphere of *normality* after some years, tending to become increasingly like the surrounding villages, with some production and trade adapted to the circumstances. If a training programme places itself in the middle of the emerging formal and informal structures, it should be able to read the markets and respond with training that is relevant and appropriate even in that situation.

The restriction on movement imposed by the Tanzanian authorities is a crucial factor in this respect. If the refugees had the opportunity to trade freely with the surrounding world, they could do much to improve their existence. In the case of the failure of the current peace initiative, the international community, and especially UNHCR, must work at all levels to have Tanzanian authorities lift the restrictions.

Conclusions

The SAEU scholarships allocated to vocational training have reached a small number (25) of refugees, many of whom have been in Tanzania for a long time or were even born there. The selection process is fairly good, and costs are not excessive. The extent to which graduates find jobs after training is not known.

The training programmes in the camps have made widespread use of the human resources available in the camps and have achieved rather good results at low cost. However, vocational training has not been given the highest priority among a range of activities competing for the time of the implementing NGO staff. A common and more consistent approach by the NGOs in the planning, coordination, selection of trainees, monitoring and evaluation could have led to the achievement of a higher degree of impact in the form of employment and economic activity, as well as of sustainability. Better targeting through the formulation of clear objectives and definition of target groups would facilitate this process.

Prospects for repatriation

The visit to Bujumbura revealed that the private and public sectors in Burundi suffer badly from international isolation. The levels of all economic and social indicators have dropped. Economic life is running at a low ebb – imports and exports are either restricted by law or constrained in other ways. Virtually all donor-financed development projects have stalled. And there is a full stop in recruitment to the public service.

The office of the World Bank was consulted on the issue of potential growth sectors in the economy after a return to peace. The main export items are agricultural products (coffee, cotton and so on), and it was difficult to identify any sector with rapid growth potential. Assuming the need for the reconstruction of the infrastructure, the public works sector could experience growth in both income and employment terms. In this connection, the Bank is at an advanced stage of preparation (appraisal stage) of a project that will help the Burundian government to set up an AGETIP (Agence d'exécution des travaux d'intérêt public) structure to implement labour-based public works. (The first AGETIP was established in Senegal, later to be followed by similar structures in several African countries.) The appraisal will obviously depend on the progress of the peace talks. In time, it should be able to provide employment to large numbers of people on works such as feeder roads and other infrastructure through the application of labour-intensive technology known in French as HIMO (Haute intensité de main d'oeuvre).

A visit to the Ministry of Reconstruction revealed very little in the way of concrete plans to absorb large numbers of returnees. The UN system has produced a joint emergency plan for Burundi to be presented to donors for funding to the extent of US$86 million; only a small part of this has been pledged so far. Other initiatives are under way, notably the one put forward by Nelson Mandela and French President Jacques Chirac. The success of these undertakings remains to be seen; they again will depend much on the progress of the peace process.

Training in Burundi

A private training institution owned by a former refugee seemed to be doing very well training people in business management, but the owner complained about the embargo constraining the possibilities for expansion. This institution had strong links to industry, and its curriculum included the placement of students in companies for practical training. Most of the students were reported as finding employment after graduation. On the other hand a government institution along the same lines, set up under the auspices of the university, suffered from the lack of all kinds of resources, as well as a lack of employment opportunities for graduates.

The type of vocational training institutions most relevant to the present study is offered by the Ministry of Youth, Sports and Culture which in 1991 combined under the name of 'centres d'enseignement des métiers' (CEM) a range of centres and structures first set up under other ministries. Graduates are issued with a *certificat d'aptitude professionnelle.*

The CEM number 127, out of which 67 are considered to be functional. The rest are to a large degree destroyed, and the degree of functionality of the others can be questioned. Many instructors have left or fled, some have been killed, and appointing any replacements has been impossible due to the recruitment freeze, meaning that some centres try to function with two or three instructors instead of 10 or 12. As could be expected, the state of the equipment leaves much to be desired, and there are no funds to maintain or replace defunct equipment. Training materials are at best in short supply but more often non-existent, meaning that instructors use their own hand-written notes and drawings, which the trainees copy into their exercise books (a common situation in many training institutions in Africa, but unfortunate and inefficient all the same). There can hardly be said to be any common standards. The links between the centres and the local enterprises are weak, and no industrial attachment forms part of the courses. Not surprisingly, employers hold the certificate awarded in low esteem, and few graduates find jobs after graduation.

An extraordinary and very positive exception to this state of affairs was found in the 'Centre de formation et de perfectionnement professionnel' (CFPP) in Bujumbura. There are four such centres in Burundi with autonomous statutes, though receiving a government subsidy. The CFPP is recognized as the best of its kind in Burundi, and benefits from an autonomous status that allows it to generate income through consultancy work. Most of its students have completed grade 8 or 9, and the 27-month course includes alternating periods of enterprise placement, maintained through continuing close links with industry, large as well as very small. All its graduates find jobs. It has been in existence since 1986 and possesses vast experience in the micro- and small-enterprise sector. This institution is referred to in more detail below, as a potential resource in support of a training programme for the refugees.

Reconstruction

With a peaceful transition, an enormous amount of physical reconstruction and rehabilitation will have to take place in Burundi. Agriculture will have to be brought back into production, and schools, clinics, the water supply systems, roads and other infrastructure will have to be constructed. Assuming that some private investment and donor-financed development assistance will also come in, there will be a booming market for construction work. Improved agricultural and horticultural practices and agriculture-related services can also be expected to find markets. This again will generate business for the small-scale manufacturing and service sectors.

Previous Burundian governments were able to contain the rural–urban influx to such a degree that Burundi remains one of the least urbanized countries in Africa, the urban population accounting for only 8 per cent of the total, against 33 per cent in sub-Saharan Africa as a whole, according to the World Bank. With an introduction of multi-party politics, and an estimated annual growth of the labour force of 100,000 young people, this pattern is almost certain to change. The implication of increased urbanization for training is that there is scope for some training in urban-oriented skills.

A range of training activities, existing ones as well as new initiatives, were discussed in the refugee camps and in Burundi, and almost all were found to have potential in a situation of repatriation. The main immediate limitation lies in the market constraints in the camps in case of prolonged stay. However, this must be accepted as a fact of life and, in the interim, ways and means must be sought to exploit all market niches to their full potential.

Scenarios

Repatriation in 2001. The UNHCR country operations plan (COP) expects an estimated 150,000 Burundians to be repatriated in 2001, given a successful outcome of the peace negotiations, the rest following in 2002 and 2003. Under this scenario, there would still be a case for carrying out training for at least one to two years at a rate of say 2,000 people per year.

Repatriation in 2001–05. The medium-term view assumes partial failure of the negotiations, but a gradual scaling down of atrocities. The scenario justifies the introduction of an expanded training programme, perhaps targeting 4–5,000 persons per year.

Repatriation in 2003–10. The longer-term perspective assumes failure in the current peace effort but also fatigue among the political opposition, forcing it towards piecemeal agreements that would encourage gradual repatriation to apparently secure provinces. With some 10,000 entering adolescence per year at the current level of caseload, a training programme targeting 4–5,000 annually would remain necessary.

Whether UNHCR and its partners can handle the training of so many people is a question yet to be answered. A training programme of this magnitude would have to balance carefully long- and short-term courses, as well as economic and social objectives. In recognition of the fact that vocational training is not the solution to all problems, UNHCR should also consider other activities of a more social nature to be offered to the young refugees.

The prolonged stay in Tanzania associated with the second and third scenarios (partial or complete failure in the peace effort) would require the maximum pressure to be applied to the Tanzanian authorities for the lifting of the restriction on movement by the refugees.

A future training programme

It is assumed here that large-scale repatriation will only occur in the medium or longer term, and that an expanded skills training programme is therefore relevant and necessary.

The programme takes as its point of departure the assumption that there are both economic and social objectives that are valid but not easy to accommodate within a single vocational training programme. It is therefore proposed that the programme should consist of two main parts:

- Vocational training, aimed at the provision of skills for (self)-employment – the economic objective;
- Non-vocational activities, aimed at occupying youths not interested in vocational skills training with positive activities for the body and mind – the social objective.

Vocational training

Modalities. There are three basic modalities of relevance here, which can be applied on their own or in any combination that is found to be useful:

- Institution-based training (IBT)
- Group-based training (GBT)
- Enterprise-based training (EBT)

Pre-entry ***institution-based training*** is exemplified in the description above of the CEM in Burundi. Although institution-based training need not be in such a problematic state, the lack of interaction with private enterprise is common and limits the graduates' chances for gainful employment. The scholarships for vocational training in Tanzanian institutions sponsored through SAEU also fall in the institution-based training category.

Group-based training is the way in which training is already organized in the refugee camps, where people are encouraged to work in groups or cooperatives. This has the advantage of the group being able to share tools and equipment; it can also help to cultivate a spirit of working together, and often allows for the integration of disabled members in the group. On the other hand, the group is likely to dissolve at the time of repatriation, and the extent to which an entrepreneurial spirit is fostered under group-based training is limited. Those groups which are formed are also the basis for assistance to income-generating activity which often follows group training.

Somali refugees learning blacksmith crafts. Hagadera Camp, Kenya. UNHCR/07.1999/B. Press

Enterprise-based training in the present context refers to training undertaken within the very small enterprise, normally in the form of a traditional apprenticeship. This is by far the most common mode of skills acquisition in Africa. Enterprise-based training is currently not included in the training programmes taking place in the camps. The advantages of enterprise-based training are that trainees are exposed to the real constraints and challenges faced by and within the small enterprise; the training is very practical; and the products will have to be sold. The inherent risk in enterprise-based training is the possible use of trainees as cheap labour by some employers.

A strong focus on self-employment through enterprise-based training will offer opportunities to those with entrepreneurial drive to get a training that will effectively help them to set themselves up and succeed on their own. The business perspective must be applied persistently throughout the selection, training and follow-up stages.

There is space for both group-based training and enterprise-based training in the training programme. Enterprise-based training makes use of a new resource that can help the programme expand, namely the individual micro-entrepreneurs not currently participating in training, apart from training their own apprentices.

In addition to enterprise-based training and group-based training there are numerous training opportunities elsewhere in the camps. This is particularly the case with the NGOs that are engaged in practical work such as construction of wells, roads and buildings, or in logistics such as transport. It is common for refugee labour to be used in these activities and some training does take place, but not in any coordinated fashion. This should be taken up with the NGOs and form part of a training programme.

Agriculture and horticulture are supported as income-generating activities, and some training is given in this context. This could be organized as an integrated group-based training activity with specified training tasks for groups according to the agricultural calendar.

Strengthening theoretical instruction. The programmes could benefit from becoming harmonized. The scale of the proposed training programme justifies an effort to establish classroom training programmes in the subjects and trades that are in highest demand. A suitable physical structure for this purpose (training centre) should be established in each camp and equipped with standard teaching materials and reference books. While the training centre need not be overly sophisticated, it will need to be equipped with a strongroom in which to keep tools and other valuables.

The majority of in-service training will continue to take place on the job, whether as group-based training or enterprise-based training, interspersed with trainees attending theoretical courses at the centre. These courses would be organized in modules of a duration varying between one day and two weeks.

The training centre will also organize upgrading courses for those already skilled, giving preference to the trainers but being open to others as space allows. Initial subjects would include quality control (organized according to trades) and business skills (mixed groups). The upgrading programme will be open to organizing other courses in subjects in high demand among small entrepreneurs.

Certification. UNHCR and the implementing NGO will issue certificates of attendance to those who graduate from a course. The certificate will be based on common syllabi applied throughout the camps, and will mention the topics covered in the training. Standards which are currently applied in Burundi will be adopted as much as possible. Cooperation with a Burundian institution will facilitate the integration of Burundian standards.

However, while most people like to have a piece of paper to show that they have some particular skills, it should not be forgotten that the training programme is basically an informal one. Burundian employers do not hold the official certificates from the CEM in high esteem – what matters is what a person can do, that is, the capacity they have to apply their skills. Also, for the self-employed, who will make up the majority, the certificate is not the most essential asset. The quality of the training, rather than the paper qualifications, remains the most important thing.

Support to enterprise-based training and group-based training. The lack of incentives for trainers is a problem that needs to be resolved if a wider training programme is to succeed. In the case of enterprise-based training, the individual artisans should be encouraged to take in apprentices, and must be supported with tools and training materials for the trainees. The level of support will be negotiated in each case between the NGO and the entrepreneur, with a view to keeping it as economical as possible. The products resulting from this will belong to the enterprise. A contract will be signed between a craftsman and the NGO, which specifies the length of the training, the subjects to be covered and the material assistance to be given.

For group-based training, the individual situation needs to be assessed. Some groups have profitable contracts and need nothing further – the principle being that they must survive with their business like everyone else. With other groups, recompense for the trainers is clearly needed, and allowance should be provided for it. The level of recompense could be set so as to be in line with the current incentives given to refugees who carry out a number of other functions in the programmes. The same principles will apply to those responsible for training at the training centres.

Target groups. The vocational training programme targets predominantly the mainstream youth in the 15–25 age group. Where feasible, individuals from vulnerable groups will be integrated in the mainstream training, and in some cases special courses will be offered to them. Gender bias towards any particular trade will be actively discouraged.

Market orientation. Market responsiveness is a key factor in successful enterprise development. Markets change constantly, and so must the training. The combination of courses offered will therefore be flexible, and vary between camps, as well as over time within each camp. Reading the market and looking for opportunities is a constant preoccupation of the entrepreneur, and assistance with this by the NGOs can be very valuable. While previous efforts to market refugee products in Dar es Salaam should be followed up, the local markets represent a much larger clientele and must be actively explored.

Selection of trainees. If training for self-employment is seen as comprising three stages – selection, training and follow-up – then it is well known that damage done in the earlier stages can rarely be rectified later. A consistent focus on the goal, namely to become a gainfully self-employed person, must be maintained throughout the stages.

The selection of trainees is particularly important. Selection of candidates must be improved, with emphasis on their potential for entrepreneurial activity. It may be suspected that in the past some have joined training programmes with the short-term objective of getting access to micro-project assistance rather than to acquire a competency. That will rarely lead to any successful enterprise being created.

Improved selection will try to avoid this through interviews that will assess the person's intentions and entrepreneurship potential. The master craftsmen to whom they will be attached will be the judges and decide whom they want to accept as their apprentices. A pre-defined trial period should also be introduced, after which, if the trainee is found not to be suitable, for example because of absenteeism, or lack of interest or aptitude in carrying out instructions, s/he can be discontinued and replaced by another.

Areas of training. As mentioned, the composition of courses must be market-responsive and therefore flexible. Many possibilities seem to exist, some of which need to be further explored.

Agriculture and non-farm rural activities. Although classified as an income-generating activity (not as vocational training), the example of the *horticulture* project in Mtabila should be replicated *as a training activity,* wherever land and water are available. It involves a lot of training and has high potential for both improving own consumption and sale.

Education and training of carpentry in the camps will give refugees valuable skills that will facilitate their reintegration and enable them to contribute to the reconstruction of their home communities. Refugees from Burundi and Rwanda, Ngara Camp, Tanzania. UNHCR/08.2000/L. Boscardi

Zero-grazing, whereby cattle are raised and fed in cowsheds and do not graze, should be suitable for Burundi where land is scarce. However, land is also very scarce in the camps, and it will be difficult for individuals to grow enough elephant grass to ensure sufficient supply for a zero-grazing livestock unit (conditions differ from place to place but as a rule of thumb, 1 hectare is required per unit). It could *perhaps* be tried with women's groups, especially where a women's centre exists, if sufficient land could be allocated for this particular purpose. The principle would then be that an organized group of four to five women would build the cowshed and grow elephant grass in a sufficiently large designated area. When they were ready, a suitable non-indigenous breed of cow (probably Friesian), already in calf, would be supplied. Expert advice from Tanzania should be sought on teaching the women how to keep the animal(s), make use of milk and manure, how to detect illness and acquire veterinary assistance, and so on. However, great care should be exercised before venturing into this activity.

Crafts such as ***blacksmithing*** *and* ***soldering*** are necessary for the production and servicing of farm implements and should also be supported.

Carpentry has high potential in Burundi and should continue and expand, but with a strengthened attention to quality. Furniture catalogues (such as that of the Swedish IKEA company, whose straightforward designs offer good examples for copying) should be made available as an inspiration to carpenters.

Masonry has not been promoted for environmental reasons (the shortage of fuelwood for firing bricks). However, since there is a ready market, it is proposed that masonry is taken up in all camps, based on the production of cement-stabilized soil bricks as an alternative to fired bricks. The bricks should be mainly for training purposes but could also find a market for direct sales. Different models of presses for compaction must be studied in order to find one that is suitable for rural conditions, that is, sturdy and durable. A small feasibility study, or pilot project, should be carried out to establish the types of soils that are suitable, as well as the amount of cement required for different levels of loadbearing capacity.

Simple ***plumbing*** could also be tried, although the market for that is small in the camps. Sanitation blocks and improved latrines might still be required at a certain scale. The training of ***electricians*** is ***not*** encouraged under camp conditions.

Small-scale manufacturing and services. Tailoring remains a useful trade and should be supported. In relation to tailoring, short courses focusing just on ***ironing*** clothes can be envisaged as appropriate to some with low education levels.

Also ***textile printing*** is an option, as cotton is grown and ginned in Burundi. Since khanga and kitenge material is highly subject to the whims of fashion, it would be advisable to start with items such as table cloths and curtains.

Baking has proven to be successful in Mtabila and can easily be replicated elsewhere.

Sandal-making using old tyres is being done. However, *shoemaking* to a higher standard is also possible and may be tried out. *Shoe repairing* remains an important small-scale service that is often carried out by the disabled and should be supported.

Education and training of bicycle repair has provided refugees with valuable skills. Refugees from Burundi and Rwanda, Ngara Camp, Tanzania. UNHCR/08.2000/L. Boscardi

Bicycle and radio repair has been tried with success and should continue to be supported.

New activities that may be considered include ***sign writing*** and ***photography***. Both are inexpensive and should find markets even in the rural areas. Full courses in ***motor mechanics*** are expensive and difficult to organize in a camp. However, tyre repair, panel beating and windscreen repair might work, possibly in cooperation with NGOs engaged in logistical work.

Finally, there is ***hairdressing***, which should have a great future, judging from all the hair-and-beauty salons to be found on every street corner in Bujumbura.

Follow-up. Follow-up to enterprise-based training is mainly carried out with the aim of assisting in the search for market opportunities. Where possible, newly trained people should have access to contracts from NGOs and their staff.

Follow-up to group-based training should mainly be through income-generating activities, while the more commercial contracts are given to graduates of enterprise-based training.

The level of support should be negotiated with a view to keeping it as low as possible, for two reasons: to minimize influencing the market mechanism, and to allow the maximum number of people to share the limited resources available.

Non-vocational activities

Sports. There is very little recreational activity to occupy the refugees. This is especially a problem with the youths, and the organization of team sports in the camps would be an appreciated and relatively inexpensive supplement to vocational training. There would in fact be a training element included in the form of training coaches and referees.

It is proposed that a sports club be organized in each camp, focusing on ball games such as football for the boys, volleyball for the girls or mixed teams, basketball and the like, after consultation with the refugee community. Simple facilities should be established, some using voluntary labour. The clubs should be staffed with refugees receiving incentives.

The clubs should arrange competitions and tournaments, if possible with the outside environment. In addition, the clubs should help the primary schools to organize sports lessons and competitions.

Internet cafés. At first sight, refugee camps are not the first places one would associate with computers and Internet access. Is that because of the focus on basic necessities such as food distribution, which tends to draw attention away from such sophisticated activity which would presumably be for the very few? Or is such activity just irrelevant under camp conditions?

While opinions are divided, there is general agreement that Africa is falling behind in a global development where information technology becomes increasingly essential. One facility that has taken root in most African cities however, is Internet cafés, as an economical way of sharing resources and gaining access to the technology. There are many young people in the refugee camps, as in the surrounding Tanzanian environment, who could benefit from getting to know about computers and the Internet, but have no chance of doing so. In addition to the Internet café being used as such, its facility can obviously also be used for general computer training.

The possibility merits consideration, not least since it is understood that a potential donor has indicated willingness to offer resources to UNHCR with the specific objective of giving refugees access to computers and the Net.

There could be a problem with the Tanzanian authorities, which may not agree with such sophisticated equipment going to the refugees, when their own smaller towns lack electricity and other basic facilities. However, the argument in favour of installing Internet cafés outside the camps is as valid as that for installing them inside them, and UNHCR already allocates considerable resources to the development of refugee-affected areas. If this idea were to be pursued, it should therefore also include establishing Internet cafés in the towns of Kasulu, Kibondo and Ngara (and possibly Kigoma).

The idea is not so far-fetched as first appears. There is no need for fixed telephone lines – a satellite connection can be established as with mobile telephones. And electricity can be provided by generator – this is important, since air conditioning is required for the sake of the equipment. Likewise, the building must be dustproof and secure.

It can be done, and it is recommended that it is tried in the Burundi camps and the Tanzanian towns mentioned above, as a part of the training programme.

Liberian refugees in a training workshop. UNHCR-GTZ run technical school. Gueckedou, Guinea. UNHCR/03.1998/B. Clarke

Objectives

When setting objectives for an expanded training programme, the following must be accepted as principles:

- There are both economic and social objectives and separate targets should be set for each type;
- Not all youths have the drive and potential to become successful micro-entrepreneurs;
- Not all youths (or their parents) are interested in vocational training;
- In view of this, a training programme should offer other activities in addition to vocational training.

Below is an outline of a programme that builds on those principles. The outline sets targets for one year at a time for all the concerned camps; these targets will then be broken down between the camps according to their population size.

The overall objective of the programme is *to provide refugees, and in particular the youth, with skills that will be useful for them on their repatriation to Burundi.*

In order to achieve this, four immediate objectives have been formulated:

1. To establish and manage a camp-based training programme.

This entails creating a coordination structure across the camps; establishing a training centre in each camp; identifying training opportunities with the NGOs that are engaged in logistical work in the camps and ensuring that these are used in a systematic way; organizing market surveys and inventories of potential trainers in each camp; and testing new technologies with the help of consultants.

2. To enable youths to become self-employed through enterprise-based training.

This is an economic objective. It would set as a target the annual graduation of 1,000 youths from enterprise-based training (assisted apprenticeships) with refugee micro-entrepreneurs, supplemented with theoretical instruction at the training centres.

3. To provide different target groups with employable skills through group-based training.

This objective is also predominantly economic. It combines targets of 1,000 mainstream youths with 500 with special needs (from vulnerable groups). A third target is to have 5,000 people attend short horticultural training sessions each year through a considerable expansion of the land allocated to horticulture in each camp. The mode of training is group-based training, with supplementary theory at the training centres. Group instructors will receive monthly incentives at an agreed level.

4. To occupy out-of-school youths who otherwise have very little to do.

The target here is to engage 5,000 youths in sports activities through the establishment of sports clubs, and to help primary schools to have, for example, football competitions. The second target is to extend computer and Internet use to 1,000 youths per annum through the establishment of Internet cafés in seven refugee camps and three Tanzanian towns. Under the supervision of the responsible NGOs, refugees receiving incentives will largely run the activities.

Coordination and management of training programme

A strong coordination structure for training needs to be established. It is proposed that UNHCR appoints a staff member at the level of field officer to oversee the coordination, while each NGO involved in training will appoint its own training coordinator, the purpose being to benefit from each other's experience in the replication of existing, and establishment of new, activities. The structure will also seek to harmonize practices with regard to compensation and support.

The coordination and management structure is illustrated in Figure 1.

Figure 1: Training Programme Organization

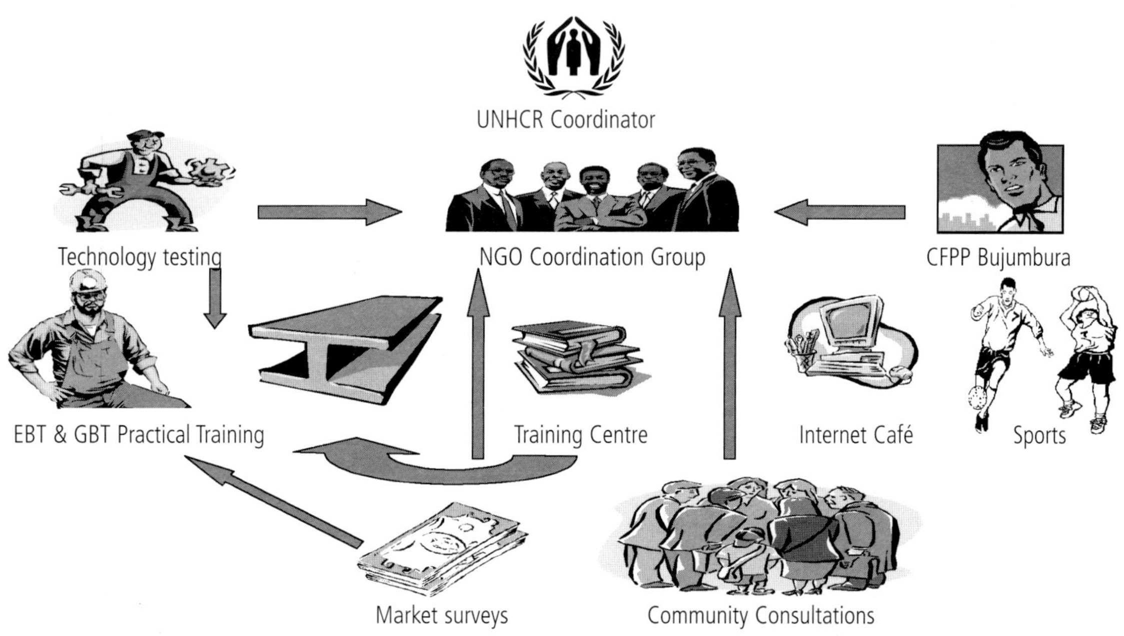

The NGO Coordination Group, under the supervision of the UNHCR Training Coordinator is in charge of the day-to-day management and general progress of the programme. It will consist of the UNHCR Coordinator and representatives of all NGOs involved in training in camps for Burundians. It will have monthly meetings.

The summary terms of reference for the Coordination Group are:

- Ensure close cooperation with the Tanzanian authorities in all matters related to training
- Ensure close consultation with refugee communities
- Ensure that uniform structures for incentives and other financial/material support apply in all camps
- Promote uniform training programmes (syllabi) across camps
- Consult with other NGOs engaged in practical work in the camps with a view to identifying training opportunities
- Establish a common certification system for attendance, mentioning the subjects from the syllabus covered in the training
- Detailed planning of the activities in terms of timing, budgeting, and distribution of resources between camps
- Promote training for self-employment in the selection, training and follow-up stages
- Initiate testing of new technologies with potential for application in the training programme
- Carry out proactive marketing surveys and actively assist refugee producers in finding new markets or expand existing ones
- Initiate the establishment of training centres in all camps and supervise them
- Initiate the formation of sports clubs, and promote school sports activities
- Coordinate the use of local consultants

The link to Burundi will be secured through cooperation with the Centre de formation et de perfectionnement professionnel (CFPP), in Bujumbura. CFPP will be able to provide assistance in ensuring the relevance of the training to Burundian markets and the supply of training materials, as well as in pedagogical and technical subjects. It is proposed that CFPP be contracted to carry out three visits per year (for two persons) and to provide ongoing support on request.

Assistance will be sought from Tanzanian specialists on a consultancy basis, for example when new technology such as the brick press is introduced, or when zero-grazing is under consideration.

Project design

The logical framework of the project is presented in two tables. Table 5, giving a project design overview, combines the objectives with their corresponding *outputs* and *activities*, and indicates the types of *inputs* needed to produce the outputs (quantification of inputs comes later in the budget section). In Table 6, which sets out a logical framework, the objectives and the outputs are shown together with the objectively verifiable indicators (OVIs), which will be monitored in order to assess whether or not an objective is being reached or an output is being produced. The means of verification (such as reports, manuals, etc.) for monitoring the OVIs are also indicated, as are the assumptions upon which the objective/output is based.

Monitoring and evaluation

The coordination structure will also ensure that consistent monitoring is carried out that will facilitate:

- Comparison of costs per activity based on cost-per-month-per-trainee
- Early awareness of market opportunities
- The extent to which trainees set up their own enterprise
- The extent to which new enterprises survive

Consultancy assistance will be required to help set up a consistent monitoring system. It is recommended that a programme review take place early in 2002.

Workplan

A tentative workplan for the year 2001 is presented in Table 7.

Indicative budget

A cost analysis of the four project elements reflecting the four objectives is attempted in Table 8. It is indicative at best and depends on a range of external factors.

The main assumptions are the following:

- There will be sufficient interest on the part of the communities, youths and potential trainers to make it possible for the programme to work
- NGOs will have (or will be given) the necessary capacity to coordinate and manage the programme in a consistent way
- NGOs will always seek cost-effective solutions (rather than seeing the indicative budget as written in stone)
- The refugee trainers will be given incentives at the levels already set
- Land will be made available for a substantial expansion of horticultural training
- New market opportunities can be identified with a determined effort
- A source of funding for the Internet cafés has already been identified

The indicative budget is followed by Table 9, which gives the distribution of targets and budgets between camps, based on targets and unit costs for each element, and divides the numbers according to the population size of each camp. This means that, for example, out of a budget allocation of US$90,000 for enterprise-based training, with a total of 1,000 trainees, Nduta, allocated US$12,600, will train 140 youths, while Lukole, allocated US$29,700, will train 330. Again, as populations change, these figures are indicative and subject to agreement by the Coordination Group. The distribution key will then have to be modified. Clearly, the limitations of land availability will influence the distribution.

Table 5: Project Design Overview

Objectives	Outputs
1. To establish and manage a camp-based training programme	1.1. Coordination structure 1.2. Training opportunities identified with NGOs engaged in logistical work in camps 1.3. Inventory of potential trainers 1.4. Training centres in each camp 1.5. New technologies tested
2. To enable youths to become self-employed through enterprise-based training	2.1. 1,000 youths graduate annually from enterprise-based training
3. To provide different target groups with employable skills through group-based training	3.1. 1,000 youths and 500 people from vulnerable groups graduate annually from group-based training 3.2. 5,000 people receive horticultural training annually
4. To occupy out-of-school youths who have otherwise very little to do	4.1. Sports training and contests 4.2. Internet cafés established

Activities	Inputs
1.1.1. Appoint training coordinator for each camp 1.1.2. Organize monthly meetings 1.1.3. Organize CFPP inputs for Burundi relevance 1.1.4. Prepare annual training plan with budget and distribution between camps 1.2.1. Consultations with NGOs to identify training opportunities 1.3.1. Carry out survey of available skills for enterpris based training and group-based training in all camps 1.4.1. Build and equip training centres 1.4.2. Hire trainers 1.4.3. Organize skills upgrading courses at centres 1.5.1. Procure and test brick-making and other equipment	• Staff costs – UNHCR, NGOs • Travel costs for meetings • Fee for CFPP • Construction training centres • Equipment training centres • Refugee staff incentives • Consultants for technical testing • Brick-making and other equipment
2.1.1. Community consultations 2.1.2. Carry out market survey 2.1.3. Select candidates jointly with enterprise-based training trainers 2.1.4. Sign contracts with enterprise-based training trainers 2.1.5. Supervise training and provide theoretical instruction 2.1.6. Follow-up with business advice and contracts	• Staff costs – UNHCR, NGOs • Refugee staff incentives • Tools and materials support to enterprise-based training
3.1.1. Community consultations 3.1.2. Carry out market survey 3.1.3. Select candidates jointly with group trainers 3.1.4. Hire refugee group trainers on incentive basis 3.1.5. Supervise training and provide theoretical instruction 3.1.6. Follow-up with advice and income-generating activities support 3.2.1. Secure land for horticulture in all camps 3.2.2. Organize horticultural activities as group training	• Staff costs – UNHCR, NGOs • Refugee staff incentives, including group trainers • Tools and materials support
4.1.1. Community consultations 4.1.2. Organize football and volleyball clubs in each camp 4.1.3. Organize other team sports as required 4.1.4. Organize school and club competitions 4.1.5. Train trainers and coaches 4.2.1. Engage consultants, identify venues, procure equipment 4.2.2. Set up Internet cafés in camps and nearby towns 4.2.3. Carry out computer/internet training	• Staff costs – UNHCR, NGOs • Refugee staff incentives, including group trainers • Tools and materials support • Consultants' fees • Rehabilitate buildings • Internet equipment

Table 6. Logical Framework

Objectives and Outputs	Objectively verifiable indicators
Objectives	
1. To establish and manage a camp-based training programme	• A coordination structure exists and is functioning
2. To enable youths to become self-employed through enterprise-based training (EBT)	• Enterprise-based training works • Selection criteria ensure candidates with potential for self-employment go for EBT
3. To provide different target groups with employable skills through group-based training (GBT)	• Group training continues to work • Sufficient numbers of trainers and trainees participate
4. To occupy out-of-school youths who have otherwise very little to do	• Good response from youths to sports offers • Interest in using the internet
Outputs	
1.1. Coordination structure 1.2. Training opportunities identified with NGOs engaged in logistical work in camps 1.3. Inventory of potential trainers 1.4. Training centres in each camp 1.5. New technologies tested	• NGOs in each camp appoint training coordinator • Monthly meetings held • CFPP missions take place • 200 training opportunities identified • Inventory survey conducted • Training centres established and functioning • Brick presses in use in camps
2.1. 1,000 youths graduate annually from enterprise-based training	• 1,000 youths graduate from EBT • New markets are found • Follow-up with advice and contracts
3.1. 1,000 youths and 500 people from vulnerable groups graduate annually from group-based training 3.2. 5,000 people receive horticultural training annually	• 1,000 youths and 500 vulnerables graduate from GBT • New markets are found • Follow-up with advice and income-generating activity • 5,000 people participate in horticultural training
4.1. Sports training and contests 4.2. Internet cafés established	• Sports clubs organised and functioning • Club and school competitions are held • Coaches are trained • Internet cafés are established and functioning • Computer training is carried out

	Means of verification	Assumptions and risks
	• Minutes from monthly meetings • Six-monthly training progress reports	• NGOs have basic capacity to coordinate training programme
	• Site inspection • Selection criteria • Contracts with EBT trainers	• A potential for self-employment exists • Micro-entrepreneurs are willing to take in trainees for EBT
	• Site inspection • Progress reports	• Group training can work side by side with enterprise-based training
	• Site inspection • Progress reports	• Recreational activities can contribute to development of positive attitudes to the benefit of the communities
	• Annual training plan with budget for each camp • Progress reports • CFPP reports • Inventory survey report • Activity report from training centres • Technology feasibility report	• UNHCR makes coordinator available • NGOs make coordinators available • CFPP interested to assist • Potential training opportunities with other NGOs exist • Funding available to establish training centres • Environment-friendly technologies are feasible for camp use
	• Progress reports • Performance questionnaires filled by EBT trainers	• 1,000 apprenticeships can be found • Serious selection criteria are applied
	• Progress reports • Performance questionnaires filled by GBT trainers • IGA reports linked to training	• Group trainers are willing to work for incentives offered • Land for horticulture can be allocated
	• Progress reports • Site inspection	• Youths will respond to sports offers • Tanzanian authorities agree to internet idea • Suitable facilities can be established

Table 7: Workplan 2001

Activities		2000 Nov.	2000 Dec.
Objective 1: Establish and manage camp-based training programme			
1.1.1	Appoint training coordinator for each camp	■	■
1.1.2	Organise monthly meetings	░	░
1.1.3	Organise CFPP inputs for Burundi relevance	■	■
1.1.4	Prepare annual training plan with budget and distribution	■	■
1.2.1	Consultations with NGOs to identify training opportunities	■	■
1.3.1	Carry out survey of available skills for EBT and GBT		■
1.4.1	Build and equip training centres		
1.4.2	Hire trainers		
1.4.3	Organise skills upgrading courses at centres		
1.5.1	Procure and test brick-making and other equipment		
Objective 2: Youth self-employment through enterprise-based training			
2.1.1	Community consultations	■	
2.1.2	Carry out market survey		■
2.1.3	Accept applications and select candidates with EBT trainers		
2.1.4	Sign contracts with EBT trainers		
2.1.5	Supervise training and give theoretical instruction at centres	░	░
2.1.6	Follow-up with business advice and contracts		
Objective 3: Employable skills through group-based training			
3.1.1	Community consultations	■	
3.1.2	Carry out market survey		■
3.1.3	Accept applications and select candidates with group trainers		
3.1.4	Hire group trainers on incentive basis		
3.1.5	Supervise training and provide theoretical instruction	░	░
3.1.6	Follow-up with advice and IGA support		
3.2.1	Secure land for horticulture in all camps		■
3.3.2	Organise horticultural activities as group training		
Objective 4: Sports and Internet			
4.1.1	Community consultations		■
4.1.2	Organise football and volleyball clubs in each camp		
4.1.3	Organise other team sports clubs as required		
4.1.3	Organise school and club competitions		
4.1.4	Train trainers and coaches		
4.2.1	Engage consultants, identify venues, procure equipment		■
4.2.2	Set up Internet cafés in camps and nearby towns		
4.2.3	Carry out computer/internet training		

Key: intensive level of activity ■ ongoing activities ░

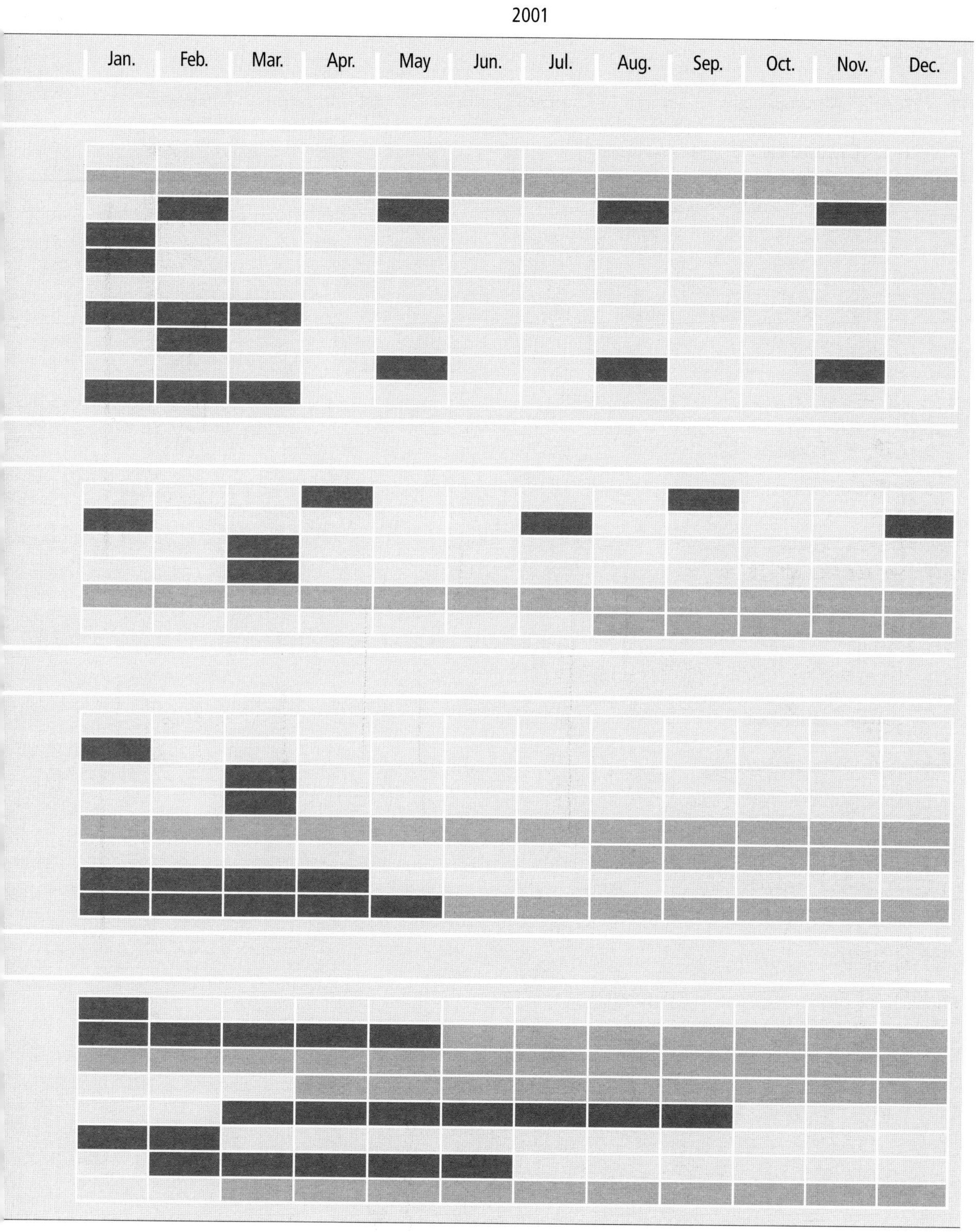

EBT: enterprise-based training GBT: group-based training IGA: income-generating activity

Table 8: Indicative Annual Budgets*

Costs by objectives (US$)				
	Project elements	Quantity	Unit cost	Total cost
Objective 1:	**Coordination**			**106,000**
	• NGO national staff	6	3,300	19,800
	• Refugee staff incentives	50	300	15,000
	• Construct & equip training centres	8	3,000	24,000
	• Travel for meetings	1	1,000	1,000
	• Local consultants (months)	12	600	7,200
	• CFPP visits	3	5,000	15,000
	• Brick presses	8	3,000	24,000
Objective 2:	**Enterprise-based training**			**90,000**
	• Tools/materials	1,000	60	60,000
	• Classroom training	1,000	10	10,000
	• Follow-up contracts	100	200	20,000
Objective 3:	**Group-based training**			**155,000**
	• Tools/materials	1,500	40	60,000
	• Classroom training	1,500	10	15,000
	• Follow-up income-generating activity	1,500	20	30,000
	• Horticulture	5,000	10	50,000
Objective 4:	**Sports and Internet**			**180,600**
	• NGO national staff	15	3,300	49,500
	• Refugee incentives	30	300	9,000
	• Sports equipment	7	300	2,100
	• Internet equipment	10	7,000	70,000
	• Internet café buildings	10	5,000	50,000
Total				**531,600**

* Buildings and equipment are one-time investments
* Internet cafés could be phased over two to three years
* Most construction and some equipment can be financed as income-generating activity

Costs by category (US$)				
Personnel	**Construction**	**Equipment**	**Tools and materials**	**Follow-up**
19,800				
15,000				
	18,000	6,000		
7,200				
15,000				
		24,000		
			60,000	
				20,000
			60,000	
				30,000
			50,000	
49,500				
9,000				
		2,100		
		70,000		
	50,000			
115,500	**68,000**	**102,100**	**170,000**	**50,000**

Table 9: Distribution of Targets and Budgets Between Refugee Camps

Overall population		
Camp	Population	Percentage
• Mtabila 1 and 2	56,000	16
• Muyovosi	35,000	10
• Nduta	48,300	14
• Mtendeli	41,000	12
• Kanembwa	18,000	5
• Karago	35,000	10
• Lukole A and B	116,700	33
Total	**350,000**	**100**

Distribution: Target populations and budgets		Total	Mtabila	Muyovosi
Objective 1:	Coordination			
	Budget US$	106,000	16,960	10,600
Objective 2:	Enterprise-based training			
	• *Target population – youths*	*1,000*	*160*	*100*
	Budget US$	90,000	14,400	9,000
Objective 3:	Group-based training			
	• *Target population – youths*	*1,000*	*160*	*100*
	• *Target population – vulnerables*	*500*	*80*	*50*
	• *Target population – horticulture*	*5,000*	*800*	*500*
	Budget US$	155,000	24,800	15,500
Objective 4:	Sports and Internet			
	• *Target population – sports*	*5,000*	*800*	*500*
	• *Target population – Internet*	*1,000*	*160*	*100*
	Budget US$	180,600	28,896	18,060
Total Budgets US$		**531,600**	**85,056**	**53,160**

	Nduta	Mtendeli	Kanembwa	Karogo	Lukole
	14,840	12,720	5,300	10,600	34,980
	140	*120*	*50*	*100*	*330*
	12,600	10,800	4,500	9,000	29,700
	140	*120*	*50*	*100*	*330*
	70	*60*	*25*	*50*	*165*
	700	*600*	*250*	*500*	*1,650*
	21,700	18,600	7,750	15,500	51,150
	700	*600*	*250*	*500*	*1,650*
	140	*120*	*50*	*100*	*330*
	25,284	21,672	9,030	18,060	59,598
	74,424	**63,792**	**26,580**	**53,160**	**175,428**